非常建筑

YUNG HO CHANG / ATELIER FCJZ

DESIGN as EXPERIENCE RESEARCH

images Publishing

Contents

Experience of In-Out-Door

Experience of Learning

Experience of Lifestyle

Experience of Mountain and Water

Design as Experience Research

Yung Ho Chang

In the Chinese language, the name of our practice, Feichang Jianzhu (FCJZ), can mean different things in different contexts. The phrase can be spoken as a noun to mean "extraordinary building" or as an adjective that expresses the description "very architectonic." The interpretation that my architect father jokingly claims is his favorite is "abnormal architecture," which is perhaps the least complimentary one of all. However, increasingly, I find myself in agreement with him, since at FCJZ, besides space and its enclosure, we tend to wonder if we can in fact "design" the way in which people encounter the world and live their lives; in other words, we seek to design experience—tangible, physical experience.

If the experience within a building needs to be materialized in a customary manner, we assume the typical role of an architect (with pleasure); however, if the experience calls for more than the standard, requiring a different final outcome, then we may wear a few hats, switching between the architect hat and other designer hats to tailor the products. For example, we may produce utensils for eating, or come up with alternative formats for reading—but of course, while still always using the knowledge and methods of an architect, inevitably resulting in finished creations that are quirky and maybe a bit "off;" maybe even slightly on the abnormal side.

This volume of design work—simultaneously normal and abnormal—is organized around an agenda of experience. Forty-four projects are grouped into the following nine themes: City, Everyday, In-Out-Door, Learning, Lifestyle, Mountain and Water, Movement, Stories, and Time and Space. These categories reflect our vast range of research interests within experience design, as well as beyond, and through them we ask:

Can we design cities?

Can we design lifestyles?

Can we design time?

How much outdoor life can we have?

How does the cyber experience impact the material one?

Do we still need typology?

Do we still need methodology?

Did we ever need a pure architectural experience?

Is programing a part of design?

Is total design possible?

What is history? Knowledge or part of the present?

What is perspective? A tool or an idea?

What does the East and West divide mean?

This list of questions is by no means conclusive and we are not sure if we will ever find answers to some of them, but these challenges drive our practice. Every time that we discover something unknown to us on our way to reach a possible solution for a problem, we know that we have put a step—be it big or small—forward.

The Work of the Atelier FCJZ: Innovation and Tradition

Kenneth Frampton

Architect, Historian and Critic of Architecture

Emeritus professor, Graduate School of Architecture, Planning and Preservation, Columbia University

Growing up in the midst of the Cultural Revolution, Yung Ho Chang was educated as an architect at the Nanjing Institute of Technology (Now Southeast University), and thereafter in the US at Ball State University and the University of California in Berkeley, from which he graduated in 1984. Subsequently he founded with his wife, the architect Lijia Lu, an atelier under the name Feichang Jianzhu (FCJZ), the first independent architectural practice in the People's Republic of China.

Having studied in the States during the heyday of postmodernism, from 1981 to 1984, Yung Ho Chang would have been familiar with Paolo Portoghesi's Venice Biennale of 1980, which featured the scenographic so-called Strada Novissima, lined on both sides with hypothetical shopfronts designed by a rising generation of postmodern architects, many of whom came from the States and influenced by Robert Venturi, took a *collagiste* approach to the design of these decorative façades, ostensibly referring to past and present stylistic tropes.

Something of a similar postmodern manifestation, but this time in terms of an assimilation and transformation of explicitly modernist ideas, was an assembly of model houses, each built to the designs of an Asian architect and erected in the so-called Commune by the Wall sponsored by the developers Zhang Xin and Pan Shiyi, and completed just prior to the millennium.

Yung Ho Chang's canonical Spilt House was realized on this site in 2002. Zhu Jing Xiang has suggested that there is an uncanny intimation that this radical work was the result of some natural disaster, as though a subterranean creek had turned into a torrent and divided a single house into two parts that were still "hinged" together about a triangular patio. And it is perhaps this sense of trauma that makes this house a postmodern work as didactic in its own way as the modern utopian vision of the Rietveld Schröder House of 1924.

Its significance in this regard is confirmed by the fact that it is constructed out of the two materials with the least embodied energy, namely walls of rammed earth and a skeleton frame of wood. Equally significant is the fact that this work was preceded by the Shan Yu Jian House, which had been designed by the atelier for an even more dramatically mountainous site in the vicinity of Beijing. This stone-faced house realized in 1998 is articulated about three separate levels, as it steps down the mountain under a single mono-pitched roof, with each level giving rise to a separate attic room accessed by its own stair and looking south over the top of the roof.

Here, as in the Split House, we already encounter FCJZ's preoccupation with the stair as the quintessential element involved in the diagonal movement of the subject through space. An expressive staircase is a key symbolic element in the Hebei Publishing Building of 2003, and it is already there along with an atrium in the seven-story Morningside Mathematics Building built for the Chinese Academy of Sciences in Beijing, designed by the atelier at the end of the '90s. A generous stair hall with large half-landings, linked by a dynamic, free-standing stair, is also the central unifying feature in the masterly six-story laboratory building erected on the Novartis campus in Shanghai in 2016. This exemplary feature, which is otherwise only a means of access, is rendered as a semi-public space within which research scientists and technicians may take "creative" breaks. It is fitting that the thick upstands of the staircase and its landings are finished in light bamboo as opposed to the laboratories, where an efficient transparent machine-aesthetic prevails throughout. Apart from continuous horizontal glazing, the elevations of the building are faced in traditional gray terra cotta tiles, along with louvers in the same material shielding the upper reaches of the fenestration. The building opens to a courtyard landscaped by Zhu Yufan and bounded by "traditional" tiled roofs, onto which the ground floor dining space opens. Here, tradition and innovation are fused together so as to create a new synthesis.

In their King's Joy restaurant, completed in Beijing in 2012, tradition unavoidably took precedence in the conversion of a large, two-court *hutong* house[1] into a luxury restaurant, treating the first court as an open-air honorific entry and the second as a large, covered dining room, with a fully-glazed, steel-framed zenithal light spanning clear over the space.

In this work, as elsewhere in modern work throughout China and Japan, Hans Wegner's Chinese inspired modern bentwood chair of 1944 is adopted as a dining chair throughout the restaurant, the modern Danish tribute to the legacy of Chinese culture, complimented here by equally refined wood-brick and tiled screens designed by FCJZ.

Landscape comes particularly to the fore in the work of the atelier in the so-called Green Campus Redux, a reworking of an existing college campus in Beijing where the atelier was commissioned to refurbish the space in order to make it more accessible and comfortable for the students and the general public alike. The result is a landscape that has been treated as if it were a park or the garden of a villa, rather than a campus.

The pre-existing walkways are here paved in brickwork, laid against the direction of pedestrian movement and left ragged at the edge so that the paving merges into the greensward. Timber pergolas are erected over these walkways so as to break up the campus into large rooms, and natural light filters through the orthogonal latticework of these pergolas according to the position of the sun. The overall result seems closer to the spirit of Japan or, by the same token, to Dutch Neoplasticism rather than to the Chinese garden tradition. The vertical supports of the pergolas come down on one side to support cantilevered benches introduced so as to afford a place for people to sit in the shade. The metal jackets protecting these scantlings as they come down to the ground recall something of the Jugendstil. The atelier's description of these pergolas says everything about the way they have envisaged their vegetal integration over time.

> "We see architectural elements...as a way to articulate the natural and the man-made and use small pieces of timber to construct a double-layered structural system which on the one hand provides a roof and seats

1.There are three courtyards in this project: in addition to the side courtyard at the entrance and the indoor dining courtyard covered with a glass roof, there is also a traditional open courtyard.

for users and at the same time invites vines and other plants to grow over. The new wood pergolas have a much lower profile than the previous stone verandas (and) thus a more intimate scale. They embrace the landscape in the middle and extend into the open green in a dovetail manner in various locations."

In a 2012 retrospective on the work of the atelier, Yung Ho Chang would characterize their production as "materialist." In this regard he has been as much a designer of clothing, furniture, and tableware as he has been an architect in a strictly professional sense and in this respect, it could be said that the work of Atelier FCJZ has been more Italian than either Chinese or American.

This aspect of the studio's production has been at its most exuberant and elegant in the design of clothing. This allowed them to approach in the most direct way possible their long-standing aspiration for their designs to be inseparable from the sensuous experience of the subject. This desire for an immediate all-enveloping, tactile appropriation of a work comes particularly to the fore in their 2D-3D Qipao clothing line, the prototypes of which were based on the traditional *qipao*, dating back to the early days of the Republic and ultimately to the traditional male garments worn in Manchuria.

This was the model for their attempt to create a casual, loose fitting, multipurpose garment stylistically appropriate for a contemporary feminine urban lifestyle. The atelier will embrace this "experiential" line again in their design of urban cycling wear which may stem from Yung Ho Chang's nostalgia for the sustainability of cycling, the universal way of getting around during the Maoist period that is still in extensive use even now, despite the ascendancy of the automobile and the ubiquitous piles of abandoned bicycles all over China.

These are shades of a similar ecological respect for the bicycle in other FCJZ projects such as their spiraling, circular Bike Ring designed for Xiamen in 2019 or their territorially-scaled, double-level, reinforced concrete Qinpu Bridge projected for Shanghai in 2016 with a varying section designed to separate bicyclists from automobiles. All of this relates back, as the clairvoyant Zhou Rong suggests, to the Duchampian wheels of Yung Ho Chang's first realized work, the short-lived, eco-revolutionary Xishu Bookstore of 1996.

The design of clothing resurfaces in one form or another in the work of FCJZ as is evident from the sets and costumes that they designed for a dramatization of the Wei-Jin period legend, entitled *Seven Sages of the Bamboo Grove*, recounting the adventures of seven spirited literati. In this instance, the loose-fitting costumes were made by cutting openings at random out of a tube of polypropylene fabric, which apart from added color guaranteed the uniqueness of each costume by virtue of being worn in unpredictable ways, enabling each actor to express changes in their corporeal posture and shifts in their psychological mood throughout the performance, much like the abstract stage set of tall thin poles of varying diameter, which could be construed, when seen across the all-round acting arena, either as a palace or as the mythical bamboo grove.

As far as the design of furniture is concerned Atelier FCJZ has been at its most lucid and elegant in their design of bent plywood furniture, the result of their collaboration with the Qumei firm, which has pioneered the production of bent plywood in China. For this manufacturer, the studio designed its Bend It Like Yoga line of furniture, wherein bent plywood tables and chairs assumed anthropomorphic form. Apart from these pieces, FCJZ also designed bent plywood pushcarts for serving cakes in the Shanghai 21Cake chain of coffee bars and bakeries.

Yung Ho Chang's cultivated hyper-awareness of the continuity of the past in the present, irrespective of the divide between East and West, finds a particularly ironic expression in his redesign of the traditional Chinese "*cheng* table" of which he wrote:

> "The *cheng* (leg bracket) for this table is of a much larger size than the traditional ones and formally more expressive. Ultimately the *cheng* table redesign is an attempt to blur the divide between the traditional and the modern by simply taking a precedent and pushing its logic further."

In this way, the extended leg brackets reinforced the surface of the entire table, making it into a stressed-skin structure, similar to the monolithic character of reinforced-concrete constructions.

Of late, Atelier FCJZ has made increasing use of concrete, going from its use of long-span, gently-arched concrete slabs in its museological interpretations of the traditional Chinese covered bridge (in Annan in 2010 and in Jishou in 2019) to its current extensive use of concrete cast from timber-boarded formwork, the so called *bêton brut* method first used by Le Corbusier to cast the concrete of his Unité d'habitation Marseille of 1952. This material has led Yung Ho Chang to associate concrete with the Chinese character for earth, *tu*, combined with the character for wood, *mu*, to yield his idea of *tu mu*. This mythical fusion is demonstrated in the tactile opacity of the four *bêton brut* houses that he built at Ningbo in 2021. At the same time, exposed reinforced concrete was indispensable for the realization of the anti-perspectival No Name Art Museum, under construction in Zhejang in the same year, in order to house the life work of the legendary painter Wu Dayu.

As with other contemporary architectural firms using concrete, the atelier is confronted with the paradoxical postmodern dilemma posed by this material, because while it has been associated with the liberative legacy of the Modern Movement during the first half of the twentieth century, we now have to acknowledge that its production is environmentally problematic. However, it is the limitless sculptural potential of this material that emerges in the beautiful folded-plate monitor lights that admit zenithal light to the studio workshops of the Liangzhu campus, under construction for the China Academy of Art at Hangzhou, as a new comprehensive university of design accommodating 4,000 students in five- to ten-story dormitory blocks, interspersed within a linear, layered matrix of vaulted, top-lit, open-planned, teaching spaces. This work promises to be the twenty-first-century equivalent of the progressive pedagogical tradition of the Bauhaus built at Dessau in 1926 and the Hochschule für Gestaltung erected outside Ulm in 1955.

Given its long-standing penchant for the design of clothing, it is hardly an accident that Atelier FCJZ should design a range of overalls to be worn by the future students, inspired, it would seem, by images such as those of the eccentric H.H. Richardson wearing his monk's habit or a staged shot of a group of students wearing the hypothetical overalls, an image appropriately reminiscent of shots of groups of students taken in the Vkhutemas during the heroic decade that followed the Russian Revolution.

Over the past thirty years, this uniquely talented partnership has been able to produce a ludically exuberant body of work over an exceptionally wide range, one which not only represents the image of another modernity, but also constitutes a vital and environmentally valid material culture for the future of Chinese society.

Conceptuality, Urbanity and Materiality—
Reading the Practice of Yung Ho Chang and Atelier FCJZ

Li Xiangning

Architectural critic and curator
Dean and professor, College of Architecture and Urban Planning, Tongji University

"Towards a Critical Pragmatism: Contemporary Architecture in China," an exhibition that I curated, which opened at Harvard University in 2016, was the first large-scale collective exhibition of contemporary Chinese architecture in the United States. Sixty works of contemporary Chinese architecture were selected; one each from the sixty most representative Chinese architects. Coincidentally, the oldest architect among them, Yung Ho Chang, was born in 1956 and had turned sixty that same year—an age that represents the length of an era in Chinese tradition. This coincidence lent a special historical relevance and symbolic meaning to the exhibition. There is no doubt that Chang has influenced a whole generation of younger architects and their experimental, critical ways of thinking. In addition, he is an important driving force behind, and witness, to the contemporary transformation of Chinese architecture.

Most of the literature on contemporary Chinese architecture highlight one particular event that represents the onset of a prosperous age for contemporary architecture: the founding of an independent architecture studio by Chang shortly after the reform and opening period in China. In the decades that followed the founding of the People's Republic of China in 1949, Chinese architectural practices constituted mostly state-owned, large- and medium-sized design institutes. Though private architectural firms began to emerge in the 1980s, agencies that were truly independent from the state-owned system gained public prominence only after Chang, along with his wife and partner, Lijia Lu, set up Atelier Feichang Jianzhu (FCJZ) in 1993 and returned from the United States to begin their practice in China. From the 1980s to the mid-1990s, the discussion of experimental architecture in Chinese magazines, such as *The Architect* and *World Architecture Review*, essentially revolved around the practices of individual architects like Chang, Wang Shu, and Liu Jiakun. That trend pointed at the emergence of another mode of practice that was counter to state-owned architectural design institutes. They challenged the mainstream model through their experiments, while referencing the latest Western architectural theory and practice. They sparked a wave of architectural culture in China, enthusiastically embracing architecture as a new, fascinating, and thought-provoking contemporary culture.

Chang was a role model for the younger generation, and his career inspired both emerging architects and students at that time. Born into a family of architects, he belonged to the first group of students who studied in the US after the Chinese Cultural Revolution. He won multiple awards in international design competitions during his studies, garnering widespread admiration from his peers. During the 1980s and 1990s, he played a major role in directing the attention of Chinese architectural students toward international architectural dynamics and the active participation in international student competitions. His design proposal of Vertical Glass House, submitted to the Shinkenchiku Residential Design Competition in Japan, was finally completed in 2013 and presented at the West Bund Biennale in Shanghai, two decades later. Even today, his work continues to present a strong criticism of (and challenges) professional conventions and rigid models of architecture.

To the younger generation of Chinese architects, the ultimate significance of Chang's success lies in how it allows them to envision a path of independent architectural practice that pursues experimental value and criticality beyond an institution of mainstream architectural design. Chang was also the first Chinese architect to receive international recognition. In fact, he was, for the most part, the sole representative of Chinese architects in international architecture exhibitions before 2000. In 2005, he became the head of the Department of Architecture at the Massachusetts Institute of Technology (MIT), United States, setting the precedent of a Chinese architect leading an international architecture institution, and Atelier FCJZ progressively became a bridge between young architecture students, international architectural education, and independent practices. The mindset and design experience imparted by Atelier FCJZ has helped many young architects succeed in their independent practices and become influential in the field of contemporary Chinese architecture.

Reading Chang can be a difficult task. When he returned to China from the US in the early 1990s, his professional practice of nearly three decades covered everything from architecture to interior, clothing, furniture, and stage design, as well as media and contemporary art. It's a complex system with an internal logic that requires careful examination.

Over the thirty years of his design practice, Chang's works always seemed to focus on three particular topics. These three aspects—conceptuality, urbanity, and materiality—may also be clues to understanding the continuous development and evolution of his design thinking and practical concerns.

Conceptuality

Chang's architectural practice shares certain similarities with that of American architect Peter David Eisenman. Like Eisenman, Chang combines architecture with philosophy. Chang's works can't be interpreted at a physical level without an understanding of his underlying thought system. In other words, Chang's architectural works are both buildings in the traditional sense, and part of a self-referential discourse system. Compared with Eisenman's dry and abstract theoretical system, the structure of Chang's architectural philosophy is full of forks in the road, tricks, humor, and sly reflections. Its rich charm induces visitors to lose themselves within. Conceptuality is the common thread that runs through the entirety of his architectural practice to this present day. For Chang, architecture is a projection of ideas and an expression of an architectural language system that is independent of construction and use. This kind of conceptual approach can be presented in a multitude of ways: as

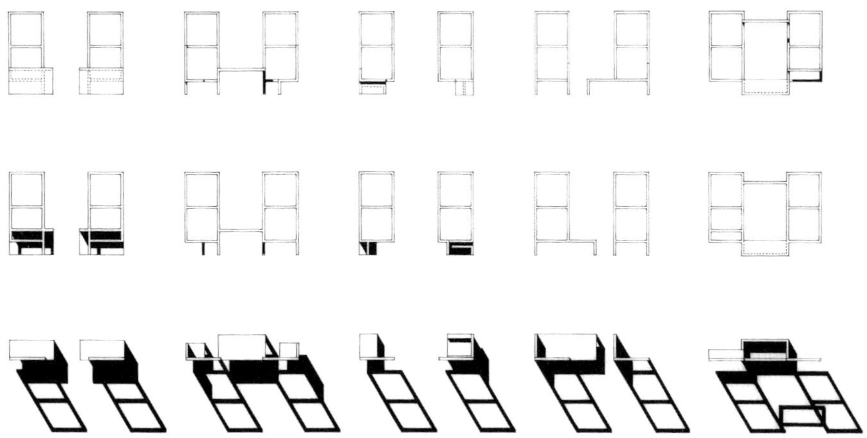

1 Window-Furniture, 1989–91

2 Kinder-Window-Garten, 1992

a narrative—similar to Chang's humorous writings—as a language of architectural ontology, or as the high abstraction shown in the practice of conceptual architecture in contemporary art.

Chang's early years in the United States triggered his close attention to theories and concepts. In his article, "Journey to Cranbrook," he explores the nature of "theoretical architecture." His study of the "Laboratory of Uncertainty" at Ball State University, Indiana, United States, under Rodney Place, gave rise to his exploration of everyday objects like bicycles and their possibility to dominate the leading narrative of a space. These ideas would later permeate into his designs, such as Bike House and the Book-Bikes of Xishu Bookstore. Chang's other design concepts draw inspiration from art installations, literature, and film. Japanese director Juzo Itami's *Dandelion* and Hitchcock's *Psycho* and *Rear Window* have also influenced Chang's works, such as his kindergarten project in Luoyang, Henan Province, (images 1 and 2, page 14) and the viewfinder concept of the villa in Persimmon Grove, Beijing, China.

Such concepts are able to be more story-like and easily understood by laypeople outside of the architectural profession, as they often revolve around familiar visual images or objects. Conversely, conceptual construction can be more abstract, due to its relation to the autonomy of architecture and the proposition of modernity. In this sense, Chang's explorations and practice have contributed significantly to the ontological transformation of contemporary Chinese architecture.

In his article, "Learning from Industrial Architecture," Chang points out that the most important success of modernism was to "eliminate the interference of meaning; architecture is the building itself, an autonomous existence. It is not a tool to express meaning or its supporting explanation." These ideas may be easily accepted today, however, in China during the 1990s, after years of being greatly influenced by formalism, postmodernism, and deconstructivism, Chang needed to be thoroughly distinct in his pursuit of basic architectural issues, and in the cautious, if not suppressed, use of formal language, which relates to the creation of beauty, representing the pride of an architect. Even fellow artists found his most essential architectural values hard to accept, while well-known art critics thought Chang's architecture to be "just a boring, if not ugly, square box." It was miles apart from Frank Gehry's free-flowing style of architecture favored by artists and the public. It was the independent architects under his banner who brought some of the basic values of Western modernist architecture back to the Chinese architectural circle, which had missed out on these important lessons.

Urbanity

Rem Koolhaas had once said that size matters. Where mega architecture is concerned, Bonaventure Hotel in Los Angeles, United States, designed by architect John C. Portman, was regarded by American literary critic, Fredric Jameson, as a

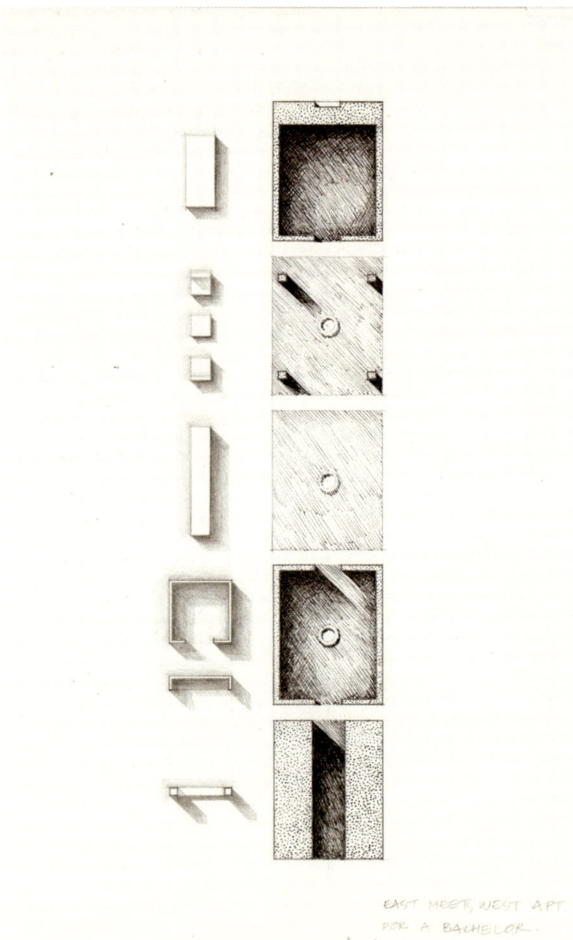

3 Sketch for Bachelor Apartments—Four Rooms

4 Presentation drawings for Bachelor Apartments—Four Rooms

miniature city. In contemporary China, thirty years of rapid urbanization has concurrently resulted in many transitions from buildings into miniature cities, resulting from the scale of such projects. The urbanity of contemporary Chinese architecture may be an important source of ideas for Chinese architects, including Chang. Compared with urbanization as a concept of urban planning, Chang's practice shows urbanism as a concept that analyzes the city from the perspective of the built environment.

Even early into his architectural practice, Chang continuously paid close attention to the metaphor of architecture as a miniature city. For him, even a small building could project the idea of an expansive urban structure. I have always been very fond of the floor plans in Atelier FCJZ's designs. These floor plans best reflect Chang's thinking. We Chinese architects are trained to treat buildings as a complete unit, with each room representing a smaller division of the whole. Chang's early practice with conceptual installations resulted in his preference for treating each small unit, such as a room, a staircase, or a small corridor, as a separate architectural body, while the whole building became a miniature city of architectural complexes. This tendency first emerged in his Four Rooms project (images 3 and 4, page 16), as part of a conceptual design competition, and became apparent in the carefully balanced combination of plans in the Morningside Center of Mathematics at the Chinese Academy of Sciences in Beijing, where the five primary functions—workshops, bedrooms, conference center, management office, and computer room—were deliberately treated as separate small buildings and connected through individual hallways. The precise control of the relationships between the building's parts on a small scale created a clear rhythm for this "mini-city."

In his article "Small City," Chang argues that the key to urbanity is neither scale nor facilities, but density. Many of his works explore density at different levels. In the design of Hebei Education Publishing House, the density of the building forms a "vertical city" by superimposing its different functions. Similar concepts are also present in his project in Paju Book City in South Korea. In the plan for Jiading Mini-Block, Chang tried to maximize the use of the construction site to form an ultra-dense community within the industrial park through unique designs under unified planning conditions, creating the experience of an organically growing community.

The following two projects represent a logical synthesis of his explorations of urbanity. The scale of the two projects couldn't be more different: the first is the single-floor No Name Art Museum, while the second is the Liangzhu Campus of the China Academy of Art, a university as an ad hoc construction of a "town" in its true sense. The former reflects the obsession of Atelier FCJZ for simple spatial elements and small prototypes—such as boxes, corridors with a sense of perspective, tapered camera obscura, and long buildings with single-pitch, vaulted roofs. These miniature buildings are connected in a series by corridors and courts, creating open areas that allow for a variety of different functions, like observation, transportation, recreation, performance, breathing, and meditation. These spaces combine to resemble a unified courtyard and display scenes of "mysterious" lighting reminiscent of a painting of a town square by Italian painter Giorgio de Chirico. The Liangzhu campus is really a small city, transforming the vertically concentrated teaching spaces of a traditional campus into a continuous horizontal complex, spreading out in all directions.

Materiality

In 2012, at the Ullens Center for Contemporary Art (UCCA) in Beijing, Chang titled the retrospective of his personal and Atelier FCJZ's work "Materialism." For the six main parts of this exhibition, he completed six different construction processes with varying materials like concrete, gypsum plaster, and raw soil. This is perhaps the best example of his pursuit of materiality in architecture.

The return to materiality may be Chang's way of rethinking and transcending conceptuality. Although his early work depended on construction, it was clear that conceptual considerations outweighed specific construction methods and materials. After completing his work as the head of the Department of Architecture at MIT, Chang again focused his work on the construction practice itself (image 5). The "materialism" was not so much a metaphysical proposition of rethinking architectural values, but rather his point of interest and a shift in his work's focus. The attention toward materials in his recent works mainly manifests in two aspects: an updated use of new and traditional materials in construction, and an exploration of architecture beyond its traditional housing and cultural functions, rather, as a possibility of urban infrastructure. In many of his design projects, these two aspects are intertwined.

In Split House at the foot of the Great Wall in Beijing, Chang began experimenting with the traditional use of rammed earth as a building material. Designed for the 2010 Shanghai World Expo, the Shanghai Corporate Pavilion utilized large amounts of polycarbonate on the surface of the building. This recyclable material used for CD cases offered an answer to a demand for the environmentally friendly practices of green buildings and the use of solar energy. In a series of subsequent works, Chang began to introduce the results of his laboratory research on materials and construction technologies, which resulted in the 2017 Brick Pavilion in Shenzhen and the Fiberglass House in Nanjing, which was topped off in 2018. The Concrete Vessel at the 2019 House Vision Beijing showcases the development and innovation of concrete with the use of 3-mm porous glass-fiber reinforced-concrete (GRC) panels, which provide breathable building envelope. His interpretation of clay bricks applied to high-rise buildings, as in Maison de la Chine at Cité internationale universitaire de Paris, France, was highly anticipated, as well as the reinvention of concrete materials in the Liangzhu campus of the China Academy of Art.

5 Atelier FCJZ office in Old Summer Palace, Beijing, China

Chang's earliest use of Chinese building materials can be traced back to his research into bamboo. In his 2000 work, Bamboo City, he explored the use of living bamboo as a material for façades and derived concepts of urban infrastructure of greenery from the plant's way of growing. This possibility of combining infrastructure and building was also demonstrated in some of his recent projects. The entire Bridge Museum in Anren, Sichuan, resembles a bridge with its long-span structure. Its function as an exhibition hall is superimposed over its infrastructural function as a pedestrian bridge. This idea has been fully embodied in the newly completed Jishou Art Museum in Hunan. The bridge's upper concrete arch hosts a gallery, while the lower steel bridge retains its specific function as a pedestrian street. And because it is also required that it discharges excess flooding during natural disasters, the bridge's function is ever more rational and justified.

To some extent, the three aspects of Chang's practice reflect the changes in his academic interests and research priorities over different periods in his career. But they are not mutually exclusive. They run through his whole career and become an integrated whole.

If the methods and practical strategies of a contemporary architect were to be drawn as a gradient, the space and form of the architectural ontology would make up the center, with theory and concept on the left, and construction, engineering, and materials on the right. Most professional architects pay attention to architecture as a form of "design innovation," thus their knowledge system and architectural practice strategy inevitably appear as a kind of a spindle structure on this diagram. But Chang seldom talks about the spatial form itself. His early attention to conceptual narratives and his later fascination with construction techniques and materials have made his professional attitude take on the shape of a dumbbell-like structure, with the two ends of the dumbbell echoing each other. His considerations toward urbanity, materiality, and infrastructure represent an important manifestation of his conceptuality.

Yung Ho Chang is unique. A close observation of the trajectory of his own academic and practical development has helped to construct a Yung Ho Chang that is both an architect and an architectural thinker and writer. His variety of interests and practices, the breadth of which stretches across different fields is rare among contemporary Chinese architects. He is also important as a pioneer of an era, and of independent practice, and thus an unavoidable figure in contemporary Chinese architecture. Many young people at Peking University (Beijing), MIT, and Tongji University (Shanghai), who studied under him, or who matured in his studio, have become stand-outs among their peers. All three decades of Chinese architects that followed him were more or less influenced by his practice and ideas. And his receiving the 2016 Building with Nature–China Architecture Media Award for Practical Achievement is simply a manifestation of this importance and uniqueness.

The Meaning of Things

Deyan Sudjic

Design/architectural critic

Former Director, Design Museum London

Throughout its long history, architecture has always encompassed design. But the balance of power between these two related fields of practice—like that between dentistry and medicine, perhaps, or poetry and prose—has fluctuated over time and across cultures. Design was an essential, if not subordinate, part of the broader range of architectural activities in pre-industrial Europe. Architectural fixtures and fittings, such as door handles, chairs and tables, fireplaces, and window frames, were tailor-made for specific projects. When the object or the project were considered important enough, a drawing (or a *dessin* in France, and *disegno* in Italy) was prepared specially by the architect or by an artist of note, for the craftsman to follow. Otherwise the anonymous craftsman worked in a vernacular tradition based on precedent and pragmatism.

The design of such items emerged from the architecture, of which they formed an organic part. They were envisaged for particular spatial or material conditions. The idea that a domestic object designed by an architect can be understood as containing the same genetic code as the architecture itself has been expressed in different ways over time. The logical extrapolation of Ernesto Rogers's famous remark about the responsibility of the architect extending "from the city to the spoon" is to suggest that from a careful enough examination of one of Mies van der Rohe's chairs, it is possible to intuit the kind of city that he might have built. Peter and Alison Smithson were also fascinated by the deeper significance of the chair and discussed it in similar terms. Certainly, Gerrit Rietveld's Red Blue Chair carries a message that strongly suggests the essence of the house that he built in Utrecht for Truus Schroeder.

From the eighteenth century onward, new methods of industrial production changed the relationship between architecture and design. The classicist British architects Robert and James Adam, for example, set up their own factories to mass produce decorative plaster ceilings, skirting boards, and fireplaces, not just for their own architectural projects, but to supply by the meter to other contractors.

Architects sometimes also continued to design fittings; Lutyens tailored light fittings and furniture for each of his buildings. But gradually, industrialization put a gap between design and architecture, and between user and maker. The factory system triggered the emergence of the designer as a distinct category of professional. In the process, the architect's role, more and more, became that of choosing and specifying mass produced objects.

The recent fascination of some manufacturers for high profile architects to design products for them—from Michael Graves's kettle to Frank Gehry's Tiffany cufflinks—has more to do with the cult of celebrity designers and the need to produce signature objects than with the traditional qualities of architecture. Objects carrying an ostentatious designer's signature became a kind of fetish in the 1980s. To compete with Philippe Starck, architects found themselves designing objects whose prime purpose was to only be a signifier, or the

1 Ancient city walls in Beijing, China, 1876

2 A *hutong* in Beijing today

3 Square River in the Old Summer Palace in Beijing

4 FCJZ office in the Old Summer Palace in Beijing

embodiment of the ritual gift giving. Starck went on to create buildings in the form of large-scale objects, which may or may not be architecture.

Yung Ho Chang's interests in designing domestic objects has unfolded against this background, but has a deeper resonance. Alessi is the Italian company that made itself famous for inviting everybody—from Graves to Aldo Rossi, Alessandro Mendini, to Toyo Ito—to design domestic objects ranging from cutlery to wristwatches. Its catalog, for many years curated by Mendini, looks more like an exhibition of the architecture of our times than a product brochure. It is not surprising then that Alessi has added Chang to its roster of designers. In the past twenty years, China has accelerated from being a consumer and replicator of architectural ideas from elsewhere, to transmitting ideas of its own.

In this context, it is important to reflect on Chang's personal trajectory. He was born in 1956. It was a trauma for him to see the demolition of Beijing's ancient city walls (image 1, page 20), which set the scene for the destruction of the *hutongs* (image 2, page 20) since the '50s. Chang left when he could, for an American architectural education, followed by a long period spent as an educator in the United States. When he finally returned to set up one of the first independent architectural offices in Beijing at the end of the twentieth century, with his architect wife Lijia Lu, China had already embarked on what might be seen as a different, but also traumatic period of physical change. The skyscraper, erected a dozen at a time had become the basic unit of architectural scale. With his background and his connections in Beijing's emerging new culture, Chang would have had the means to establish an architectural machine to turn out this kind of production, modifying its worst excesses as much as possible, and instilling some sense of quality. Instead, he struggled to make a much more careful and modest architecture, one that offers a degree of continuity and a respite from the relentless pace of change.

Chang works on what are, by Beijing standards, modest projects. In his first decade in practice, he built individual houses, a couple of art galleries, a bookshop, and some offices for a publishing company. They have elements in them that subtly hint at continuity—sometimes that continuity is with the China of the years before the twentieth century, sometimes with the much more recent but equally vanished past of the time before China's great transformation. That is the sensibility both of his architecture and his work as a designer.

His Lotus Leaf tray, made by Alessi from steel is a reminder of the way that food was once served on a leaf in place of a plate. But he also references the lotus ponds in the royal gardens of the Emperor's Summer Palace, burnt down by Western troops in 1860 (image 3), where Chang had his office from 2003–14 (image 4). The same punitive raid of 1860 also saw the destruction of much of the royal gardens of the Empress Dowager, which were rebuilt in 1888.

Chang's Lotus Leaf tray can be understood, then, not as a piece of nostalgia, or a revival of a lost tradition—though there is something of a Proustian recollection of times past in it. Rather, it is an object that is clearly of our own time, but which seeks to mend a trauma of discontinuity. The tray was based on a leaf that Chang collected, dried, and used as the basis of a digital scan that in turn was used to turn an organic form into metal.

Chang's Unit Chair does something similar by reflecting on what was once the most ubiquitous piece of mass-produced furniture in the People's Republic of China—cheap, universal, and now given a new meaning and significance. From the 1950s to the 1970s it was made all over China from wood. It was so omnipresent as to become invisible, like the blue and green uniforms adopted in the days of the Great Leap Forward. In a China full of manufacturing capacity, it is being displaced by the full range of IKEA and Muji and their local equivalents. To remake it in steel sections, in new colours, is to evoke a memory, but also to create a new design with a sense of depth and resonance.

The Cheng Table does something similar with an earlier period of China's history, as does Chang's Thick Thin Fold screen, which evokes wood and rice paper using a proprietary synthetic stone called Surrel patented by Formica. Each of them in different ways, are attempts to knit together the torn threads of a traumatized visual culture, informed by the optimistic belief that it is possible to build on trauma and draw on it to give a new depth of meaning to our understanding of the present.

China has moved remarkably quickly to develop a distinctive contemporary architecture. On my first visit to Beijing in 1992, China was at the early stage of the reform and opening-up. There were just two pieces of contemporary architecture in the entire city: I. M. Pei's ill-fated Fragrant Hills Hotel, and the newly completed Australian embassy, designed by Denton Corker Marshall. It now has some of the most conspicuous works of the world's more celebrated architects, and some of their failures too. More importantly, it has fueled the talent of a new generation of Chinese architects who have developed their own voices.

What has been slower in coming is a similar development in the practice of design in China. It's an issue which raises questions that are not confined only to China. If design is the product of the industrial revolution and the severing of the connection between user and maker, between client and craftsman, then its history in Asia, unlike that of architecture, begins either in European models, or with the moment that the economies of Japan or China or Korea developed the sophistication to move up the value chain and create consumer products with their own identity.

Chang's work, always sensitive to nuance, sometimes playful, as his interest in cake making and his fascination with detective fiction suggests, and always subtle, points to ways in which this sharp dialectic can be resolved in the most creative and intriguing of ways, by trying to create a sense of continuity that also provides the material for innovation.

5 Shoes designed by Yung Ho Chang for John Lobb

South by Southeast

Yung Ho Chang

Hilberseimer, Veranda

The world that we live in is typically described and discussed in dichotomy, specifically that of East versus West. East and West are portrayed as opposites in nearly every aspect of human life—in the way we eat, in what we wear, and in how we build. Of course differences between the East and the West exist; the following discussion does not intend to question the legitimacy of this worldview; however, I do question if the East-West dichotomy is the right approach to understanding human habitation globally, in the northern hemisphere at least.

City: In the West, one of the epitomes of modernist urbanism is the Highrise City designed by German architect Ludwig Karl Hilberseimer in 1924 (image 1). In this modern metropolis proposal, all the apartment slabs are oriented north–south. The dwelling units are exposed to sunlight in both the morning and the afternoon, while the major streets, which are parallel to the slab buildings, also get a decent amount of sunlight. In the East, the Chinese city of Tangshan (image 2) was rebuilt after the great earthquake in 1976 with a new master plan, where all the residential bar buildings were orientated east–west, which is contrary to Hilberseimer's Highrise city, but with the identical purpose of maximizing solar exposure. The High-rise City was designed for Germany, or possibly, for central and northern Europe, where the sun could be warm but never scorching, therefore eastern and western sunlight would be welcome; whereas in Tangshan and most other Chinese cities, the southern orientation is most ideal because eastern and western sunlight can generate too much heat in the rooms in the summer. A comparison of the two cites reveals a logic that can only be established if Germany and China are not viewed as being one in the west and the other in the east, but rather as one in the north and the other in the south. One's mind only needs to make a ninety-degree geographic turn to understand the discrepancy of the two urban plans that had the same concern: the sun experienced in higher latitudes is not the same as the one in lower latitudes.

Architecture: Can a building design in one region of the world be transplanted to another without any modifications?

A veranda is an open-air architectural space that wraps around a house (image 3, page 25), commonly found in the American South. If we strip away the veranda, we will likely find a brick box with evenly spaced small windows and a pitched roof—a familiar image of the northern house. In other words, the veranda is a southern architectural space that transforms a northern building type by simultaneously shading the interior rooms from the sun and providing semi-outdoor living spaces. If we look around the globe laterally, we will discover buildings with verandas in other parts of the world, from Latin America to Southeast Asia, to southern China, but always along the similar southern latitudes. Possibly originating from India, Portugal, or Spain, the word "veranda" has a warm climate origin. It may be fair to claim that in this case,

1 Highrise City (Hochhausstadt)—perspective view of North–south Street, 1924, by Ludwig Karl Hilberseimer

2 Tangshan rebuilt after 1976 earthquake

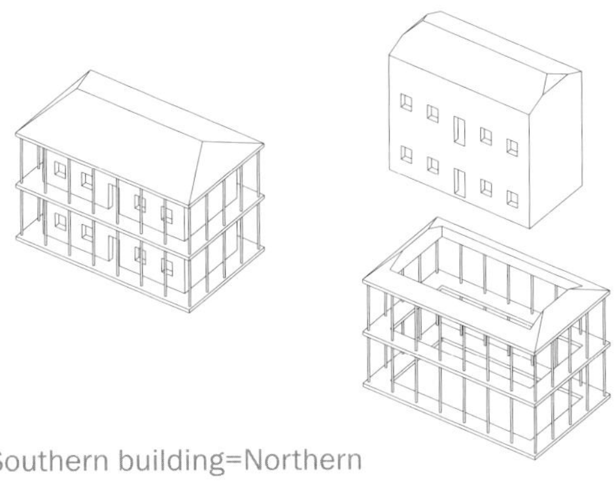

3 Southern building=Northern building+Veranda

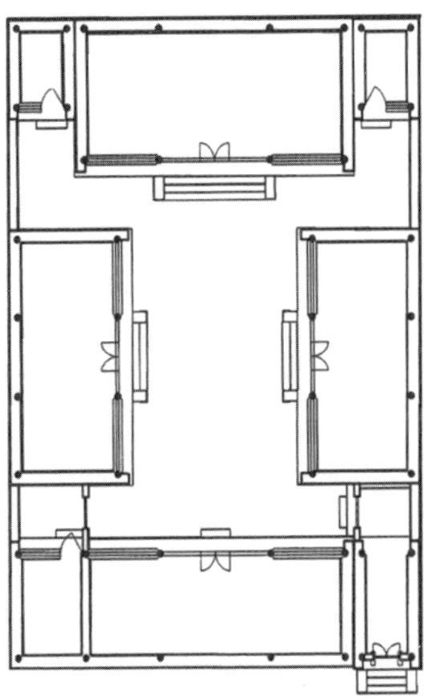

4 Typical Beijing courtyard house plan

architectural space has temperature and possesses a geographical DNA.

There are surely spatial typologies that manage to escape a latitudinal definition; the sleeping porch of California, United States, may be one of them. Thanks to warm airstreams carried by the Pacific Ocean, Californians can enjoy a relatively mild climate throughout the state that straddles numerous latitudes. For a period in the early twentieth century, sleeping porches were popular in the San Francisco Bay Area in the north to Los Angeles in the south, since resting outdoor was believed to be good for the health. Geographical features—oceans, mountains, and deserts—have profound impact on climate, and thus on architecture. They may even occasionally liberate architecture from the iron fist of latitudinal definition, like in the case of the Californian sleeping porch, but not from the reign of climate.

If the ways we live are ruled by climate, temperature, sunlight, precipitation, and other climatic factors, I would argue that we should also view the world according to the north–south orientation, rather than solely according to east–west. This discussion primarily concerns outdoor living, within the context of research on architecture in the south, with a particular focus on Southeast Asia and China.

Yuan, Schindler

I grew up in a *siheyuan* (image 4), or a courtyard house, in Beijing. *Yuan* means courtyard in Chinese, and a *siheyuan* is a courtyard enclosed on four sides. A *yuan* should not be perceived as a garden within a house—although there are likely to be a few trees and other plants—but rather as a multifunctional living space without a roof. A family eating dinner, adults entertaining friends or doing work, children playing—all such activities may occur in the *yuan*. Even in colder days, it is still possible to enjoy outdoor living under the sun. A moderate microclimate is generated by the section of the curve-linear roof slopes of the house, which keep the wind above the courtyard during the winter season. Beijing is commonly seen as a northern city in China; however, since the southern custom of outdoor living is well adapted here, perhaps it is actually the northern edge of a greater southern region?

Another more radical variation of outdoor living exists, again, in California. The Schindler House on Kings Road (image 5, page 26) in West Hollywood, designed by architect Rudolf Schindler for self-use, has no indoor living rooms in the conventional sense. Instead, there are four equal work-live spaces for each of the two married couples sharing the house. Two courtyards, one for each couple, furnished with fireplaces, serve as the living rooms, where the inhabitants held social gatherings. Obviously, Schindler wanted to take maximum advantage of the mild and arid southern Californian weather in organizing the architectural spaces of the house, while also revolutionizing domestic life. There are also sleeping porches on the rooftop. However, when I use the word courtyard here, I am not certain if it is the correct term as Schindler's courtyard has no enclosure, lacking the inherently urban quality of the inwardly organized Chinese *yuan*. Maybe it is better to refer to it as an open or sub-urban courtyard. Patio was the word Schindler used to label the space on his drawings, and perhaps the more accurate expression. If so, should the Beijing *siheyuan* then be considered an enclosed patio? My effort to use the same word in English—"courtyard" or "patio" or some other semantics—aims to put these outdoor living spaces from diverse regions on a comparable platform. Yet, it might be wiser to withhold labels so that our imagination will not be bound by the *yuan*, or Schindler, and we open up to more possibilities to invent and reinvent exterior spaces for habitation.

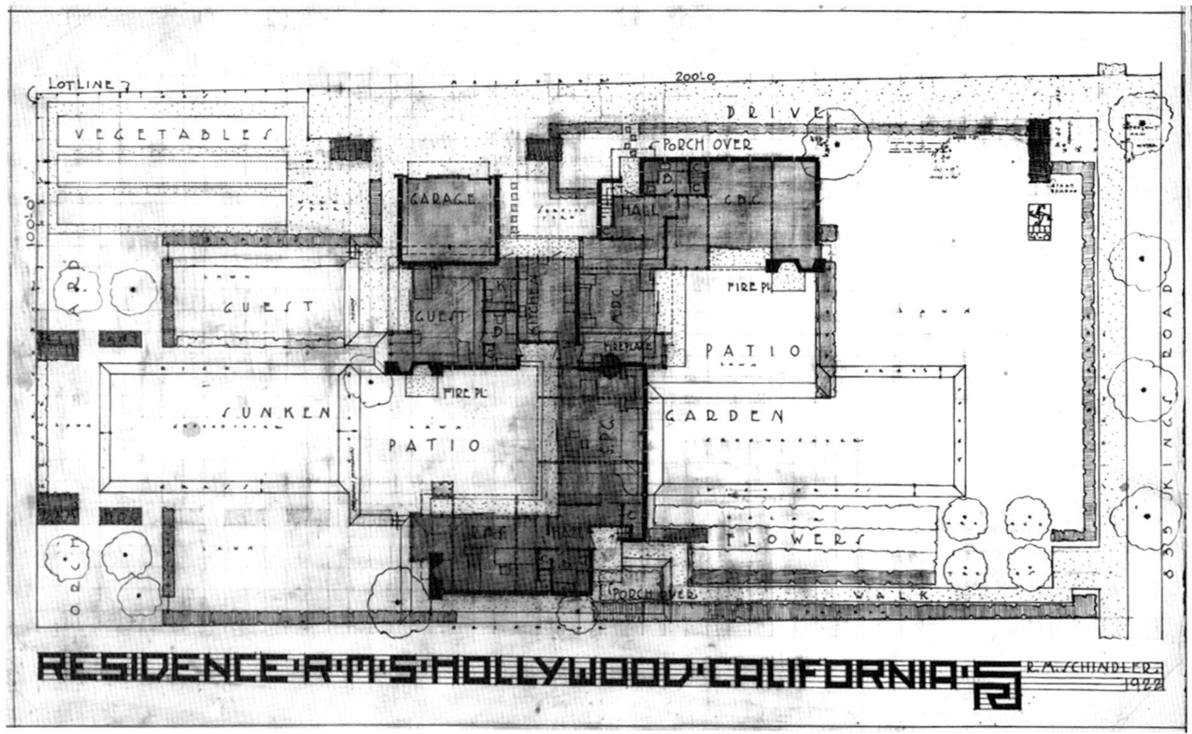

5 Plan of Kings Road House, West Hollywood, California, United States, 1922, by Rudolph Schindler

Bawa, *Tyukanriuiki*

Sri Lankan architect Geoffrey Bawa found the weather of his home country so agreeable that he would design rooms opened directly to the outside, much like the parlor in his own house in Colombo. His commitment to outdoor living would often not allow him to tolerate even a single layer of glass in between and to drive only convertible cars. When Bawa renovated the old Lunuganga rubber plantation into his weekend garden villa, he only added an outdoor "room" to the main house (image 6), which was essentially a roof without walls, where he worked, relaxed and entertained. There is no English vocabulary that defines such an architectural space—a pavilion could be enclosed, a porch is transitional, and a patio has no roof. The Italian term *loggia* might be the closest thing, but a *loggia* typically opens only on one side, whereas Bawa's room opens on two adjacent sides. The fact that Italy has an open room like the *loggia* and England does not indicates the geographical locations of the two countries. Further south than European countries, China has a rich lexicon for such roofed but open spatial conditions: The *tang*, like the *loggia*, may open on one side or two opposite sides; the *ting* opens all sides and is always arranged with a concentric plan, and the *xuan*, usually rectangular in shape, opens on all sides. All of them are occupiable rooms, legitimate and clear. It may be rhetorically unproductive to differentiate semi-outdoor and semi-

6 The added "outdoor room" at Lunuganga plantation, Sri Lanka, 1948–98, by Geoffrey Bawa

7 Part of "*Songs of the Twelve Months (September)*" painting, Qing dynasty

8 *Copying Wang Wei's Wang Chuan Painting* by Guo Zhongshu, Northern Song Dynasty

indoor spaces. The Japanese phrase *tyukanriuiki* covers it all, meaning in-between zone or gray space.

I am interested in the gray space, not only from a typological point of view, but rather, I see in these spaces a human desire to be close to nature.
The conduciveness of the climate of a region is subjective. Colombo, at latitude six degrees north, was hot for me, while Beijing at forty degrees north could be cold for a visiting Sri Lankan. However, nature fascinates us all. During China's Qing dynasty, a popular painting theme was the "Songs of the Twelve Months." The architecture in these paintings would often have large open windows or be without walls, even during the snowy season, as depicted in the paintings (image 7). Is it a realistic portrayal of life in the past? I doubt it. But the aspiration to live without a boundary between the inside and outside is evident. Wang Wei, a Tang dynasty poet and, in a way, a Bawa-like figure in Chinese history, acquired an estate and wrote a poem for each of the buildings he built. Here is one of the most well-known:

Ginkgo Pavilion

Ginkgo cut for beams,
cogon tied for roofs.
Cloud between pillars disappears,
gone raining over earth. (image 8)

This is a simultaneously imaginative and realistic account of a piece of architecture: with building materials and components named, the construction process is revealed in the first two lines. The poem's verses suggest that the building is so high up in the mountains that clouds can dwell inside, and the room must be so wide open that clouds may come and go as they wish. It is a *xuan*.

Like Bawa, Wang invited nature in. A *xuan* or an open room was one way to extend this invitation. The *yuan* or a courtyard was another. Another classical gray space is the *yan-xia* or a space under cantilevered eaves or an overhang, which is always situated between indoor and outdoor spaces. There is also the *lang*, a covered open space of a linear form. The *lang-xia*, or under the *lang*, is an other member of the veranda clan. There are also variations such as the *lang-zi*, which is a covered walkway, or the *lang-qiao*, a covered bridge.

Mies, Umbrella

One courtyard house I walked through repeatedly in my mind's eye is the unbuilt Three-Court House by Ludwig Mies van der Rohe, designed in 1938 (image 9, page 29). Sometimes, I imagine that there is no glass wall between the inside and the outside; other times, I rearrange the domestic functions within, as the original plan is vaguely programed, similar to rooms in a traditional Chinese house. The house embodies the idea of living close to nature, with a touch of zen. The design displays many previously mentioned in-between spatial types, such as the *yuan* and *lang-xia*, and even a degree of openness that is similar to the *xuan*, but with a glass barrier. It, however, is unlike any of the type of courtyard/patio houses we have seen so far. Firstly, in this house, the interior and exterior spaces are completely equal in terms of architectural significance. In fact, they are part of the same large courtyard space defined by the peripheral walls, and together form a holistic piece of architecture. Secondly, with specific programmatic functions left out from the drawings, one may be led to conclude that it may or may not be a house; it is a piece of pure architecture. To my knowledge, Mies never spoke East-West, let alone gray space, although his critic Werner Blaser might have done a fair share of cultural comparison on his behalf. However, it is obvious that Mies was fascinated by the intermediate zone, which might have led him to the terrain incognito.

When *yan*, or eaves, surround a building, such as in a traditional Chinese temple, gray spaces are located on the edge. It creates an umbrella-like structure and the building begins to project a publicness. In reality, gray spaces are often situated in the transition and serve as a connection between the public and the private: the Qilou shop houses of Guangzhou, which are buildings that straddle the sidewalk; the five-foot-wide walking pavement of Singapore; the colonnade of Bolonga, Italy; the arcades of Paris, France—just to name a few, are venues where such gray spaces can be found.

The gray space does not belong exclusively to the architecture of the private domain. Furthermore, this may be where we can begin to construct a better relationship between our public and private lives. While outdoor living is more prevalent in southern regions, a gray space can be found both in the north and the south. To superimpose a North–South divide over other existing divides is not my intention. I'm simply sharing an interest in outdoor space; Mies was a northerner from Germany, I am a northerner for China. My wish is to discern the finer shades of architectural spaces through the global climatic diversity, so that we may build more responsibly for the world.

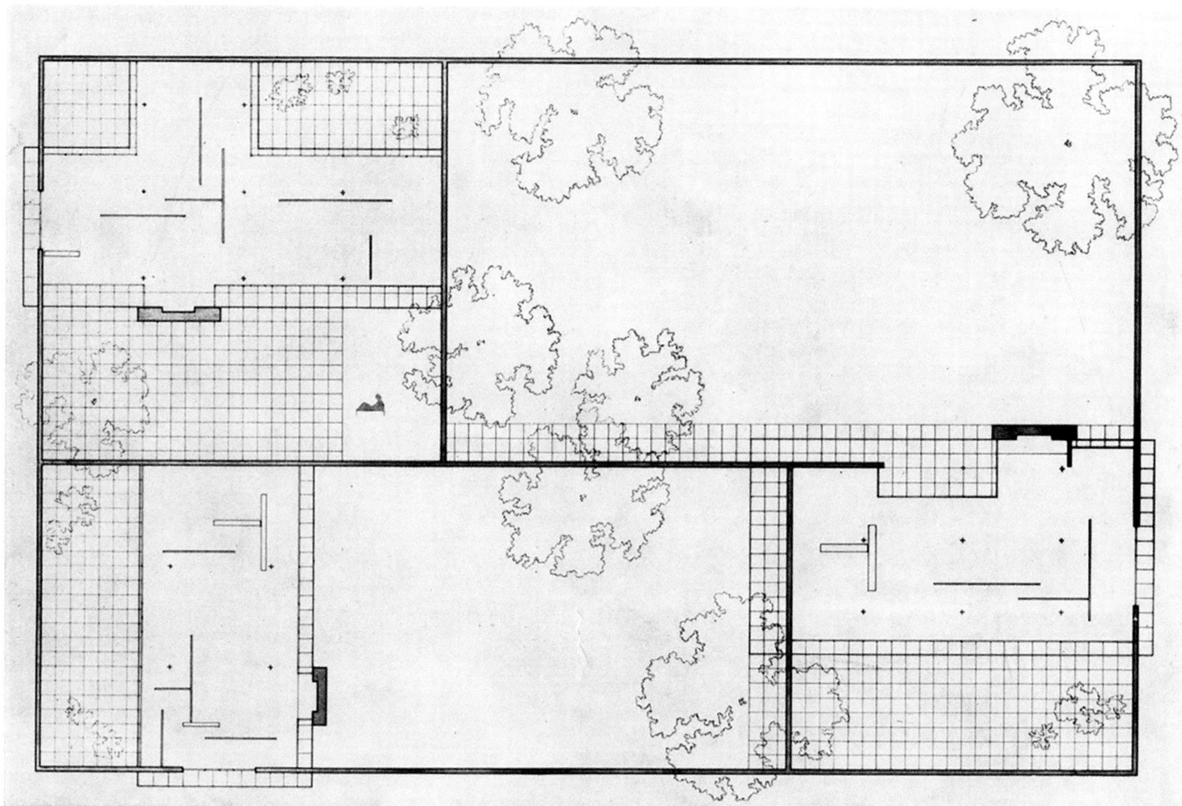

9 Plan of Three-Court House project, 1945–46, by Ludwig Mies van der Rohe

[EXPERIENCE of CITY]

Morningside Center for Mathematics

Chinese Academy of Sciences, Beijing, China

1998

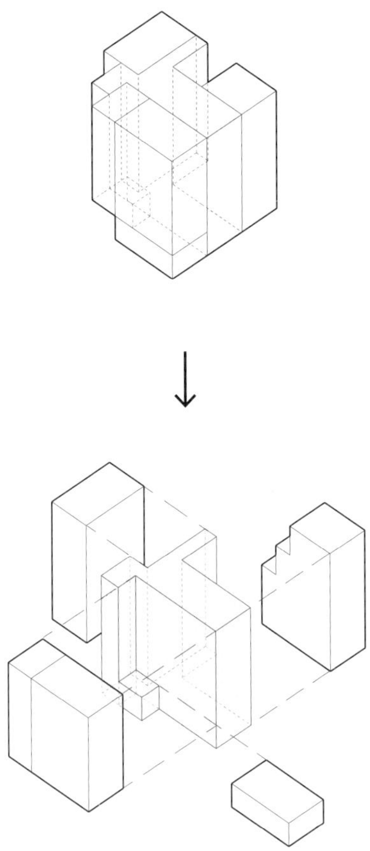

Buildings in the building: The program asks for a singular volume on a tight site to accommodate all the daily activities of the mathematicians, except dining, which is housed in a facility next door. A live-work arrangement limits researchers' opportunity to go into the city. In order to bring only a minuscule amount of urbanity into the building for the center's residents, we turn the seven-story structure into five internal buildings according to their different uses. The buildings-in-the-building are defined by stacks of floors and different architectural qualities, such as private spaces in the individual research stack and the dormitory stack opens on one side, while the stack containing the public spaces open on two opposite sides. The semi-public spaces, also forming a separate stack, are translucent on two opposite sides. The mini towers are then connected with passages, light wells, and bridges over a sky-lit "gap," which may be seen as a traditional courtyard—but squeezed to fit into the contemporary city. Through such design, it is hoped that one may blur the experience of going from one room to another, with that of going from building to building.

Window unit design: Conceptually, we also reorganized the functions of a typical window—a fixed glass pane for light and view, an operable opaque aluminum panel for natural ventilation, and an aluminum louver for air conditioning.

v View from northeast

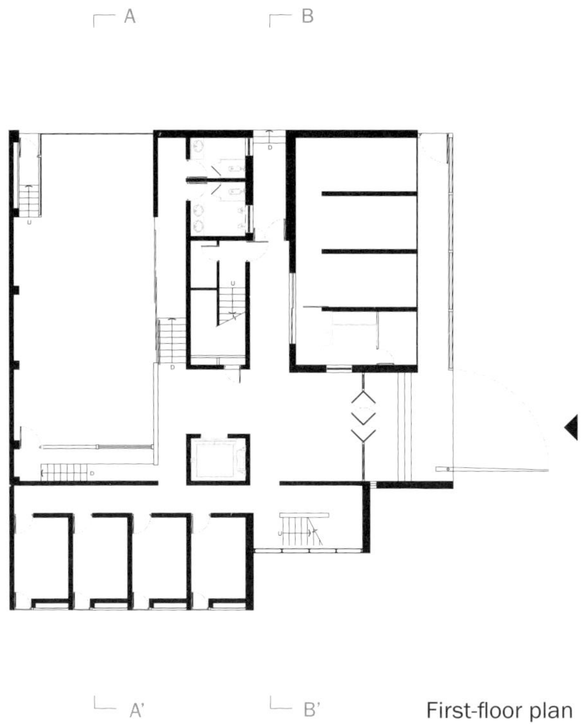

First-floor plan

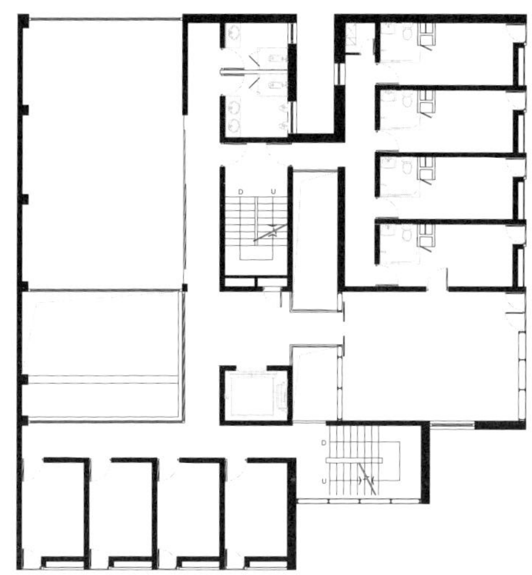

Second-floor plan

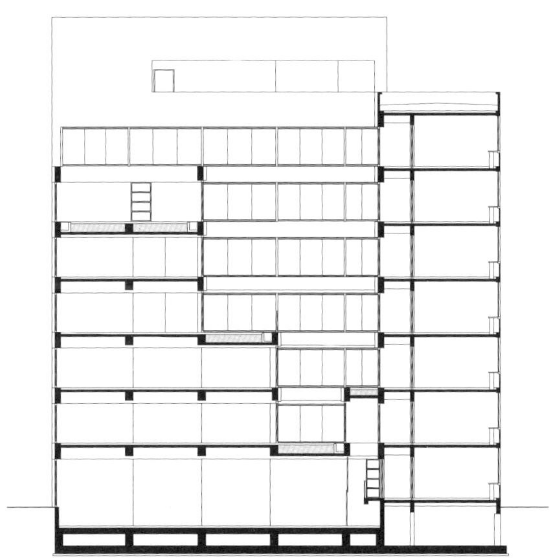

Section A-A'

Section B-B'

> 1 Conference room
> 2 Staircase
> 3 Atrium
> 4 Roof terraces between mini towers

1		
2	3	4

Individual research room interior

v Elevation/window detail

v Passage outside entrance

[EXPERIENCE of CITY]

Museum Bridge

Anren, Sichuan Province, China

2010

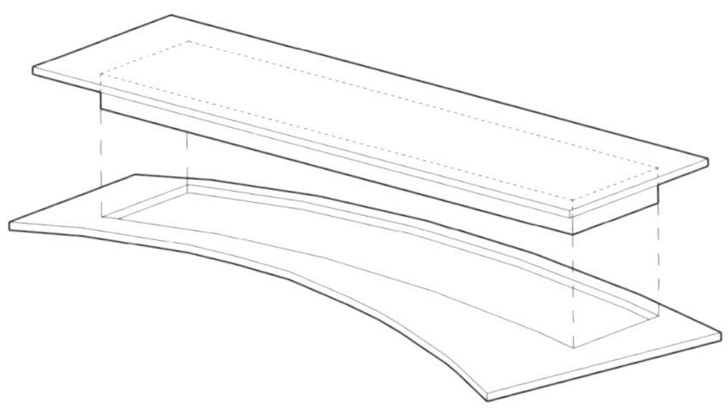

Beyond typology: The Museum Bridge is a combination of two building types. Apart from being one of the museums in the Jianchuan Museum Cluster in Anren, Sichuan Province, it is also a piece of urban infrastructure, extending as a pedestrian bridge over a creek between the museums. We consider bridges as part of urban public space and extensions of the streets in particular. In this case, the museum is not only a component of the bridge, but also a programmatic linkage between two sides of the riverbank. Therefore, the Museum Bridge possesses the characteristics of both a gravitative museum and an uplifting arch bridge.

Genealogy as form generator: In formal language, this museum echoes the style of Chinese architecture from the 1950s to the 1960s. Moreover, it reflects the classical DNAs of the Socialist Realism from the Soviet Union by assuming a tripartite composition. However, each of the three elements are also redefined: The roof becomes a plane with cantilever eaves, not unlike that of traditional Chinese wooden architecture; the body, penetrated on the roof by four skylights, takes the form of a closed box carrying cultural relics; and the base is transformed into a group of slanted concrete columns on the bridge piers. It was envisioned that the Museum Bridge would attain a form of temporal duality—both modern and historical.

Structure and materials: The Museum Bridge is made entirely of concrete. At the bottom of the building are thirteen groups of columns in different angles on the river banks, and they support the museum box above. The material of the façade is fair-faced concrete that is molded by formwork lined with bamboo splits. Due to the coarse construction quality, an intense textural quality is created.

COMMENTS

Guo Yimin
Associate Professor, School of Architecture, Southeast University
Director of the Structural Architecture Research Center

Geometry and technology; floating and support; the spiritual and the daily life; the abstract and concrete—the defamiliarization created by these compositions of opposing characters is not coming from nowhere. In the Museum Bridge, through a series of manipulations, such as superposition, replacement, and juxtaposition, the existing concepts and characters have been turned into new meanings.

> View from northeast

The Hall of Supreme Harmony, Palace Museum, Beijing, China: classical DNAs

National Museum of China, Beijing, China: classical DNAs via the Socialist Realism from the Soviet Union

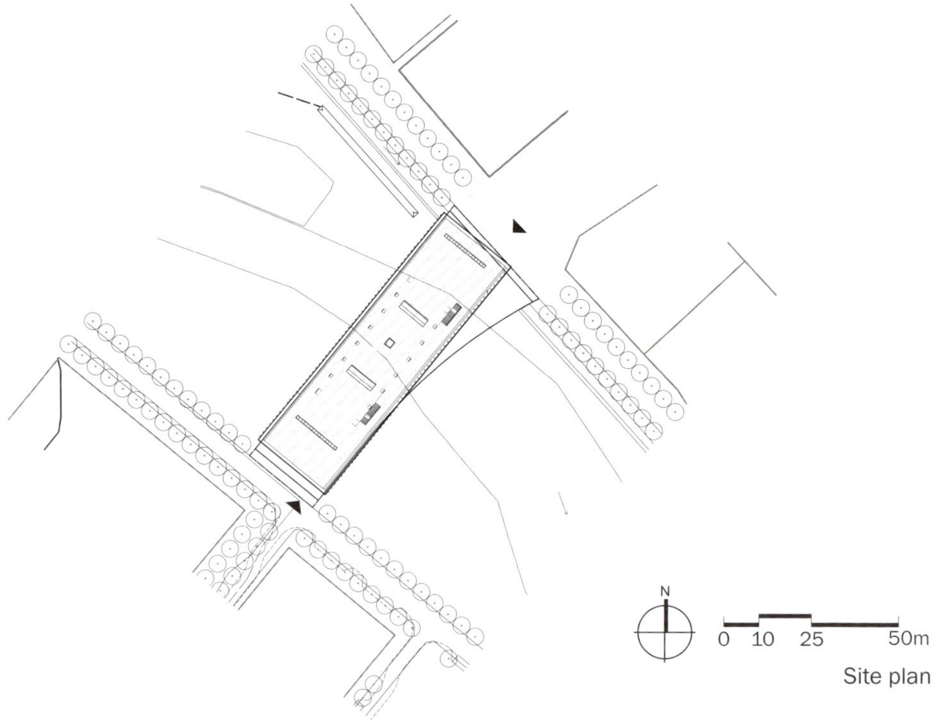

Site plan

v Distant view of Museum Bridge

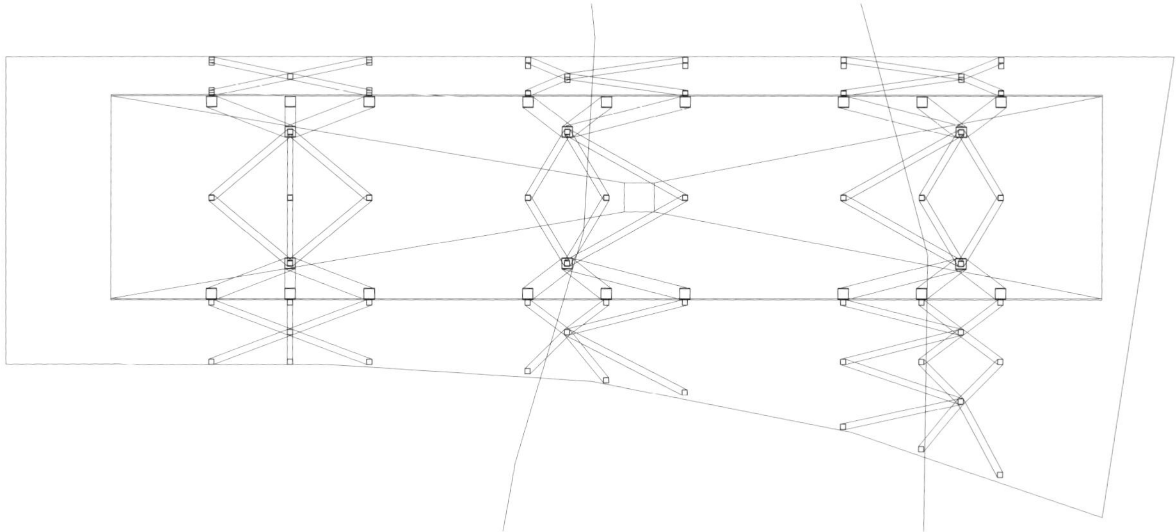

Under-bridge plan

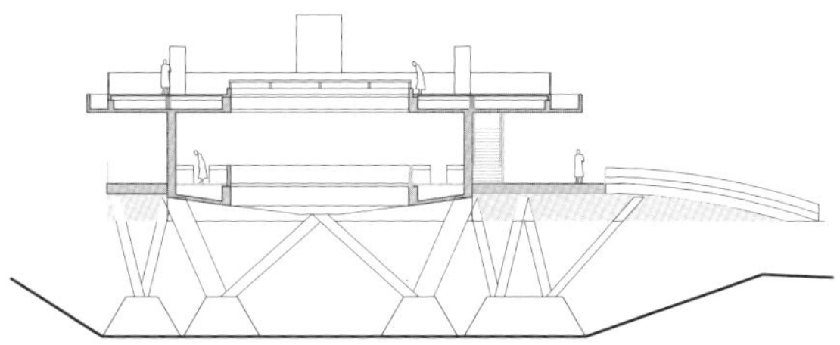

Cross section

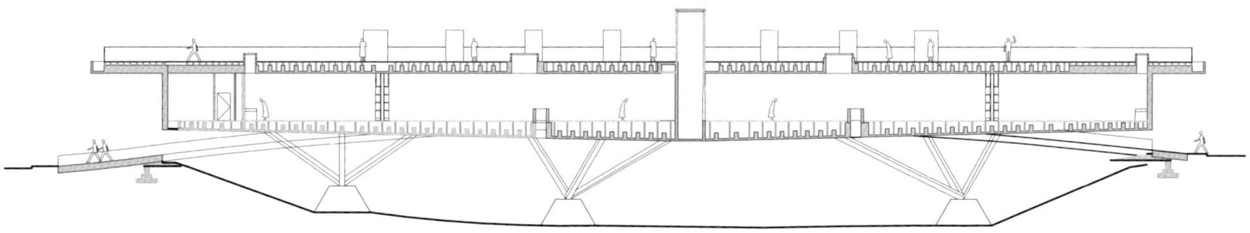

Longitudinal section

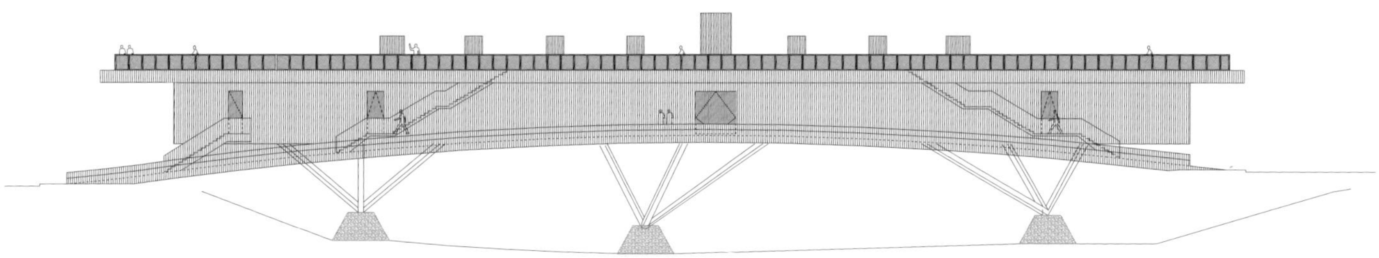

South elevation

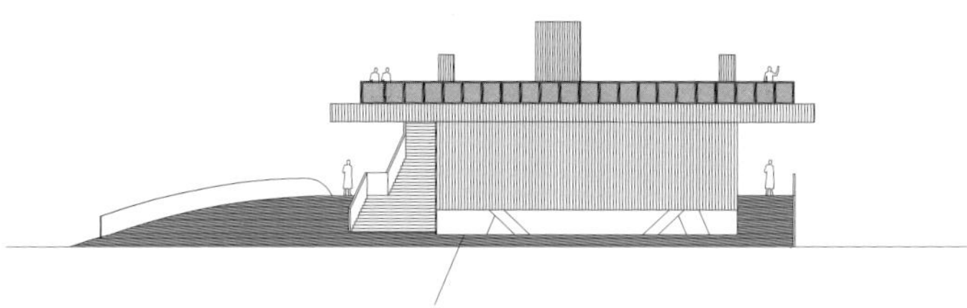

East elevation

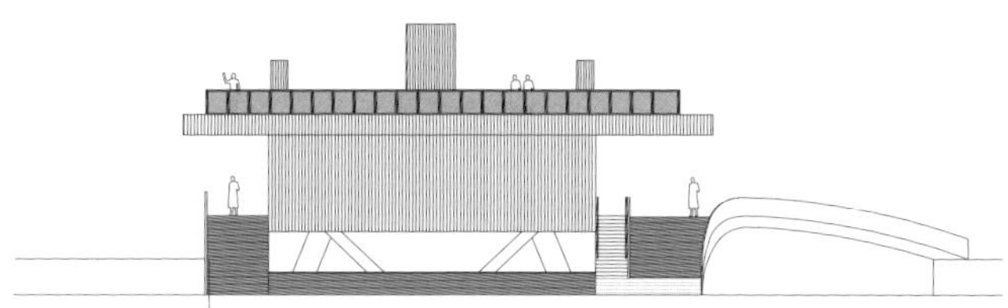

West elevation

0 4 10 20m

< On the Museum Bridge looking south

Paving the river pebbles walkway

Concrete cast with bamboo formwork

v River pebbles on top of balustrade, ground, and steps

v Main staircase to roof terrace

Space in exhibition hall

Exhibits installed

v Exhibition hall with natural light

Frames from film *ENJOYING* by Atelier FCJZ

v Creek under the bridge

[EXPERIENCE of CITY]

21Cake, Huangpu Shop

Shanghai, China

2016

A site with limitations: In a shopping complex in central Shanghai, the space for 21Cake measures 33 square meters and has a narrow linear configuration and two bends, and a column in the middle.

A challenge goal: We were asked by the bakery chain, renowned for its design innovation, not only to transform an unusable space to become usable, but also to create a state-of-the-art cake and coffee shop within.

Shop as shop window: Because of the shallowness of the space given, the entire store is treated as a fully equipped shop window with two counters—one facing the street and the other facing the inside of the shopping center. Even though the space is too tight to accommodate seating for the customers, a Corian wall has been installed, so that customers may lean against it as they enjoy the confections; along the window is also a cantilevered table made from the same material. Similar to a shop window—perhaps even resembling a billboard—there are signs and product information displayed using LED lights on the translucent interior wall, which passersby along the street can easily read. On the sidewalk, furniture pieces provide rest stations for customers, as well as pedestrians. As small as it is, we hope this store engages the city in a big way.

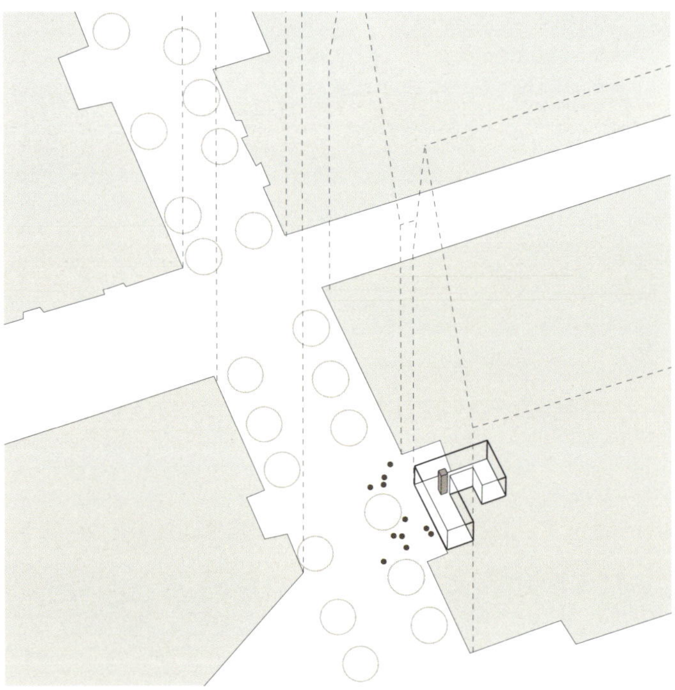

v The shallowness of the shop led it to be creatively transformed to be part of the street space

> View of the shop from the street

21cake
廿一客
21cake
雨水

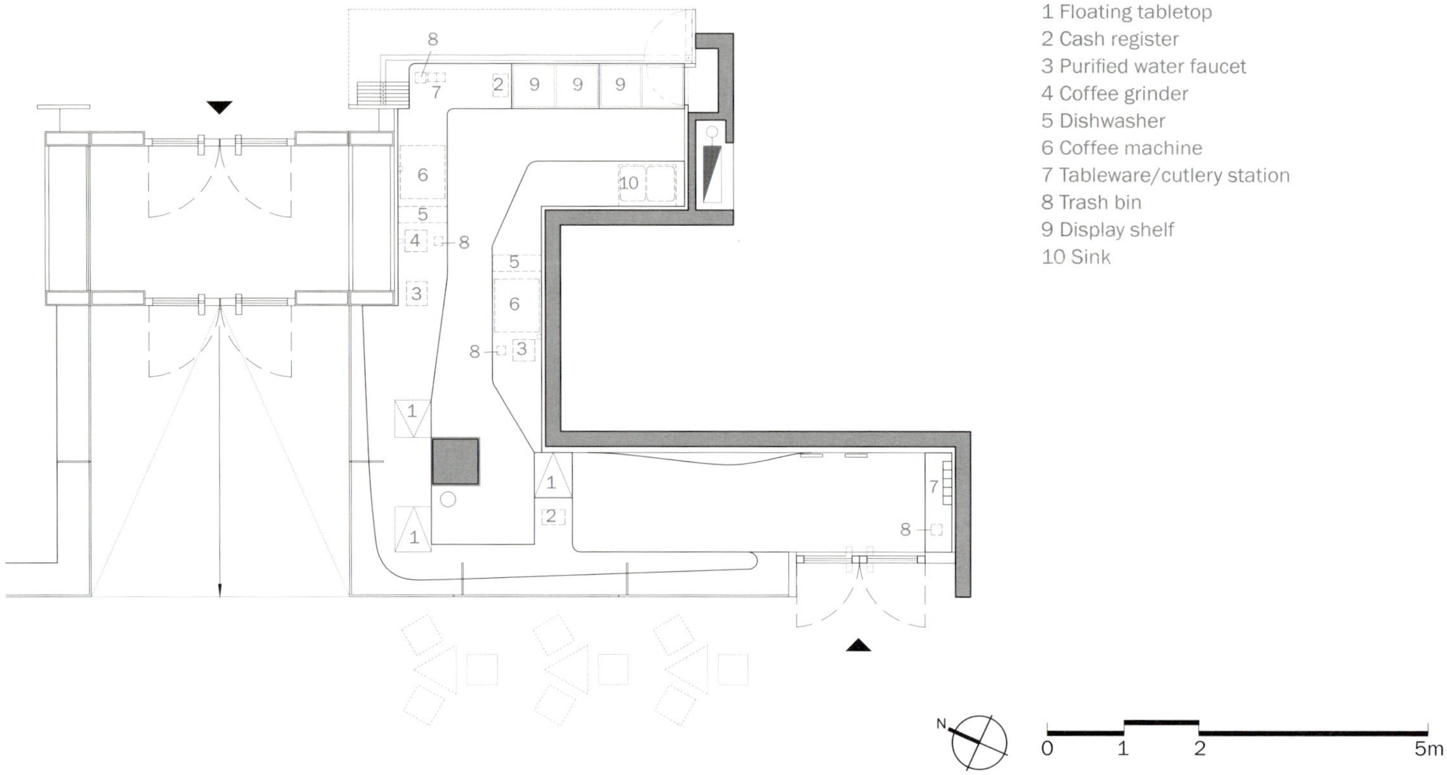

1 Floating tabletop
2 Cash register
3 Purified water faucet
4 Coffee grinder
5 Dishwasher
6 Coffee machine
7 Tableware/cutlery station
8 Trash bin
9 Display shelf
10 Sink

Plan

v View of concertina store shutter from inside the mall

Closed

Open

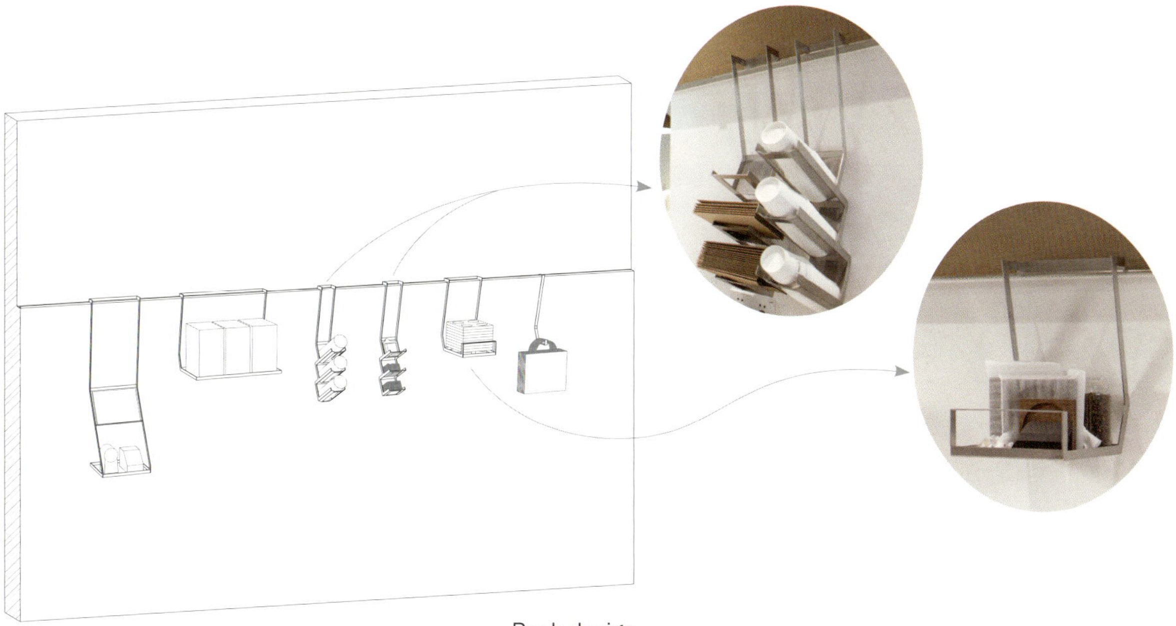

Rack design

A curve designed in the wall for leaning against

v Customers leaning against Corian wall and counter

[EXPERIENCE of CITY]

21Cake, Baoshan Shop

Shanghai, China

2020

The interior design of 21Cake's Baoshen store in Shanghai is based on the idea of *da shitang* and *da fanzhuo*, meaning big canteen or communal dining hall and big shared dining table, which were common in China throughout the 1950s to 1970s. We wanted to express how a bakery could also be a community center. The design of this shop is meant to be a prototype that can be used in other branches in the future.

In the center of the shop is a bean-shaped *da fanzhuo* or puzzle-piece table, which is made up of ten small tables. The "pieces" (or tables) can be taken apart and rearranged as desired. This concept supports customers' various spatial needs in the bakery throughout the day, for example, small tables for individuals to have breakfast in the morning or big tables for gatherings of various sizes later in the day. It can also be arranged to host a baking class, with just a few students, or a birthday party with a large crowd. Other than using it for dining, the *da fanzhuo* may also be configured for the purpose of displaying the bakery's products, like breads and cakes.

v Interior view of store, with the *da fanzhuo* assembled as one big table

On the floor, underneath the *da fanzhuo*, copper strips are overlaid on the terrazzo to outline and map the configuration of the table above, which serves as a kind of "user's manual" for arranging the furniture. The lighting fixtures above the *da fanzhuo* are flexible and can be adjusted according to the positions of the tables.

The *xiao tuiche* or little pushcart is another innovative element in the design, and is a concept borrowed from the traditional style of serving dim sum. These carts allow customers to be served at their tables by the service team. They can also be used to display fresh bakes at the entrance, as well as other locations in the store for sampling. The *xiao tuiche* are made of bent plywood and are designed in three different models—for bread, cake, and ice cream, respectively.

For the overall design of the space, we used terrazzo, wood, and stucco as main materials; all in warm hues to create a relaxing and homey feeling for the neighbor-customers.

Close-up of the *da fanzhuo* plan on the floor

v *Disassembled da fanzhuo*, with lighting adjusted according to the table arrangement

< The bean-shaped *da fanzhuo* occupies the center of the shop

With the *xiao tuiche*, or pushcarts, customers may be served at their tables

v Close-up of *da fanzhuo*

v A row of *xiao tuiche*

[EXPERIENCE of CITY]

Jishou Art Museum

Jishou, Hunan Province, China

2019

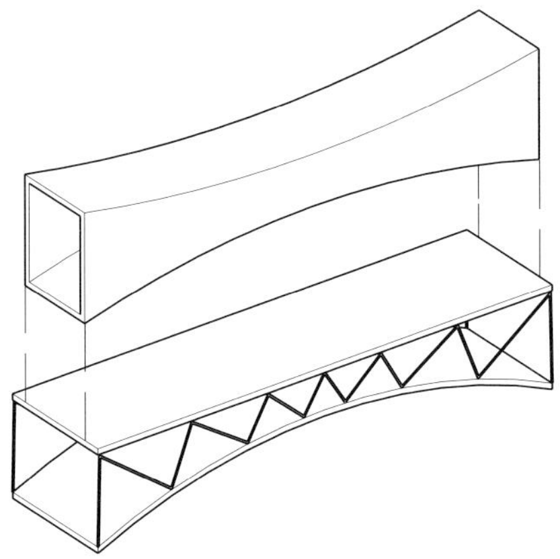

COMMENTS

Jiang Jiawei
Postdoctoral Fellow, School of Architecture and Urban Planning, Tongji University

Jishou Art Museum closely follows the dwellings on both sides of the Wanrong River. Its scale and color fit perfectly into the existing appearance of the town. There are many ethnic minority groups, including Miao, Tujia, Dong, and Yao, who have lived in the adjacent regions, like western Hunan, eastern Guizhou, and northern Guangxi since ancient times. They are brave and bellicose and often attach meanings to their surroundings. The *fengyu* bridges in their stockaded villages were the social centers for the people. Today, such cultural images remain as a collective memory, although their mythological meaning have faded away. They strike a chord with the local villagers and continue to create a sense of nostalgia. The art museum enters the ancient town as a modern institution and facilitates the old village's modern transition, while still evoking past cultural images in the form of an unfamiliar structure. In other words, this does not simply challenge their preconceived ideas, but also reimagines their symbolisms.

A social cause: The city of Jishou, where the Jishou Art Museum is located, is the regional capital of Xiangxi in western Hunan Province and a minority autonomous zone. Initially, the municipal government was considering parcels of lands in the development zone outside the urban core for the museum, however, we proposed to build the art museum in the center of the old town because we believe that a cultural facility should be easily accessible. The Wanrong River runs through the middle of Jishou, therefore designating the most central location for the art museum as being over the water. This also allows the art museum to double as a pedestrian bridge. By situating it so, we hoped that people in Jishou would not only make a special trip to the museum to view art, but would also encounter art on their way to work, school, or to the store, as they use the bridge.

Urban intervention: Typical contemporary cultural institutions in China, such as museums and theaters, are treated as freestanding monuments, away from communities. We think that an art museum should not be isolated from its users. The Jishou Art Museum is inserted into the existing urban fabric with buildings along the Wanrong River that house shops, restaurants, and B&Bs (often with the owners living upstairs). Hence, the front entrances of the Jishou Art Museum on both riverbanks are part of the mixed-use street walls and are integrated into everyday life.

Reinterpretation of tradition: Covered bridges called *fengyu qiao*—meaning wind-and-rain bridge—have long been a tradition in the mountainous regions of China. They are not only used for getting across rivers or valleys, but also serve as public spaces where travelers can rest, and where vendors set up stands to sell their wares. Our design creates a contemporary interpretation of the age-honored building type. With this project, we introduce art as a new program on a covered bridge, while maintaining pedestrian traffic, ultimately translating the formal language of the *fengyu qiao* into a modern one.

A bridge building: The art museum is composed of two bridges that are stacked one over the other. The lower level is an open steel truss structure that resembles a covered street for pedestrians and also allows the flow through of water when the river floods; the upper level is a concrete arch that was cast-in-situ, with a painting gallery inside. In between the two bridges, glazed walls and a tiled shading system enclose the art museum's main hall for temporary exhibitions. Supplementary spaces, such as the entrance halls, administrative office, shop, and tearoom are situated in the two bridgeheads at either end. People can enter the museum from either side of the river.

Jishou Art Museum is in debt to the artist Mr. Huang Yongyu for his initiation and donation.

> Bird's-eye view

Jishou Art Museum as an insertion in the existing urban fabric

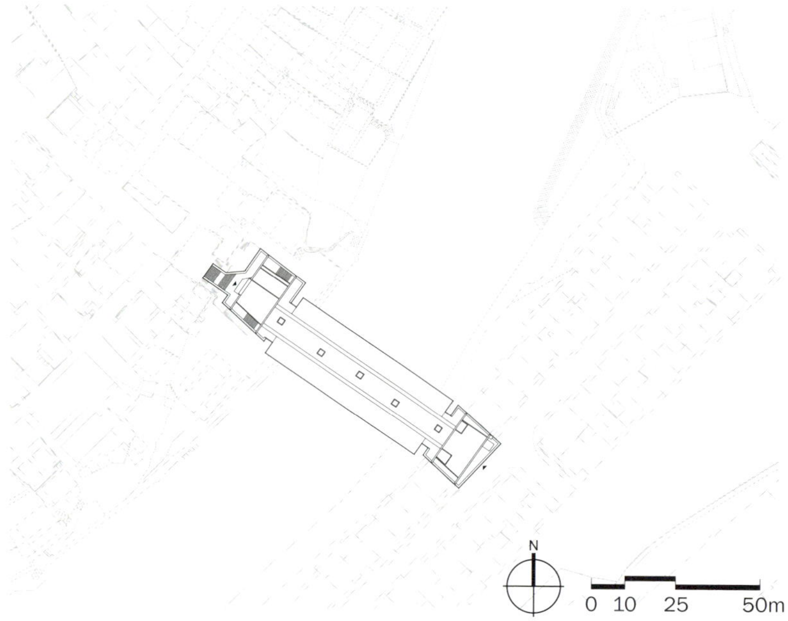

Site plan

v View over Wanrong River

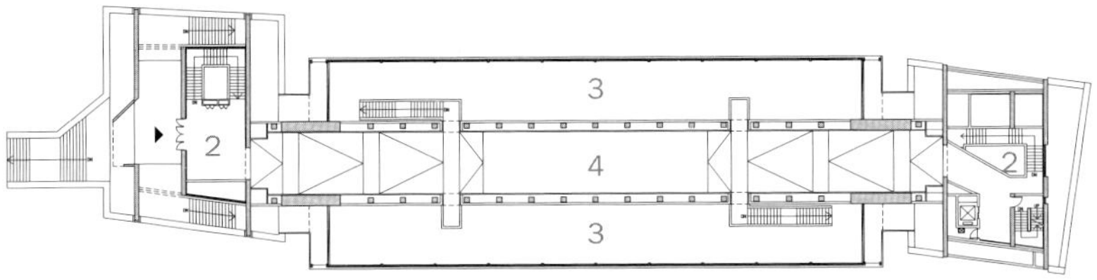

Third-floor plan

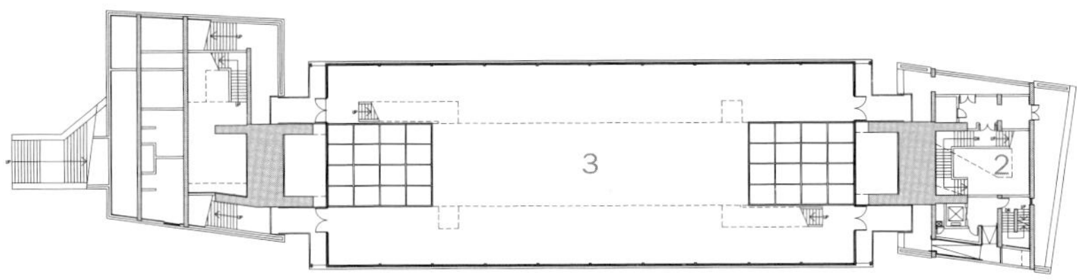

Second-floor plan

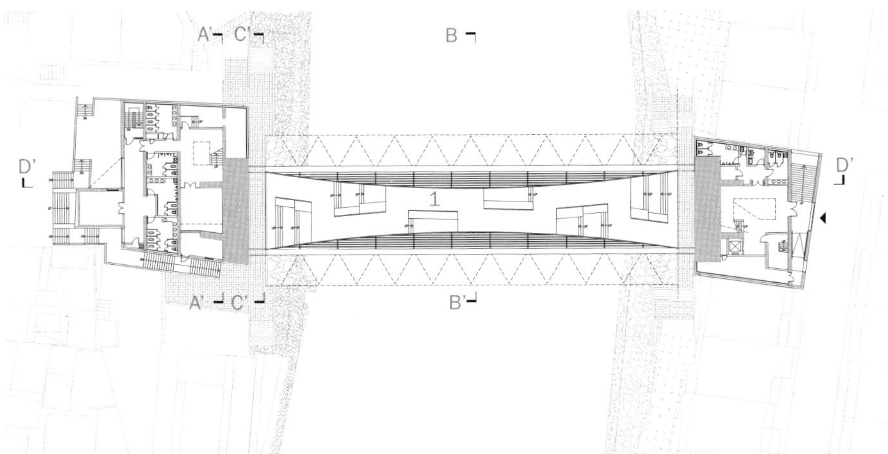

First-floor plan

1 Pedestrian crossing level
2 Lobby
3 Great exhibition hall
4 Painting gallery

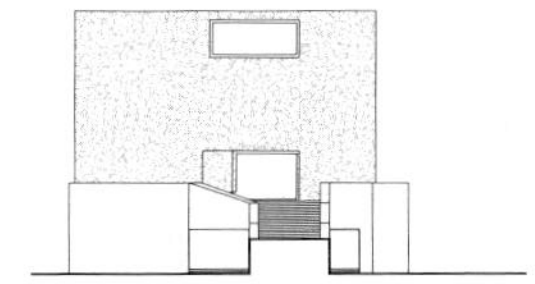

West elevation

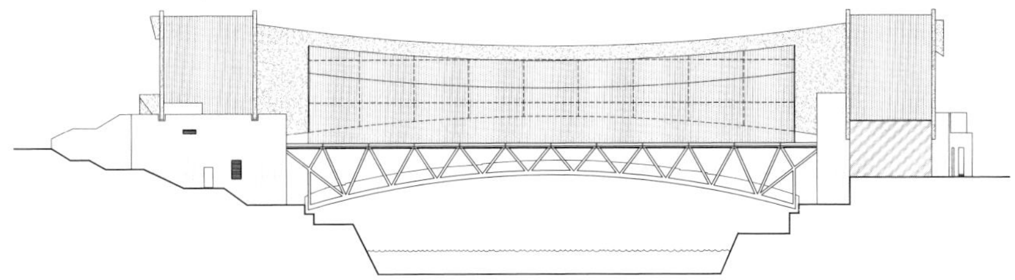

South elevation

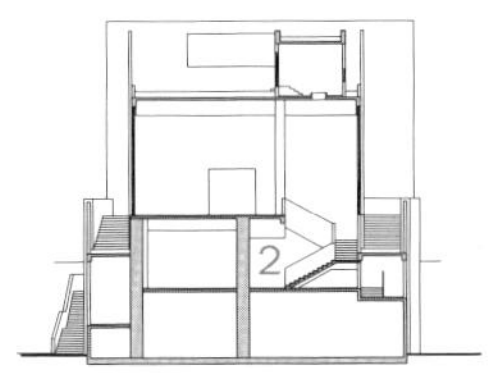

Section A-A'

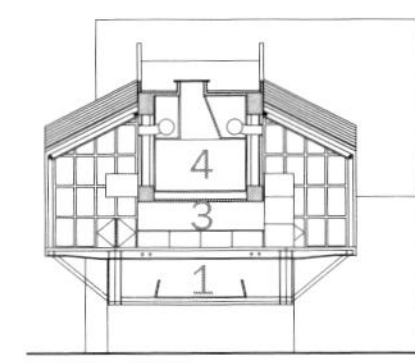

Section B-B'

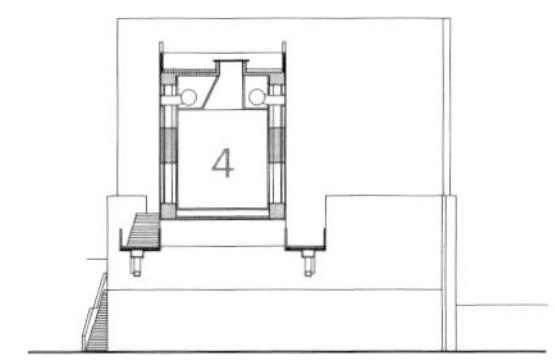

Section C-C'

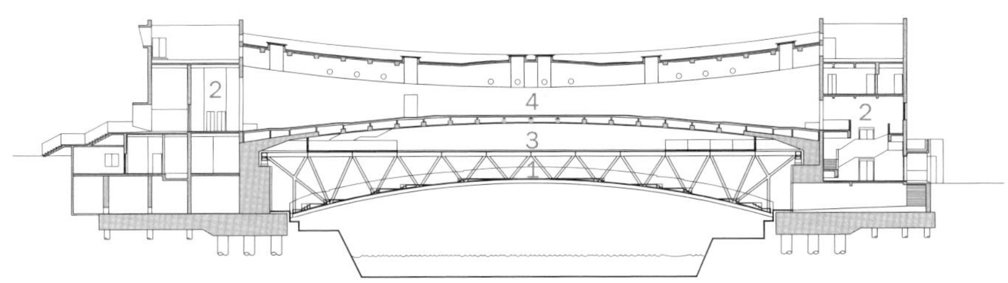

Section D-D'

Fengyu qiao

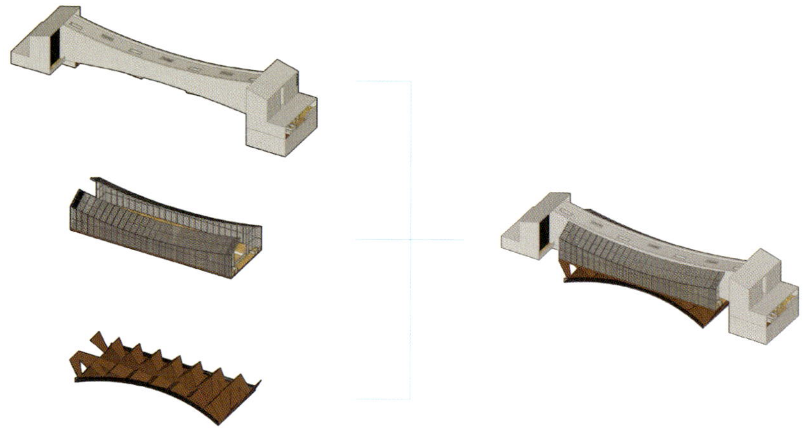

Conceptual diagram of a double-decker design: concrete bridge over steel bridge

∨ Pedestrian bridge level

Social life on a *fengyu qiao* (left)
Social life on Jishou Art Museum pedestrian bridge level (right)

v Pedestrian bridge level with skylights looking into great exhibition hall

1 < 1 Third-floor painting gallery inside concrete bridge

2 < 2 Great exhibition hall under concrete bridge

Transitional space with post-tensioned prestressing bolt for concrete bridge structure on left wall

v Staircase in east lobby

v East entrance lobby

< Great exhibition hall

v Looking out from the west entrance

v Looking at the museum from a nearby street

< East entrance
> West entrance

Close-up of west façade

v Walkway outside the museum

Close-up of tiled shading

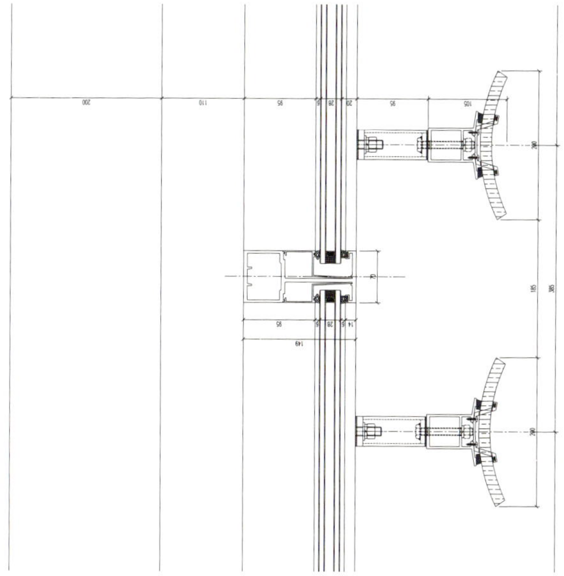

Curtain wall plan showing tiled shading

∨ Riverside façade with tiled shading

∨ Looking at the great exhibition hall from the third-floor balcony

[EXPERIENCE of CITY]

Zigzag Tower

Zhengzhou, Henan Province, China

2019

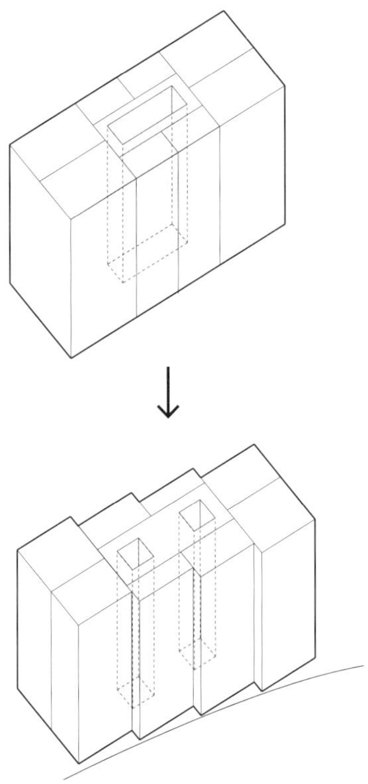

Typological analysis: Speculative office tower design is usually dictated by a set of conventions developed primarily with concerns for safety and natural light. For this project in the eastern district of Zhengzhou, Henan Province, after analyzing various precedents, we decided to accept the prototypical rectilinear plan with central cores as the starting point of our design, while looking actively for opportunities for modifications.

Site geometry: The opportunity to modify the prototype was presented by the site itself—a slightly curved rectilinear parcel that is a part of a monumental ring around an artificial lake. We believe the curvature, however subtle, should be acknowledged and so transformed the typical rectangle of the plan into a zigzag. By doing so, we also created a sense of verticality with an otherwise square volume.

Floor plan and space: The zigzag configuration offers a floor plan with multiple corners and better views, as well as a sense of an open space as the aggregate of a number of smaller increments. In the section, we devised an atrium between the two cores that penetrates all the floors. There are two sets of bridges that span the central void so that the verticality of the building and the drama of the space can be experienced from within.

Structure and economy: The structure is a beam-free reinforced-concrete slab system with central cores and peripheral columns and allows a totally open and flexible space, which can be divided into offices of diverse sizes. Without beams, we were able to reduce the floor height—but not the ceiling height—and include an extra floor within the building height limit.

Façade: Peripheral columns, for load bearing and natural ventilation, are placed in an alternate pattern on the outside of the building enclosure, further reinforcing the vertical composition of the volumes. On the upper floors, every two columns twist and converge into one toward the ground, so as to have greater indoor-outdoor contact on the lower floors.

> View from outer ring road

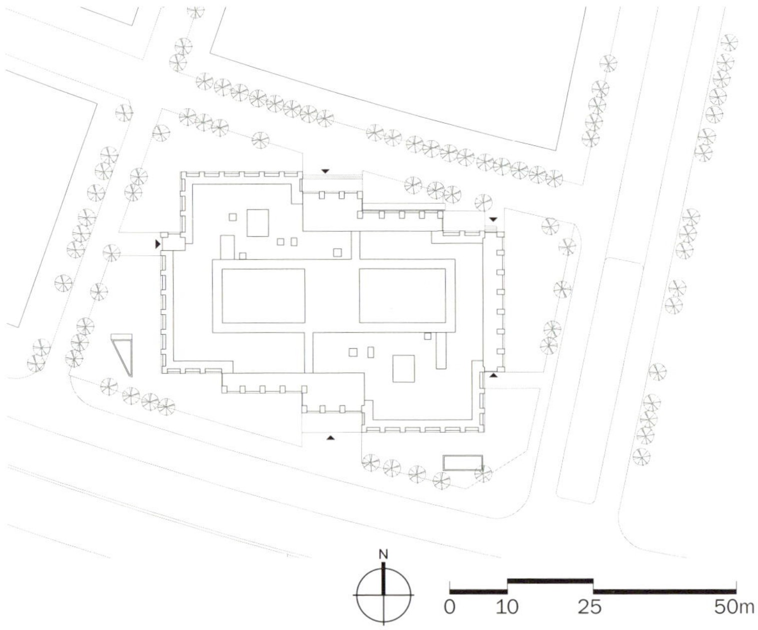

Site plan

Aerial view of rooftop

v Bird's-eye view of master plan

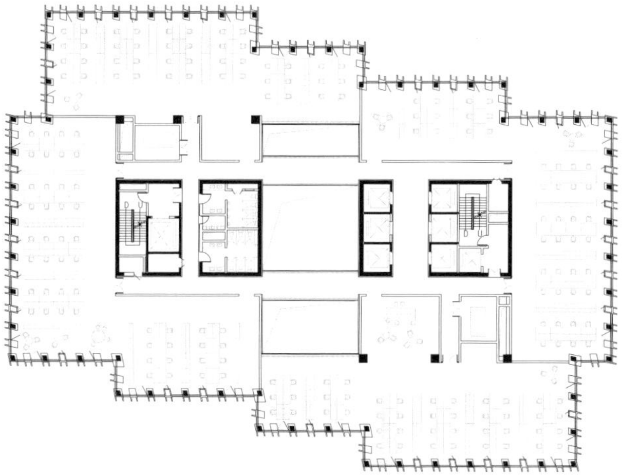

Typical-floor plan

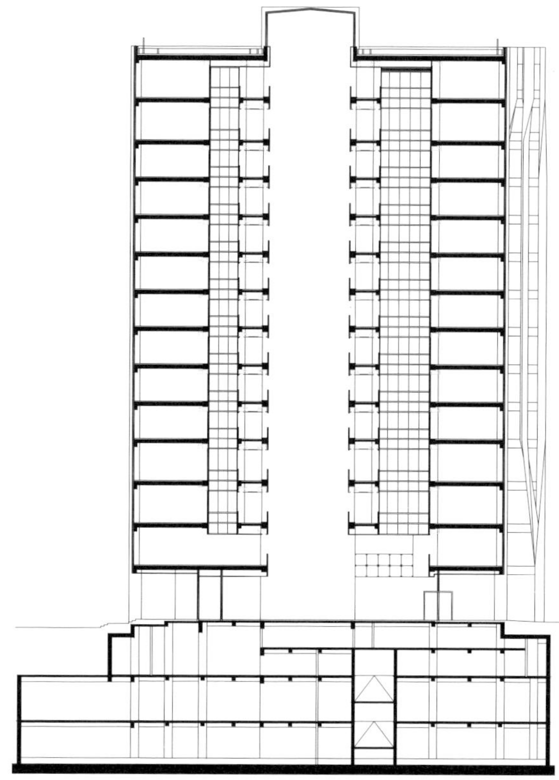

Section

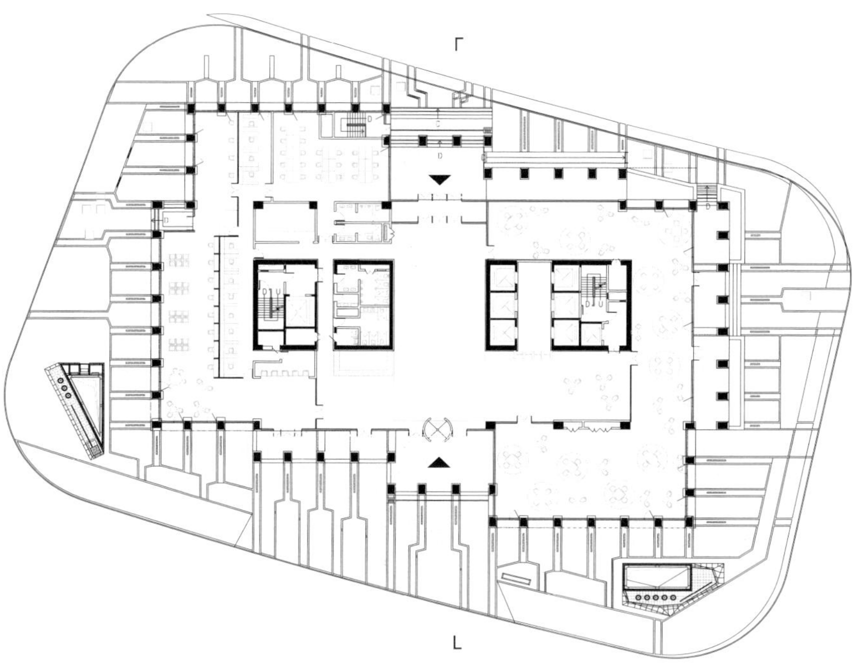

First-floor plan

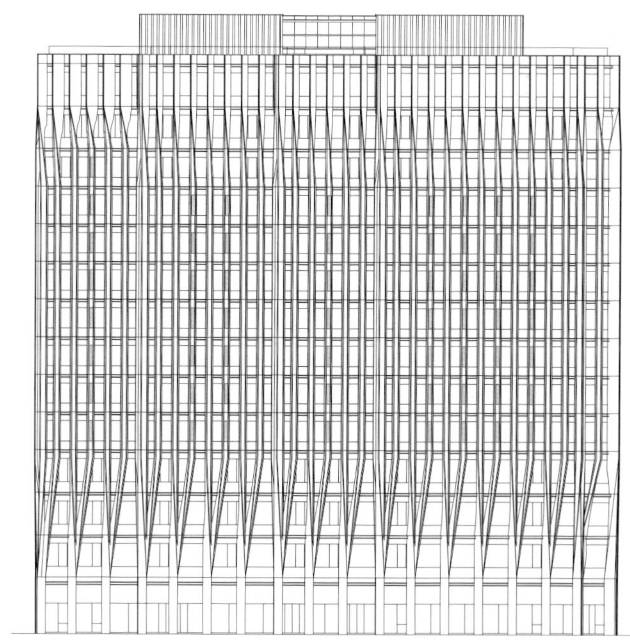

South elevation

0 4 10 20m

Structural system

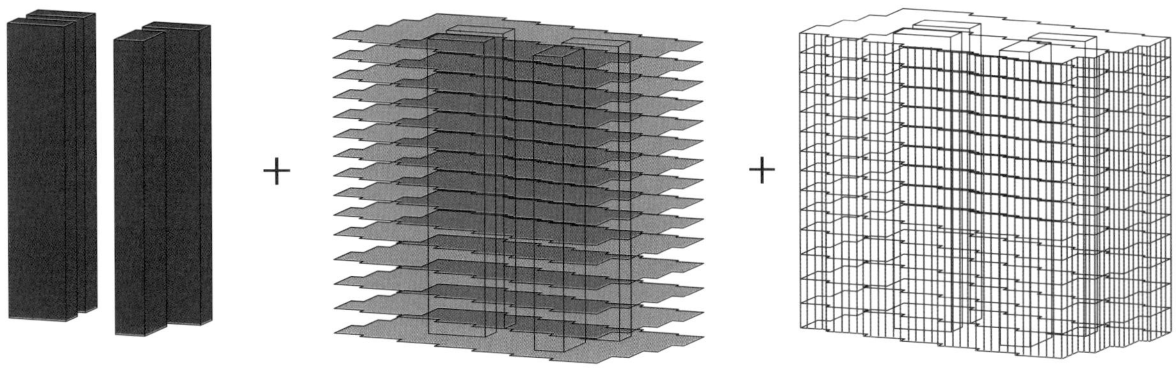

Core Flat slab floors Peripheral columns

v Upper part elevation details

Conceptual sectional diagram

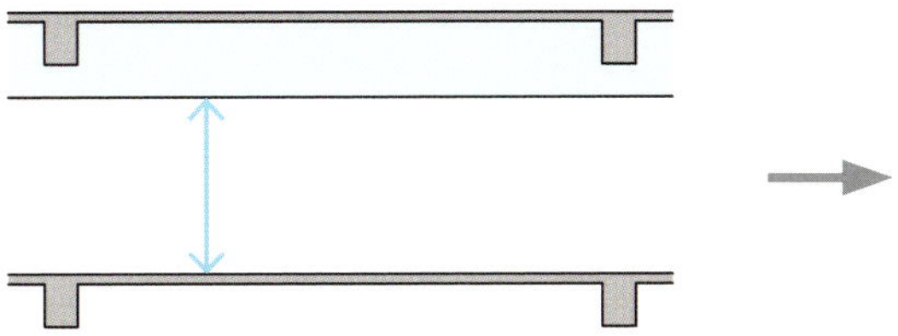

Beams intrude into the MEP space lower the ceiling and in turn reduce the height of the usable space.

A beamless structural system integrates the structure with the MEP space, thereby increasing the height of usable space.

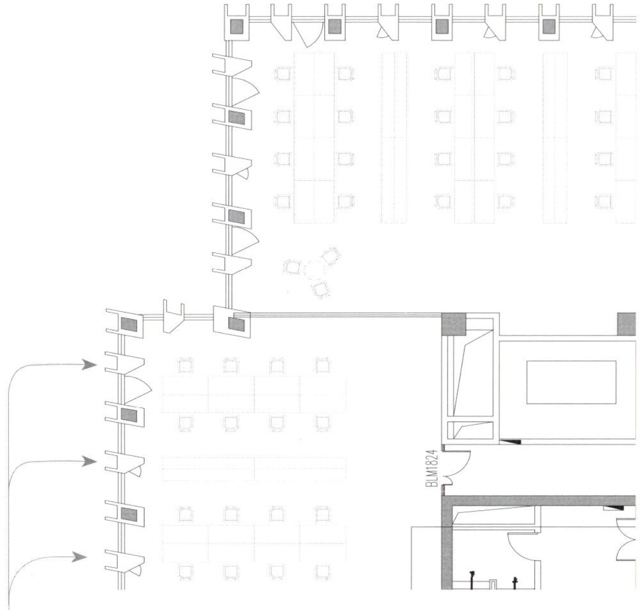

Partial plan of a typical floor

v Lower part elevation details

v Natural ventilation shafts from inside

1 < 1 Interior atrium

2 < 2 Bridge crossing atrium

> Sunlight accentuates the folding of the aluminum cladding

[EXPERIENCE of CITY]

Jiading Mini-Block

Shanghai, China

2020

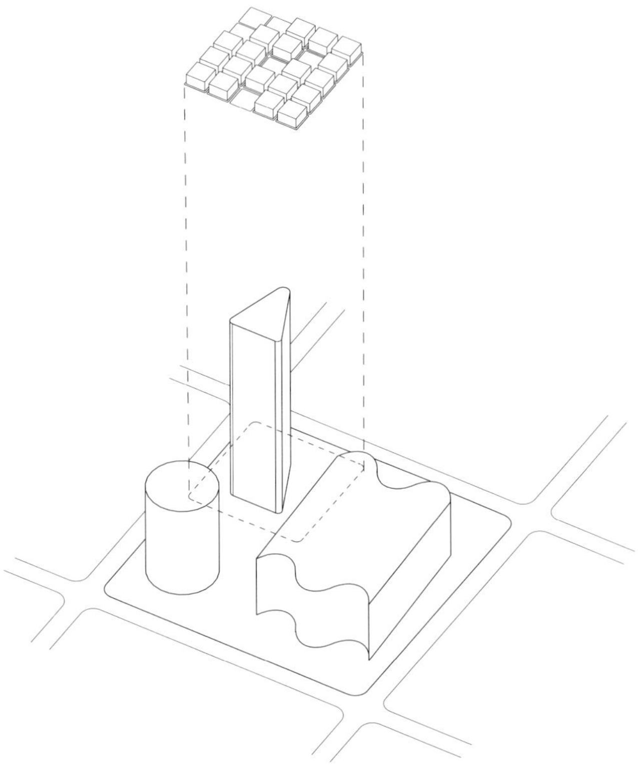

The challenge: The size of a typical block in new Chinese cities starts from approximately 500 by 500 meters. Such largeness, compared to the range of standard blocks in European cities, is a result of scaling cities for cars rather than people and accelerating the development of these cities. The problem of the "mega block" is twofold:

1. It is anti-urban—it does not produce a walkable city, and at the same time diminishes the quality of urban spaces.
2. It produces high carbon levels as its dependence on cars pollutes the air, as well as produces traffic congestion. Once a city is built based on such an inhuman spatial scale, it would be very difficult to remodel it into a livable environment.

It is crucial, therefore, to reconsider block size, before more mega blocks are realized in the ongoing urbanization of China. In other words, the block size has to be reduced to make a city both human and clean again.

The project: While our practice has not yet had the opportunity to plan an entire town or city, we were given the chance to design a R&D park outside of Shanghai in 2008, in the satellite town of Jiading, the Industry 4.0 Demonstration Base. The urban dimensions of this district for high-tech companies—a total of 24.67 hectares—prompted us to experiment with a smaller than usual block size. How small can a block be? We were aware that a block is part of the urban fabric and defined by streets and that the size of a block is determined by density, scale, and program.

An office park is typically suburban and accessed by the occupants/tenants by private cars. Once there, they would spend almost the entire work day in their office before driving home. There is little room for urban and social life. To achieve urbanity within an office park may be too tall an order, but we could definitely, at least, encourage the occupants to come out and walk around during their lunch break. But before defining the block, we first had to take on fabric and street.

The fabric: In the master plan, we tackled the issues of density and program and proposed a low-rise (with only four stories), high-density (average master plan FAR 1.2/block FAR 2) carpet with mixed programs, which would be mainly offices for high-tech companies with public/commercial facilities on the street level, and some residential elements on the top floor, such as rental apartments and hotels, but not condominiums, given Chinese zoning regulations.

The street: The primary urban space in this work-oriented area is the street, which has been designed to be ten meters wide and spatially defined by the three-meter-wide covered walkways on the ground level of the buildings. As the project is situated in the southern Yangtze River region, a cantilevered canopy or arcade protects pedestrians from the long rainy season and excessive sun in the summer.

The block: After establishing that each company may own a floor area of up to 4,000 square meters, retail outlets and eateries would desire corner locations, walkability, and connectivity between blocks—thereby having more building-street interface in general—we set the block size at 41.2 by 41.2 meters, which is an antithesis of the typical 500-meter and above mega block; we, therefore, referred to it as a "mini block." For reference, we searched globally for a city with a comparable block size and discovered in downtown Portland, Oregon, United States, a vibrant, livable city center with approximately 40-by-40-meter blocks. Other important dimensions of the mini block are as follows—

Grid: approximately 50 by 50 meters, from street center to street center.

Block/building module: 41.2 meters break down into five 8-meter column-to-column bays, plus 0.6 meters on each end for any potential architectural articulation of façade. A measurement of 41.2 by 41.2 meters meets the floor area ratio of 4,000 square meters per block to allow a block to be occupied by a number of small firms, or one large company. It is a single-building block.

While the majority of block-buildings are similar in size, each one is designed differently, in terms of floor plan and elevations, which allows the development to meet the varied space and identity needs of the businesses, while enriching the experience in the urban spaces.

First four mini blocks: For the architectural design phase, we began with four mini blocks. We were asked to facilitate a number of public functions, such as a convention center and a hotel, the spatial demands of which resulted in eight-story buildings. To be true to our master plan, we designed two separate pieces of architecture—four-story block-buildings on the ground and another four-story continuous loop building that "floats" on the top of the mini blocks.

This allows the mini block concept to accommodate a higher density, if needed. There are twenty-two block-buildings in an area of around 70,000 square meters designed by Atelier FCJZ. The others were designed by local architectural design institutes.

The master plan: The concept of the master plan is reinforced by several other measures as follows.

Architectural design guidelines: the conventional master plan for control in China does not define the specific locations and configurations of buildings, and as a result, it controls only the floor area ratio, lot coverage, height limit, and greenery coverage, but not the quality of urban spaces. We developed design guidelines between the stages of master plan design and architectural design as a critical tool for the implementation of planning and urban ideas. Besides our own office, other design institutes/offices participating in the project needed to follow the design guidelines closely.

Integrated circulation: we introduced to some of the secondary circulatory routes the concept of "shared street," to mix street life and vehicular traffic through careful design, in order to achieve safety and accessibility at the same time. While this idea was not fully implemented, the meandering of the vehicular traffic through the street was realized.

Covered walkway system: as mentioned earlier, a 3-meter-wide colonnade or cantilevered canopy was required on the street level for all the buildings, as specified in the architectural design guidelines.

Building envelope: a setback is generally not permitted from the second floor up (as specified in the design guidelines) unless certain limited volumetric cut-outs are called for by the architectural design.

The conclusion: While the human scale remains constant, our perception of it does change, often emboldened by technological inventions like automobiles. Our ability to move faster and go further has, from time to time, made us lose sight of our bodily dimensions, imagining a scale that our physical being ultimately does not relate to. We have to reconsider the scale of buildings and cities, which are meant for human activities, or simply human life.

Jiading Mini-Block is a test in designing an urban space with a more human scale. The tenancy market responded favorably, as offices were leased out quickly. The next thing we are curious to see is whether the occupants will step out during lunch hours. With cautious optimism, we hope that there will be municipalities who take cues from Jiading and follow its lead in envisioning the creation of intimate neighborhoods, if not entire towns in the near future.

v Urban fabric made up of twenty-two block-buildings

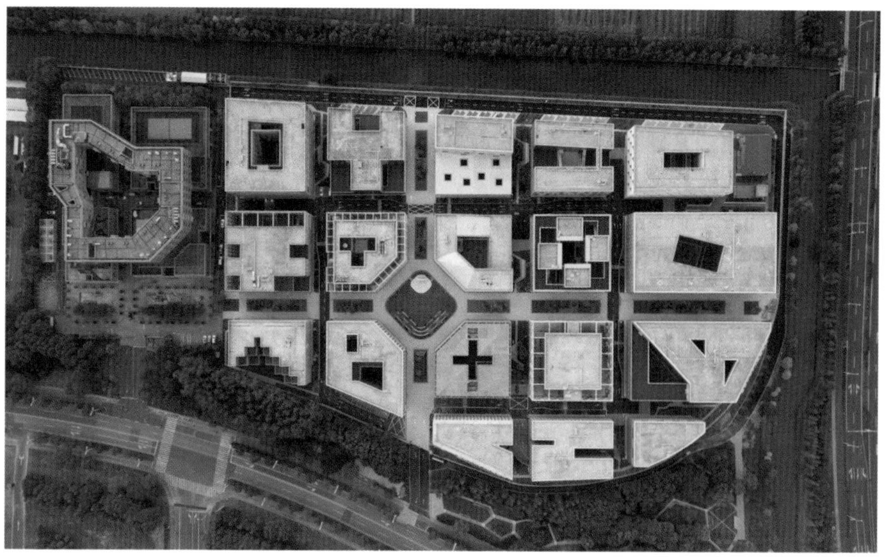

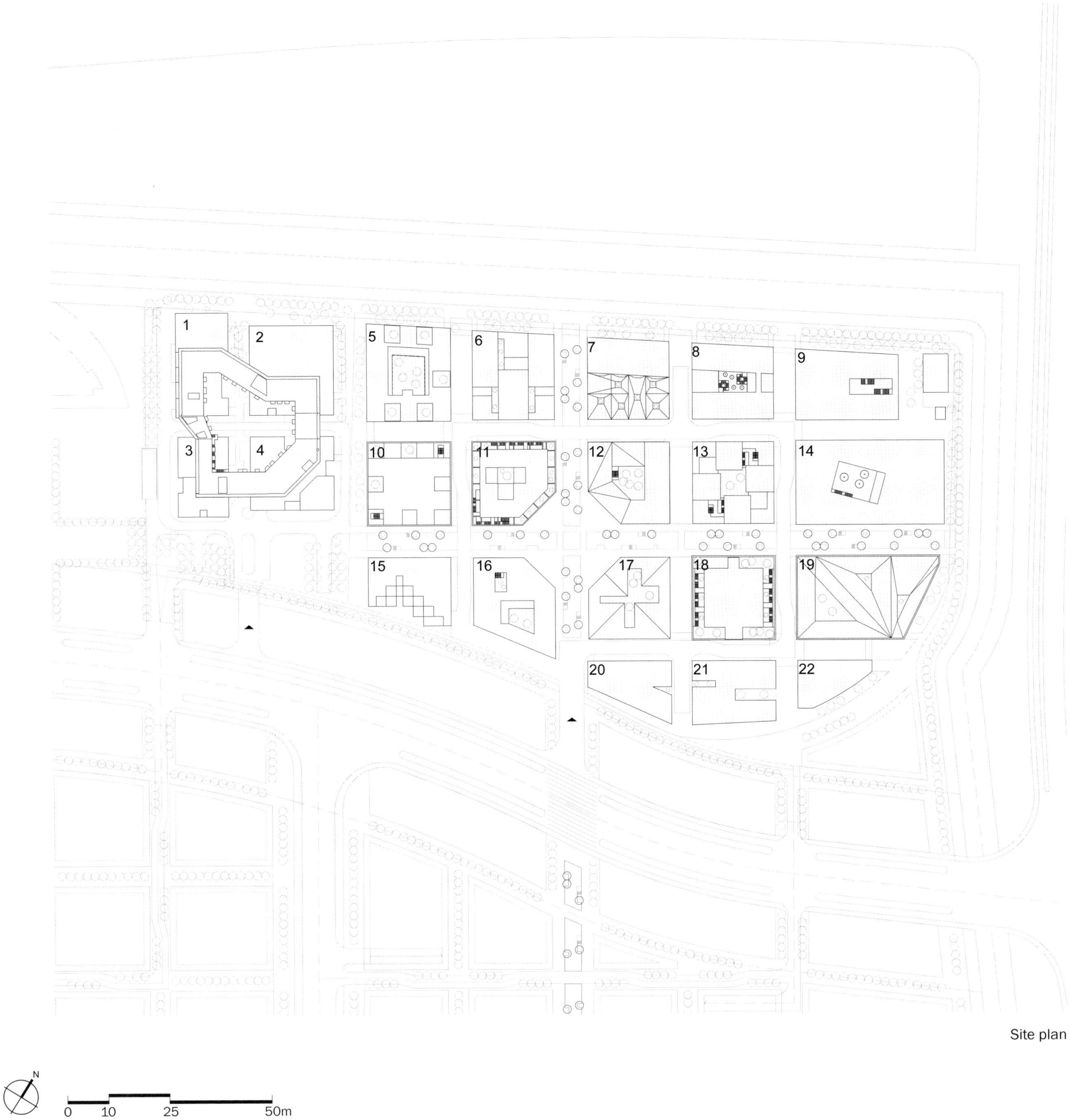

Site plan

First-floor plan

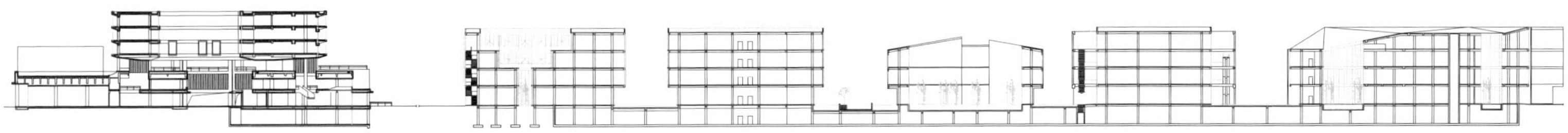

Sections

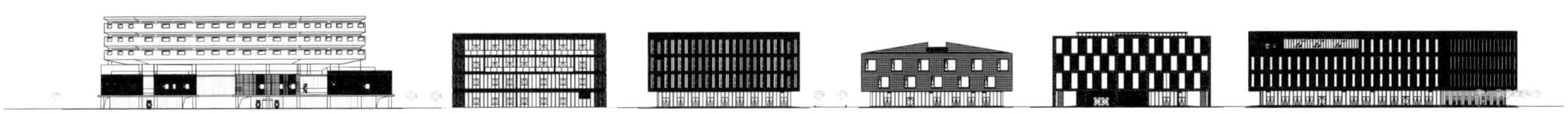

Elevations

> Under covered walkway along a vehicular street

An intersection of pedestrian streets

v Under covered walkway along a pedestrian street

出口
EXIT

< A street corner
> Changing façade design

v Block-building 15

v Block-building 8

Façade detail of block-building 11

Façade detail of block-building 20

Skylights of block-building 7

Façade detail of block-building 13

v Block-building 12

v Block-building 9

1	2
3	4

< 1 Courtyard in block-building 13
< 2 Courtyard in block-building 5
< 3 Courtyard in block-building 11
< 4 Passageway of block-building 5

v Interior of block-building 7

[EXPERIENCE of CITY]

Qingpu Bridge

Shanghai, China

Schematic design

Site: Qingpu, Shanghai, is one of the fastest developing suburban districts of metropolitan Shanghai, and part of the Yangtze River Delta, with an extensive network of watercourses. We were asked to design a bridge over one of the rivers to connect the road systems on either bank.

Program and reprograming: The initial program we received was a standard one—a bridge slab that is shared by lanes for vehicular traffic in the middle and bicycle and pedestrian lanes on the sides. Given fast-changing current-day lifestyles, two questions came to mind: If the bridge was also to be a place for people besides automobiles, could it still be defined as an infrastructure for circulation and transportation only? And should pedestrians and cars share the same space?

These questions led us to design a series of Y-shape piers with two one-way motorways placed on the top of the upper branches of the "Y," and a landscaped rolling bridge for pedestrians and cyclists at its intersection. So, the singular bridge in a typical design brief is now disassembled into three: the upper two bridges function as closed expressways, and the lower one becomes a park.

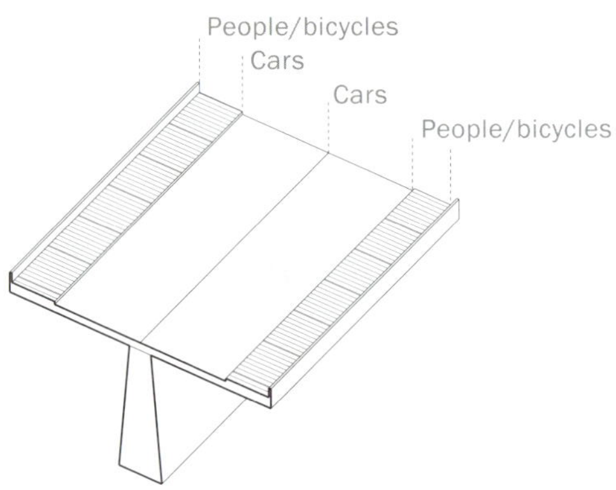

↓

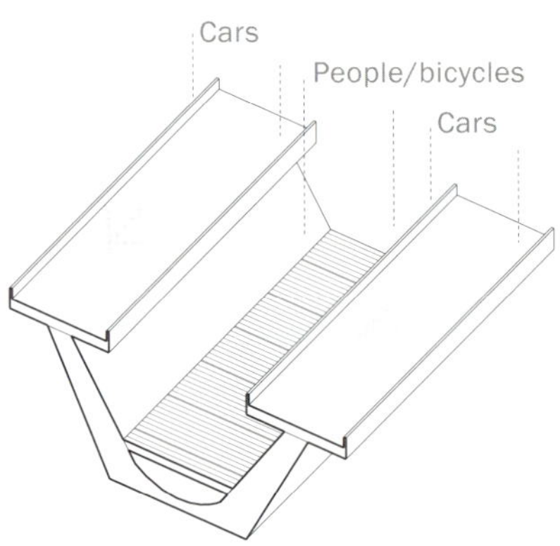

v Bird's-eye view

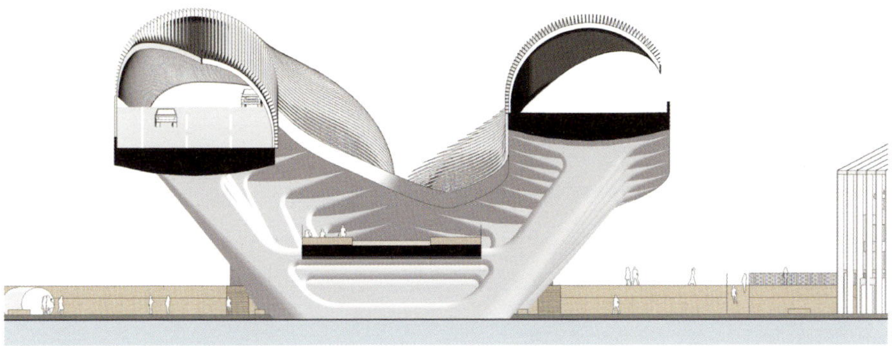

Section

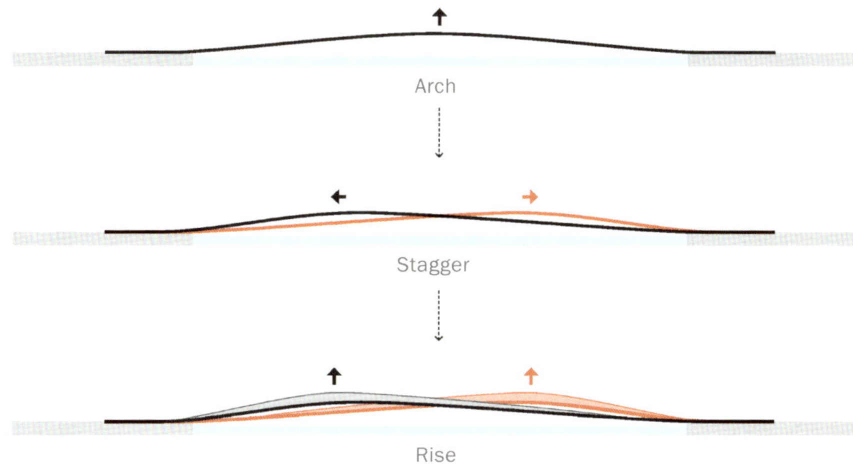

Conceptual design

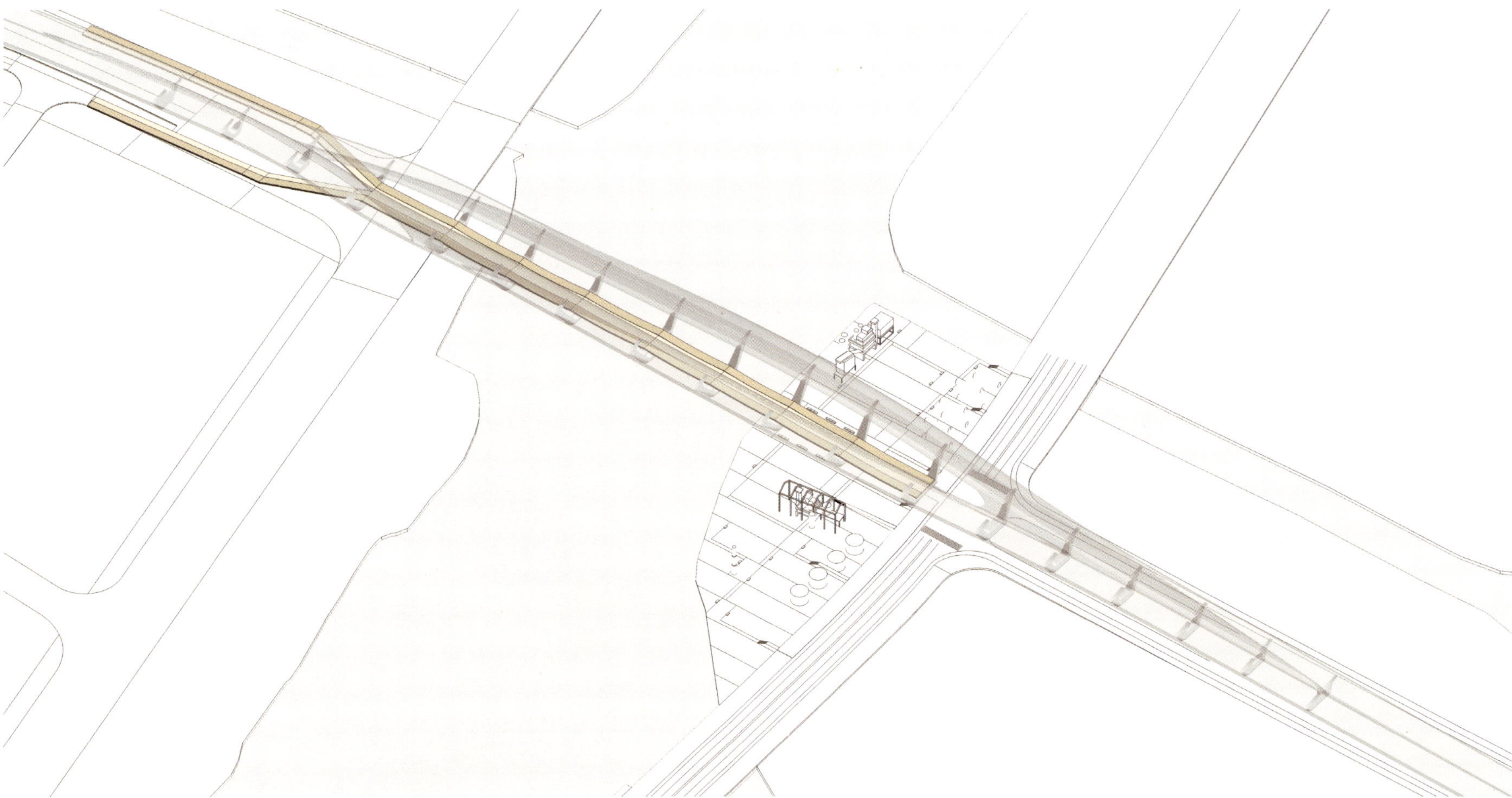

Axonometric

Elevation

> 1 River perspective

> 2 Pedestrian bridge perspective

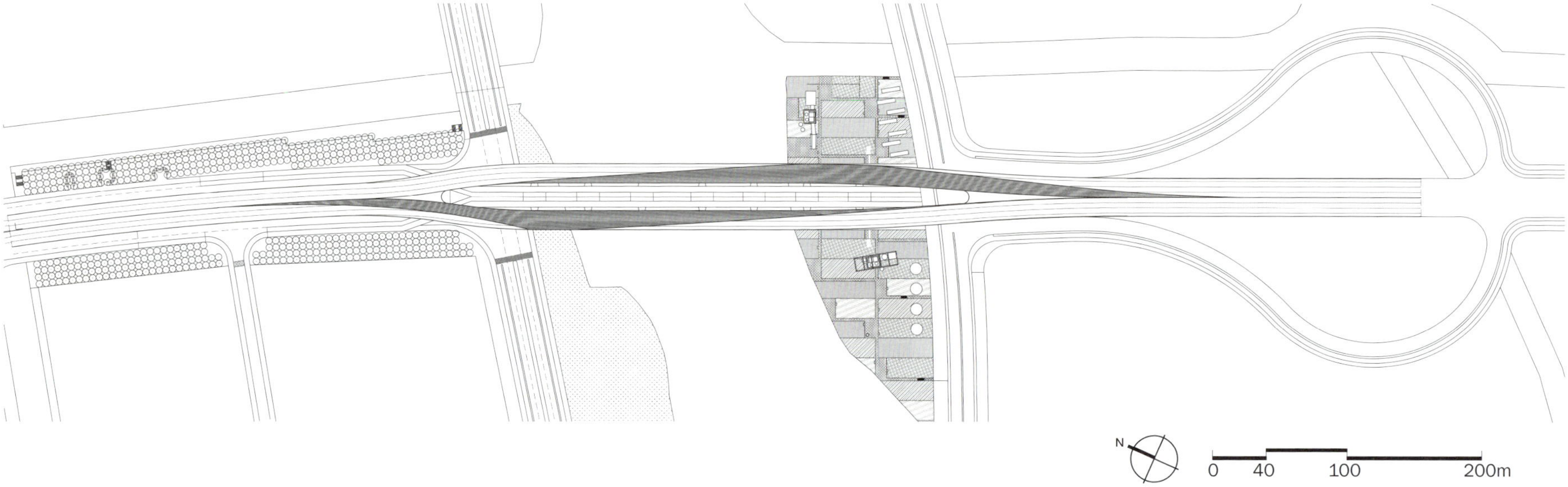

Site plan

v Pedestrian bridge perspective

[EXPERIENCE of EVERYDAY]

Thick Thin Fold

2009

A two-in-one material: The folding screen is a flexible space divider that has been used in China and East Asia for centuries. One typical version of it is a wood frame covered by rice paper—the wood provides a sturdy structure and the rice paper allows light to come through. The Thick Thin Fold is a folding screen made from one single material—an artificial stone produced by Formica and sculpted by a CNC machine, which meets both the needs for structure and translucency. The thickness of the screen tapers gradually, from 4 millimeters at one end, to 40 millimeters at the other, generating a gradation of light.

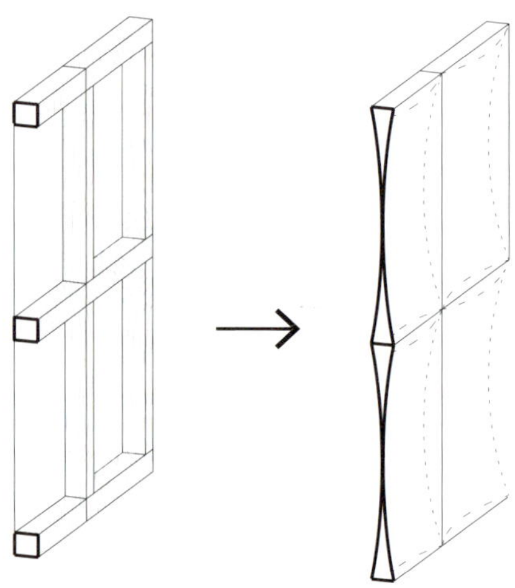

Japanese *shoji* screen

v The sheen of the material is visible only from an angle

v The material is translucent when looked at directly

> Thick Thin Fold screen on exhibition

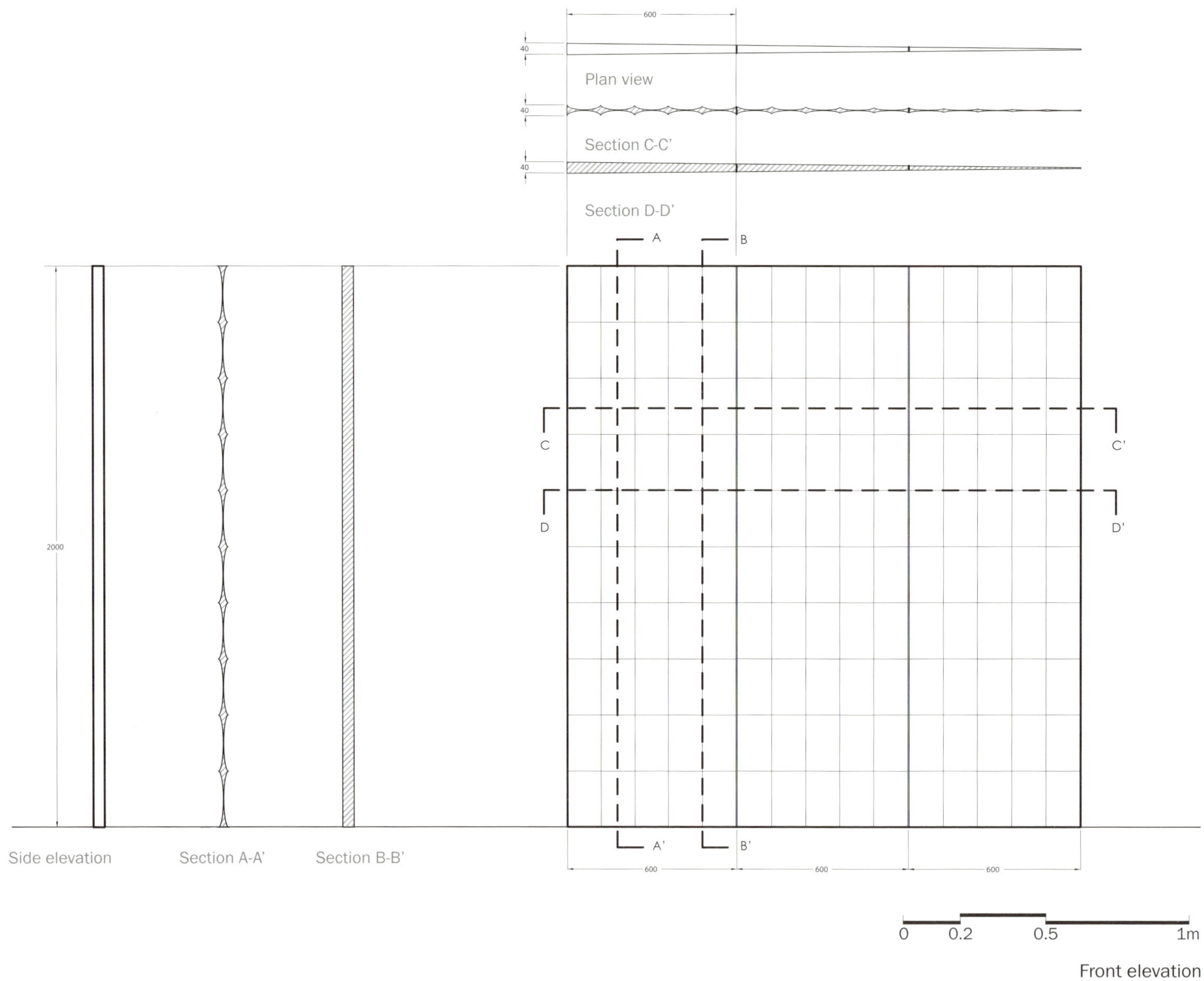
600
40
Plan view
40
Section C-C'
40
Section D-D'
A
B
2000
C
C'
D
D'
A'
B'
Side elevation
Section A-A'
Section B-B'
600
600
600
0
0.2
0.5
1m
Front elevation

Thick end detail

Thin end detail

v Transition of screen thickness

[EXPERIENCE of EVERYDAY]

Hulu

2011

Learning from *piao*: The foundation of architectural design is rooted in the understanding of everyday life. Our observations of common serving and eating utensils shaped the departure point for our dinnerware design. The traditional *piao* is a ladle created by cutting a *hulu* or gourd in half, and from that emerges a natural form appropriated by man. We sought to learn from the making of the *piao*.

Cutting a digital *hulu*: With the relevant computer program, we simulated a sliced gourd to create utensils of various shapes and sizes. We also designed stainless-steel stands to display the dinner set in such a way that the dishes, bowls, and plates are arranged and "held" together to make up the shape of a gourd. Thus, the concept of a cut gourd is visible whether the dishes are in use or displayed.

From fruit to china: Our choice of fine bone china for the dinner set expresses a series of transformations—from handicraft to industrial production, rural to urban, traditional to modern, and rough to delicate. The quality of fine bone china carries and lifts our design from concept to a new physical reality, understood only through observation, touch, and use.

A growing family: Our design of dining utensils inspired from the *hulu* and *piao* does not stop with plates and bowls. Glassware is also included in the series and features a wine decanter and glasses set, an oil and vinegar set, and a salt and pepper set, as well as a mini *hulu* made in stainless steel.

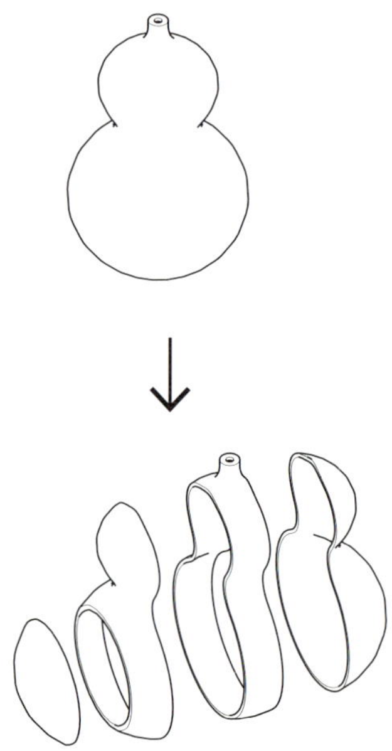

v Design sketches by Yung Ho Chang

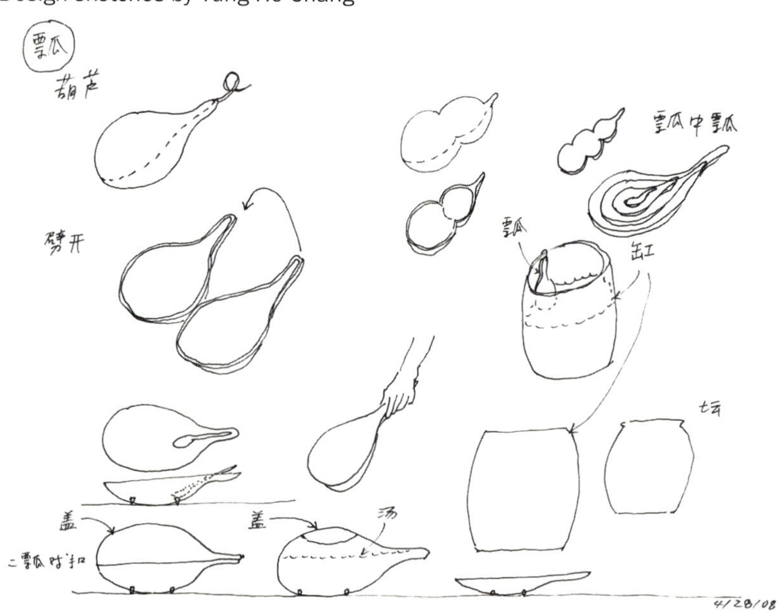

v Hulu tableware sets opened

Wine set

Oil and vinegar set

Salt and pepper set

Saucers

v Hulu tableware sets on racks

Gourd plant

Gourd fruit harvested

Gourd cut open. With inside cleaned out, one gourd becomes two *piao*

Piao in use

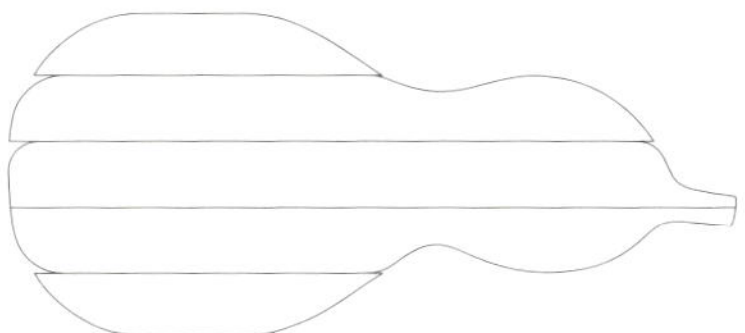

Assembled view

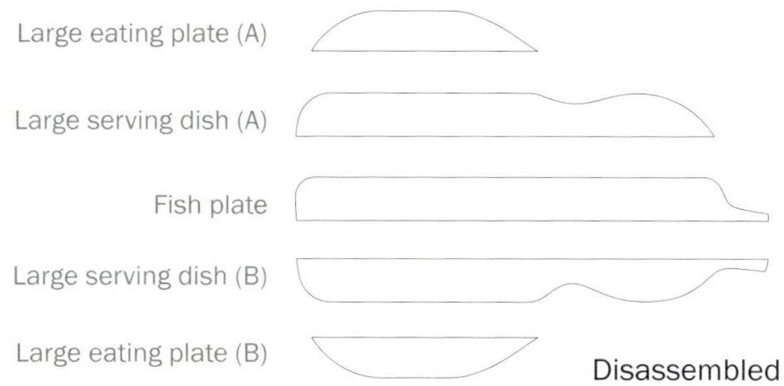

Disassembled view

v Hulu tableware in use

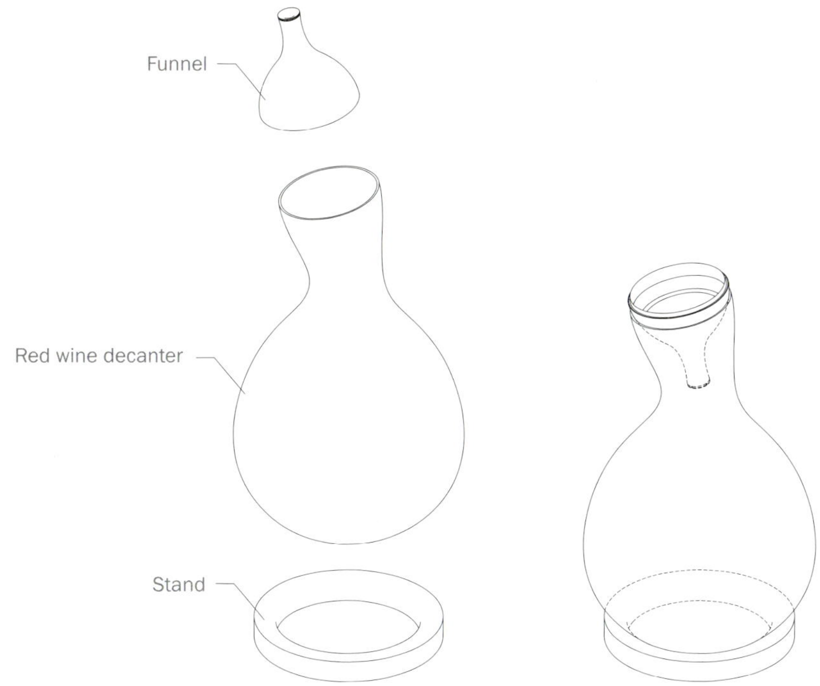

v Salt and pepper and oil and vinegar sets

v Wine decanter

[EXPERIENCE of EVERYDAY]

Lotus Leaf

2011

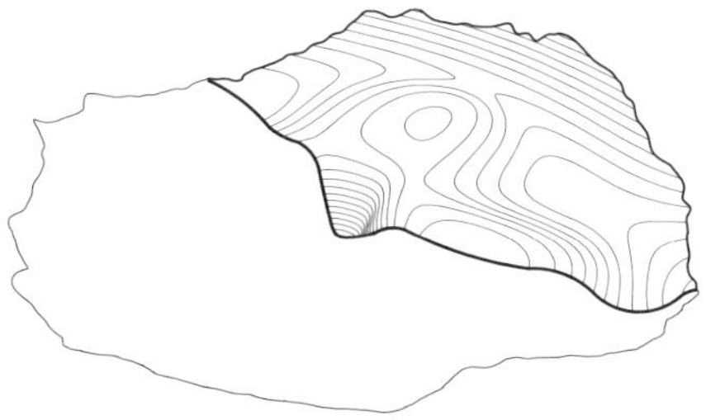

Why lotus: In China, lotus roots and seeds are eaten as food and the leaves are used to wrap certain dishes. Culturally, the lotus is also a much loved and used motif in paintings, as well as decorative items. This particular lotus leaf was picked from a pond in the Old Summer Palace in Beijing, which was built during the Kangxi period of the Qing dynasty and also where our office was once located.

A design without design: The lotus leaf was thoroughly scanned. The special qualities of the withered lotus leaf, with its shape more sinuous and its veins more prominent, are documented faithfully through computer technology. The plant is then transformed with minimal modifications; the shape of the lotus leaf is adjusted just slightly so that it can be placed stably on a flat surface.
In certain ways, the essence of the lotus leaf is preserved, even though the natural product is replaced and reinterpreted with stainless steel. In that, we design a tray by *not* designing it.

v Lotus leaf tray—front and back

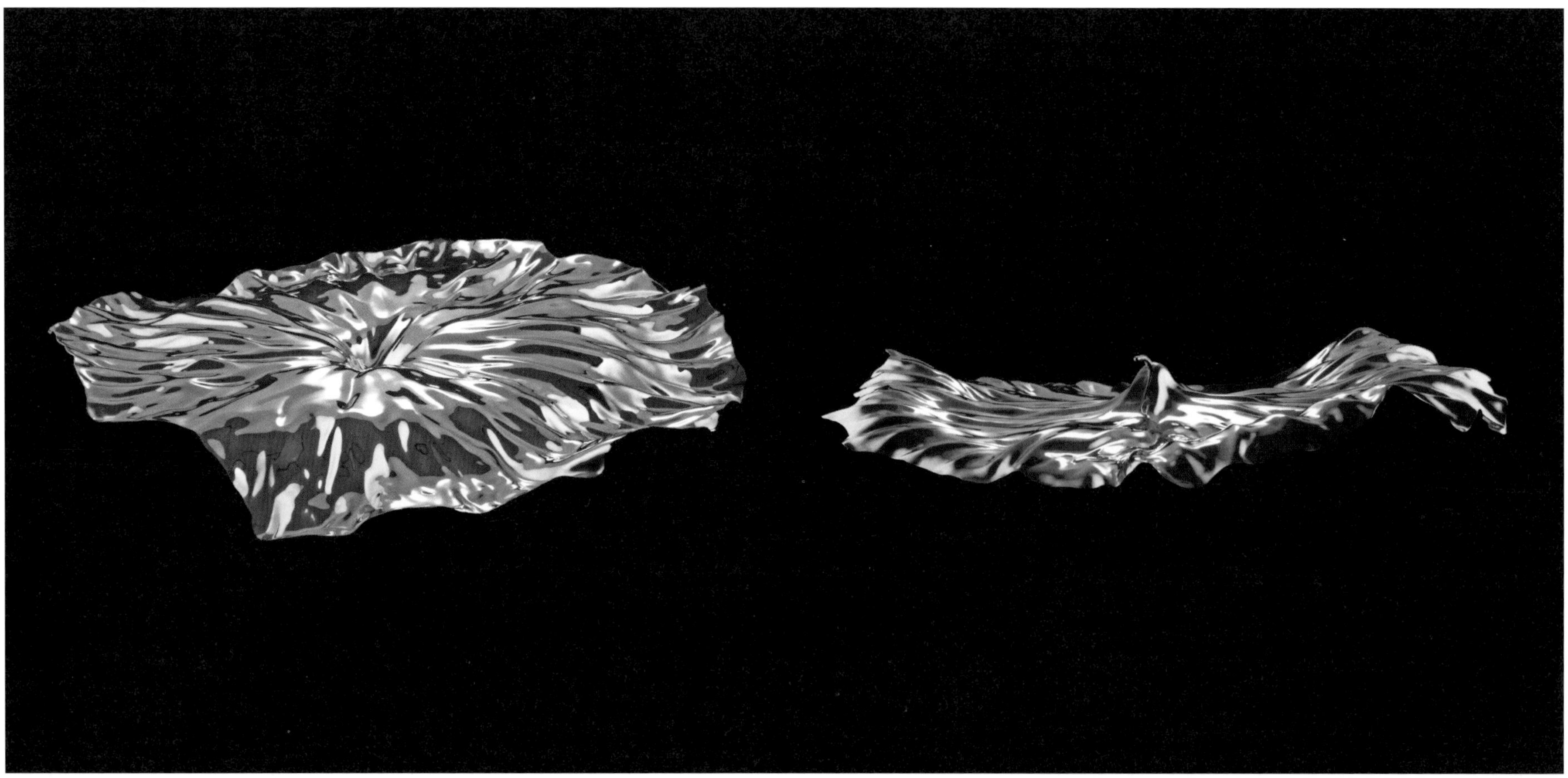

Lotus leaves in the pond

Original lotus leaf

Leaf dried out

Dried leaf scanned and adjusted

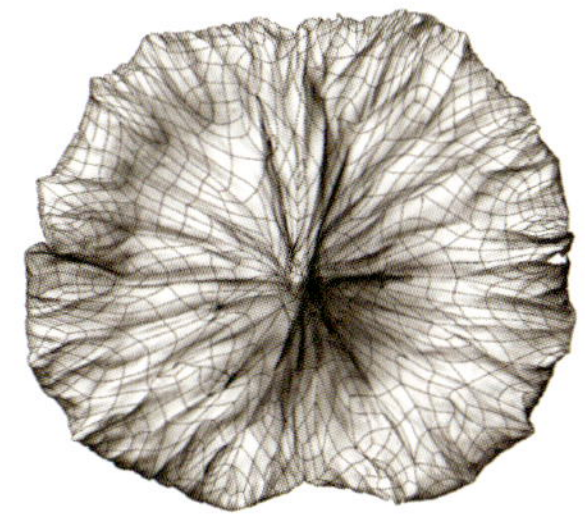

A mold made for production

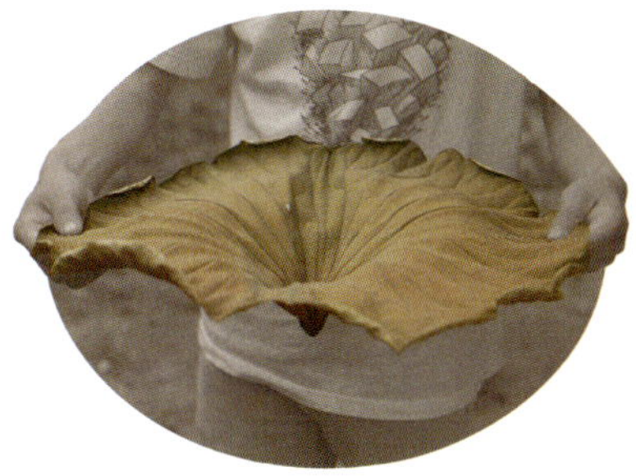

v Trays with different finishes

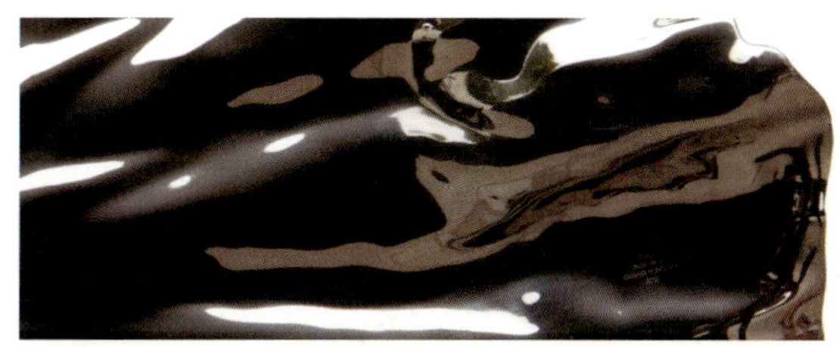

[EXPERIENCE of EVERYDAY]

Steel Unit Chair

2013

Translating wood with steel: Steel Unit Chair is a redesign of the most widely used, thus most generic, chair in China from the 1950s through to the 1970s. “Unit” refers to work unit, since the chair was almost omnipresent, used in almost every office. It was also a piece of all-purpose domestic furniture as well. The original unit chair was made of wood since wood was the only material available for making furniture during that period; our interpretation employs a 2-millimeter-thick steel angle as the material throughout. Due to the angled section of the steel, the Steel Unit Chair has a convex side that serves as a reminder of the form of its earlier wooden ancestor, and a concave side that reveals the logic of the steel work. The different colors of the two sides accentuate the dichotomy. We hope to pick up the thread of design development in contemporary China through projects like the Steel Unit Chair.

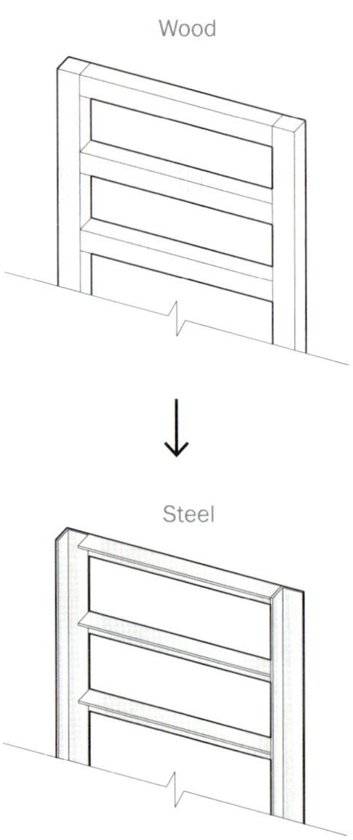

Tiny silver chair as a pendant

v Classic unit chair (left), study model (middle), and Steel Unit Chair (right)

v Steel Unit Chair details

v Steel Unit Chairs painted in different colors

[EXPERIENCE of EVERYDAY]

2D-3D Qipao

2014

East meets west in garment space: The *qipao*, a traditional dress for women in China since the early days of the Republic, evolved from the Manchurian men's robe. Today, the *qipao* is regarded as the definition of Chinese femininity and worn by females only for special occasions; it is no longer worn on a daily basis, like it was in previous generations.

Here, we attempt to connect the *qipao* with contemporary urban lifestyle and make it into something that young people can wear to work or to a party. We maintain in our design the basic shape of the typical two-dimensional cut of the *qipao*, while introducing features from the three-dimensional tailoring of the Western dress, especially where folds are concerned. The result is a series of contemporary *qipaos* that vary in formality with each piece, yet in essence, are all hybrids of two- and three-dimensional spaces.

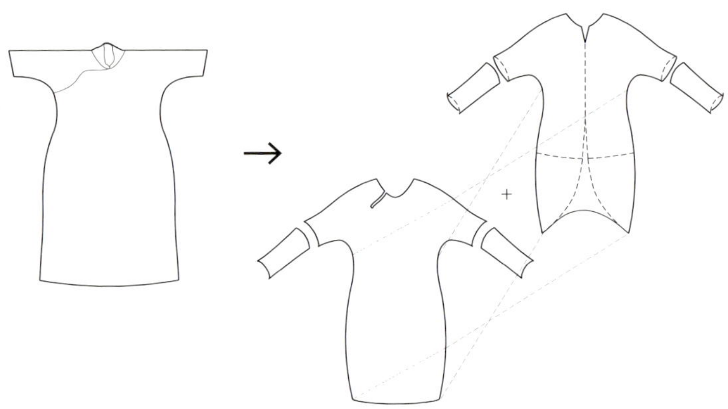

> 2D at front, 3D at back

v Design sketches by Yung Ho Chang

v A traditional *qipao*

2D cut with modern details

> 2D at front
3D at back

[EXPERIENCE of EVERYDAY]

Cheng Table

2015

Small part, big part: Classical Chinese furniture design incorporates a unique structural component known as *cheng*, which is a small curved bracing that reinforces the perpendicular joint of the table or chair top and leg. While we appreciate the ingenuity of *cheng*, we wondered if *cheng* could be more than a corner fastener, to be developed into a structural system that supports the entire table? That question became our driving force for the design of Cheng Table, where four or eight *cheng*—two from each leg, where there are eight in total—morph from bracings into interlocking beams that bear the load of the entire tabletop. The *cheng* for this table are much larger in size than traditional ones and formally more expressive. Ultimately, the Cheng Table design is an attempt to blur the divide between the traditional and the modern, simply by taking a precedent and pushing its logic further.

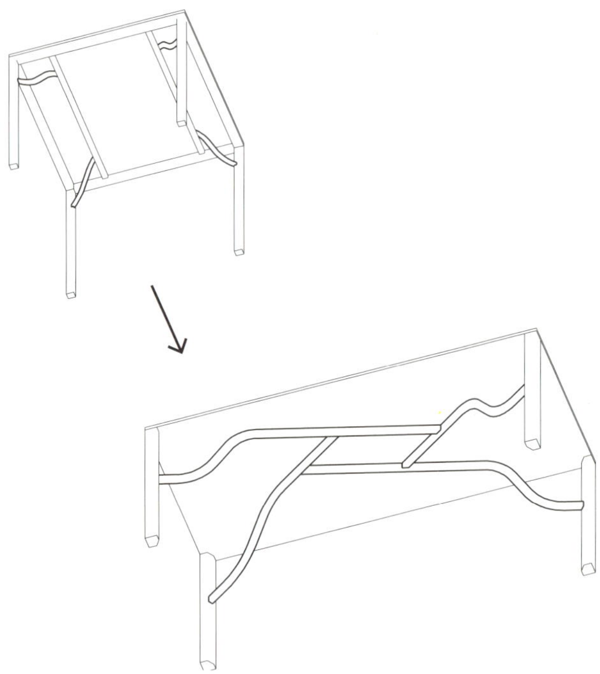

v Underside of Cheng Table

Traditional table with *cheng*

Assembling the *cheng* system

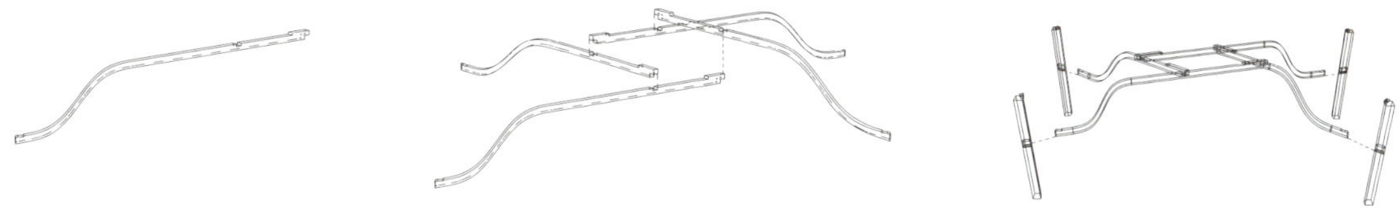

Assembling the Cheng Table

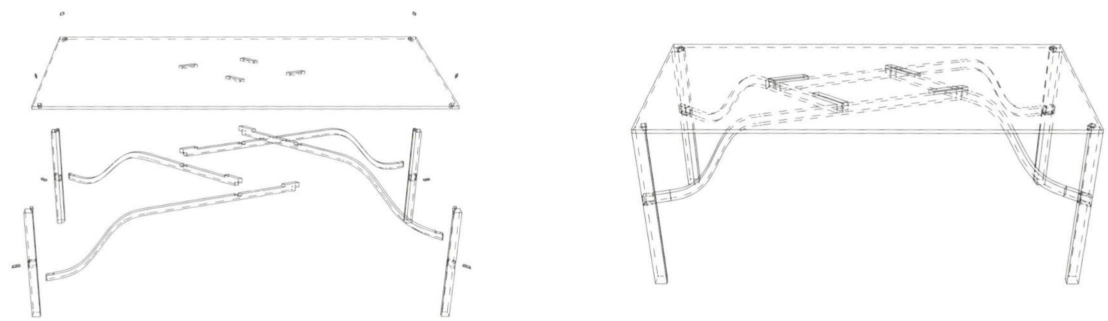

v Side view of Cheng Table

[EXPERIENCE of EVERYDAY]

Bend It Like Yoga

2016

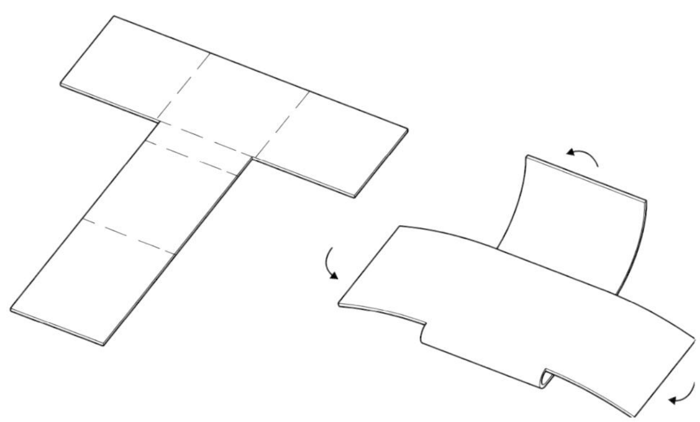

Bent plywood as a project: Bend It Like Yoga is the product of a collaboration between Atelier FCJZ and Qumei Home Furnishings Group Co., Ltd, a pioneer of bent plywood furniture in China. Bent plywood is one of the prized heritages in modern furniture design and we are fascinated and inspired to take this tradition further.

Setting up the rules of the game: Having little experience with furniture design, and wanting to avoid errors and inaccuracies from this shortcoming, we decided on using only a single piece of plywood; thus, no connection joint design was needed. Also, we wanted to achieve a degree of suppleness in the seat, and this could only be offered by a continuous plywood sheet. Of course, we also wanted to have some fun with it and wanted to test the limit of bending technology and experiment with bending the plywood in many different ways.

An open series: The strength, balance, and flexibility of the final products bring to mind the various postures of yoga asanas. The title of the series, Bend It Like Yoga, reflects our emphasis on the craft of creating, rather than implying a fixed style. Some pieces may carry genes from traditional Chinese furniture—like the *tiaoji* (long narrow table), for example; others may resemble certain European furniture typologies, such as the sofa or lounge chair. Bend It Like Yoga is a series ranging from chairs to tables, and from folding screens to stationery. Each item in the series can be a standalone piece or fused with other styles of furniture in a décor. We believe that the notion of a uniform set of furniture contradicts our multifaceted lifestyle.

Collaboration: Atelier FCJZ and Qumei collaborated closely on this series. The renowned furniture producer contributed not only their hardware, but also their software, in terms of their knowledge and experience in furniture making. We are grateful to our partners.

v Mock-ups of the Bend It Like Yoga series in Qumei's workshop

> Sofa

	2	3
	4	5
1	6	7

> 1 Wave screen
> 2 Roll arm chair
> 3 Roll back chair
> 4 X stool
> 5 X bench
> 6 Canti table
> 7 Roll ji

[EXPERIENCE of EVERYDAY]

Mille-feuille Reconstructed

2016

Quintessential problem solving: The traditional *mille-feuille* has two inherent shortcomings:

1. The crisp pastry gets softened much too quickly by the moisture of the cream between the layers; and
2. The crisp layered cake cannot be shared because it falls apart when cut.

Our approach is to solve these issues as architectural problems:

1. Separate the pastry and cream by having the cream in a "waterproofing" chocolate pool in the middle of a ring formed by pastry pieces.
2. A group of friends can together enjoy the reconstructed *mille-feuille* by each taking pieces of the pastry on the periphery and dipping it into the cream in the center. We are not redesigning the flavor of a *mille-feuille*, but have simply come up with a different way of consuming it.

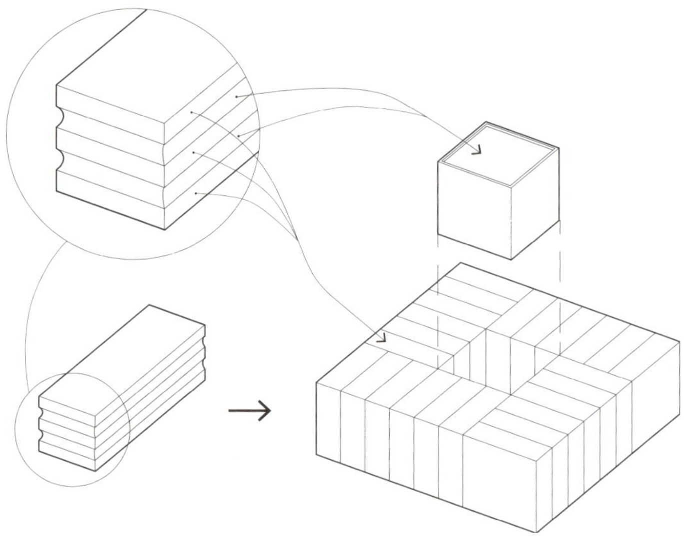

v Reconstructed *mille-feuille*

v Traditional *mille-feuille*

v Chocolate pool filled with cream, surrounded by pastry pieces

[EXPERIENCE of IN-OUT-DOOR]

King's Joy Restaurant

Beijing, China

2012

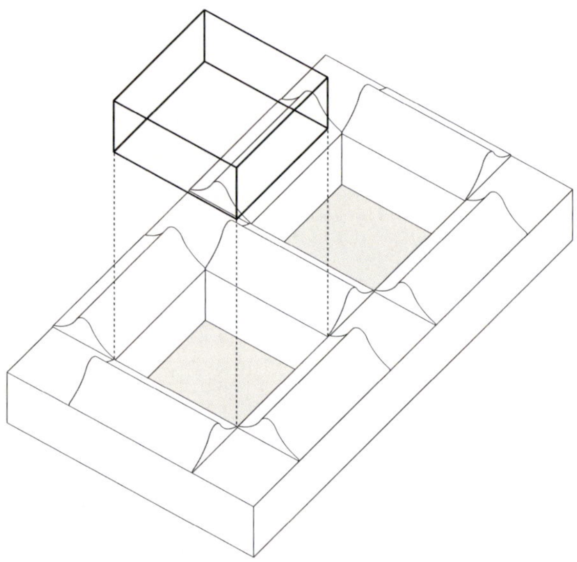

Transforming a *siheyuan*: At the entrance to Wudaoying Hutong, opposite Lama Temple, Beijing, was a newly built courtyard house (*siheyuan*) that was to be converted into a vegetarian restaurant.

Space restructured: Without changing the basic spatial structure of the courtyard house, we set out to reorganize the existing spaces. The entrance of the restaurant was moved from the center of the southern façade to the passageway on the west corner of the house, so as to allow users to pass through a series of outdoor spaces before arriving at the central courtyard. One of the original courtyards is covered with a glass roof, under which a cruciform hanging screen is employed to create a scale that is both open and intimate. This design produces a contrast between an indoor courtyard and an outdoor courtyard, with other spaces developed around them.

Materials reimagined: Our strategy was to engage traditional materials in a modern way. Mainly wood, brick, and tile have been used, which are common in traditional constructions but with unconventional applications and construction methods. Wood blocks are laid as bricks; brick corbels normally employed for the cantilevered wall become the way to build the bar counter; and roof tiles are repurposed to make folding screens, wine racks, and so on. The objective was to achieve a symbiosis of the modern and the traditional.

COMMENTS

Wang Weijen
Professor, Department of Architecture, Hong Kong University

The reversing of the logic of the material constructions, be it with the typical woodwork being made from bricks and tiles, or the piles of bricks and tiles being made from wood, arouses people's awareness of material and scale. From the partition walls, built by rotating dark wooden bricks, to the black and white ink mural in Fengzikai style, and where the folding wooden ceiling or *juanpeng* ceiling meets white concrete columns, the design cleverly conceals the original huge and awkward concrete structures in the building.

v Aerial view of the neighborhood

> Looking into the open courtyard from above, with Lama Temple in the background

京兆尹

< Entrance in courtyard
>> (Page 122) Covered courtyard showing suspended screens above
>> (Page 123) Covered courtyard

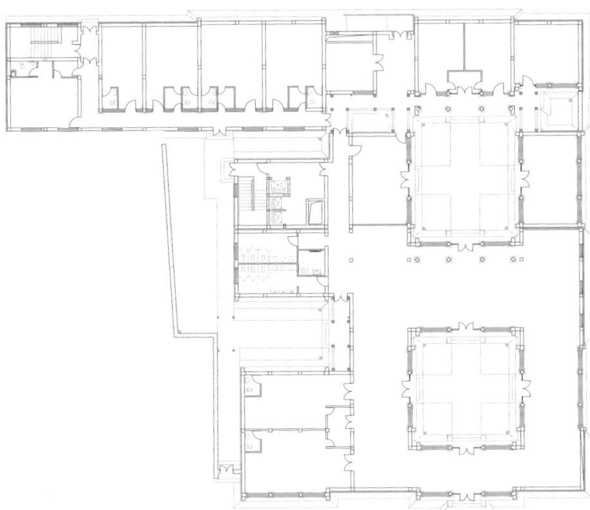

First-floor plan of the original building

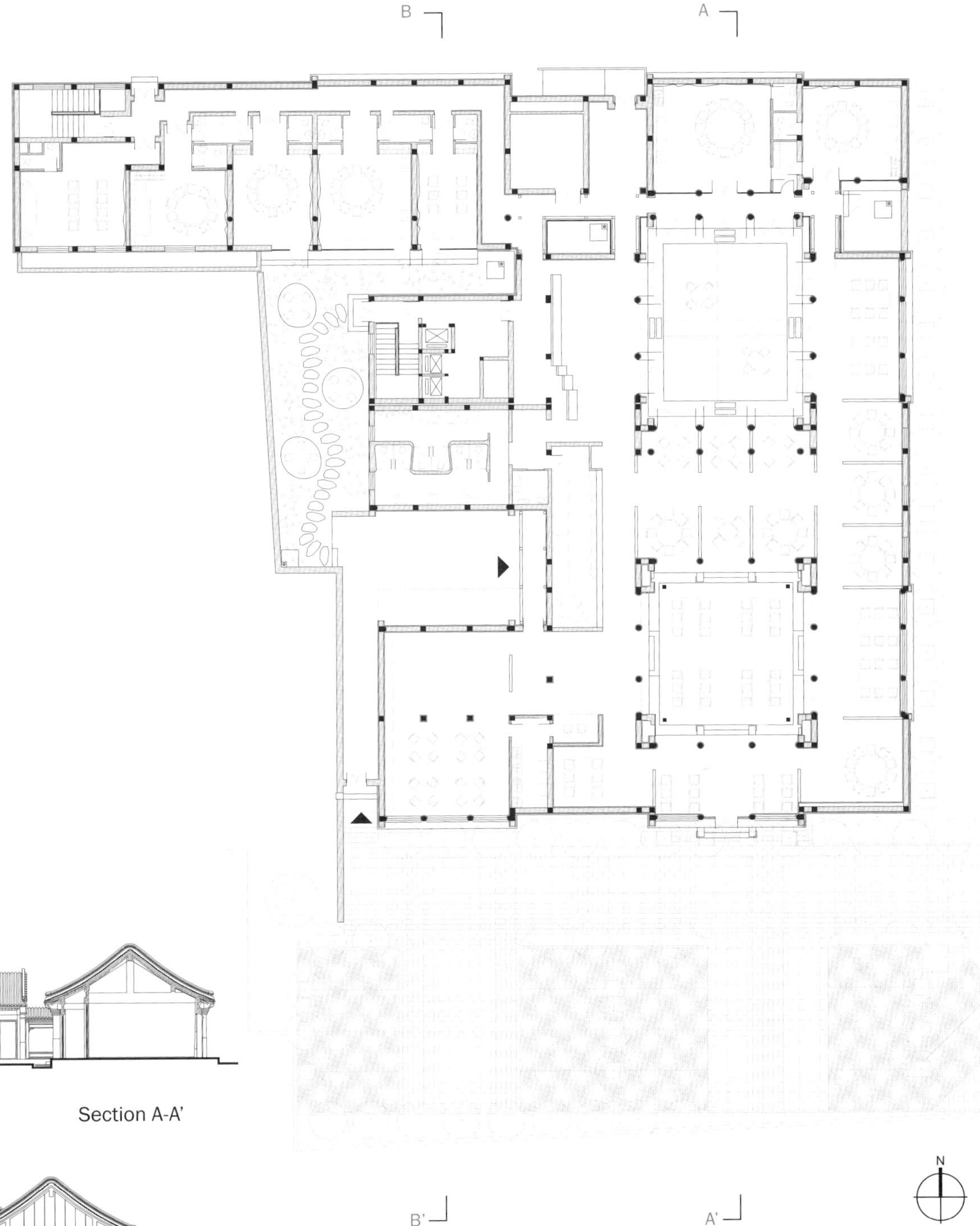

First-floor plan

0 2 5 10m

Section A-A'

Section B-B'

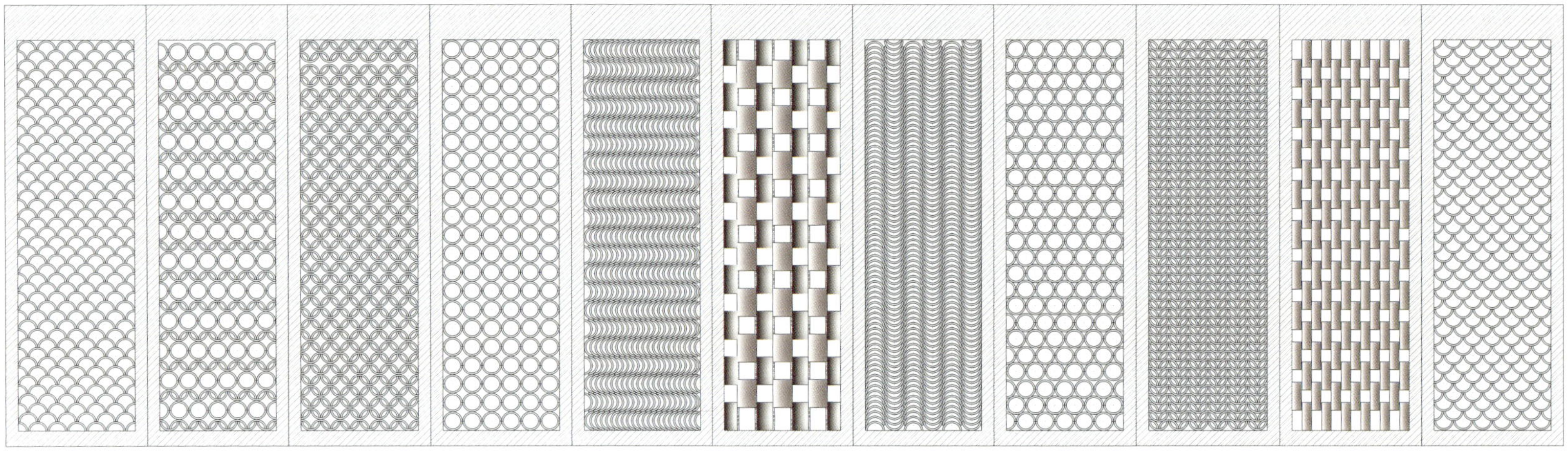

Elevation of tile screens

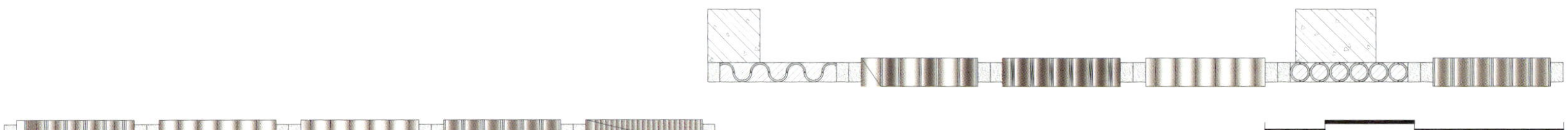

Plan of tile screens

v Tile screens

Mural on the wall by Yung Ho Chang

Tile screen detail

Private dining room

v Private dining room with curved ceiling

> Semi-private dining room

Elevation of wooden brick partition

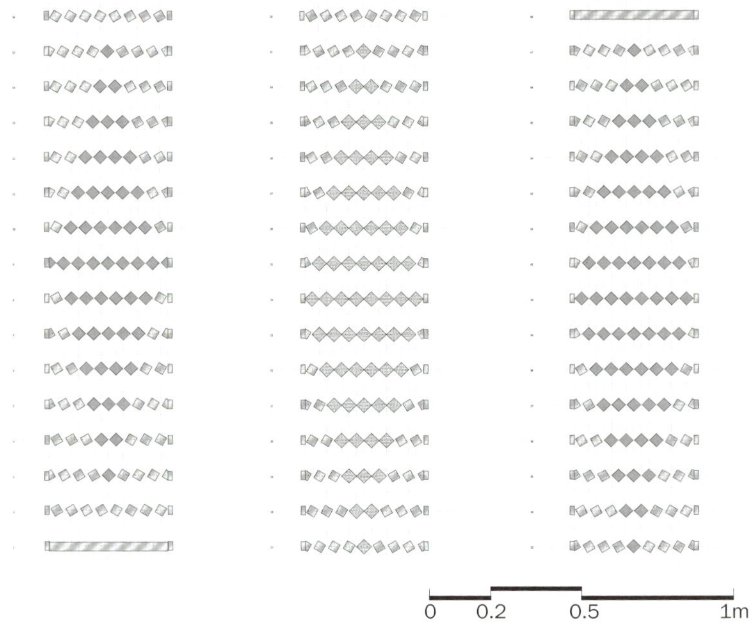

Construction details of wooden brick partition

v Semi-private dining room

[EXPERIENCE of IN-OUT-DOOR]

Campus Green Redux

Beijing, China

2015

Softening the landscape: A few years before we took on the project, the central greenery of this college in Beijing was hardened with a vast, paved plaza, numerous fountains, and stone verandas that paired with a rigid symmetrical composition. As a result of this heavy-handed design, which was in fact a makeover of the former layout, residents on the campus—the elderly in particular—seldom came to the area to relax. Therefore, we were asked to transform it yet again. It was obvious that we needed to take two main steps. The first was to soften the hardened ground, specifically by creating a gentle rolling lawn with trees that would provide shade, while changing the scale of the openness.

Constructing the interface: The second step involved the inclusion of places where people could rest, exercise, or socialize. We envisioned the architectural elements facilitating these activities, while also articulating the natural and the constructed, by using small pieces of timber to construct a double-layered cantilevering structural system (pergolas), which would provide roofing and seats for users, and at the same time encourage vines and other plants to grow along and over it. The new wood pergolas have a much lower profile than the previous stone verandas, thus ensuring an intimate scale. They embrace the landscape in the middle and dovetail into the open greenery in various locations.

We also designed two entrance gates—one for the south campus and the other for the residential quarters. By employing traditional wood and clay bricks as main materials, we extend the construction logic of the pergolas to define the interface between town and gown.

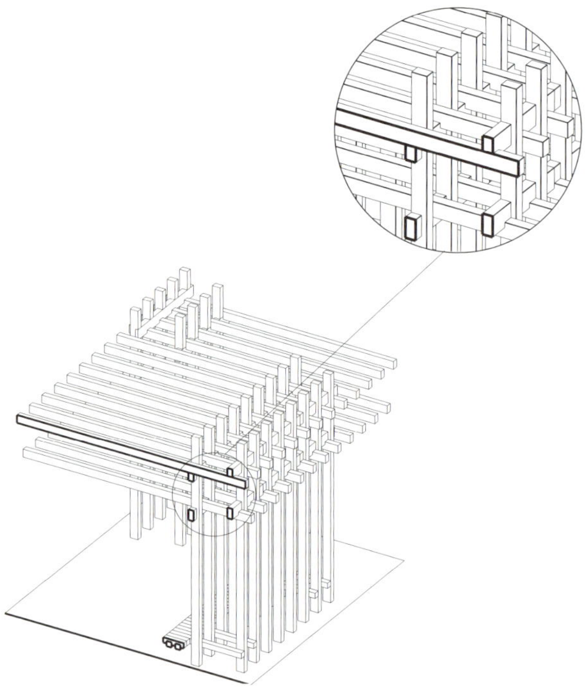

v Pergola with cantilevered canopy

> Shadow play under the pergola

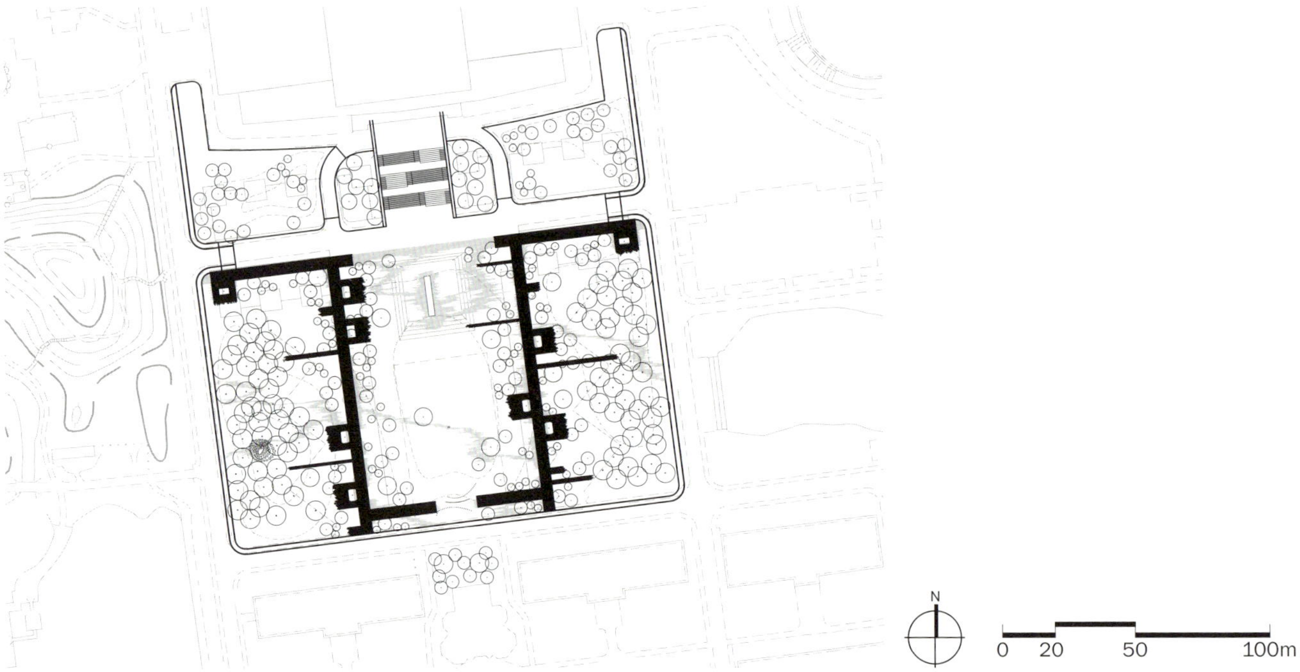

Site plan

v Pergola with staggered vertical supports

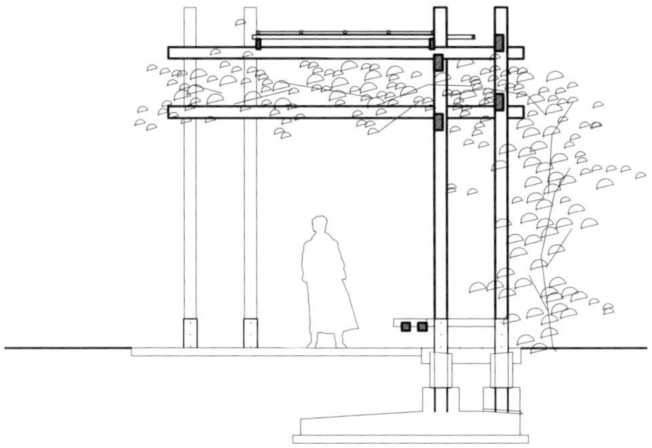

Section

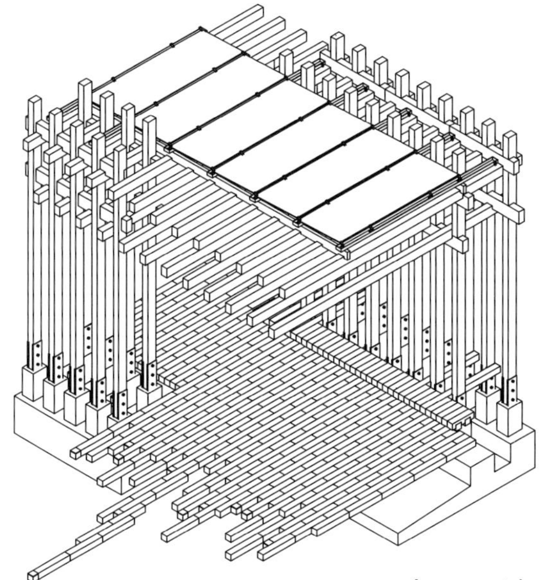

Axonometric

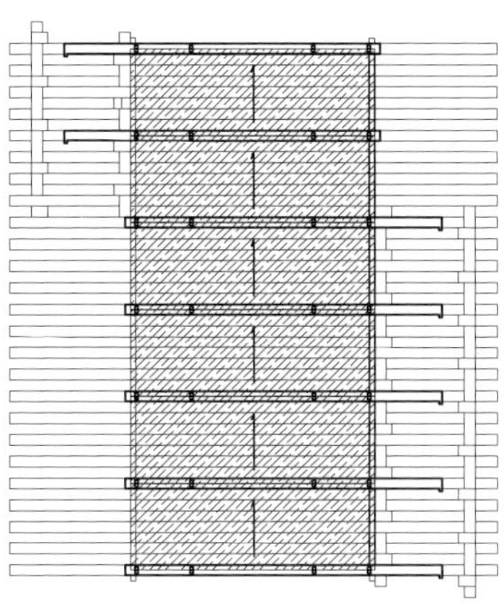

Roof plan

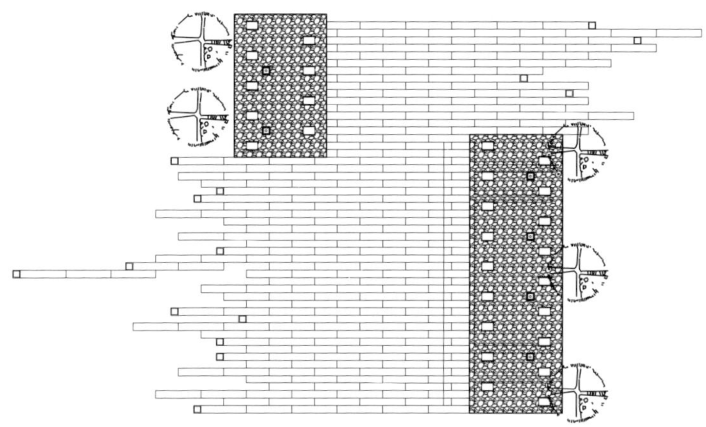

Roof plan

> 1-4 Diverse relationships between human-made and natural

1	2
3	4

Seat as part of pergola

Double-layered canopy

Close-up of pergola structure

v Between two layers of the pergola canopy

Brick work detail

v North gate of the south campus

Steel beam sandwiched with timber

Tile work detail

v South gate of residential community

[EXPERIENCE of IN-OUT-DOOR]

Novartis Shanghai Campus

Shanghai, China

2016

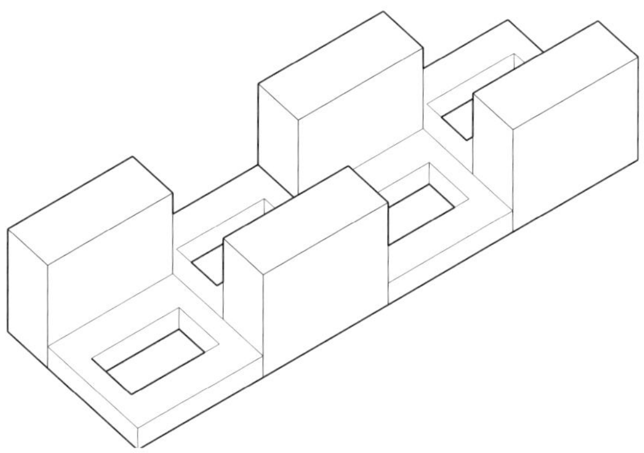

A long march in design: In 2006, Atelier FCJZ began to produce a comprehensive planning scheme, as well as architectural design guidelines for Novartis Shanghai Campus. Like Novartis Basel Campus in Switzerland, each building at the Shanghai campus is designed by a different architect. Also, a number of the spaces and the landscape of the central garden, as well as the courtyards, are designed by different designers. The direction from Novartis was to “create a livable working community that is a home-like environment, with greater opportunities to interact and cooperate.” In 2016, Novartis Shanghai completed the construction of Phase I, with a total of seven buildings.

Courtyard urbanism: In the master plan, courtyards are used to establish the overall spatial structure of the campus. Services and amenities are located within courtyards. We blur the difference between “court” and “garden” with the “court-garden” concept, which is a spatial blend of architecture and landscape. The internal and external spaces of buildings on the campus are connected with pedestrian accessibility, forming a rich, continuous system, in which the users may experience a modern interpretation of southern China gardens.

Making public spaces in a laboratory building: The laboratory building is conceived as an enclosed courtyard, with the landscape designed by Zhu Yufan. One of the campus' restaurants is located on one side of this courtyard, according to the master plan. With amenities scattered around, people on campus are encouraged to explore different buildings or move through courtyards, in the process spending more time outdoors. On the other side of the courtyard, opposite the restaurant, is a five-story laboratory tower. In keeping with Novartis's aim to create home-like laboratories, each floor inside the laboratory tower has non-lab work spaces facing the courtyard, tailoring a less formal work atmosphere within them. In the center of the building, open platforms in different sizes are stacked up in the atrium, with all the floors connected by stairs. These platforms have distinct spatial qualities, but not specific functions. While going up or down the stairs, researchers may use these platforms to rest, read, conduct discussions, or simply catch-up and interact with their colleagues.

Façade with a regional touch: To establish a sense of cultural continuity, the exterior walls of the laboratory tower are clad with gray terra cotta tiles that present the oval section in four tones of gray; the tiles gradually rotate to form a sun-shading louver in front of the windows. On the roof of the restaurant and veranda, we use yet another type of terra cotta product, so that the overall building reflects the color and texture of traditional clay bricks.

> View of lab building from courtyard

COMMENTS

Liu Jiakun
Founding Partner and Principal Architect, Jiakun Architects

The color of the terra cotta tile has undergone several changes. At first, the gray color appears as in the concept, which is a natural response to the tradition; later, it is presented in the natural color of clay, which is a complete flip, to pursue material authenticity and take into consideration Novartis's requirement of "warm and pleasant;" if I remember correctly, it once was in a warm, brown-gray, which seems to emphasize more the intuitive feeling on-site, rather than the original concept; later, the gray is stabilized, indicating that the abstract connection with the traditional building has been determined. After that, however, it follows a series of subtle changes in tones of gray.

On whether we should reference the traditional directly or abstractly, I feel that Yung Ho Chang finally made up his mind, and was pleased about it. These decisions may be very easy for some architects, but for Chang, it would likely have caused some inner struggle. Because even for references of traditional architecture, too, abstraction is hard to understand, while also being too direct, as if showing off. It is easy to make a declaration but hard to strike a balance. And the sense of proportion and inner character are the core elements of traditional Chinese spirit.

The atrium is the core of the interior space, with the fascinating platforms along the stairs enlarged to create resting spaces. The bright staff restaurant, the podium building with the pitched roof, and the simple square outdoor courtyard are equally pleasant for me. These places vaguely reveal an "old Beijing" vibe, generous and bright. Even more encouraging is that the effort toward establishing sense of proportion has not been in vain. The temperament of the building comes off as being unlike something that has been deliberately designed out, but more like a natural revelation.

v Looking into the central court-garden from above

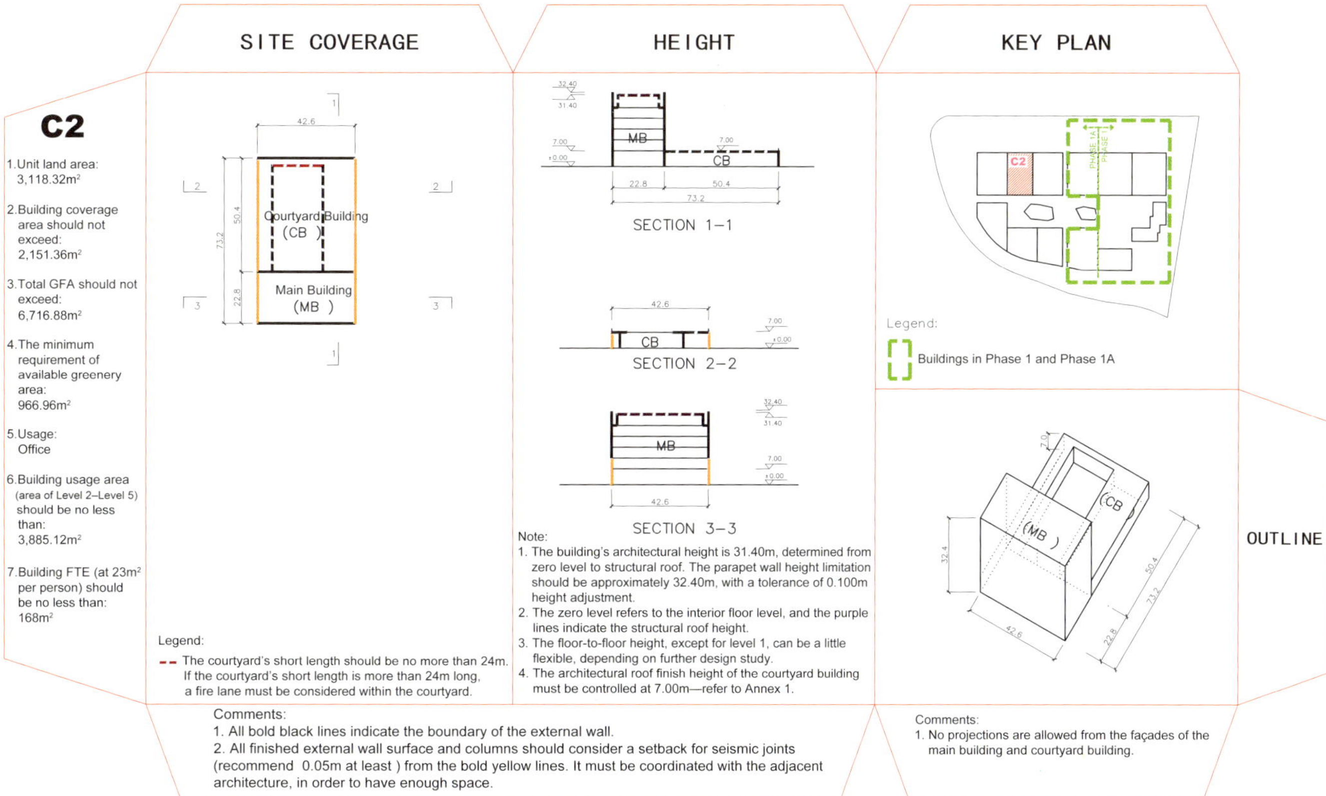

Design guidelines for building C2

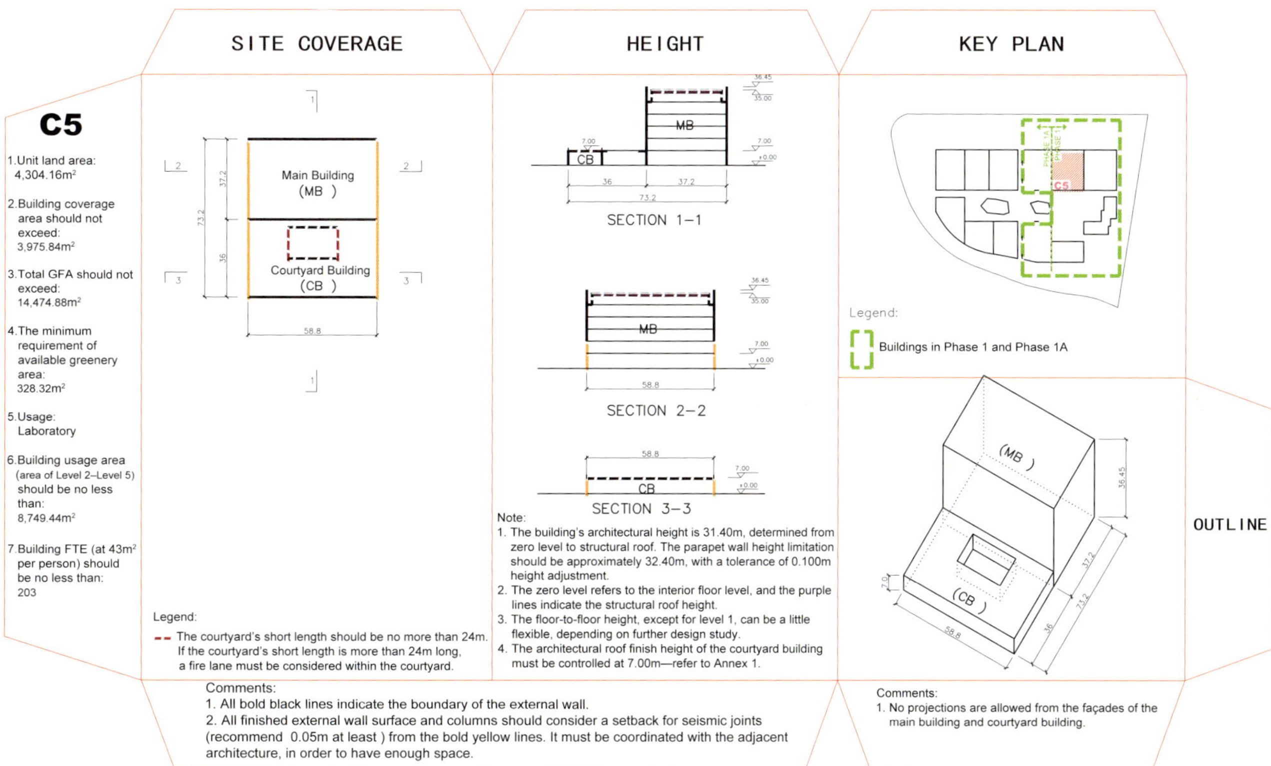

Design guidelines for building C5

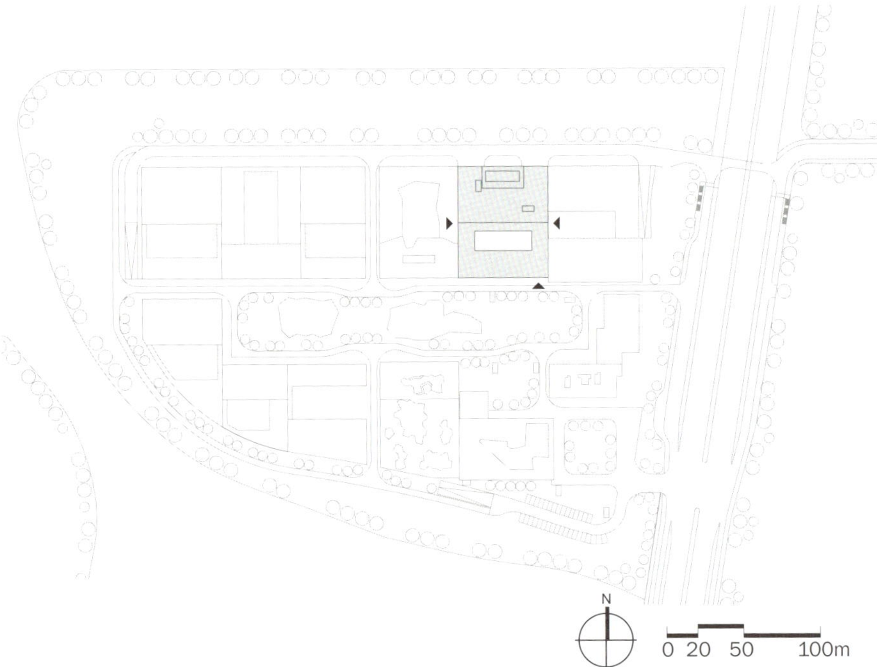

Site plan

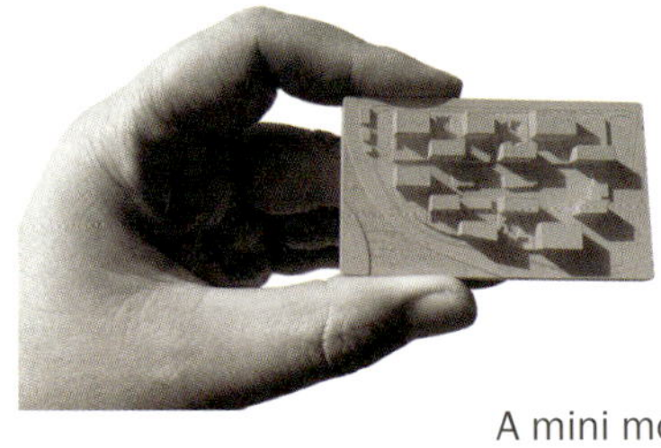
A mini model

v Bird's-eye perspective

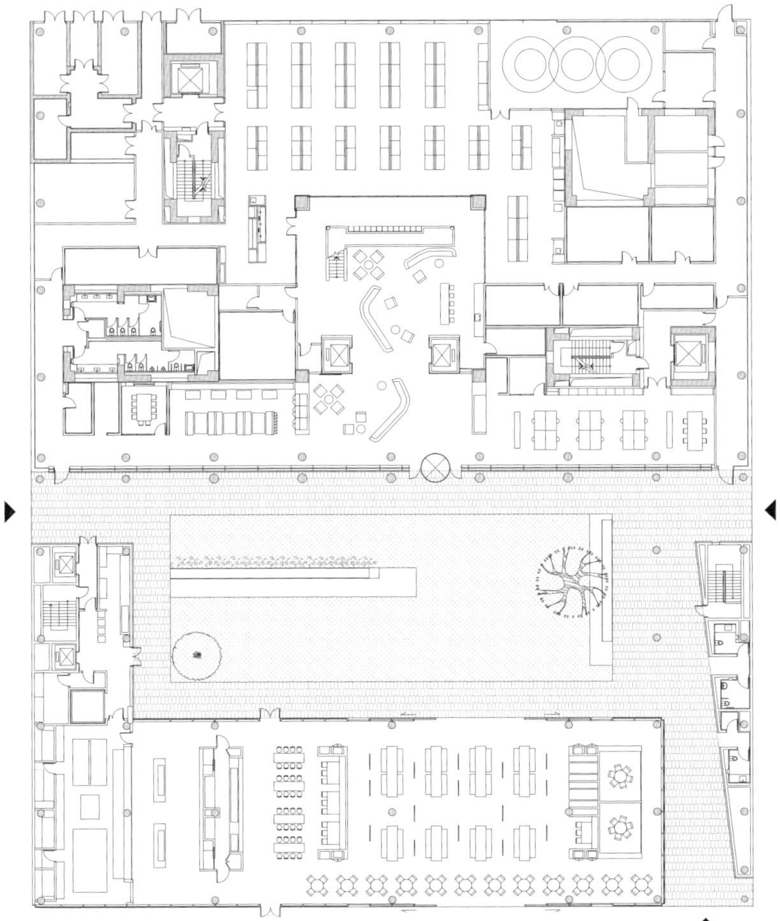
First-floor plan

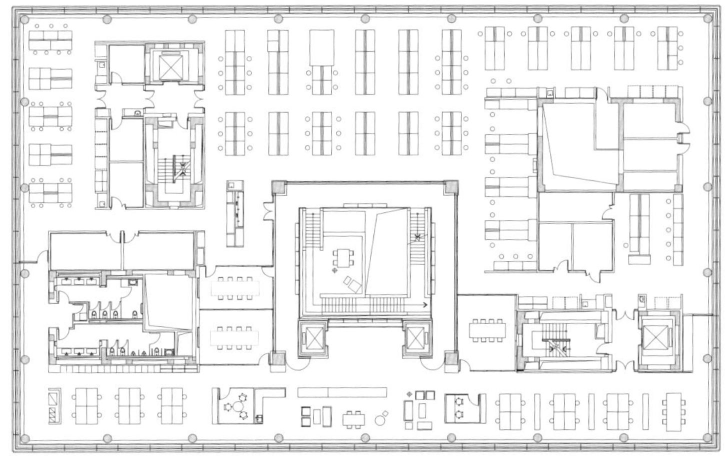
Typical-floor plan

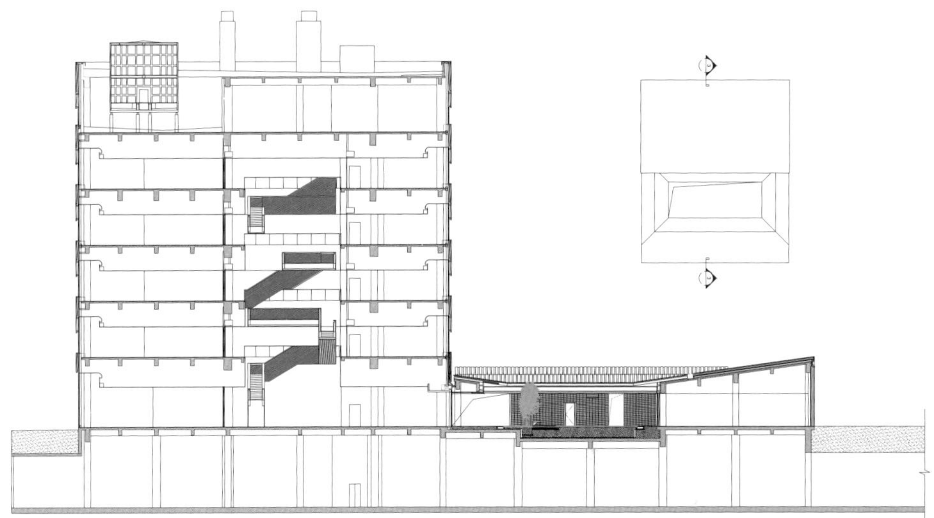
Section

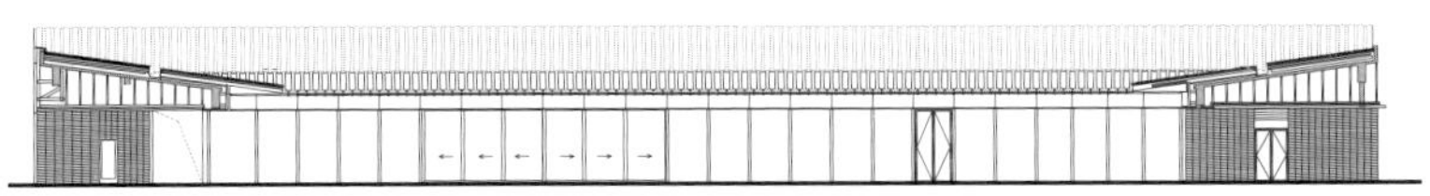
Podium building—north elevation

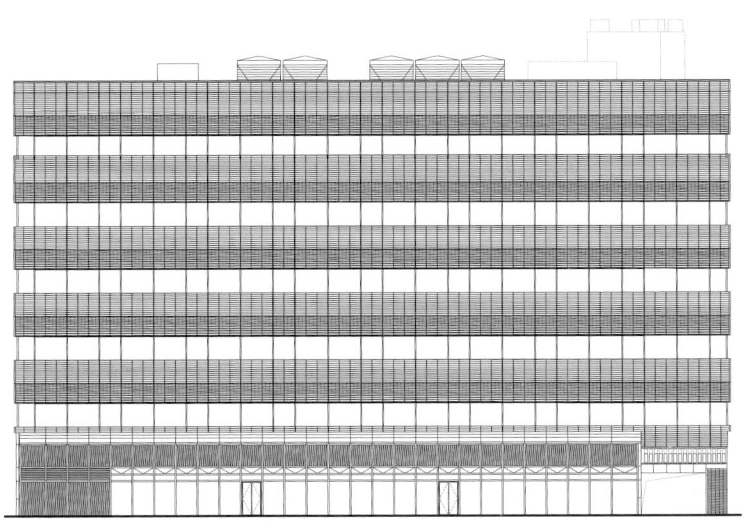
South elevation

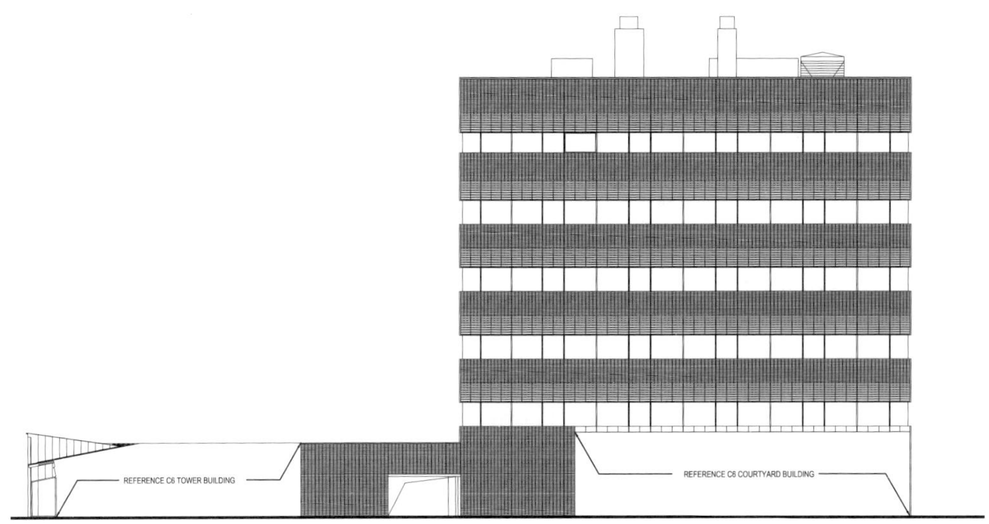

East elevation

0 4 10 20m

v Southeast corner of courtyard and courtyard entrance
v View of laboratory building from restaurant

v From covered walkway on east side, looking at restaurant and courtyard entrance
v Restaurant interior

< 1 Laboratory building façade during the day
< 2 Laboratory building façade in the evening

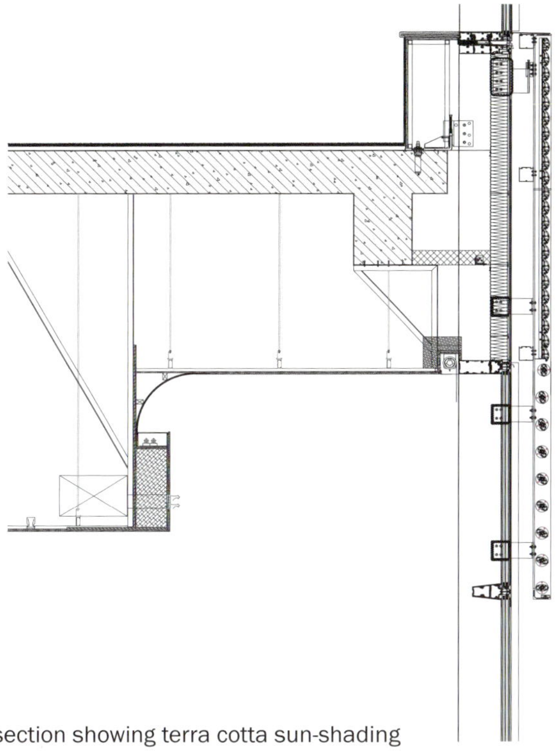

^ 1 Partial wall section showing terra cotta sun-shading
> 2 Close-up of terra cotta sun-shading device
> 3/4 Terra cotta sun-shading

< Atrium with stacked balconies
in laboratory building
> Looking down at the balconies
from above

[EXPERIENCE of IN-OUT-DOOR]

Brick Kiosk

Shenzhen, Guangdong Province, China

2017

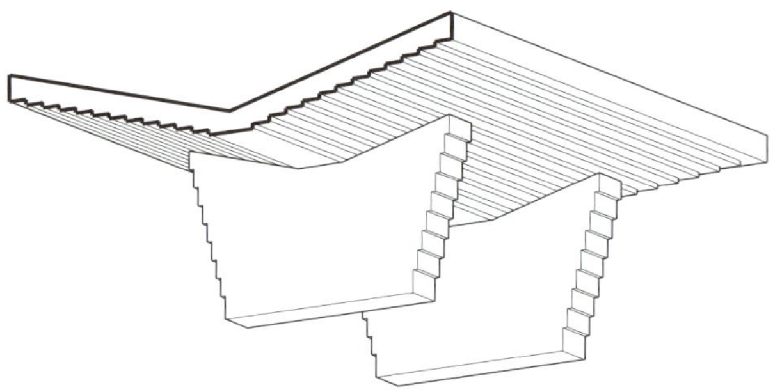

Fat pavilion: For the Shenzhen Biennale 2017, we were asked to design a small permanent structure at the entrance of Nantou Old Town, Shenzhen, which would host various exhibitions. The functionalities of this facility included providing visitors with directions, handing out maps and brochures during the biennale, and vending refreshment and snacks after the exhibitions ended. Given the requirements, an open pavilion was selected to house the various functions. When we considered permanence, it brought to mind the two most common building materials in China today: brick and concrete. So, we proposed an umbrella structure built with a combination of brick and concrete, topped with a big canopy, under which people can meet or linger while receiving information on the biennale.

Material experiment: Brick is a universally available material that shares a sturdiness with stone and concrete. Louis Kahn's famous dialog with brick reveals how the incremental assembling of the small clay block can achieve a large span with the form of the arch and poetically reiterate a time-honored constructive logic. However, we imagine that brick can also be expressed as a cantilever. This design proposition was partially inspired by an installation on the project site: a sculpture of a somewhat corpulent figure, posed in a visually striking gesture of reaching for the sky. Taking inspiration from that, we thought: we too want to be as strong as our neighbor and lift bricks and concrete skyward.

v Aerial view of Nantou Old Town with the Brick Kiosk in the foreground

> View of the Brick Kiosk on a rainy night

Cutting grooves into bricks

v Construction process

[EXPERIENCE of IN-OUT-DOOR]

Shede Visitor's Center

Suining, Sichuan Province, China

2019

A site away from our times: The project is situated in a company town in Sichuan named Tuopai, where a well-known Chinese liquor distillery, Shede, is based. The closest large cities are Chengdu and Chongqing, both approximately 200 kilometers away. Partially due to its relatively quiet location, Tuopai maintains the ambiance of both an industrial town and a rural village before the late-1970s economic reform in China. The specific site for the visitor's center is situated in front of the production campus of Shede, near a main thoroughfare, with a park and a river on the opposite side.

Liquor tourism as program: For tourists, the visitor's center is the prelude to a tour of Shede's distilling facilities. The program is well-mixed and includes a museum for liquor culture, a hotel, a dining theater, and an R&D center, among others.

Design a linear village: After a detailed study, we realized that vacationists would come to Tuopai not only because of the famous liquor brand, but also because of the pristine natural landscape, as well as the tranquil feeling of the locale. Our design should preserve these qualities. While the building complex of the visitor's center serves as a connection–transition between Shede's campus and the woodsy landscape, the architecture of the center is spatially organized as a series of smaller pavilions with central courtyards arranged in a linear fashion; its formal language is based on a low-key vernacular vocabulary of deep eaves and wood-paneled walls.

Building section: The cross section of a typical pavilion resembles that of an umbrella, with a beamless concrete roof cantilevering out from the center. The thickness of the sloping roof canopy changes gradually—thin at the eaves and thick at the base, where the air-conditioning ducts are concealed.

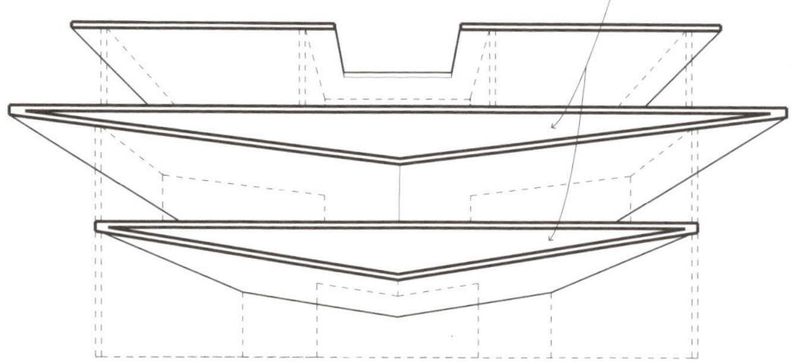

v Bird's-eye view—liquor production facilities behind Shede Visitor's Center

v Banquet hall, viewed from the north

Site plan

v View from northeast

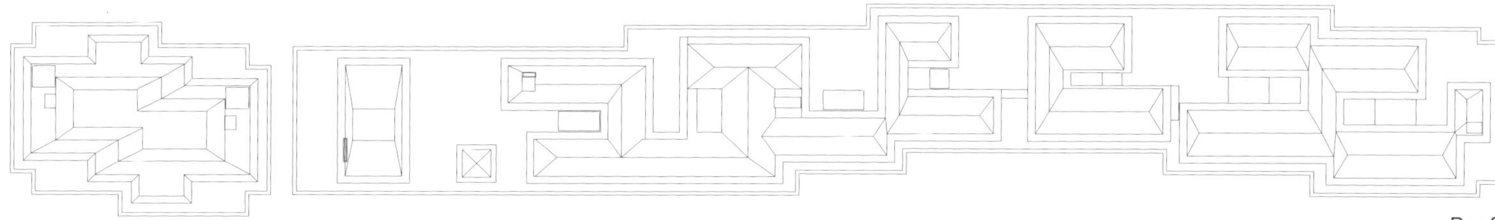

Roof plan

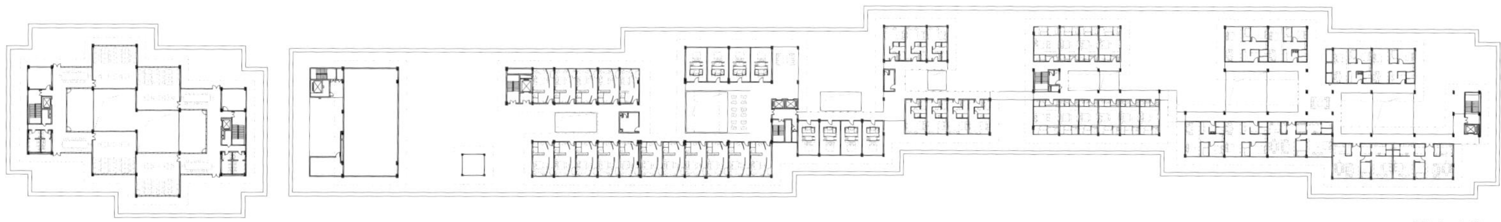

Third-floor plan

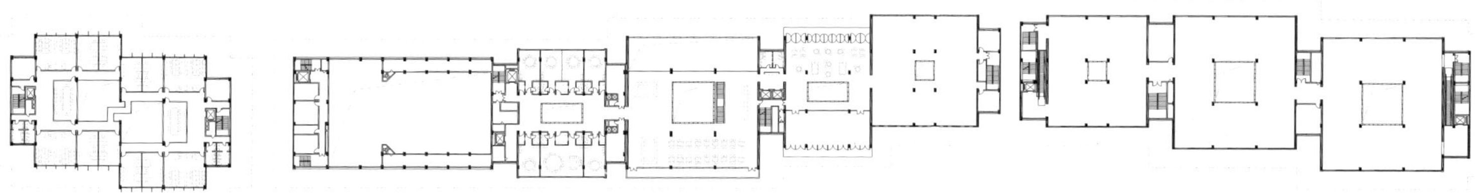

Second-floor plan

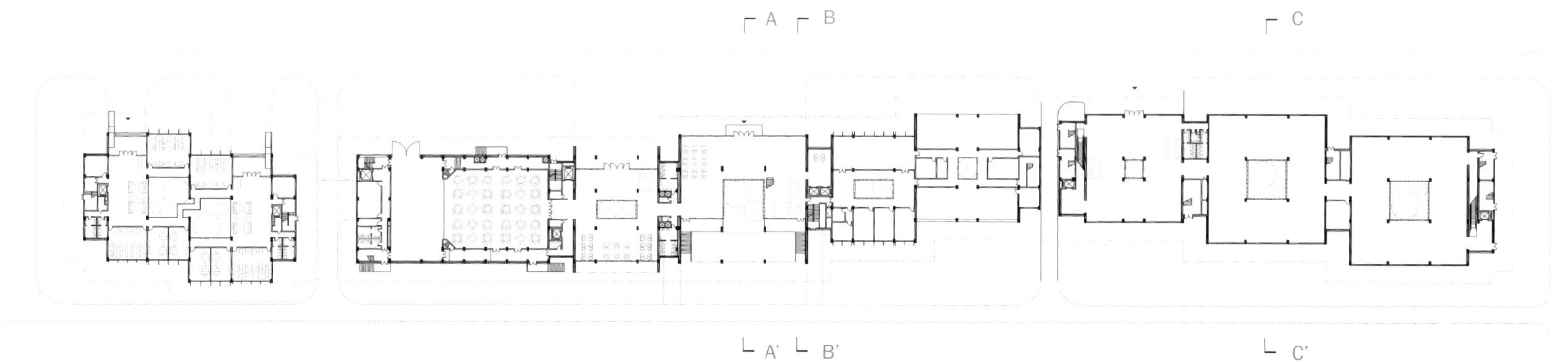

First-floor plan

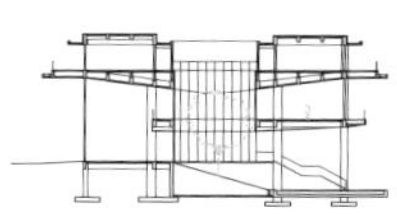

Section A-A'

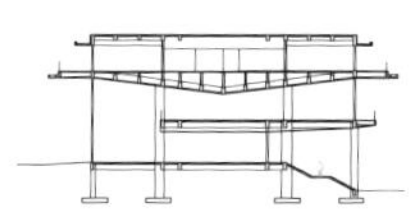

Section B-B'

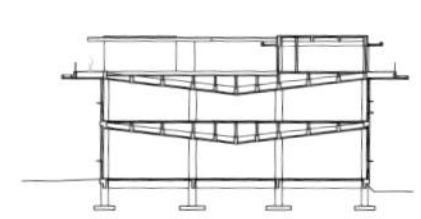

Section C-C'

Elevation

> Entrance lobby

Vernacular houses in Sichuan

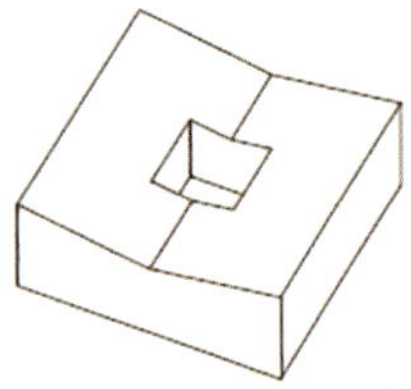

A typical volume

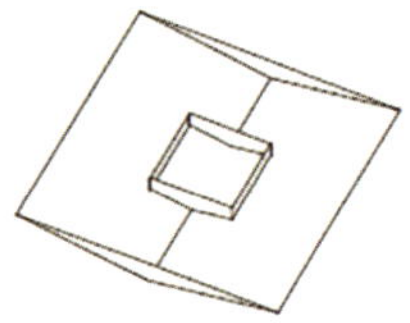

A typical floor

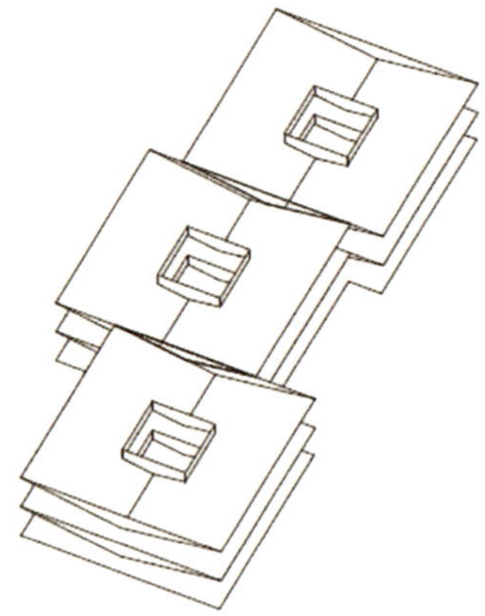

Aggregation

v South elevation

> 1 Overlooking an inner courtyard from the third floor

> 2 Exhibition hall

1

2

Section rendering

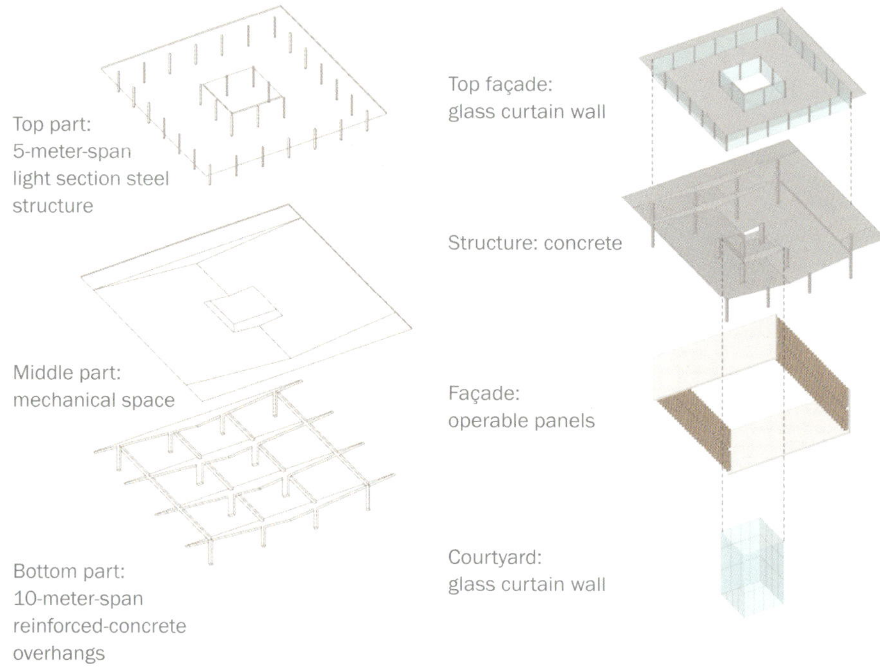

v Umbrella-like structural ceiling

v Views from the third floor

v Views from the third floor

< Elevation detail
v Between the experience center and the office building

[EXPERIENCE of IN-OUT-DOOR]

EP YAYING Fashion and Arts Center

Jiaxing, Zhejiang Province, China

2021

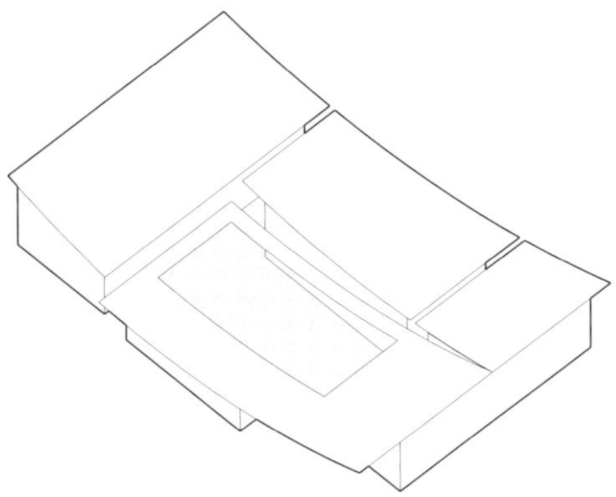

A restrictive site and a complex program

Site: The existing foundations and basements on the project site to be retained and incorporated into the new design.

Program: To provide spaces of different qualities and scales for a variety of uses: art/garment collection and display, fashion shows, procurement fairs, workshops/lectures, wine tasting, a bookstore, and restaurants and a café.

One formal gesture tying up all the pieces: We use a continuous spiral of a single curvilinear roof to unify four buildings with different foundation conditions, functions, and massing, while enclosing a courtyard in the middle. In other words, a clear formal structure unifies a complex group of parts. The large, curvy roof creates deep eaves and provides a series of semi-outdoor spaces around the landscaped central court. The ceiling system that stretches from indoor to outdoor mediates the relationship among diverse spaces.

Concrete and bamboo as *tu mu*: We use a combination of concrete frame and shear walls as the structural system and expose cast-in-situ concrete in multiple places. Both the grating on the elevations and ceilings that provide shading and screening are made of bamboo-fiber reinforced-polymer. Concrete may be considered as the contemporary version of *tu* or earth, and engineered bamboo as *mu* or timber. Together, *tu mu* meant architecture in the past in China.

v Bird's-eye view

> The inner courtyard in early spring

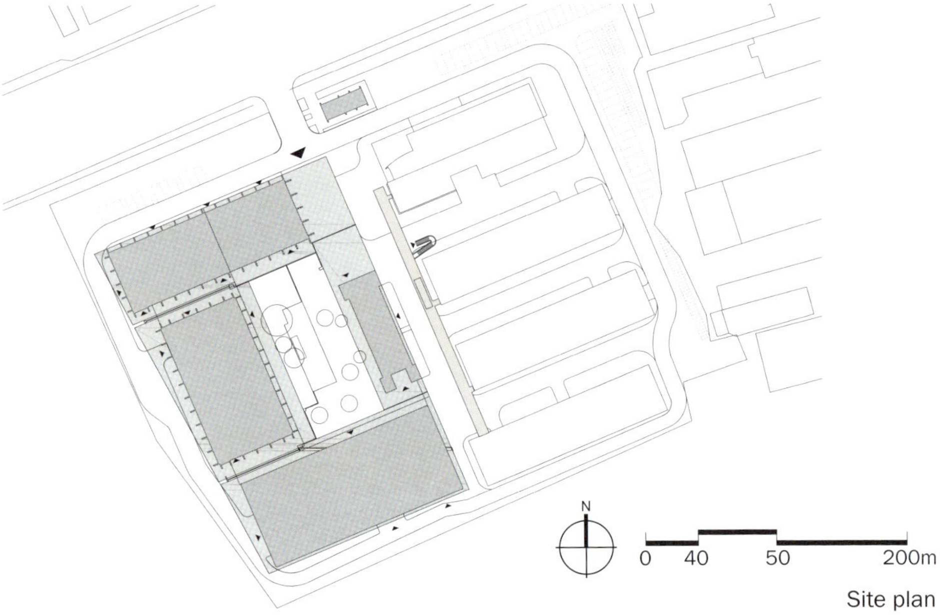

Site plan

v The main entrance

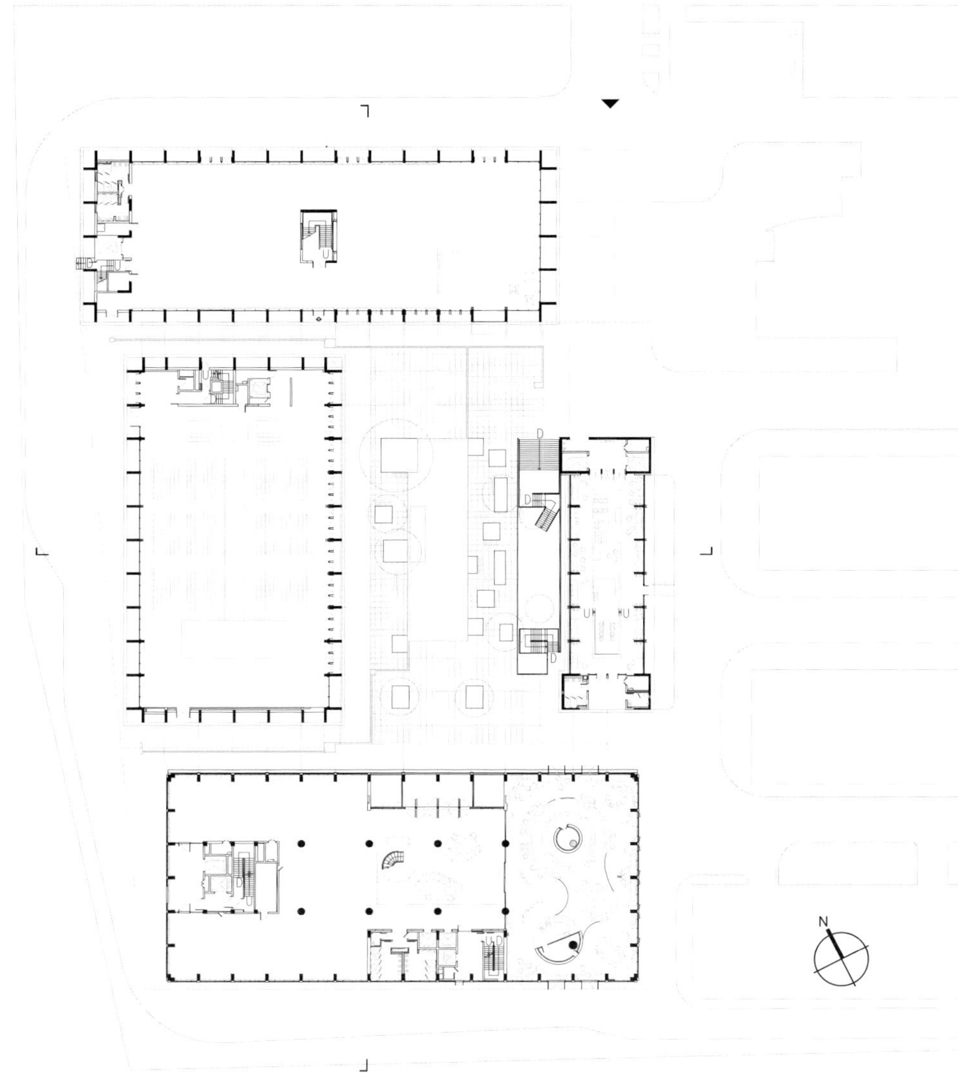

First-floor plan

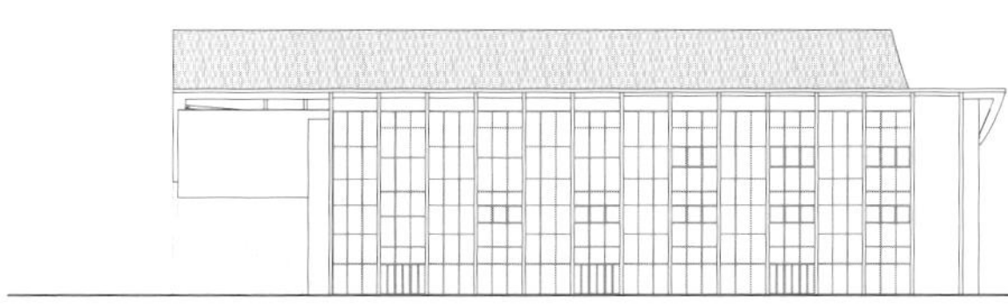

North elevation

East elevation

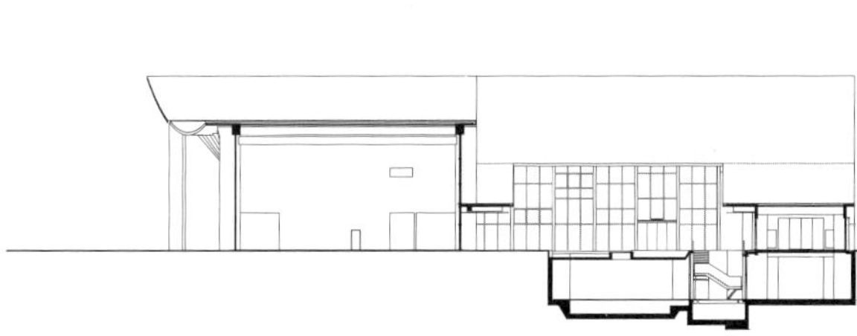

Cross section

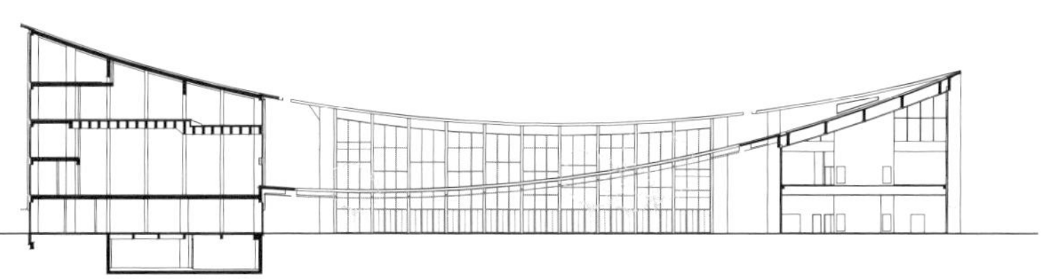

Longitudinal section

< Shear-wall-columns around the periphery
> View of the inner courtyard from the main entrance

> The curvilinear, fabric-like, double-layered cantilevered roof

>> (Page 180) The ground floor show hall and the underground ordering hall

>> (Page 181) The sunken court

The inner courtyard and the sunken court

v The semi-outdoor space below the cantilevered roof

The skylight of the underground ordering hall can be seen in the pond in the inner courtyard

A quiet corner of the inner courtyard

∨ The skylight of the underground exhibition hall is set under the pond above

The moon window of the stairwell

v Lecture hall in the main building

v Event space in the gallery

Juxtaposition of Phase 1 and the corridor building

> 1 The first floor of the corridor building
> 2 The second floor of the corridor building
> 3 Stairs to the third floor
> 4 The third floor in the form of a bridge
> 5 Open balcony on the third floor
> 6 One end of the corridor building

1	2	3
4	5	6

v The corridor building between Phase 1 and Phase 2

[EXPERIENCE of IN-OUT-DOOR]

Loop House

Beijing, China

2022

Context and site: The old city of Beijing is known for its urban fabric that is woven with *hutong* (alleyways) and *siheyuan* (courtyard houses). In a *siheyuan*, the main courtyard is situated in the middle of the house and serves as the domestic center for an extended family, which was often the scenario in pre-modern days. The rooms around the courtyard are disconnected as they would usually be occupied by the different nuclear families within the extended household. This project is located in a typical *hutong* in the central quarters of the capital city.

Program: A young couple with three small children approached us to design a *siheyuan* that offers a quintessential Beijing experience which would at the same time still fit the contemporary lifestyle of the family.

Design strategy: On the urban level, we believe that the insertion of a new component into the ancient fabric should be a seamless one, and it should accept the basic spatial structure of a traditional *siheyuan*. However, the rooms around the courtyard needed to be reconfigured into a continuous space to create a comfortable and energy-saving indoor environment that would allow the inhabitants to enjoy the courtyard as much as possible—that is, let them live around the courtyard, literally. In the end, we not only designed a dwelling for the family of five, but also a particular way of living, that could only unfold in a courtyard house, such as spending the morning in the west wing, and enjoying noon in the north, afternoon in the east, and evening in south. In a loop-shaped living room, daily life moves around the courtyard and follows the sun.

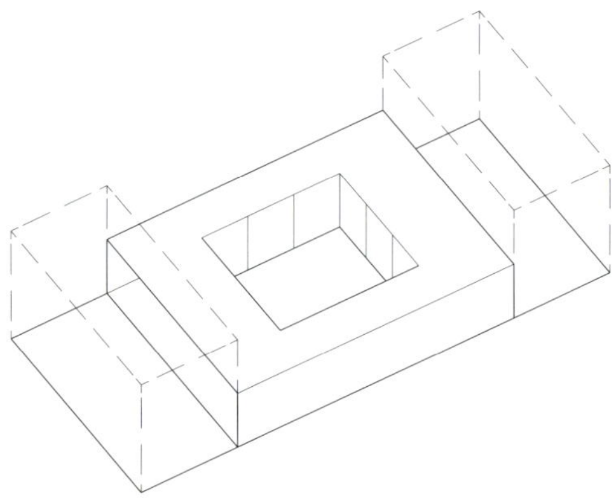

v Sunshine diagram

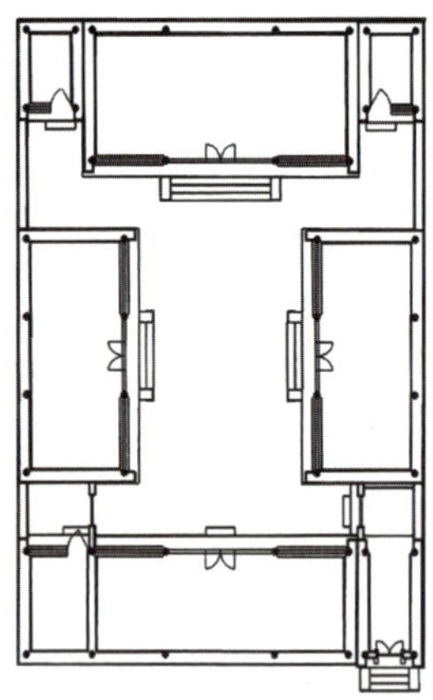

Typical *siheyuan* plan

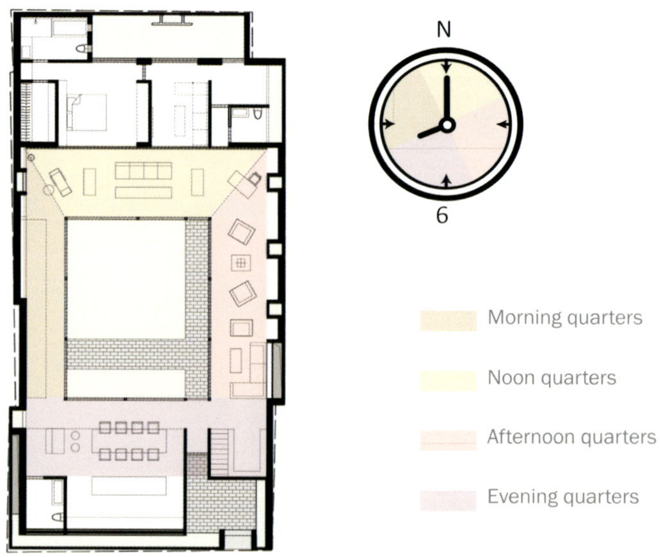

> Bird's-eye view

>> (Page 190) Afternoon sun streaming through in the east wing
>> (Page 191) Morning sun in the kitchen in the west wing

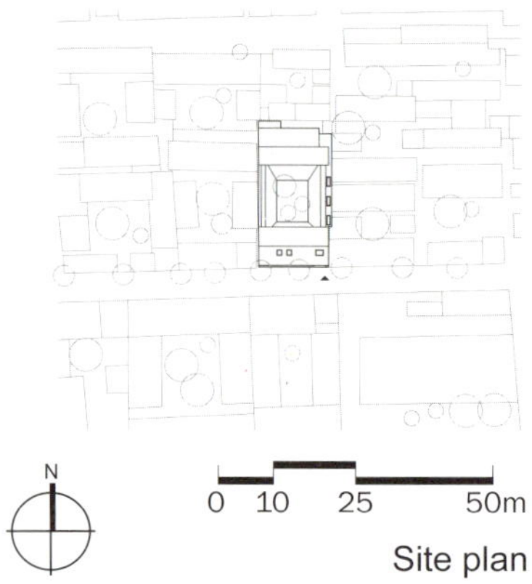

Site plan

v View of courtyard from north

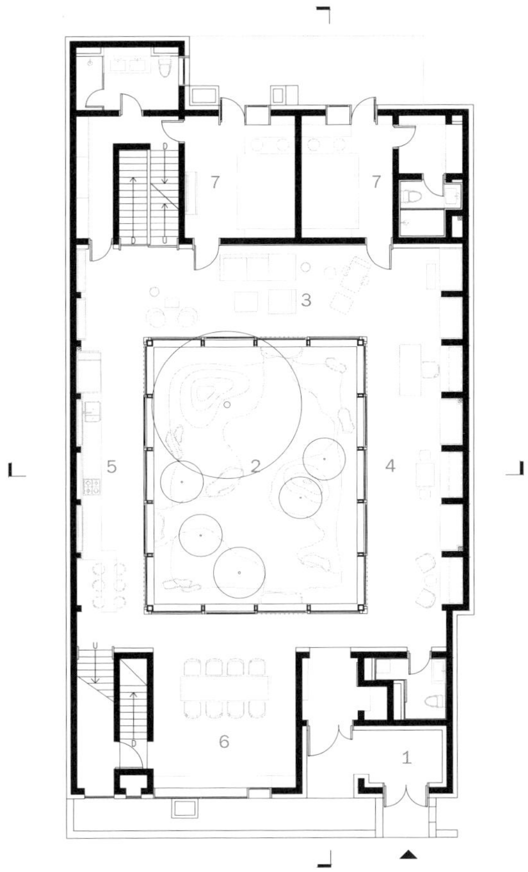

First-floor plan

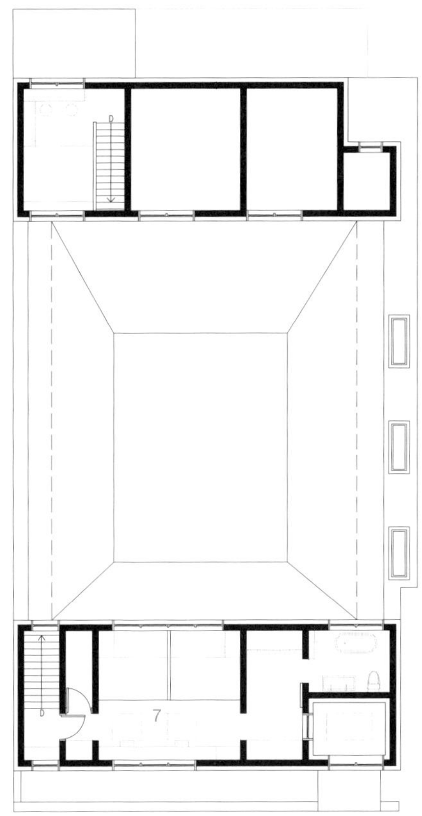

Second-floor plan

1 Entering
2 Central courtyard
3 Guest-hosting
4 Living
5 Cooking
6 Dining
7 Sleeping

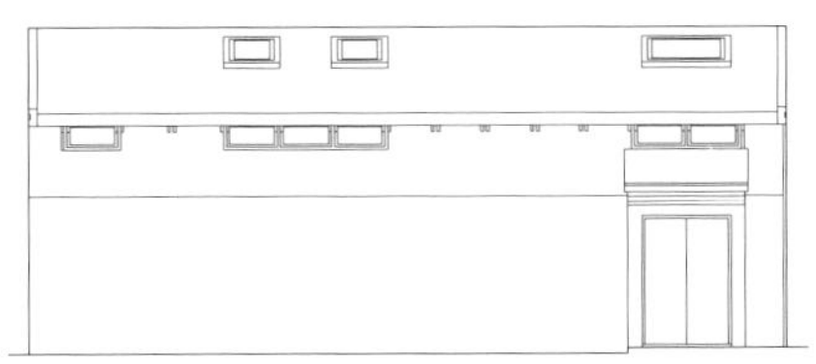

South elevation

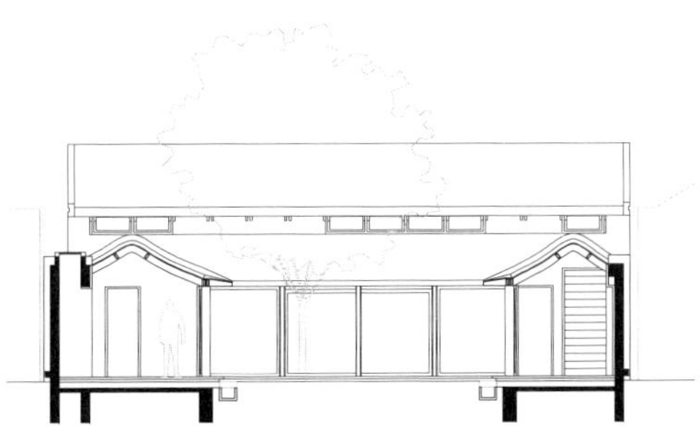

Cross section

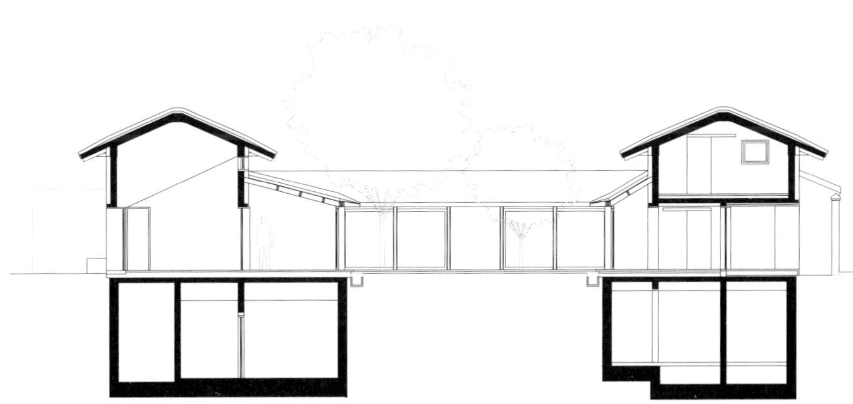

Longitudinal section

1 | 2 | 3

< 1 Early evening scene
< 2 Corner detail of eaves
< 3 A chair from Atelier FCJZ's Bend It Like Yoga collection in the house

LOC.
VISIT.

COMMENTS

Wang Junyang
Architectural theorist, critic
Professor, Nanjing University

Cité internationale universitaire de Paris (CIUP) has always been referred to as a miniature "Association of Nations." It includes more than forty apartment buildings to house exchange students from all over the world. The most famous building is, undoubtedly, Pavillon Suisse, designed by Le Corbusier, and completed between 1930 and 1932. At that time, Le Corbusier was ardently exploring modern architecture; his "Five Points of Modern Architecture," Radiant City (Ville Radieuse) master plan, piloti, and glass curtain walls are all reflected in the design of Pavillon Suisse. It can be said that—whether from a technological or aesthetic perspective—this building is full of innovation. It is also the first piece of modernist architecture in Cité internationale universitaire de Paris.

However, several problems in Le Corbusier's ideas on cities and architecture are present in this building. First, could Radiant City actually constitute a good urban model? Considering the views expressed in recent years by Yung Ho Chang regarding urban issues, this model may, in fact, require criticism and reflection. It is not surprising that in Maison de la Chine, the piloti and independent building units from the Radiant City have been replaced by the traditional courtyard model, regardless of whether the prototype for this model comes from China's Hakka courtyards, or from Georges-Eugène Haussmann's Paris city blocks (even if the ground level is only partially composed of piloti, a peripheral basic enclosure will be maintained). At the same time, a very large opening facing the sports field forms a different type of enclosure compared to traditional prototypes. The public stairs within the courtyard are ingeniously arranged at the opening, giving the building a monumental and public entrance, also forming a unique architectural highlight.

In his initial plan for Pavillon Suisse, Le Corbusier had designed a southern façade using glass blocks and glass windows that could be opened, and which were transparent; later he changed these to a glass curtain wall design. Like his Cité de Refuge in Paris, which was completed at around the same time, this design made rooms cold in the winter and hot in the summer—a problem that did not improve until the 1950s, when the curtain wall was transformed and shading issues were addressed. Different from this, Maison de la Chine awards each room a façade thickness that is suitable for its balcony or protruding window; this creates a variety of angles in the façade and makes the building's façade look like a lattice-type brick wall structure. Because the use of air conditioning is not very popular in Paris during the summer, this design is definitely helpful for improving the interior environment. It also plays a role in blocking the traffic noise from the road south of the building. Now, this "double-skin" style of façade has become ubiquitous in modern architecture.

The rooftop garden is an important factor in Le Corbusier's "Five Points of Modern Architecture," but the application of this concept is quite limited in Pavillon Suisse. By comparison, Maison de la Chine not only includes a garden in the inner-courtyard rooftop, but also makes this garden an important element of the building. One reason why Le Corbusier prefers rooftop gardens is because they are helpful in improving the insulation properties of flat rooftops. This is not an especially remarkable reason in modern times, and the garden was incorporated easily enough by Maison de la Chine. More importantly was the question of how the rooftop garden would be used. Atelier FCJZ's plan for resolving this issue was to place a ring-shaped walkway on the roof. However, as the building faces a large pre-existing sports field and the complex already has excellent outdoor walking paths, it is questionable if this walkway is even necessary. Further, if the purpose of this walkway was not only to fulfill the representation of Le Corbusier's "architectural promenade" concept, but also to serve some real sports- or exercise-related purpose (a principle of modernism), then it would seem too flat, and spatially constrained.

Regardless, this project is worthy of our anticipation on many levels.

> Southeast corner

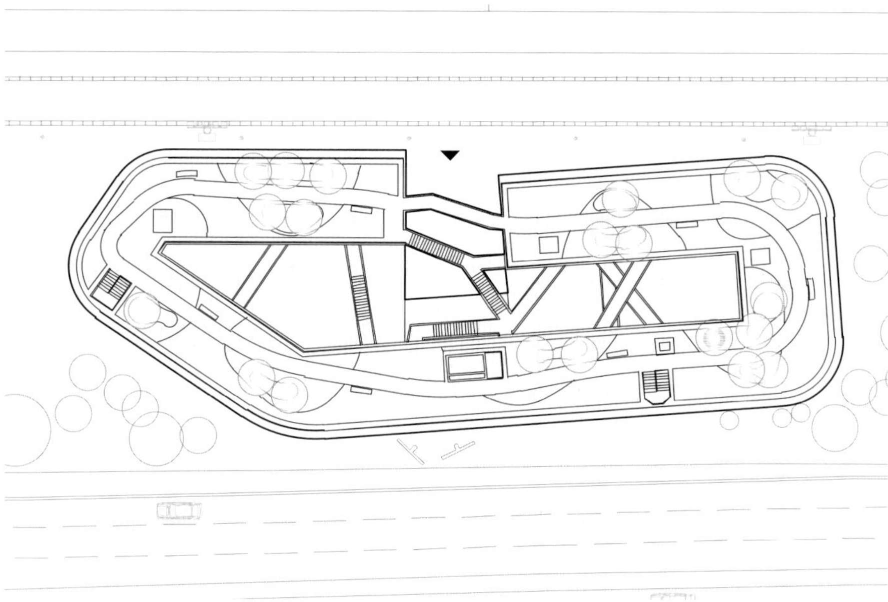

Site plan

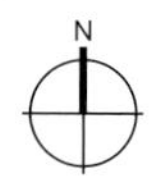

Typical-floor plan

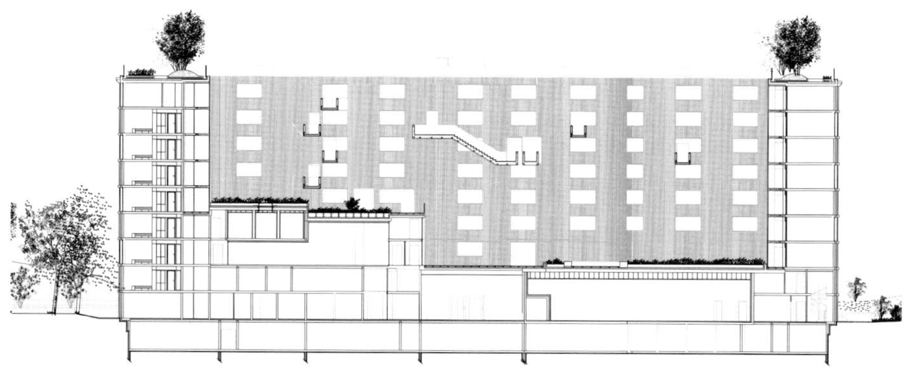

Cross section

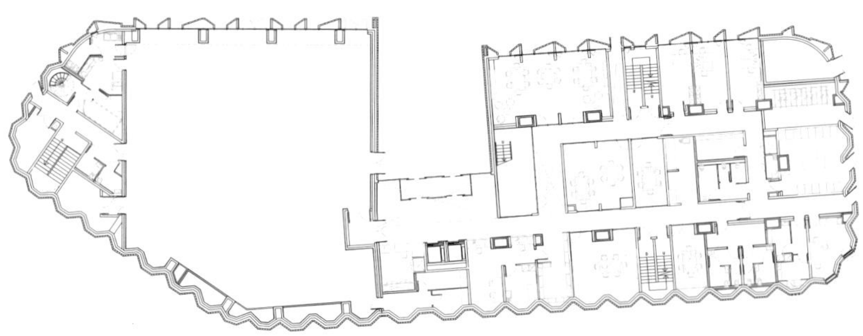

First-floor plan

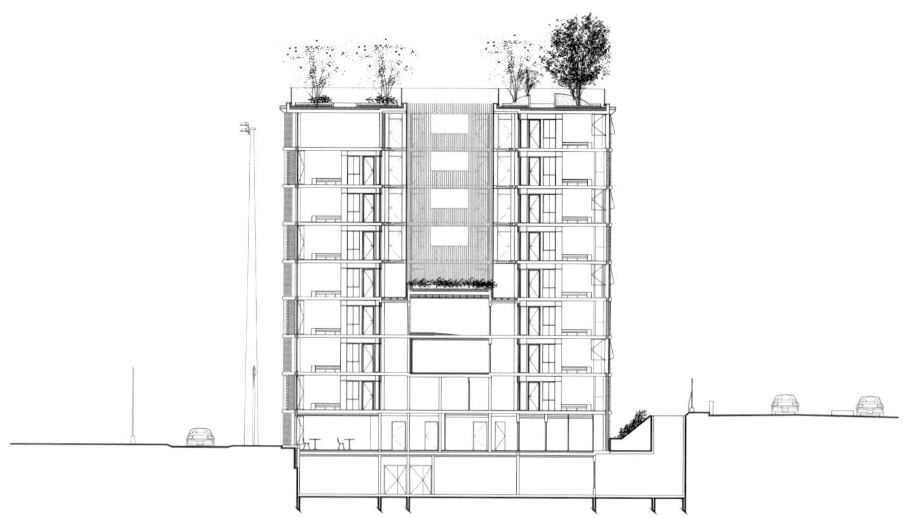

Longitudinal section

0 4 10 20m

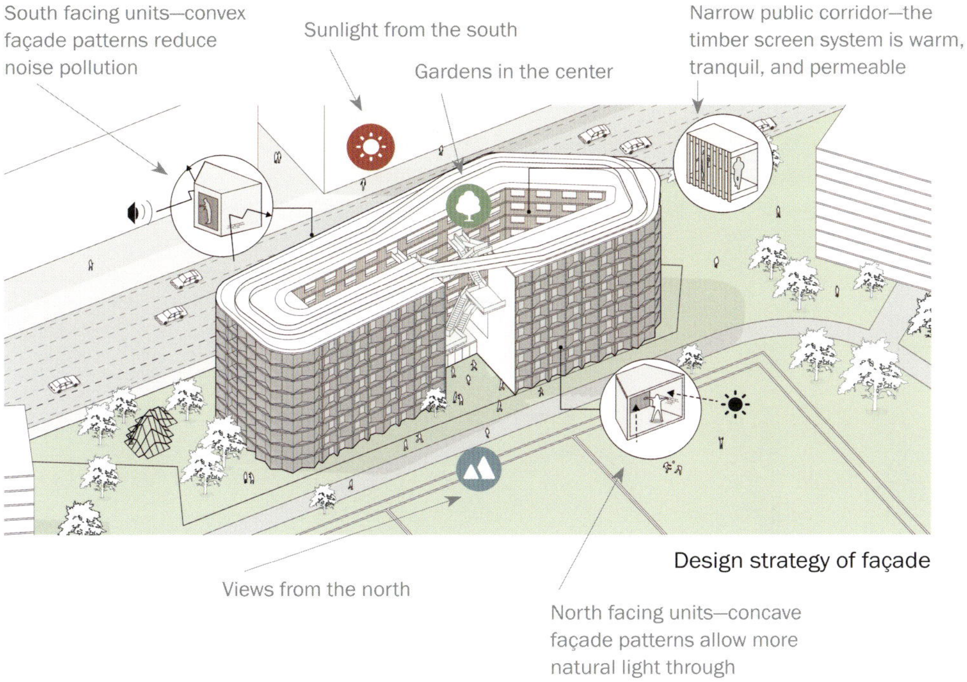

Design strategy of façade

Traditional *die se* (brick cantilever) in China

˅ Close-up of north elevation

˅ Cantilevered brick eaves using traditional Chinese *die se* laying technique

1

2 | 3

> 1 From the rooftop garden looking at the Eiffel Tower in the distance
> 2 Wood grating along the courtyard façade
> 3 Where the passage meets the stair

< On the fifth-floor rooftop terrace looking east

[EXPERIENCE of IN-OUT-DOOR]

International Exchange Center of Wenzhou Medical University

Wenzhou, Zhejiang Province, China

Under construction

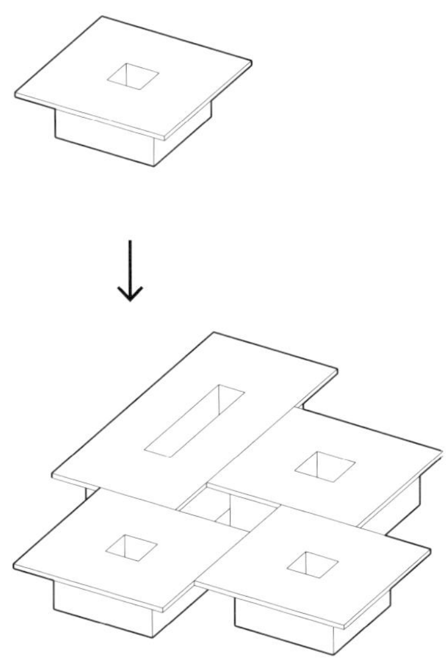

Climate and umbrella: Wenzhou, the location of this project, is a city with a mild climate. This got us wondering: given the great climate, could the human nature and behavior that pertain to outdoor living likely be more fully fulfilled here? Thus, climate becomes the driving force of this project. In order to reach the goal of integrating architecture and environment, we first organized this international exchange center with mixed programs into a cluster of eight buildings that houses a large auditorium, classrooms, a library, a guesthouse for visiting scholars, a student center, two blocks of student dormitories, and an administrative office. Breaking away from the typical enclosed architecture, we then designed each building with an umbrella-inspired section with four layers of spaces from the center to the edge: the central courtyard (outdoor); the air-conditioned area (indoor); the veranda (semi-indoor); and an area under the eaves (semi-outdoor). In each different weather condition, teachers and students can choose the most appropriate space for their study, interaction, and other activities. The large overhanging eaves—up to 10 meters deep—between two buildings form a large outdoor hall, making public activities, such as concerts or sporting events possible. It can be said that through this design, we hope to encourage the teachers and students of Wenzhou Medical University to experience a lifestyle that blurs the boundaries between indoors and outdoors, which hopefully makes them more appreciative of their geographical location.

A basic structure: For this project, we adopted the concrete frame system that is commonly used in China and achieve deep overhanging eaves through post-tension prestressing.

COMMENTS

Tong Ming
Professor, School of Architecture, Southeast University
Principal Architect, TM Studio

It seems like education can never be separated from nature and trees. It was under the Bodhi tree that the ascetic Siddhartha Gautama got instant revelation and became the Buddha; the master Confucius sat on an almond wood altar when he read books, played music, and taught his students. A tree with its spreading crown can define a micro environment among the vast wilderness. It does not only create a pleasant shade for people to rest under, but it also represents growth and development a symbolic passing of knowledge from trees to people.

The first image on the site of the International Exchange Center of Wenzhou Medical University is an area of green woods on a raised ground. Under the shade of the trees, students are scattered, resting, studying, and having picnics. The architecture acts as a kind of filling, floating in and out of the woods.

The pocket of woods on the outside also determined how Atelier FCJZ responded to the site. In this process, the huge cornices seen everywhere played an important role. The huge cornices—spreading from all four façades of the building—not only define, display, and emphasize the courtyard environment created by the four groups of woods they also build activity spaces that are both independent and connected.

We can see from this that the design of the International Exchange Center did not begin from the regular and modular architecture solids but from the four "outdoor rooms." The huge cornices floating from these four tree-filled "outdoor rooms" have been combined together, creating more "semi-outdoor rooms." The real indoor rooms take part in the creation of this image as a kind of standard and well-developed module.

Design concept sketches by Yung Ho Chang: a big canopy over the landscape

Construction in one of the courtyards

v Overall construction site

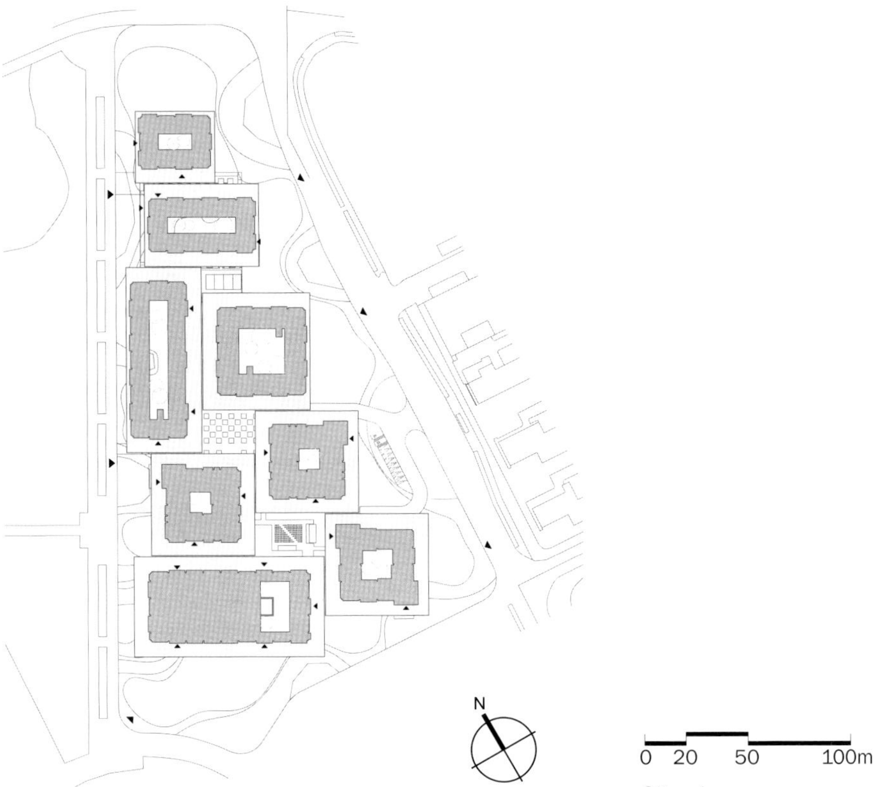

Site plan

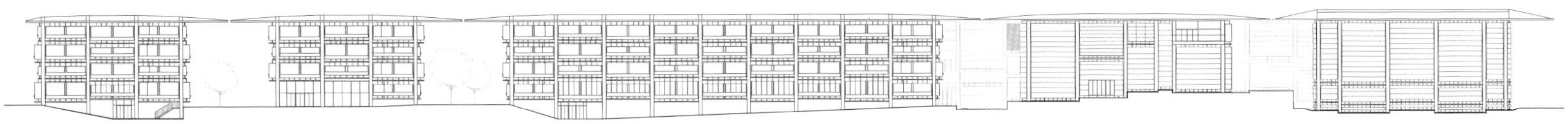

West elevation

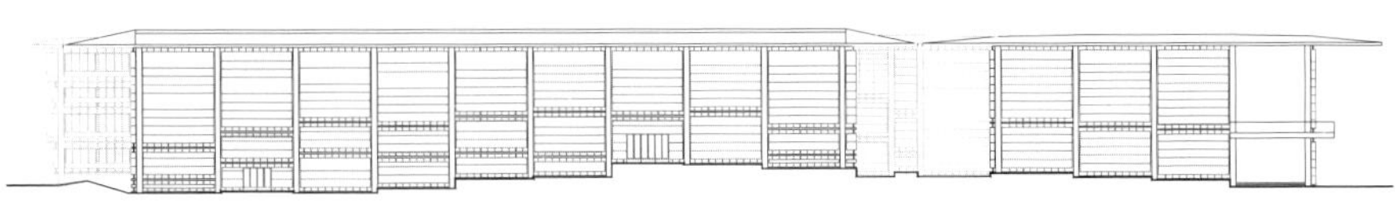

South elevation

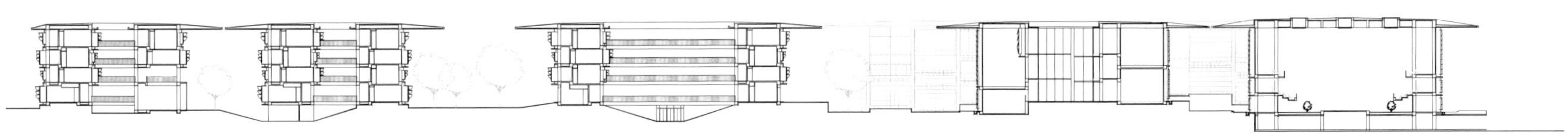

Section A-A'

0 10 25 50m

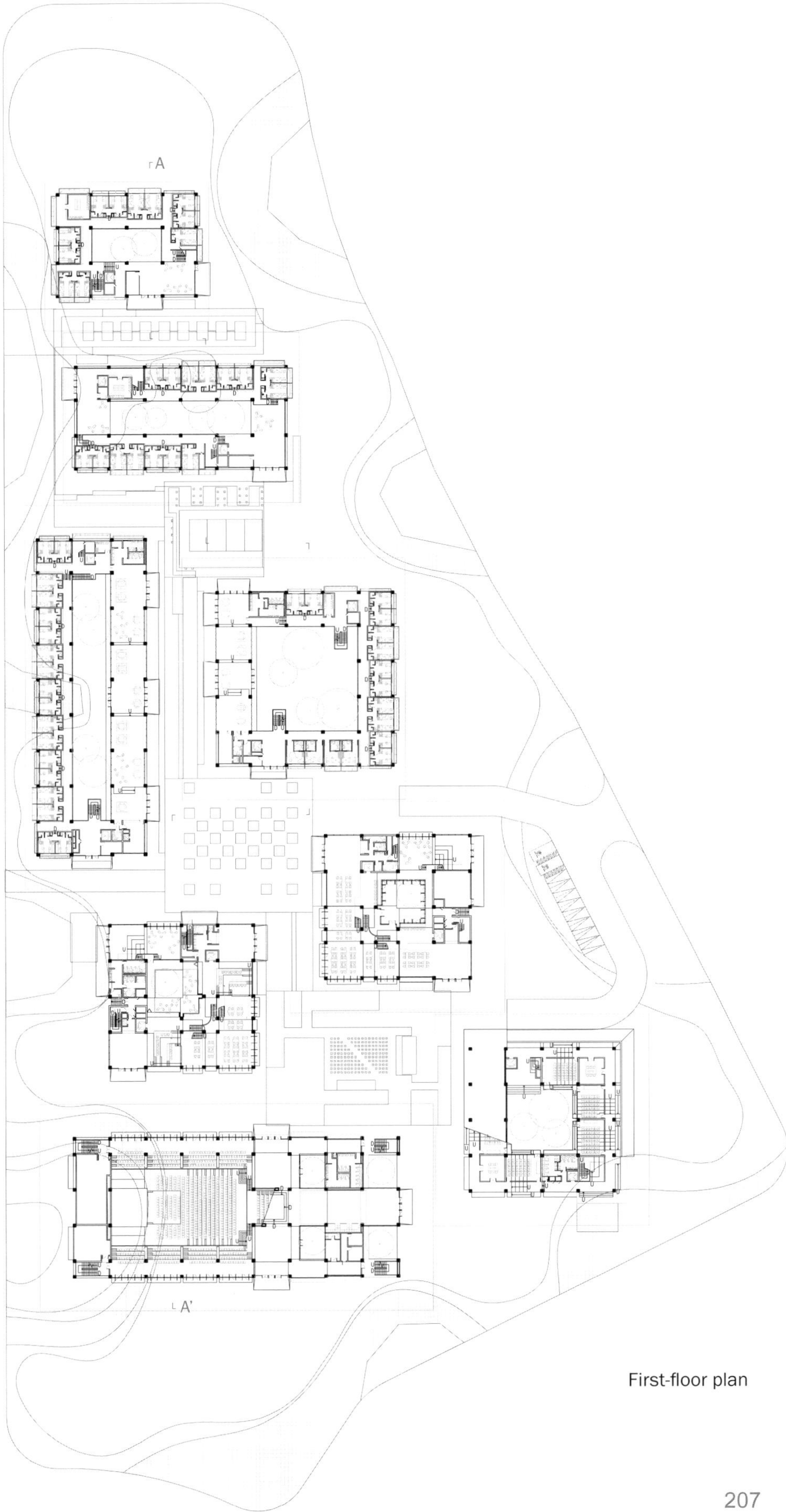

First-floor plan

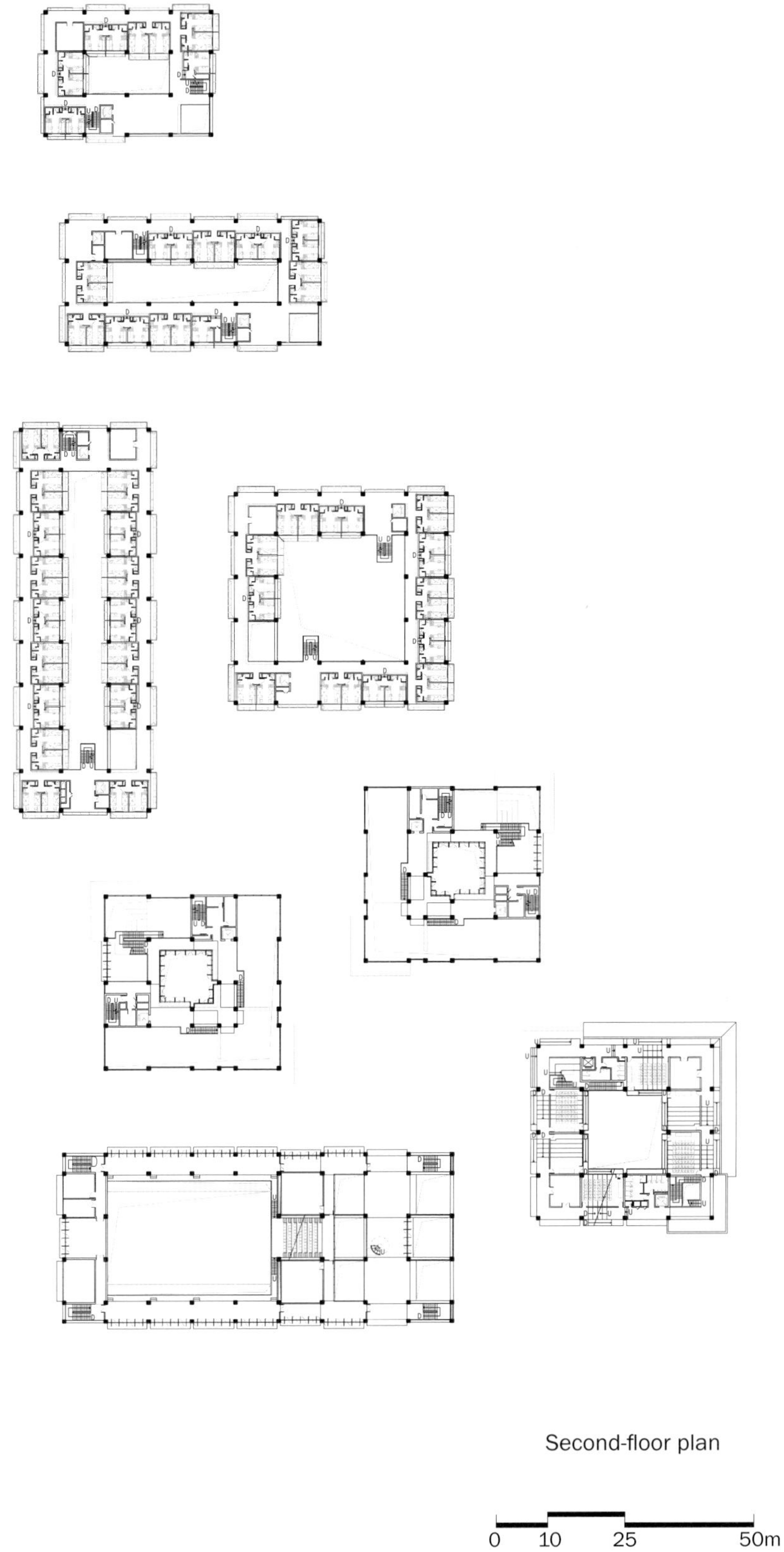

Second-floor plan

Space-layer diagrams

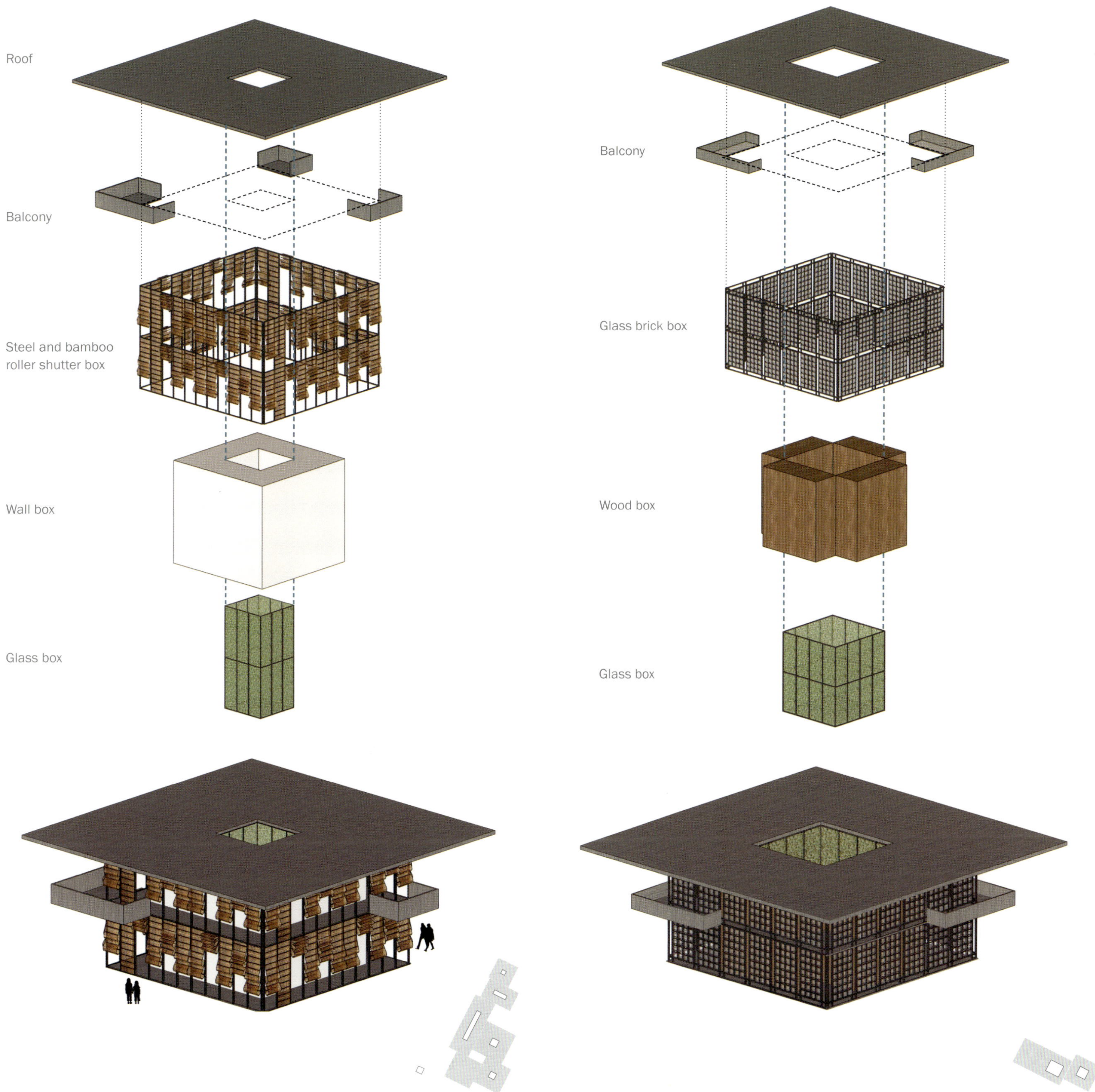

Spatial concept

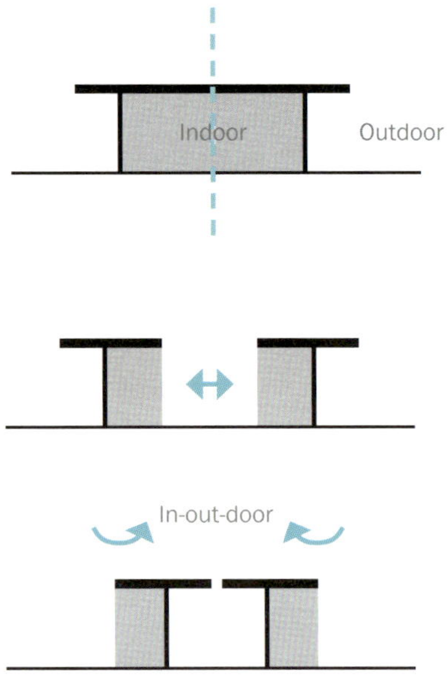

Four layers of spaces

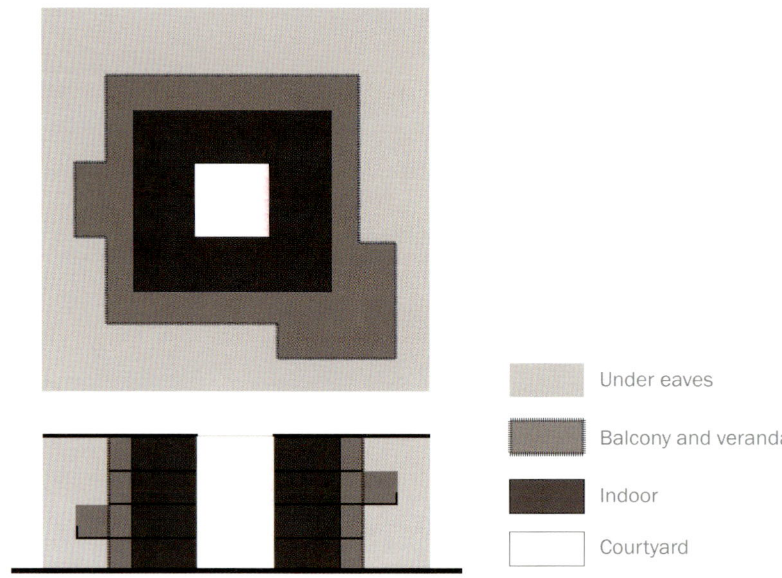

v Courtyard between buildings

v "In-out-door" space between dormitories

[EXPERIENCE of LEARNING]

CAA Liangzhu Campus

Hangzhou, Zhejiang Province, China

2021 (Phase 1), 2023 (Phase 2)

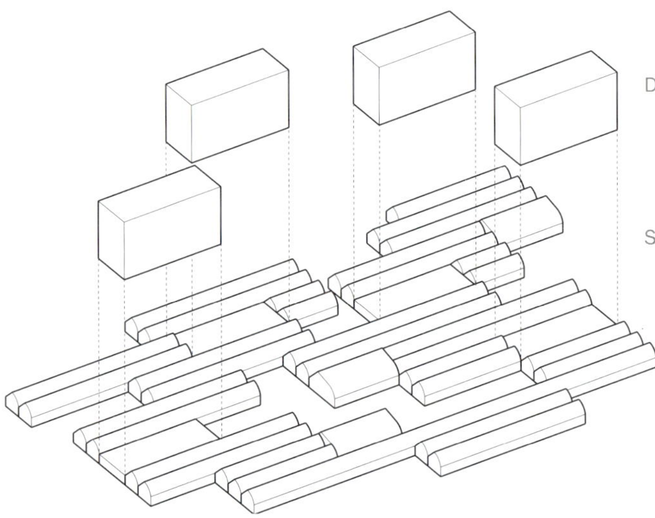

New campus, new mode of education: The new campus planned for China Academy of Art (CAA) is located in Liangzhu, Hangzhou, and will feature a comprehensive curriculum across the following schools of study: College of Innovative Design, College of Art Management, College of Foundational Education, and College of Continuing Education. It will house 3,000 full-time students and 1,000 "continuing education" students. The four main objectives of this new campus are: the development of interdisciplinary innovative talents; to promote design and informational economy; the integration of artificial intelligence technology; and to set the benchmark for contemporary design education.

Architecture that teaches: Guided by CAA's mission, we formed our own—make architecture a part of the educational system, that is, the campus design should be able to promote experimentation and the use of both the skill of the hand and the mind, as it also encourages students to interact with each other in and out of classes to nurture collaboration. While traditional classrooms are still necessary, the main teaching-learning space—workshops—at the Liangzhu campus is redefined as an open, continuous area, where classes can be held and students may work individually or in teams, reading, writing, drawing, creating, or debating. In this space, all the activities on campus are visible. We hope to blur the boundary between teaching and learning, and research and practice in this new form of learning/activity environment we have named Super Studio.

Learn-live: At the Liangzhu campus, students live upstairs of the Super Studio. The vertical stratified system of dormitory, social space, and workshops creates an architecture that embodies the concept "college as a community." Within the dormitories, there are spaces provided for students to organize interest clubs, which are, in a way, a form of "self-taught" courses. We hope to convey to the students: living is learning. This ideology makes up the anchor ideas of this campus design, together with the open workshops.

v Bird's-eye view of site (Phase 1 completed)

> Bird's-eye view of studios and dormitories

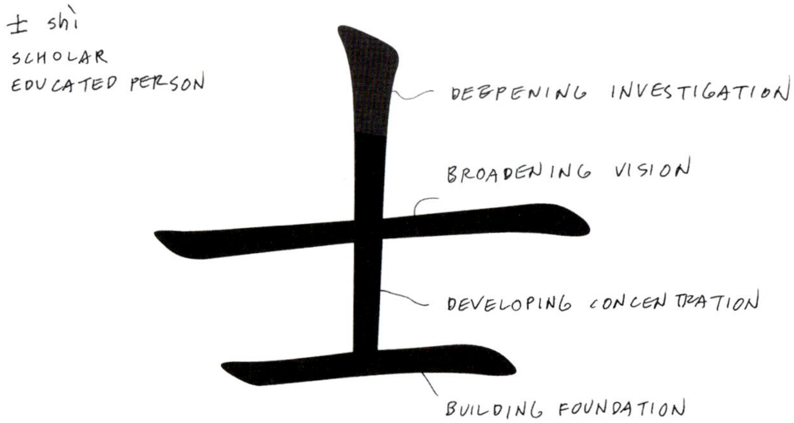

Learn-live

Concepts for educational structure

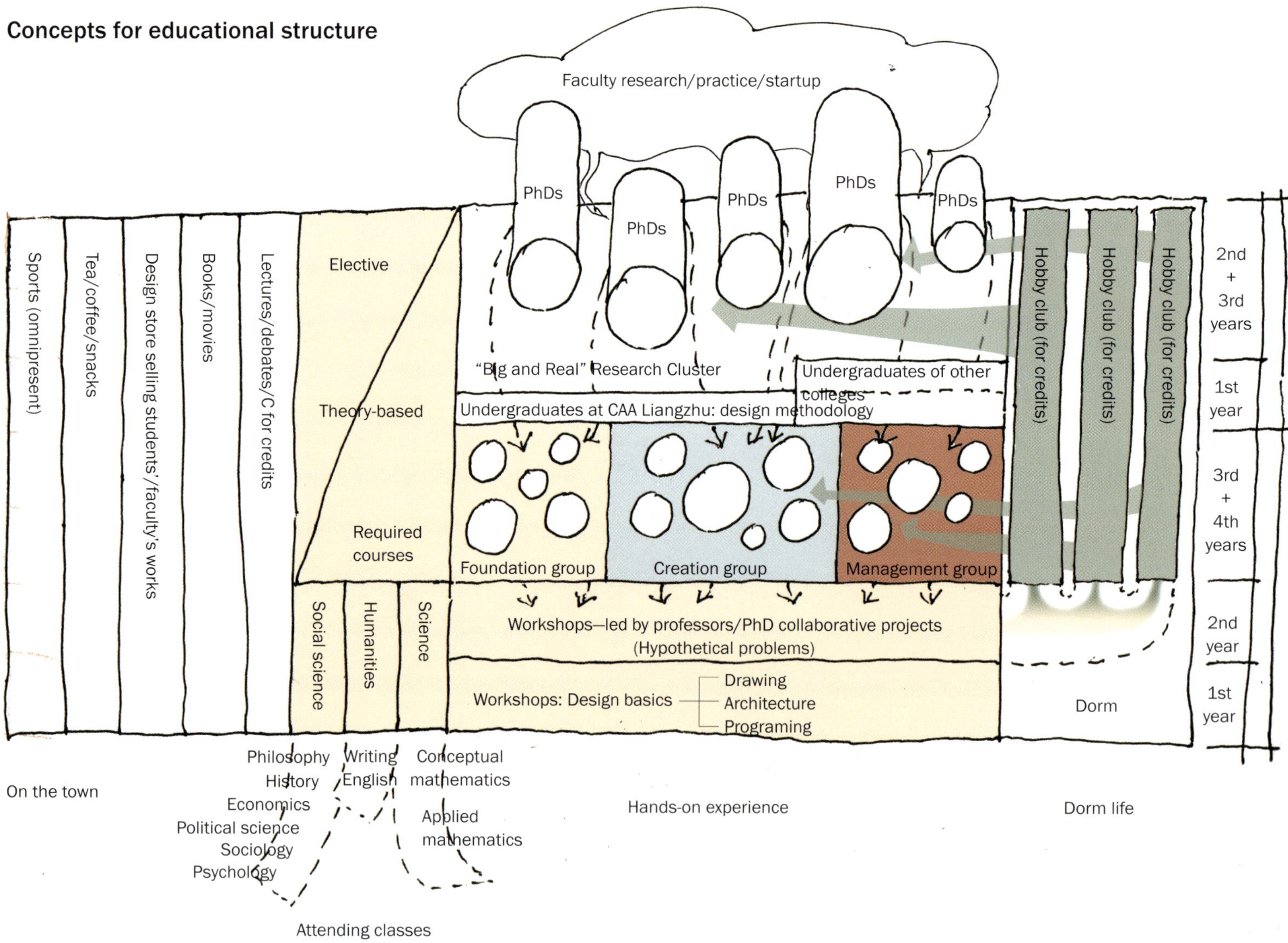

In the open studios:

What does she see?

Where is her class?

Who will she meet?

In the open studios:

Creativity Big Bang everywhere;

Learning is not limited to classrooms and may happen anywhere;

She meets her future collaborators.

Open, continuous space: space becomes field

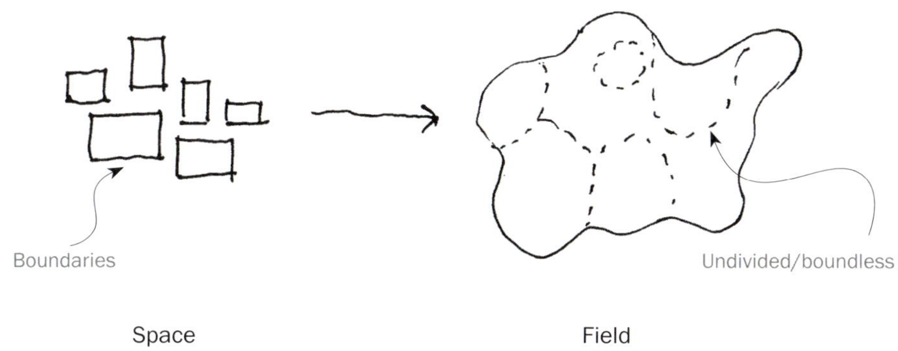

v Study models for continuous studios

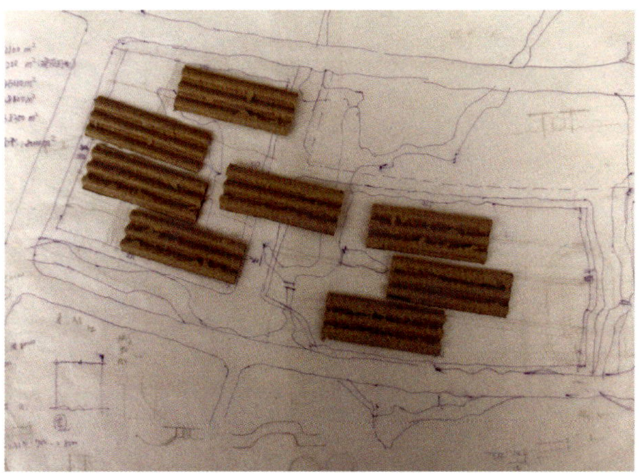

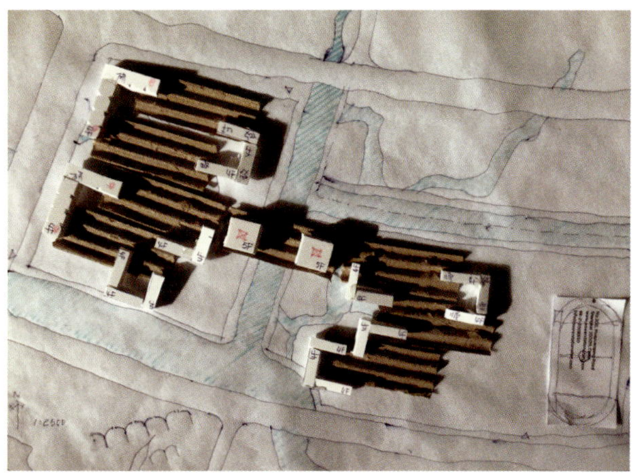

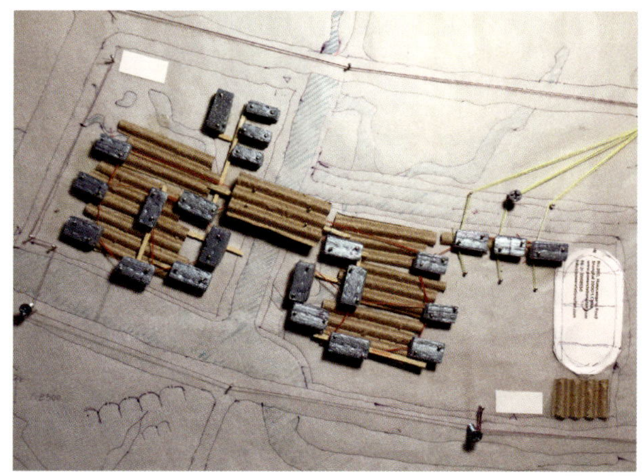

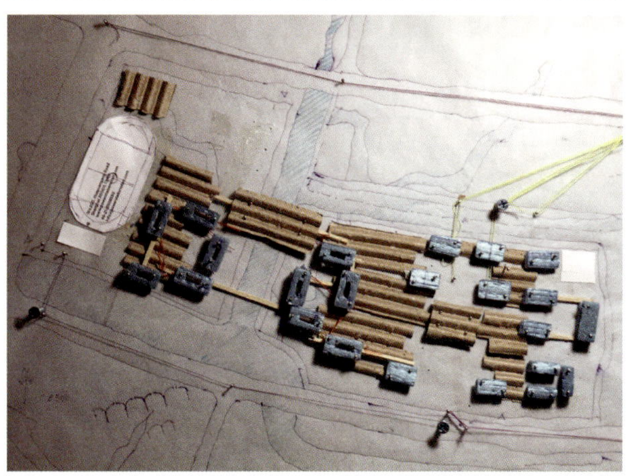

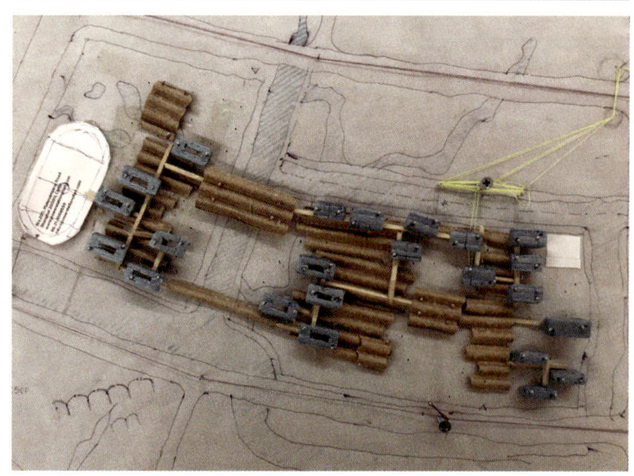

First-floor plan

v Cross section of the campus

High-rise dormitory floor plans (Building 7#)

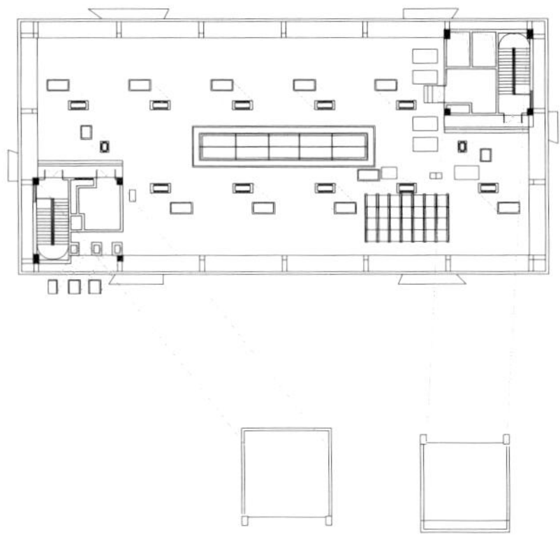

Top-floor plan

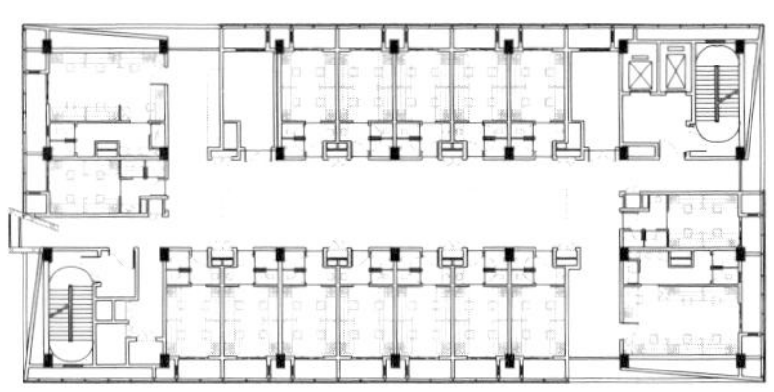

Typical-floor plan

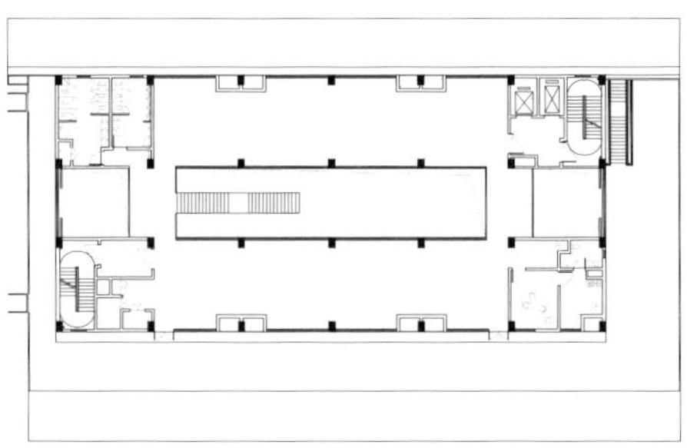

Second-floor plan

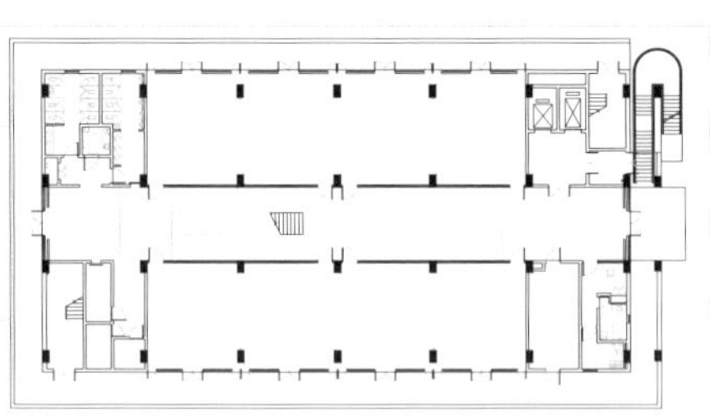

First-floor plan

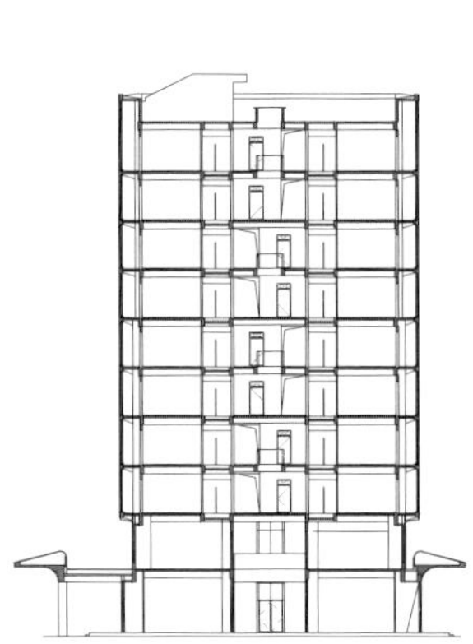

High-rise dormitory sections (Building 7#)

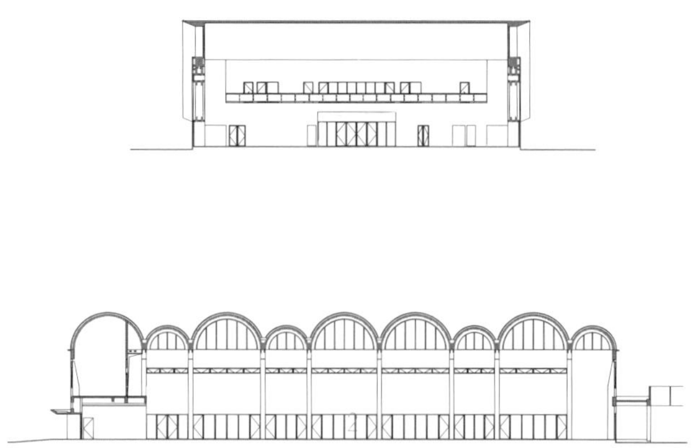

Gymnasium sections

Gymnasium floor plans

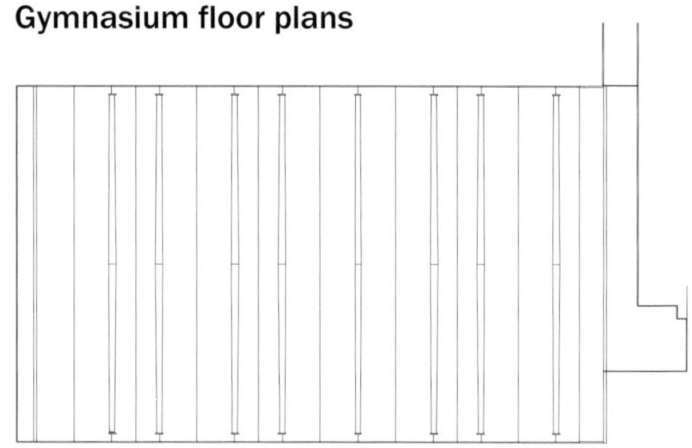

Roof plan

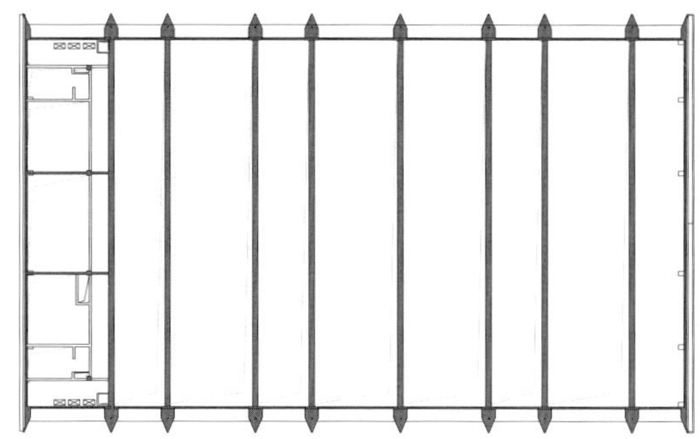

Vaults plan

Second-floor plan

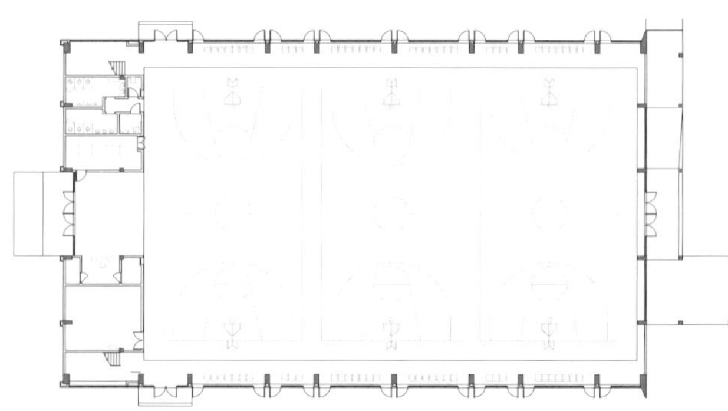

First-floor plan

Multistory dormitory floor plans (Building 8#)

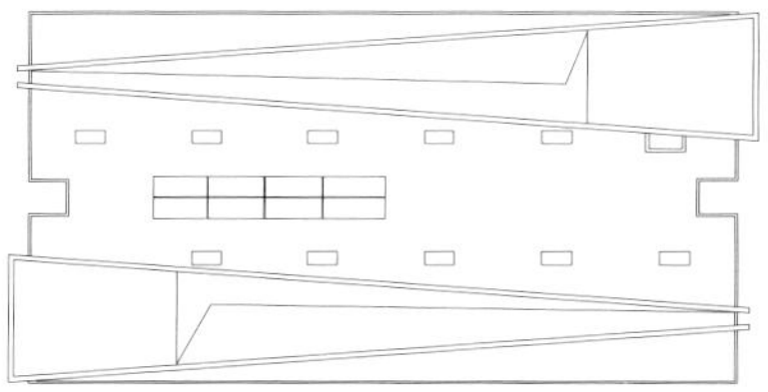

Roof plan

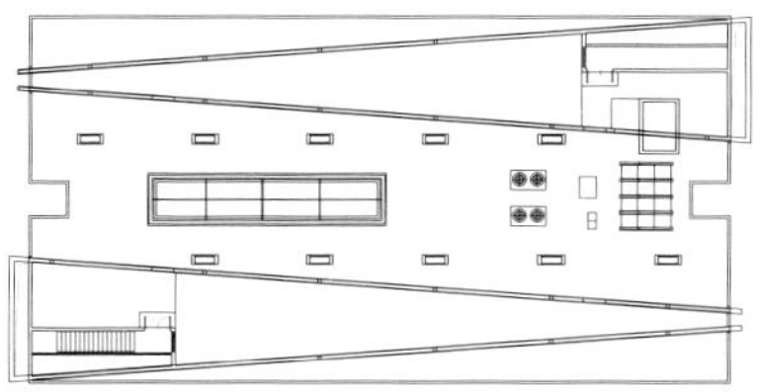

Top-floor plan

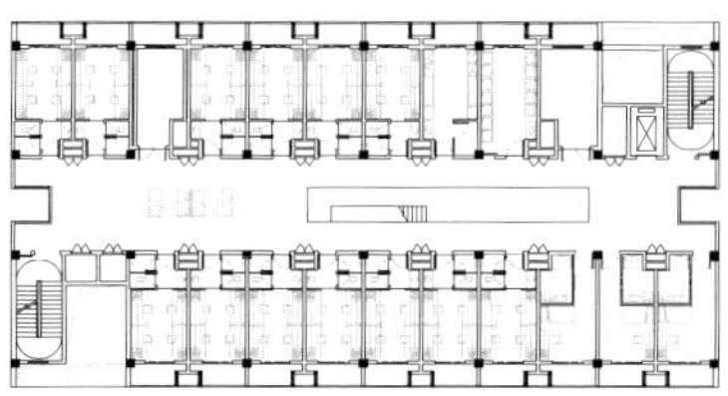

Typical-floor plan

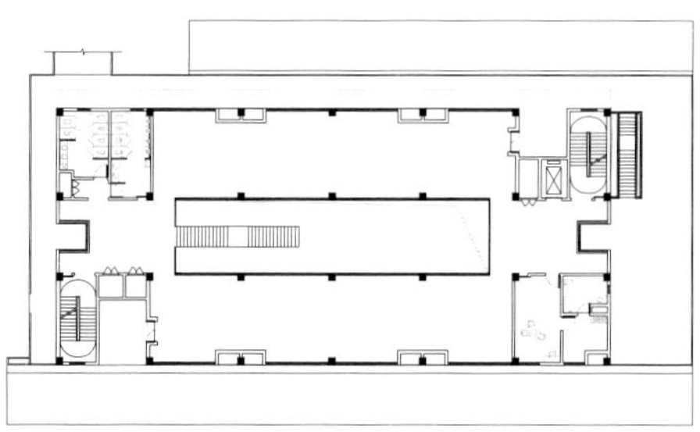

Second-floor plan

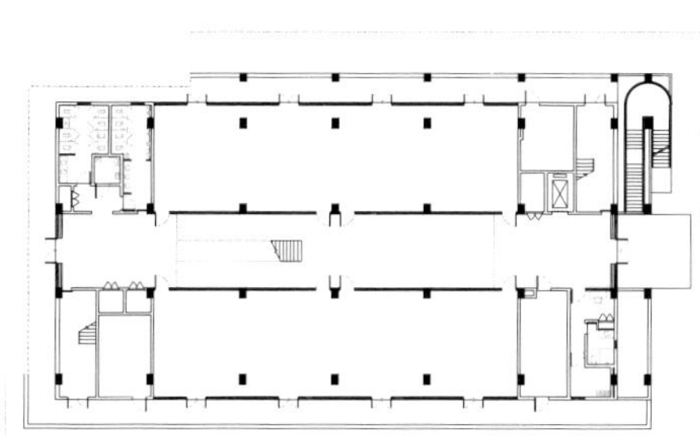

First-floor plan

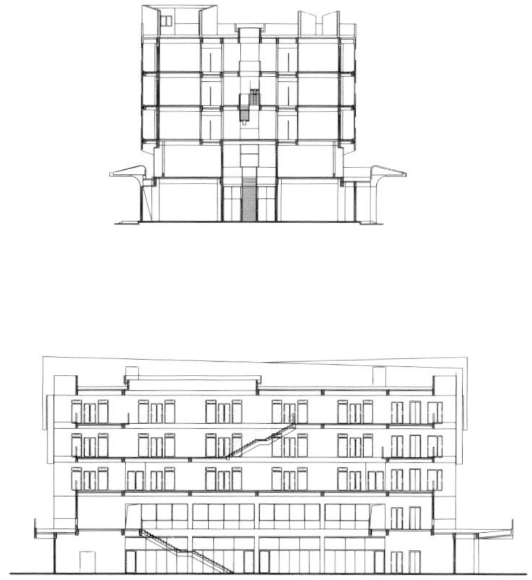

Multistory dormitory sections (Building 8#)

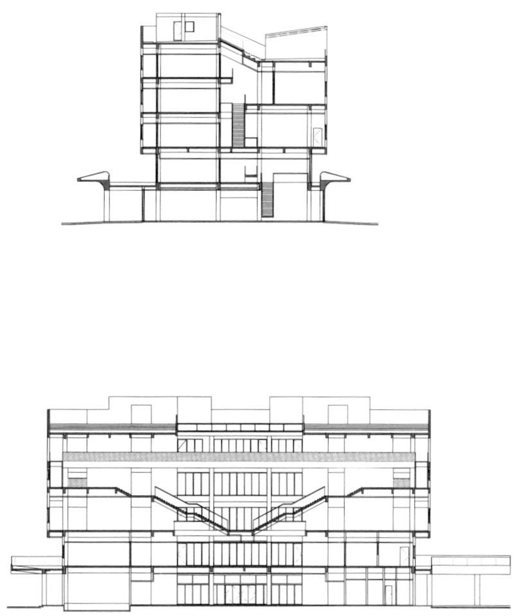

Administration building sections

Administration building floor plans

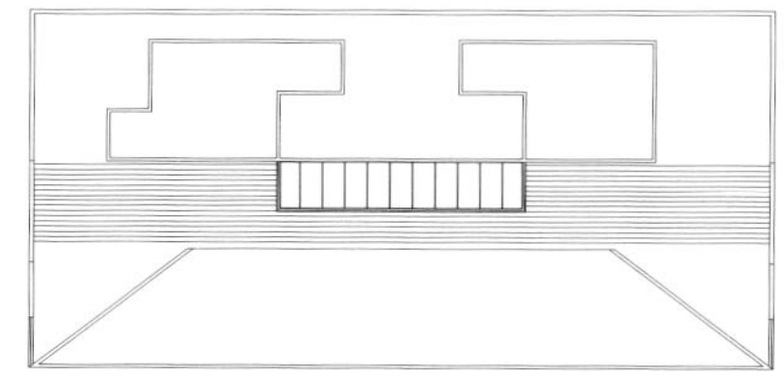

Roof plan

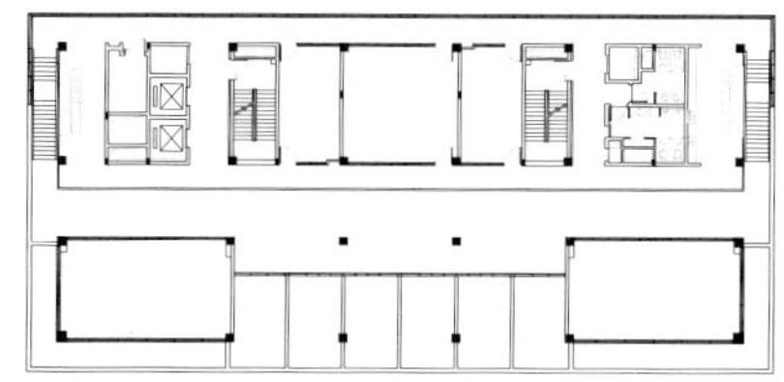

Fifth-floor plan

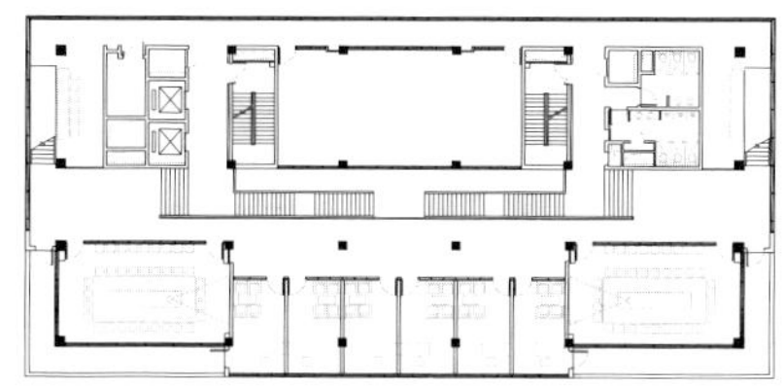

Fourth-floor plan

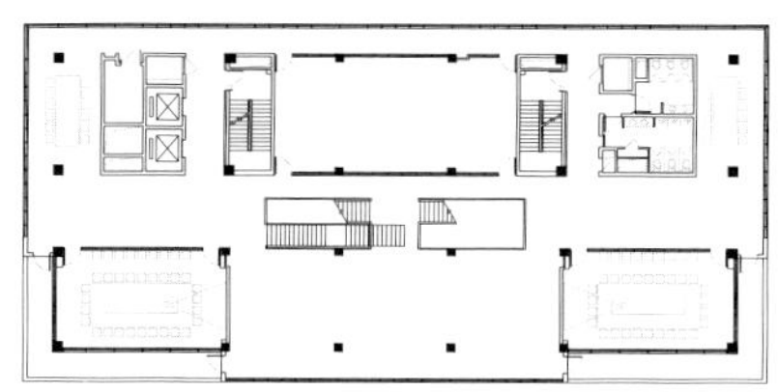

Third-floor plan

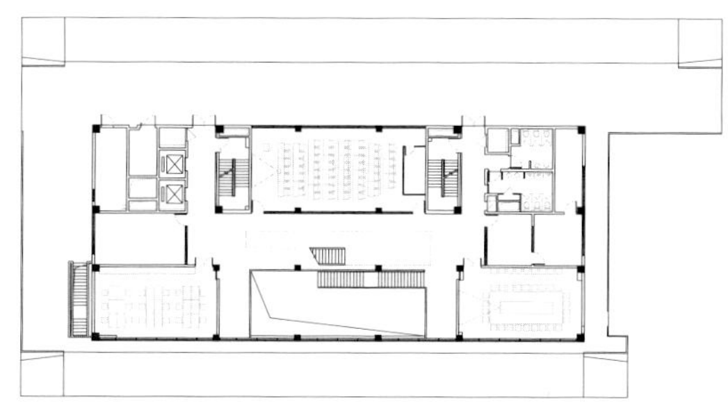

Second-floor plan

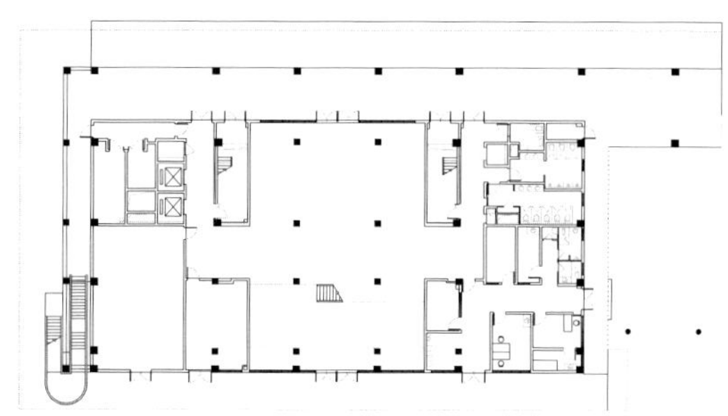

First-floor plan

> View of the dormitories over the roofs of the studios

v Partial campus fabric

< Vertical spatial organization of campus: with dormitories upstairs and studios downstairs

Close-up of elevation of high-rise dormitories

v Overlooking the first two floors of a dormitory building; the second floor will hold student interest clubs in the future

v Common space in dormitory

> Second-floor walkways

v Partial section of studio

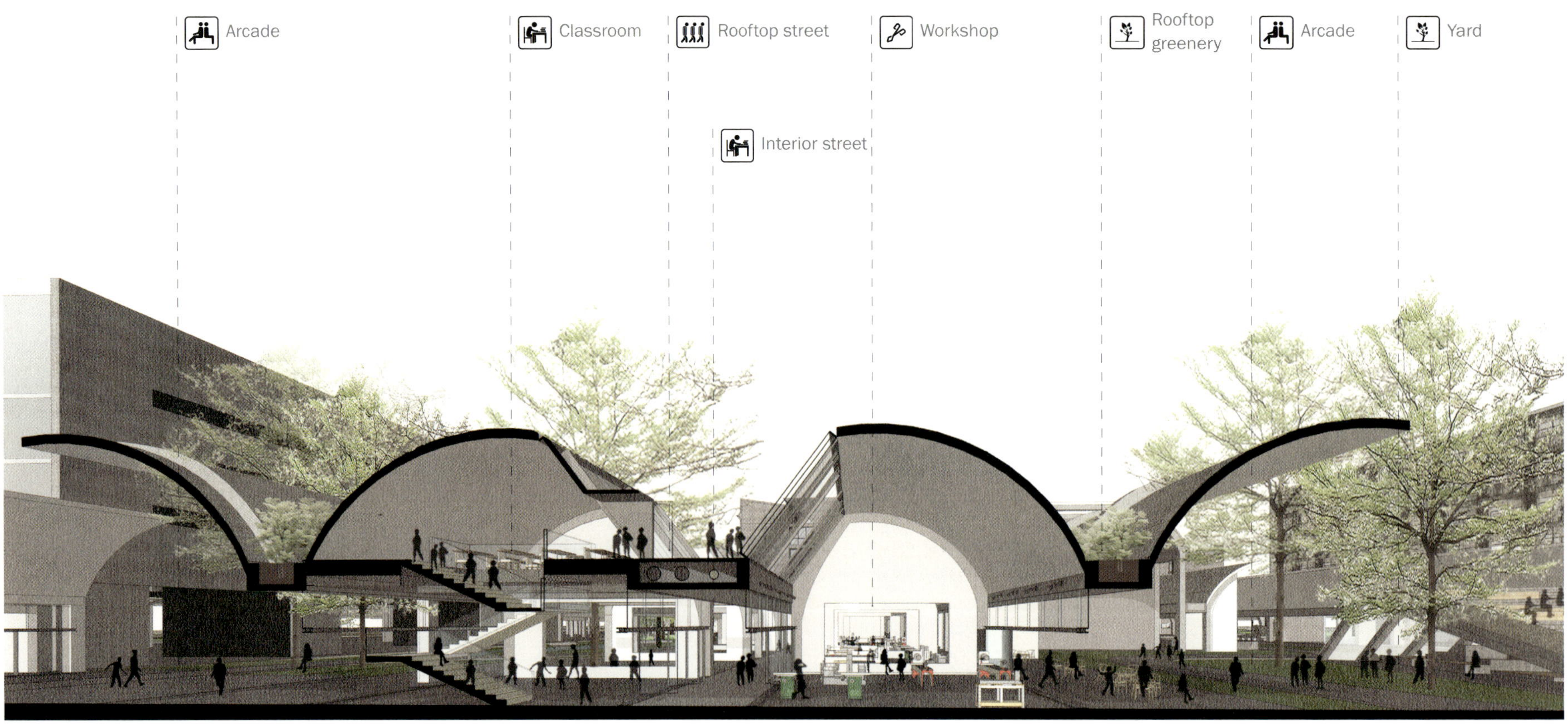

Wire mesh laying process

Preparing plaster surface

Pressing wire mesh into plaster

Corner detail

v On the exterior surface of range-finders, the wire mesh-over-plaster process was applied

v Close-up of wire-mesh-over-plaster surface

The interior of the second floor of the canteen

v Cantilevered eaves outside studios

实施校园美育
立足文化自信育新
砥砺东

< Space under the cantilevered eaves of the studios

Continuous interior space of the studios

Class in a second-floor studio

v A typical bay of the studios

v A staircase going up to the second floor in the studios

Interior of the gymnasium

v View of the gymnasium from the studio-dormitories complex

Studio smock design

Graduates of the design department of National Hangzhou Art College in 1935

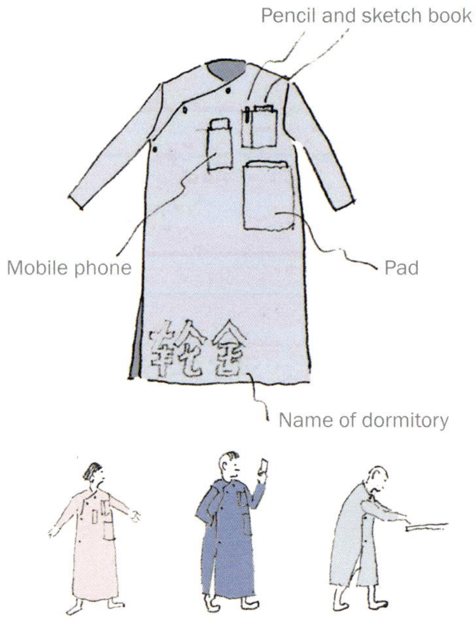

Design sketches by Yung Ho Chang

Studio smock sample

v Pond on the campus connects to the surrounding river

v Landscape water system outside gymnasium

[EXPERIENCE of LEARNING]

Open Kindergarten

Beijing, China

2022

Breaking the confines of the classroom: In China's current education system—from kindergarten to college—the classroom tends to play a central role. This enclosed space usually offers students a protective environment, but simultaneously prevents them from interacting socially and being adventurous. Our design of Open Kindergarten emphasizes spatial flexibility and devised operable walls for each classroom. When these walls are opened, each of the three floors—with four classrooms on every level—becomes a big playground, or even a community center where the children can explore and learn to make new friends.

Strategizing along a tight budget: Typically, the budget available to design educational facilities is relatively low. By focusing on space, we were able to engage the conventional structural system with common materials and produce a design that may still push the school architecture forward, however, small a step it may be.

Open class units sharing the public space

> Bird's-eye view

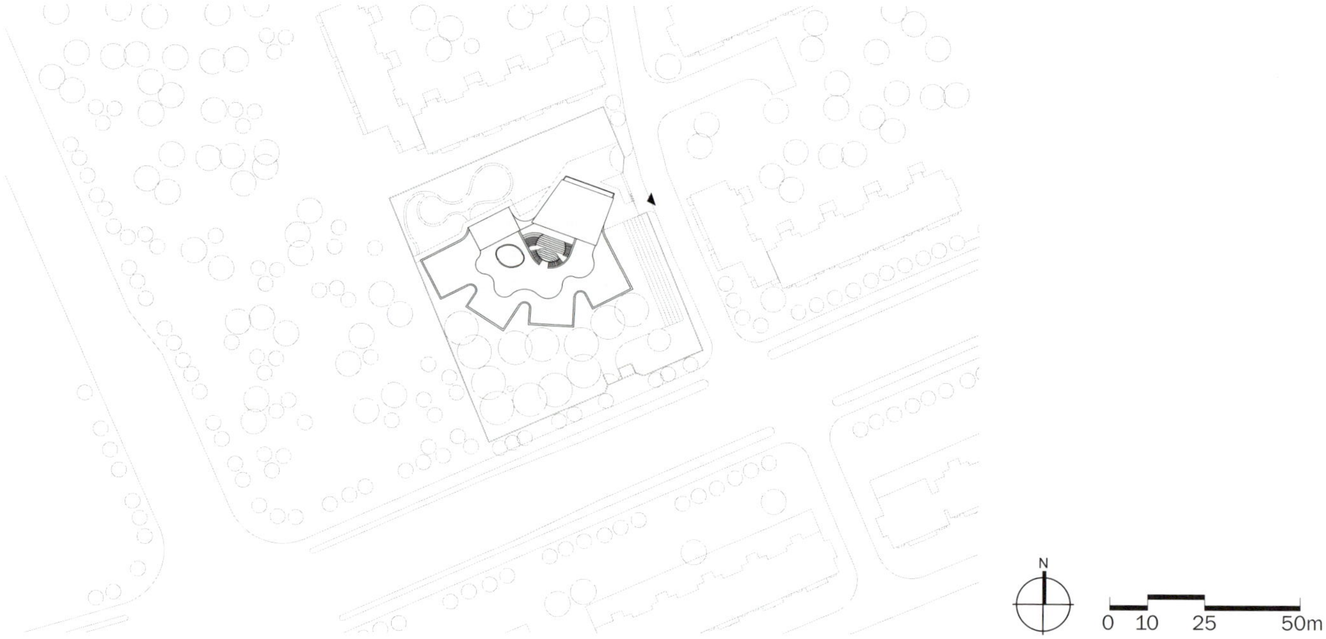

Site plan

v View from the playground on the south side

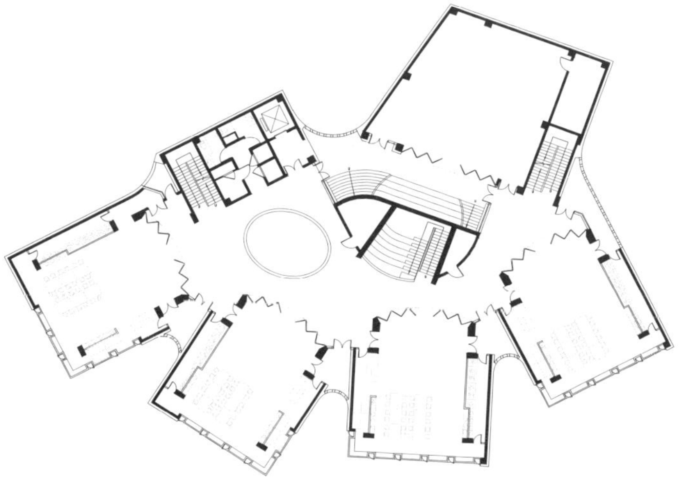

Third-floor plan

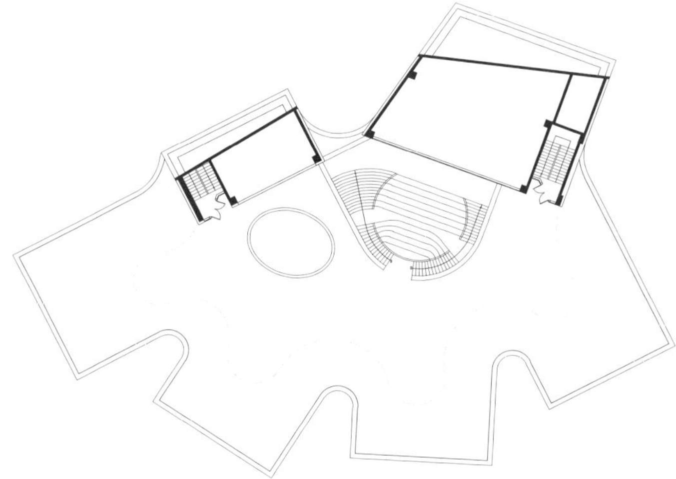

Roof plan

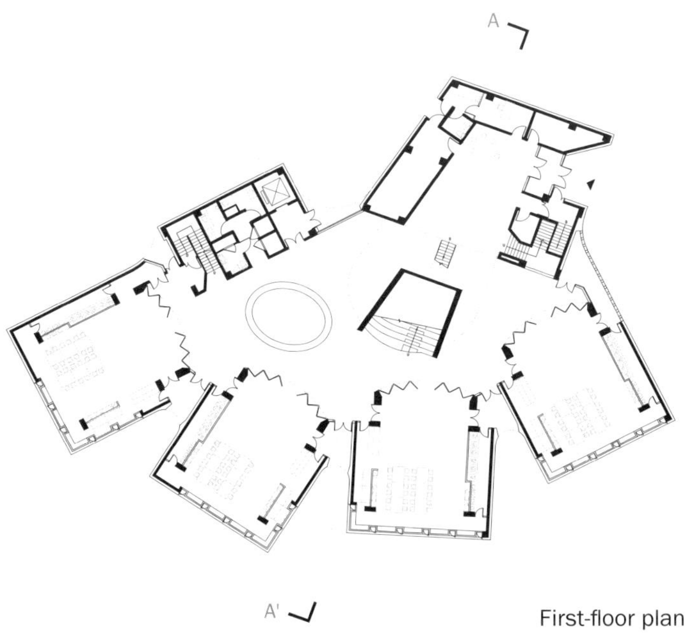

First-floor plan

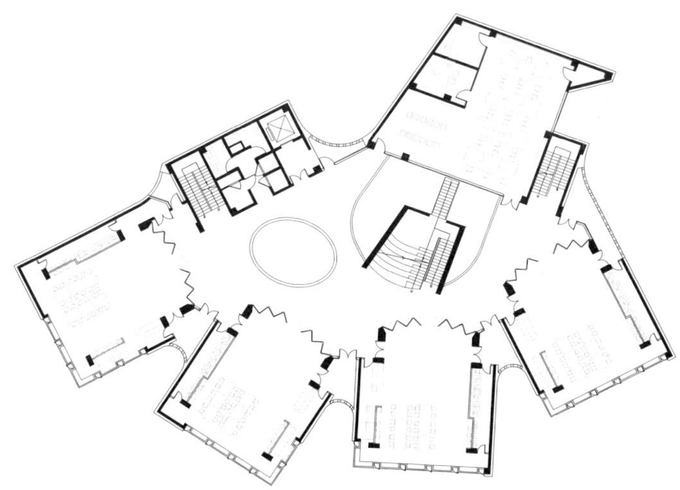

Second-floor plan

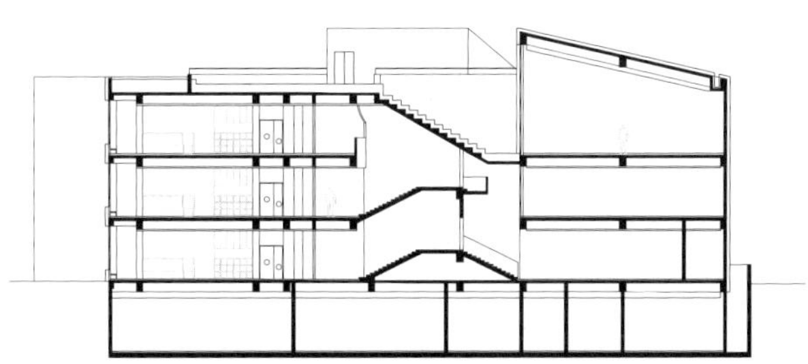

Section A-A'

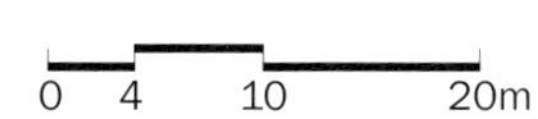

< Every class unit has two sides facing the sun to bring in plenty of natural daylight

The perforated concrete block wall creates interesting light and shadow patterns in the semi-outdoor balcony

v Main entrance

v The curved semi-outdoor balcony becomes a flexible connection between the building's different wings

> Closed/opened class partition-doors

v Class units arranged around an atrium

< View from the third-floor atrium to the terraced amphitheater

> Children can sit on the outdoor steps to watch performances and other activities, such as presentations and talks

v The open, multi-activity room on the third floor can be used as a small theater

[EXPERIENCE of LIFESTYLE]

Vertical Glass House

Shanghai, China

2013

A house with a twenty-two-year-old idea: The Vertical Glass House was first designed by Yung Ho Chang as an entry in the 1991 Shinkenchiku Residential Design Competition organized by *Japan Architecture* magazine, where it received an Honorable Mention Award. In 2013, the West Bund Biennale of Architecture and Contemporary Art in Shanghai decided to build it as one of its permanent pavilions and planned to use it as a guesthouse for visiting artists and architects in the future.

Glass house and city: The glass house has long become a typology for modern dwelling. As a contemporary urban housing prototype, the Vertical Glass House critiques modernist transparency in horizontality, which provides no privacy to its inhabitants, and attempts to re-establish the relationship between clear glass and domestic living in verticality. The transparency in this house provides two experiences: One is spiritual—due to its enclosed walls and glazed floors and roof, the house positions its dweller between the sky and the earth, creating an intimate space for meditation. The other is material—the vertical transparency of the house connects all the utilities, ductworks, and furniture pieces, including the staircase, into a systemic visualization of a machine designed for living in.

Materials and structure: The building footprint is approximately 36 square meters. The walls of this four-story residence are built with cast-in-situ concrete. Within the concrete enclosure, a singular steel post is located at the center, with steel beams dividing each level into four equal zones that frame domestic activities within each quarter. All floor slabs in the structure are made out of 7-centimeter-thick composite tempered glass. An air-conditioning system was also added to the original design.

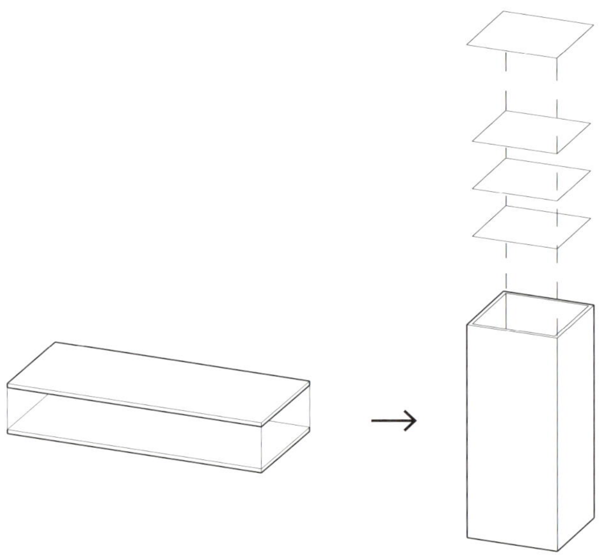

v View of Vertical Glass House from a distance

> View from boardwalk

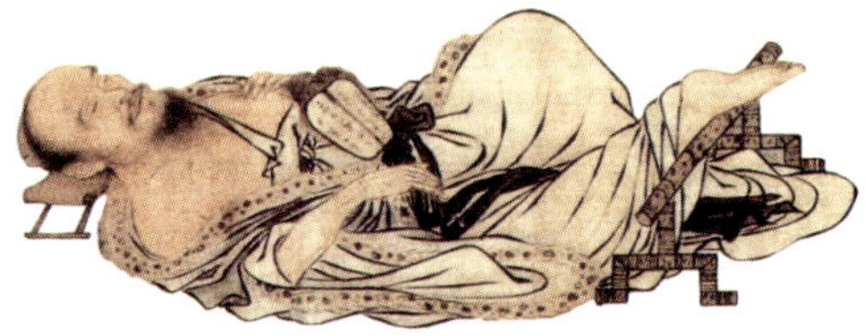

Liu Ling, a third-century literatus who always chose to be in the nude when at home, and who famously said: “Sky and earth is my house and building is clothes,” would be an ideal inhabitant of Vertical Glass House.

v Watercolor by Yung Ho Chang, 1991
(left) Day section with daylight coming in
(center) Day elevation left; night elevation right
(right) Day section with artificial light emitting from within

Sectional model

v Watercolor by Yung Ho Chang, 1991
Top: Plans (left to right): first floor (basement), second floor (street entrance), third floor, fourth floor
Bottom: (left) Looking down through all floors
(center) Looking up through all floors
(right) Space in Vertical Glass House in perspective

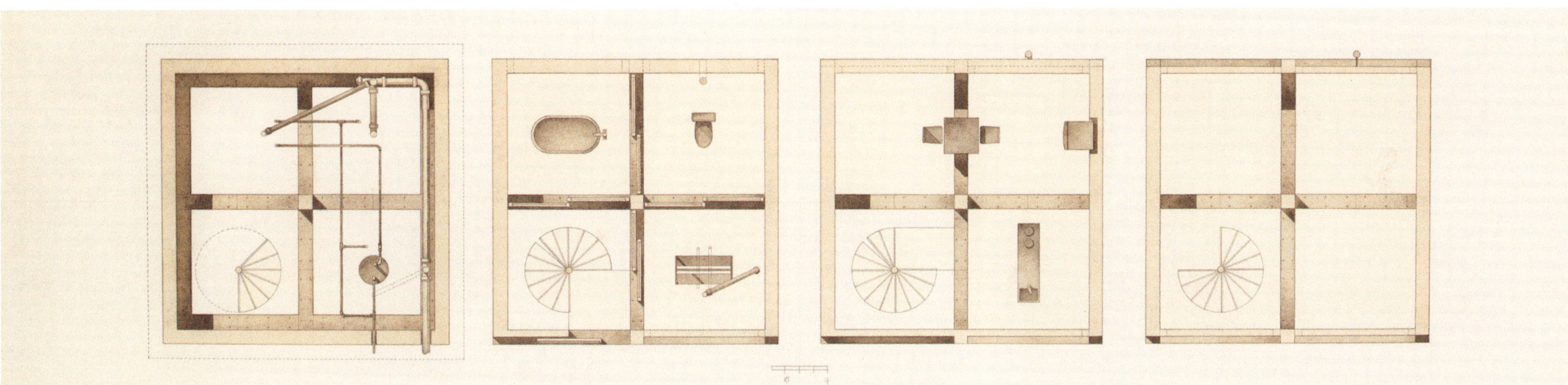

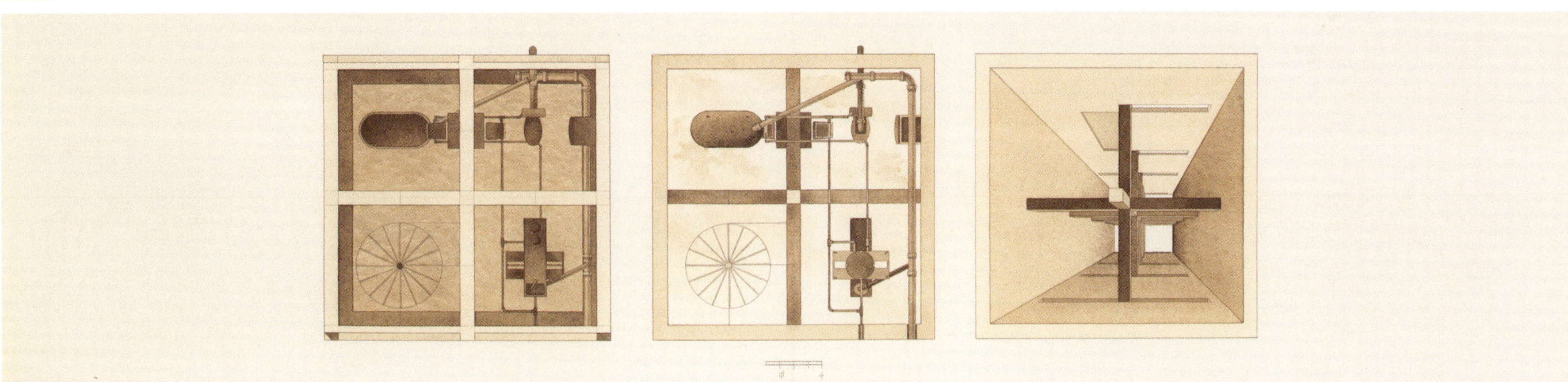

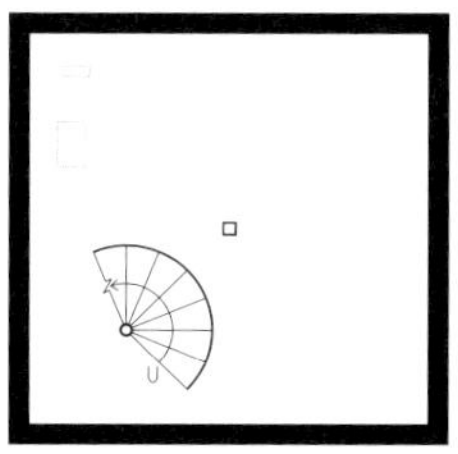

First-floor plan

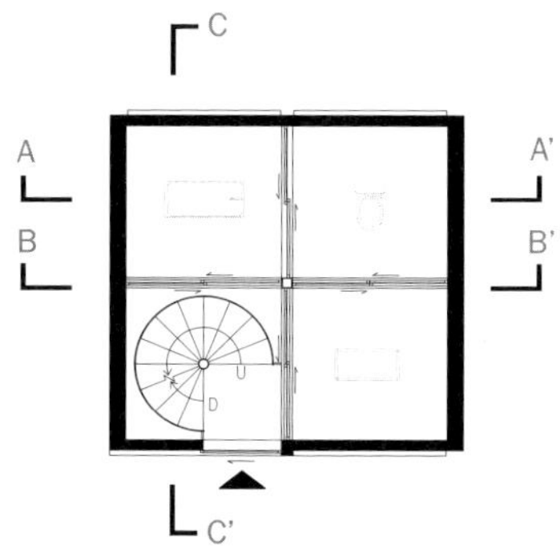

Second-floor plan

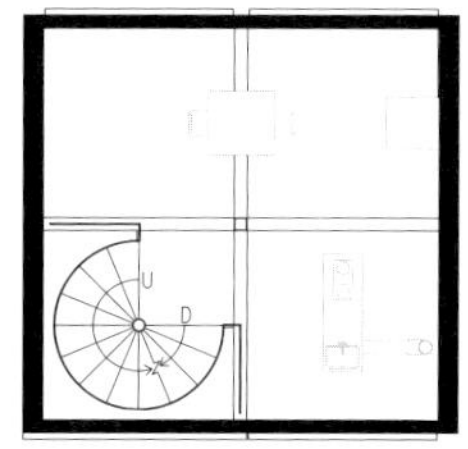

Third-floor plan

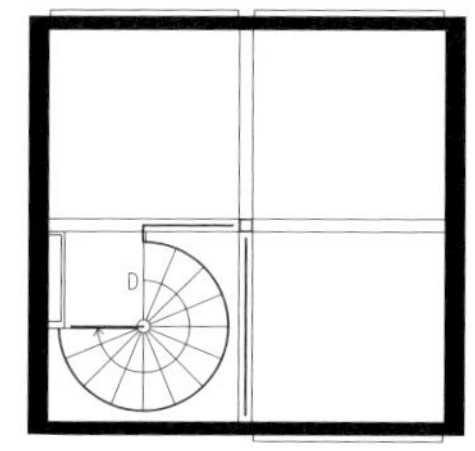

Fourth--floor plan

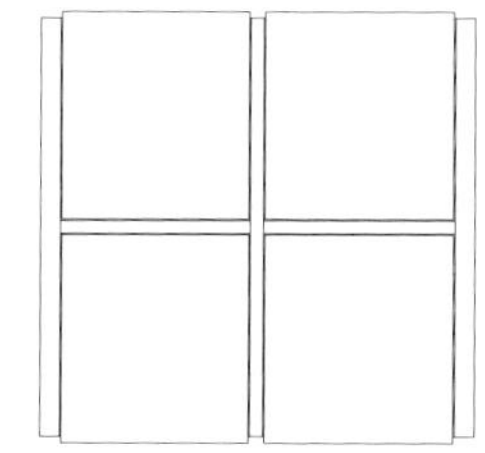

Roof plan

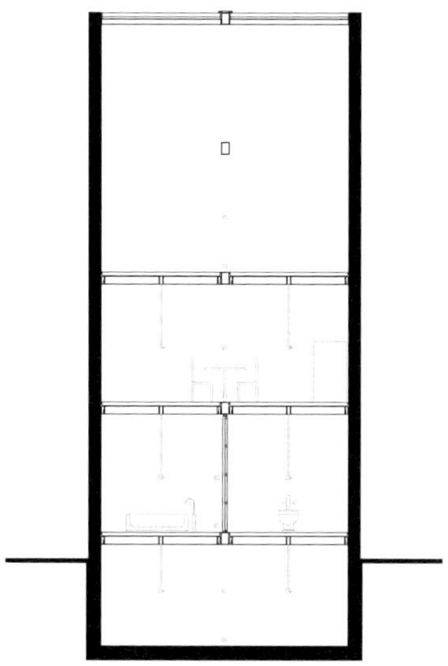

Section A-A'

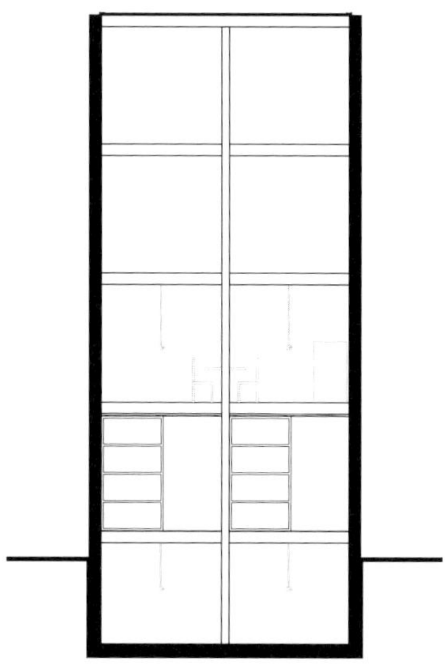

Section B-B'

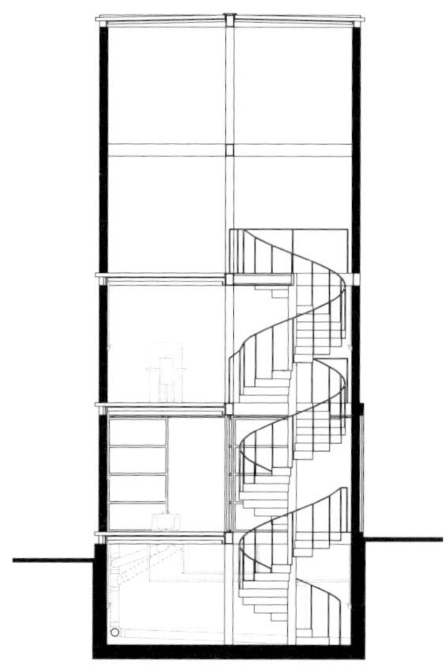

Section C-C'

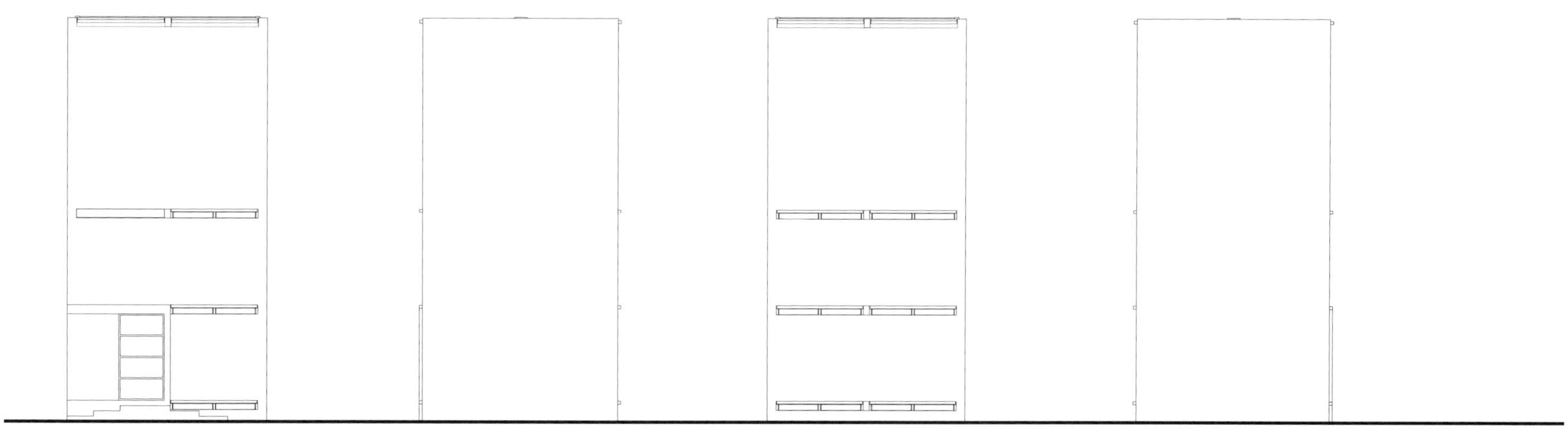

North elevation

West elevation

South elevation

East elevation

< View of entrance side

直玻璃宅 VERTICAL GLASS HOUSE

< Entrance door

> On the third floor

v Inside the second-floor entrance

v View of table and chair on the third floor from the second floor

v View of storage on the third floor from the second floor

v Counter with basin on the third floor

v View of the fourth floor that looks skyward

v Enactment of a modern-day Liu Ling

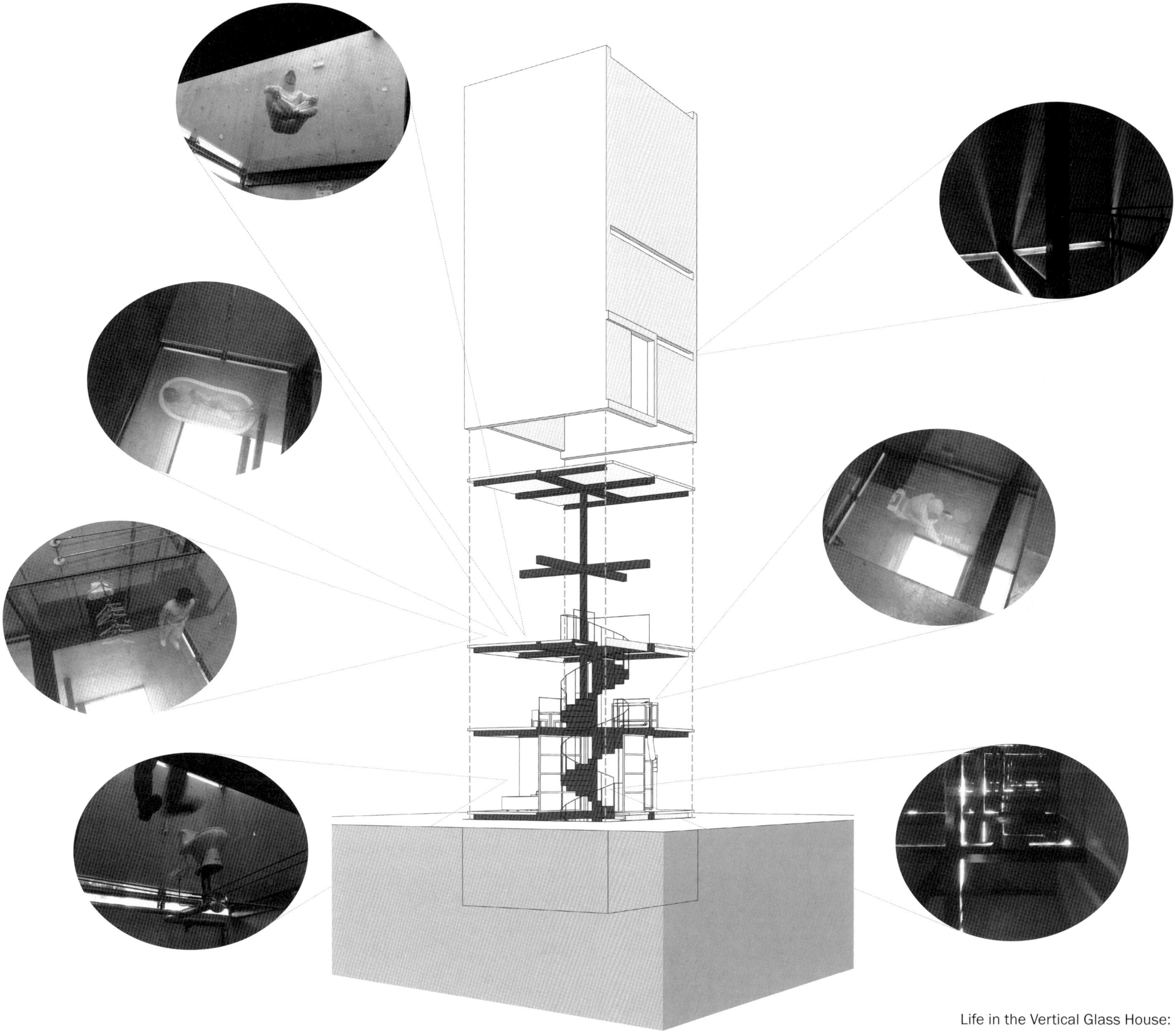

Life in the Vertical Glass House:
views from different levels

Turn and Move Toward Ontology While Holing Up in the Vertical Glass House

Wang Hui
Founding partner and lead architect, URBANUS

For many, Yung Ho Chang's controversial Vertical Glass House is perhaps only a playful sense of humor, since they often neglect the serious ontological inquiry on architecture embodied in this building on the part of the architect. One may read such inquiry in Chang's explanation of the design intentions: "Exploring the vertical transparency of architecture, which at the same time serves as a critique of Mies van der Rohe's horizontal transparency."

Transparency is one of the core issues in modern architecture. In his book *Pioneers of Modern Design: From William Morris to Walter Gropiu*s, the well-known mentor of modernism, Nikolaus Pevsner, defined the highest achievement of modern architecture before World War I as "transparency." He praised the glazed corner staircase in the Gropius House and Meyer's Cologne Model Factory for the Werkbund Exhibition (1914) by stating: "There is something sublime in this effortless mastery of material and weight."

Such sensual appeal of transparency was later described by Colin Rowe and Robert Slutzky as literal transparency, in order to differentiate what they appreciated more: phenomenal transparency, which can be found in Le Corbusier's Villa Stein at Garches, as the surface glazing on the façade of the house suggests the floor plans and spatial layout inside. Hence, transparency acquired intellectual meanings.

Mies van der Rohe brought transparency to an even higher level of rational thinking by juxtaposing transparency with dematerialization, which may be termed as conceptual transparency. Interestingly, Mies achieved his notion of dematerialization through the material measures of making intricate details, restraining the plans, and radicalizing the structure. On one hand, we admire Mies's rational approaches; on the other, the end of the Modernist transparency seems to be in sight.

To be sure, this end is only horizontal; thus, when the Vertical Glass House brings a ninety-degree turn, we find once more new possibilities for transparency on three different levels, namely sensuality, intellectuality, and rationality.

In terms of the sensual effects, transparent floors offer an entirely new visual experience and inspire imagination, which means that in this bare space, looking is no longer limited to the eyes but an exercise for the brain as well. One may imagine some dramatic events possibly unfolding in the space either above or below.

This vertically transparent space is wrapped in a concrete shell on the outside; at the tectonic details of the window slots, we can see glass brimming from inside and see through the interior spatial layout by way of phenomenal transparency. This is absolutely an intellectual game of architecture that gives this design a metaphysical flavor.

Certainly, the best way to determine the metaphysical flavor is to see if any aspiration in the realm of rationality in this building. The answer is positive. We seem to detect a certain kind of irrationality in the conceptual transparency of such a glass house, due to the irrational desire aroused by the enclosed walls and the transparent floors, something not allowed in a rational setting. Such a form of irrationality constitutes, however, a rational critique of another type of irrationality. The most irrational of all in residential architecture in China is to regulate, rationally, the private domain with standard housing units. As a counteraction, the Vertical Glass House releases the possibility of being irrational within one's personal world. In that sense, conceptual transparency pushes this dwelling design to interrogate with questions that concern architectural ontology.

In the last two decades, urbanization in contemporary China has created countless opportunities for building, yet their overly pragmatic tendency has made it very difficult for architects to seize them for design with the field of architecture in mind. The 2013 West Bund Biennale of Architecture and Contemporary Art in Shanghai presented an unusual kind of chance that Yung Ho Chang did not let down. He went back in a piece of paper architecture produced some twenty years ago, and allowed himself to watch this blazing and rowdy age from afar, and finally made a ninety-degree ontological turn.

Between sky and earth

[EXPERIENCE of LIFESTYLE]

Concrete Vessel

Beijing, China

2018

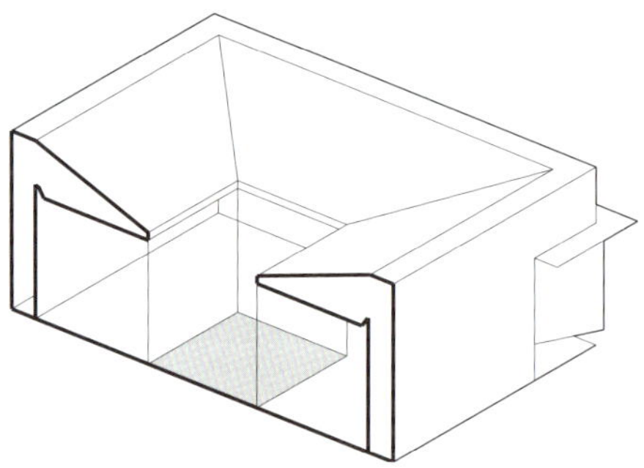

An exhibition for future living: Concrete Vessel is an experimental house Atelier FCJZ designed for the China 2018 House Vision exhibition curated by the renowned Japanese designer Kenya Hara. Our corporate partner on this project was Haier, a popular Chinese home appliance brand.

Courtyard house reimagined: As the theme of House Vision is about future living, we imagined a house that would truly embrace a version of nature that is defined by blue skies, fresh air, natural light, and living plants, which are all scarce commodities in present day. In this adaptation of the courtyard house, the boundaries between the interior and exterior spaces can be completely opened up, thus the courtyard is literally inside the house and becomes an integral part of the architecture. A continuous living space wraps around the courtyard and can be divided into either two or four rooms with sliding partitions. All required electronic functions are integrated into the building system via two counters, plus equipment placed underground.

A material that allows breaths: The structural system consists of steel columns along the periphery of the building, from which the roof cantilevers toward the central courtyard on all four sides. The material used on all surfaces inside and outside of the building, including the casings for the appliances, as well as furniture, is a minimum 3-millimeter-thin glass-fiber reinforced concrete (GRC) made from recycled construction debris. Its thinness makes this material very lightweight, and its porosity makes a breathing membrane that filters the air, while allowing natural light to come through.

Working with a materialist: The research and development of the GRC technology was conducted by Baogui Shiyi, in collaboration with Atelier FCJZ.

v Entrance of Concrete Vessel

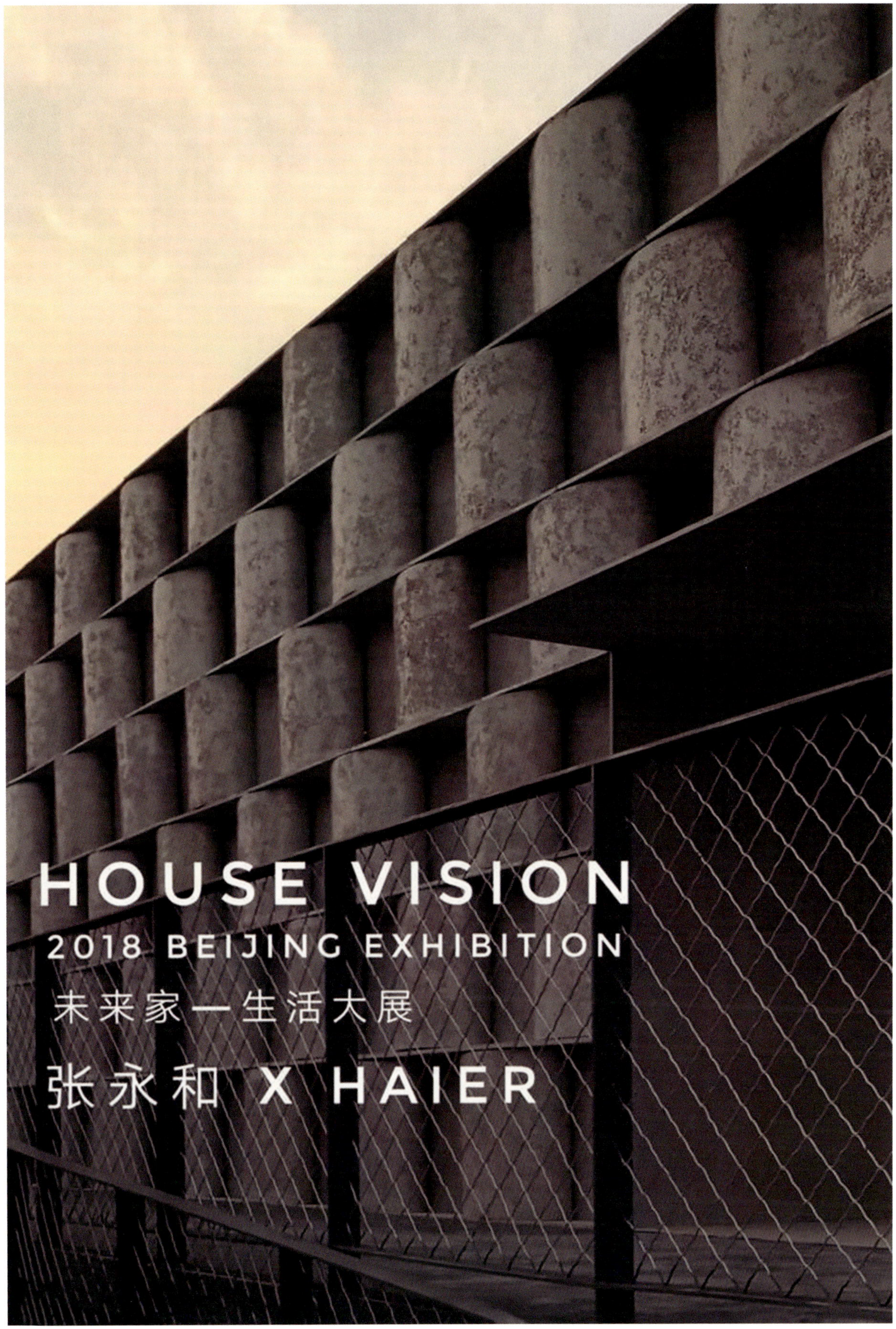

> Exhibition poster

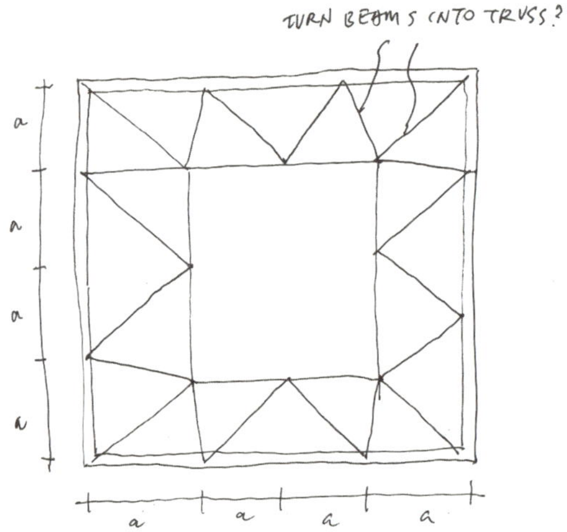

Structure sketch by Yung Ho Chang

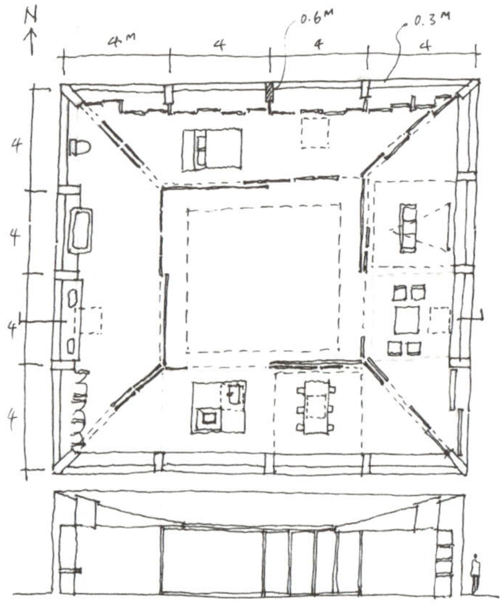

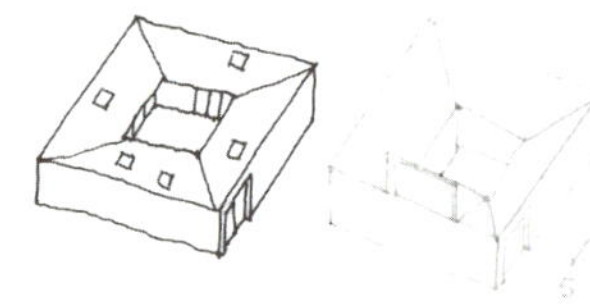

Space sketch by Yung Ho Chang

v Model for studying interior space

Lantern made from GRC by Baogui Shiyi

v Close-up of GRC

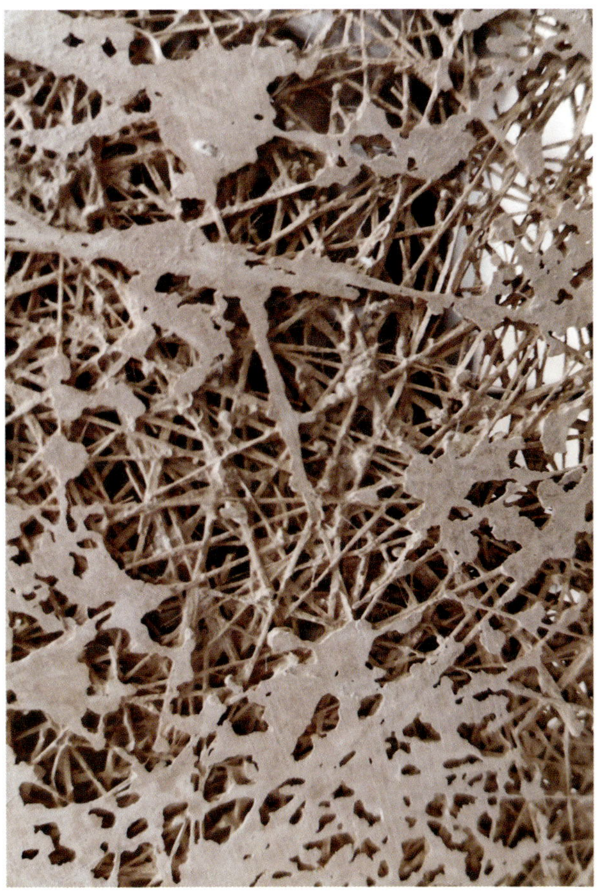

v GRC panels

< Entrance/exit with two concrete doors

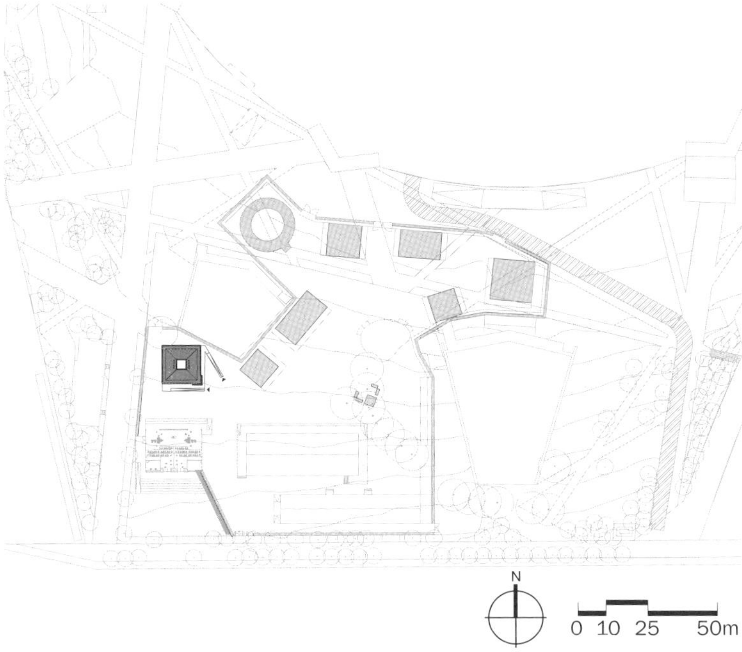

Site plan

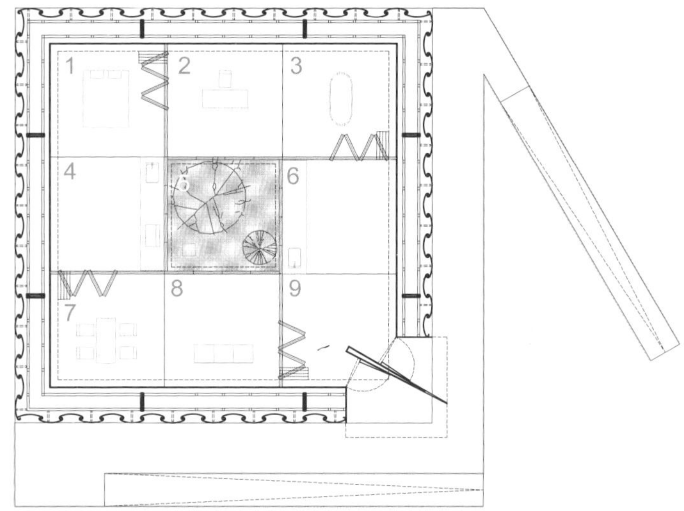

Floor plan

1 Bed
2 Desk
3 Bathtub
4 Kitchen counter
5 Courtyard
6 Wash counter
7 Dining table
8 Couch
9 Entry hall

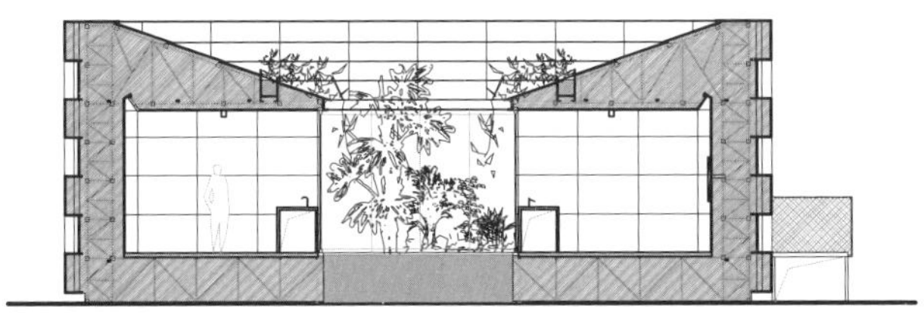

Section

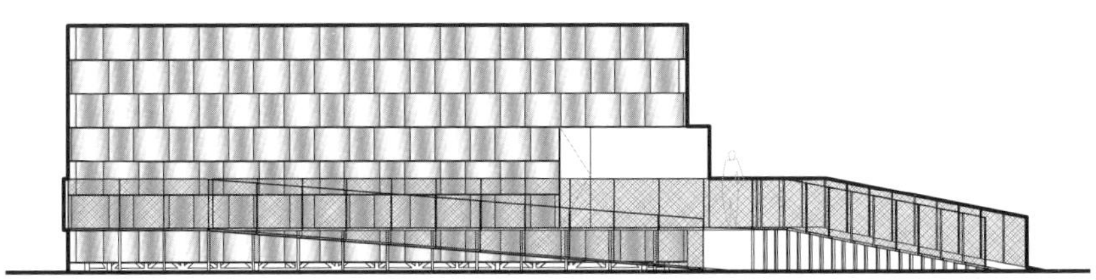

South elevation

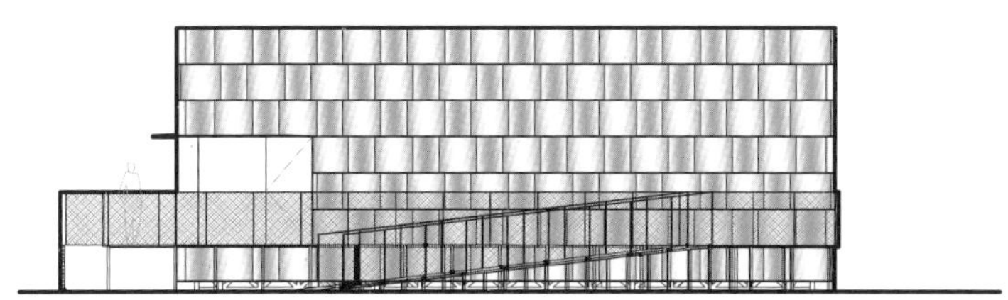

East elevation

Axonometric with roof lifted

Corner detail

GRC panels

Day

Night

v Interior; image courtesy of Japan Design Center

Possible spatial divisions

Courtyard closed by Switchable Transparent Glass (STG) in the frosted mode

Courtyard closed with STG in the transparent mode

Rooms are divided by STG in the transparent mode

Entire house is open

∨ Courtyard and living plants

∨ Interaction between indoor and outdoor

[EXPERIENCE of LIFESTYLE]

Four Studio-Houses

Ningbo, Zhejiang Province, China

2022

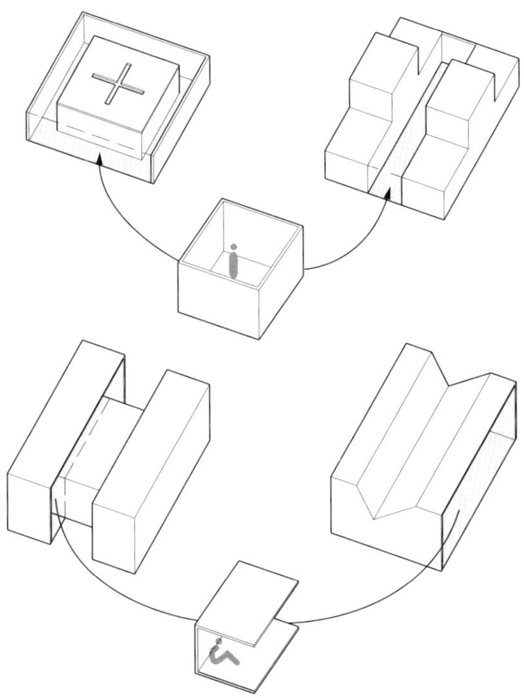

An education and art community: The Education Forum at Dongqian Lake in Ningbo is a community that includes a convention center, a hotel, an art museum, villas, and other facilities. The owner is passionate about education as well as art and built a group of studio-houses specifically to accommodate visitors, especially scholars or artists who may come for a relatively extended period of time to conduct research and/or work on creative projects.

Design as research: Three of the four studio-houses were conceived by Yung Ho Chang in the early 1990s (without client or site) as an attempt to blur the line between classicism and modernism. These "paper architecture" were in fact serious investigations on a core issue of architecture—space, but at the same time, they are also buildable propositions. This particular history of the project makes these four pieces of architecture engaging participants in the discussion and exchange of ideas on art and research at the Education Forum.

Prototyping space: The four studio-houses are meant as experiments to test out ways to organize architectural spaces. The openness of the work-live program allows us to produce four distinctly different spatial conditions. Designing space can never be separated from imagining experiences, as well as lifestyles.

The four studio-houses are named after the respective architectural element that characterizes each building's spatial organization: House with Face-to-Face Loggias, House with Cruciform Glass, House with Walkable Beam, and House with Flipped Roof.

1. House with Face-to-Face Loggias: The design imagines a symmetrical volume being sliced in the middle and pulled apart to accommodate a pool flanked by two loggias on the ground level, one on each side. The two facing loggias define the open space in between, framing both outdoor and semi-outdoor events. The inhabitant needs to cross the water court from the living quarters to work in the study on the other side and then cross it again on the way back, which creates a ritual for daily living. Sitting in a loggia and talking to a friend in the loggia on the opposite side is another pleasure the house offers. At that moment, the relationship of the loggias morphs into that of people.

2. House with Cruciform Glass: On the ground level, the spaces are organized in a pinwheel formation; on the upper level, a transparent volume is divided into four equal quarters for living, cooking/dining, sleeping, and bathing by a hollow cruciform double curtain wall that connects the second floor to the ground below. The space in the upper-floor glass house is simultaneously open and sectioned. The inhabitant may move along the outer glass curtain wall enjoying a panoramic view of the surrounding water court, which is only punctured by the sceneries through the cuts in the peripheral wall.

> Four studio-houses in the community of the Education Forum at Dongqian Lake, Ningbo, China

> View of the four studio-houses from the entry point of cluster

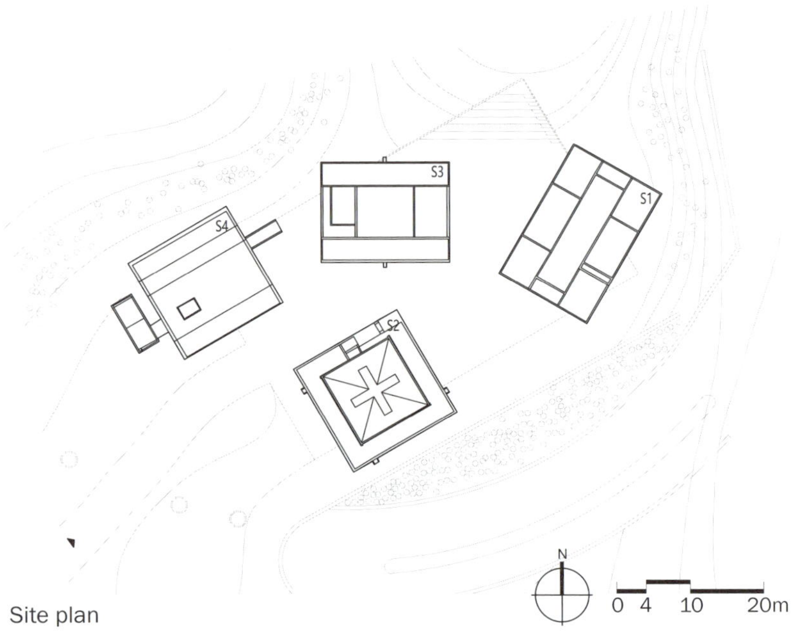

Site plan

3. House with Walkable Beam: A double-height space for a plastic art studio is bookended with two oversized porches, with a walkable floating cruciform beam in the middle. The inhabitant's creative process unfolds around the beam: Standing on or under the beam to examine his/her art on the walls, hanging work-in-progress pieces from it, or crossing the beam on his/her way to the library.

4. House with Flipped Roof: A single space is configured by an inverted sloped roof into two zones—one for work and one for living. This inhabitant lives and works in the same space, almost. Visually, live and work areas on opposite sides of the inverted roof have limited connection, yet whichever side the inhabitant is on he/she would be constantly aware of the other. This studio-house juxtaposes combination and separation.

Materiality: Reinforced concrete is used like clay to mold pure spaces. The textured surface of the exposed concrete poured in timber formwork is intended to avoid abstraction and give an expression of tangibility to the spaces.

v Bird's-eye view of the four studio-houses

> Cruciform semi-outdoor space on first floor

House with Cruciform Glass

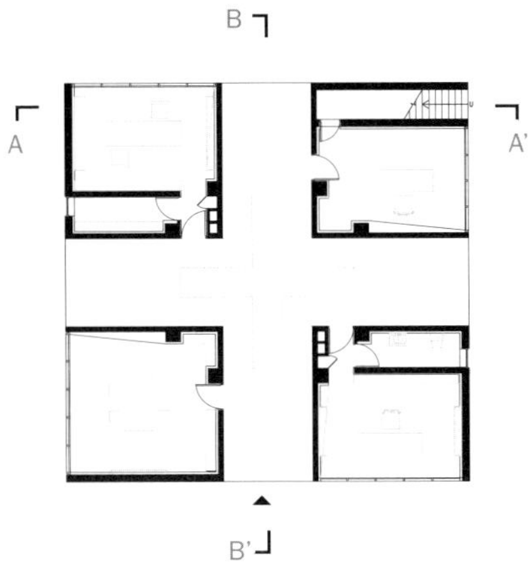

First-floor plan

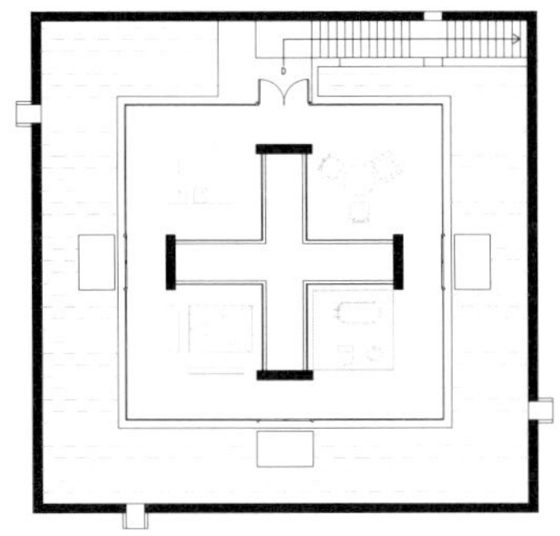
Second-floor plan

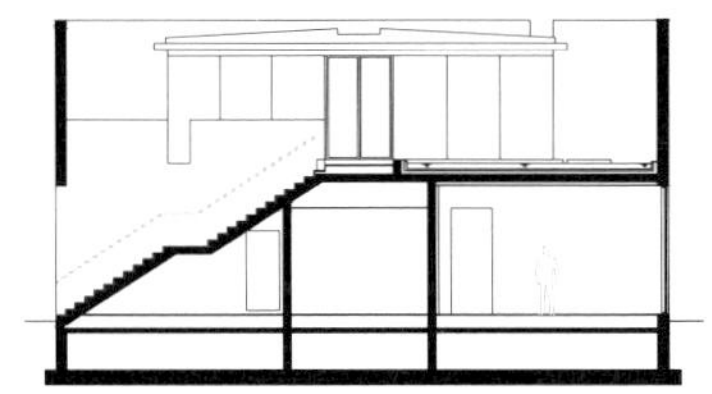
Section A-A'

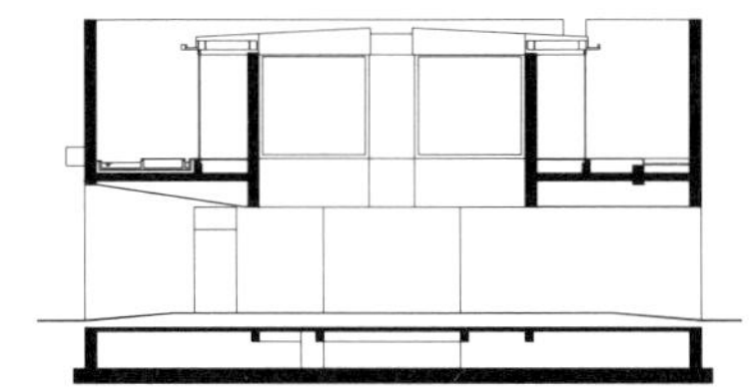
Section B-B'

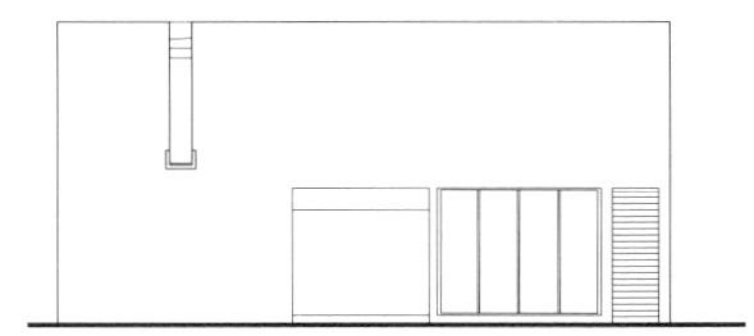
South elevation

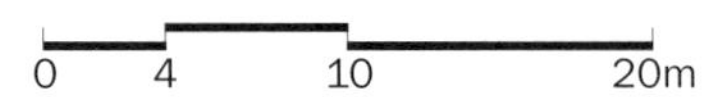

v Northeast elevation of House with Cruciform Glass, with access stair to the second floor on the right

^ Load-bearing walls are pulled in from the glass enclosure, forming transitions between rooms, and a passage along a water court
^ Stairway to the ground

< Four rooms on the second floor divided by cruciform hollow glass curtain walls

House with Face-to-Face Loggias

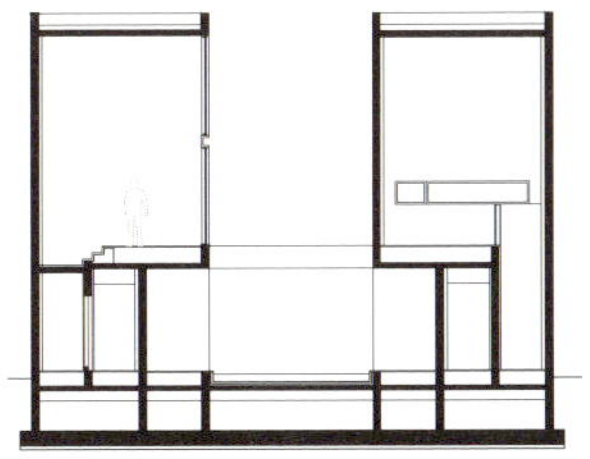

Section A-A'

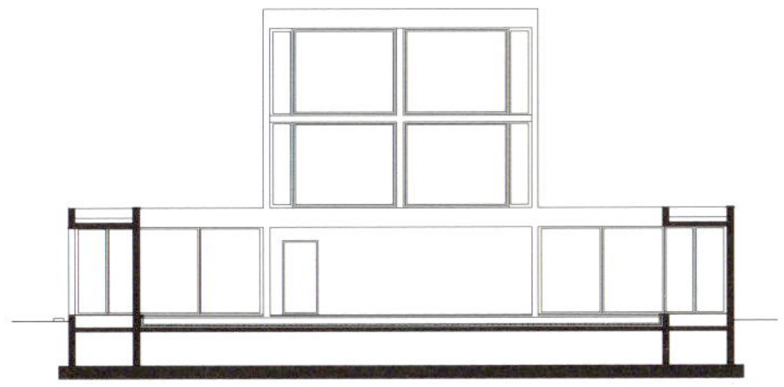

Section B-B'

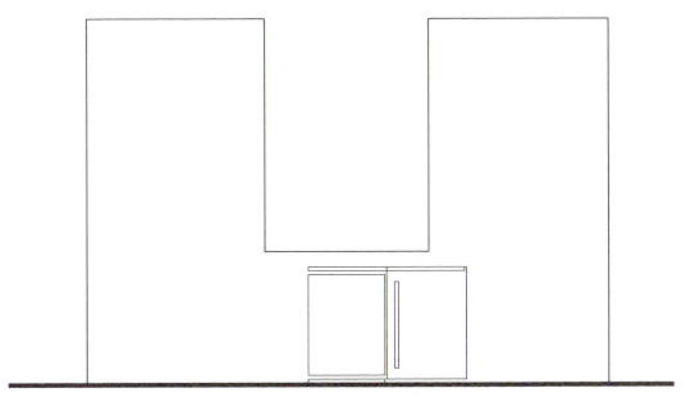

South elevation

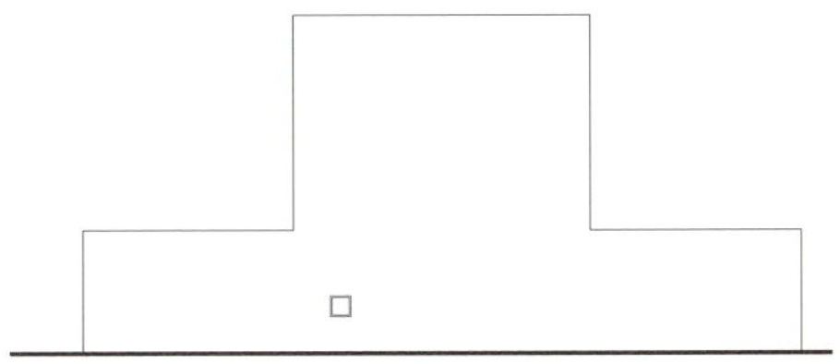

East elevation

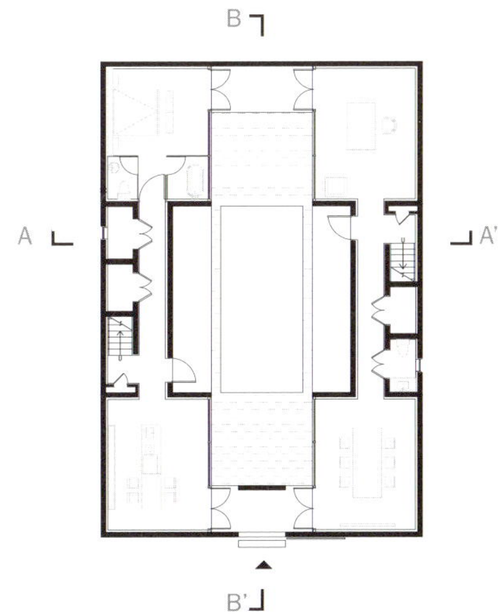

First-floor plan

Second-floor plan

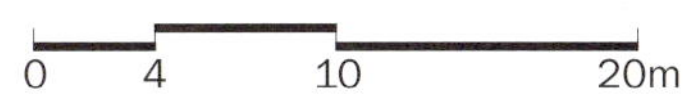

v Entrance of the House with Face-to-Face Loggias

> Living side

< Study side

> Architectural spaces molded by concrete poured into timber formwork—from indoor to outdoor

v Library on the second floor of the study side

v View of the water court and kitchen beyond from the first floor of of the study side

v The lounge on the second floor of the living side

v The kitchen on the first floor of the living side

House with Walkable Beam

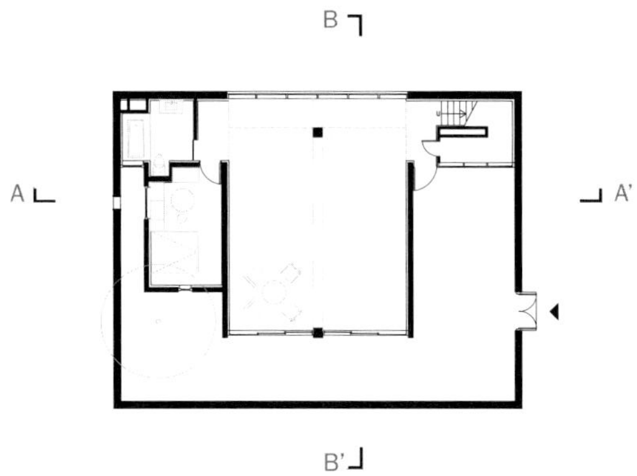

First-floor plan

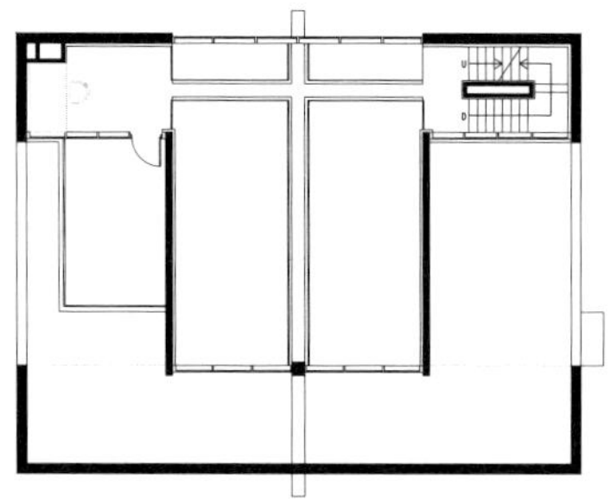

Second-floor plan

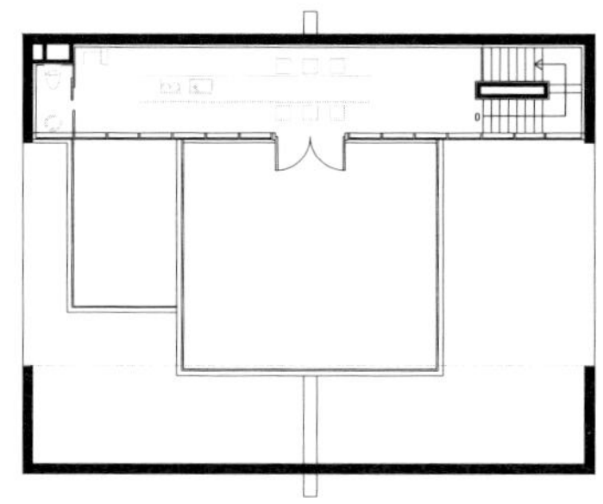

Third-floor plan

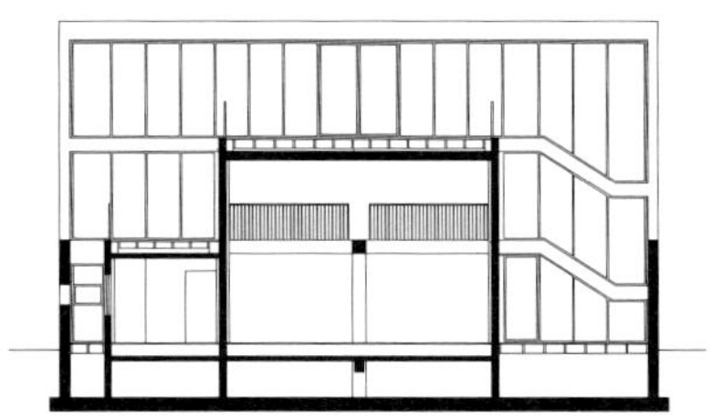

Section A-A'

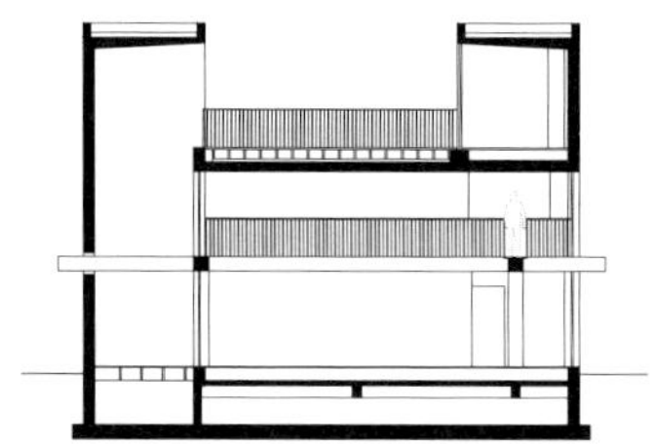

Section B-B'

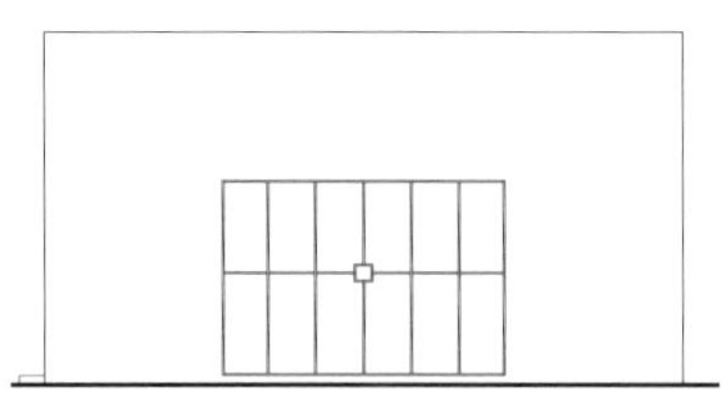

East elevation

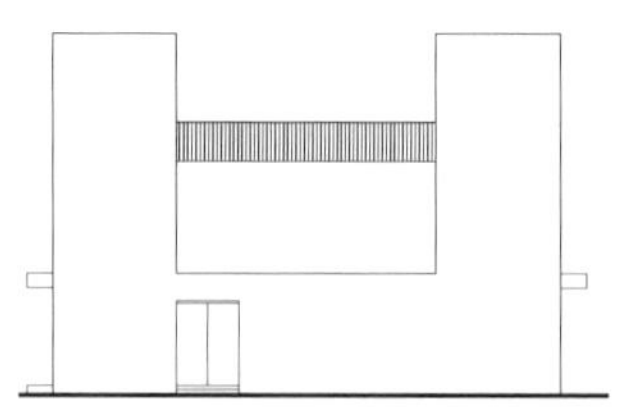

South elevation

< View of the staircase from the side yard

The end of the beam extending through the glass wall

v Beams running through the building and the porch

v View of studio interior from the porch

< View of the walkable cruciform beam

Kitchen and dining on the third floor

v View of House with Walkable Beam from the east

House with Flipped Roof

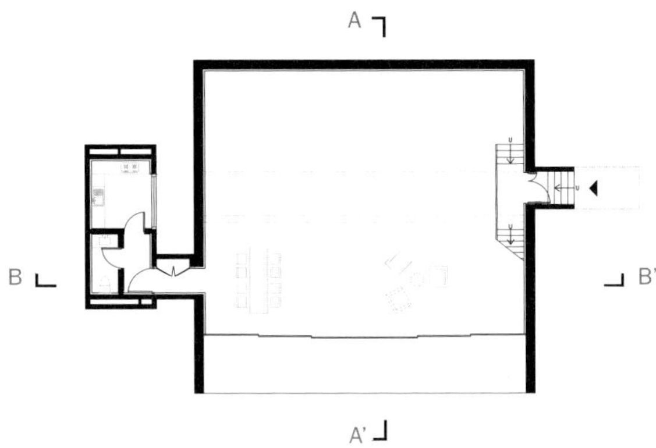

First-floor plan

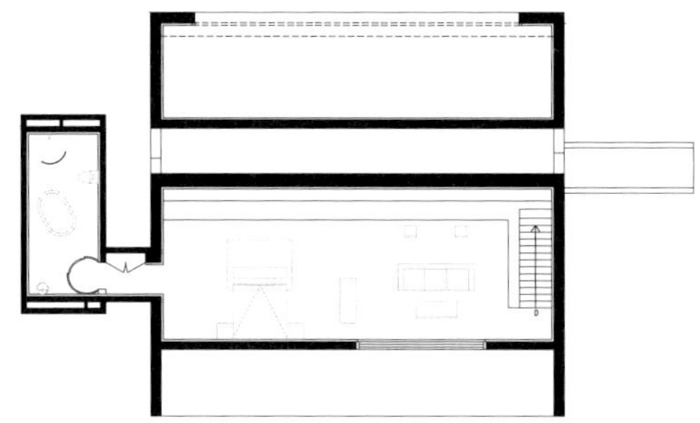

Second-floor plan

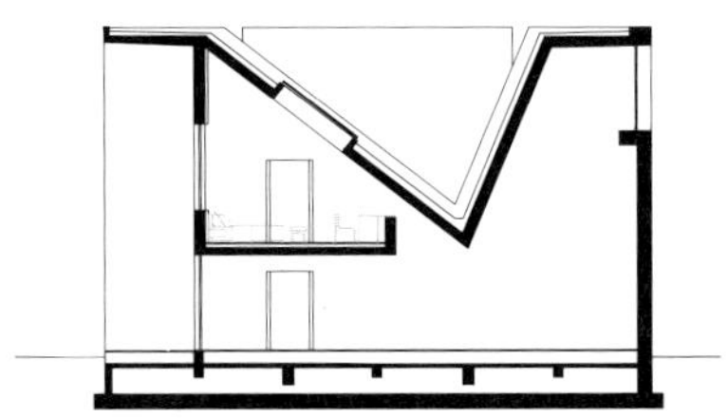

Section A-A'

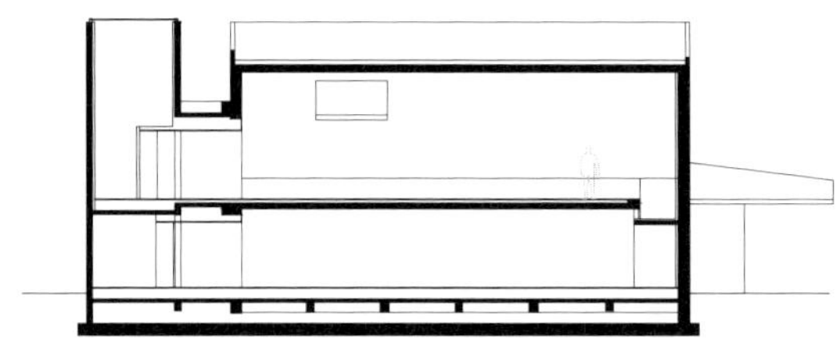

Section B-B'

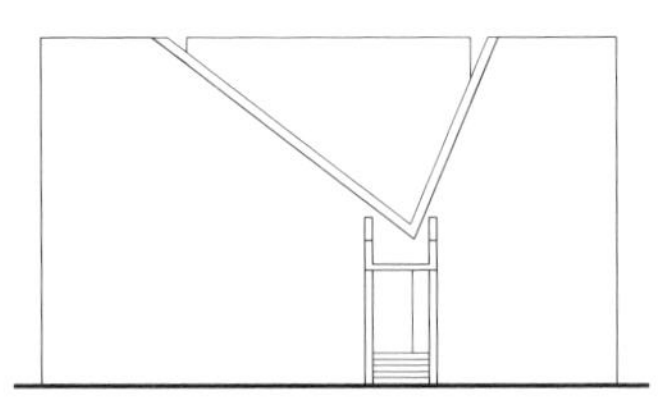

North elevation

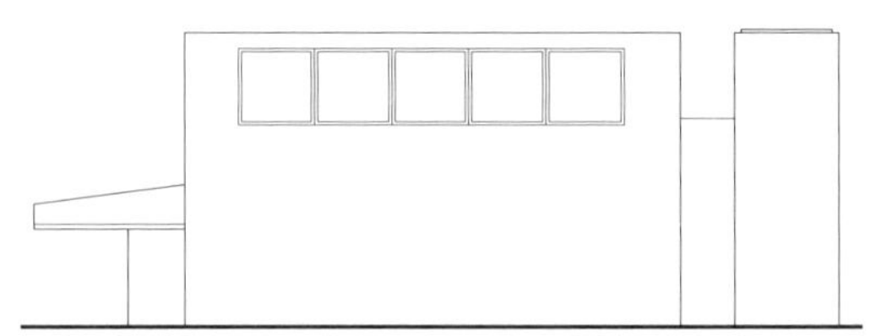

East elevation

0 4 10 20m

The water-spout-entry-porch in the rain

v Porch of House with Flipped Roof

< A single open working space on the first floor

Bathroom

v Living space on the second floor

[EXPERIENCE of MOUNTAIN and WATER]

Villa Mountain Dialogue

Beijing, China

1998

A micro-city in the mountains: The design of this country house began by ensuring minimum disruption to the existing terraced farmland, while allowing maximum interaction with the surrounding *shan shui* or landscape. This intention materializes into a big roof, which is supported on a steel frame, floating over the site as the conceptual reconstruction of the hillside. Underneath it, the notion of urbanity is translated into a spatial organization, where a continuous living space is partitioned into several areas by box-walls (mini buildings), echoing Louis Kahn's city house concept. The natural scenery on the outside is invited in through diverse glazed areas on all sides of the villa. The three attic guestrooms poking through the roof gives away the fluidity of spaces on the inside, as they present themselves as three detached micro houses on a slope. The completed house inspired the client to come up with a fitting and poetic name for the abode: "Shan Yu Jian," which means "a place for mountain dialogues."

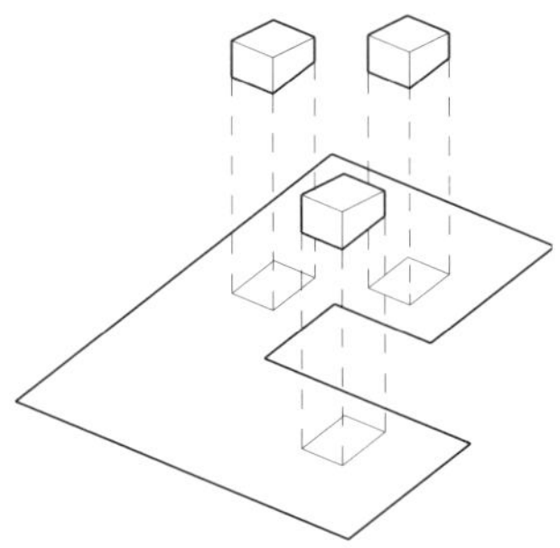

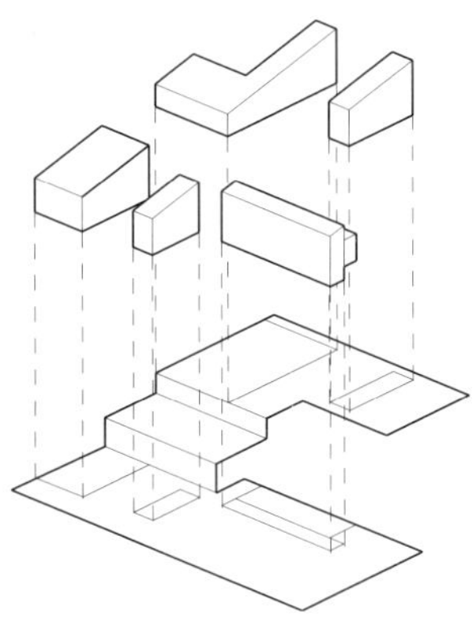

The roof of the house follows the slope of the terrain

v Mountains surrounding the villa

> View from the south

Site plan

v View from the northwest

v View from the south

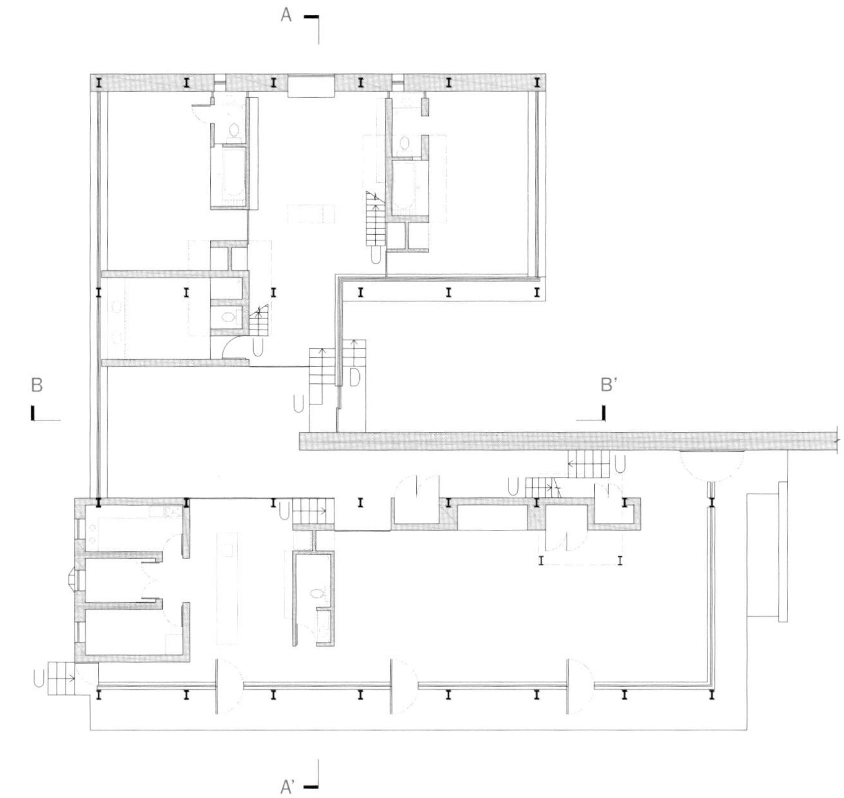

First-floor plan

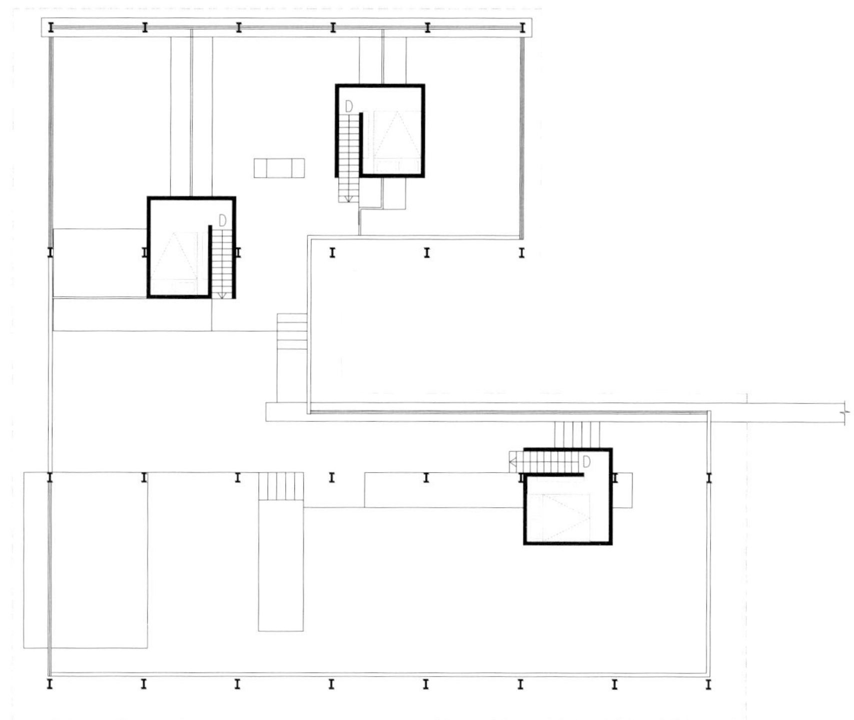

Second-floor plan

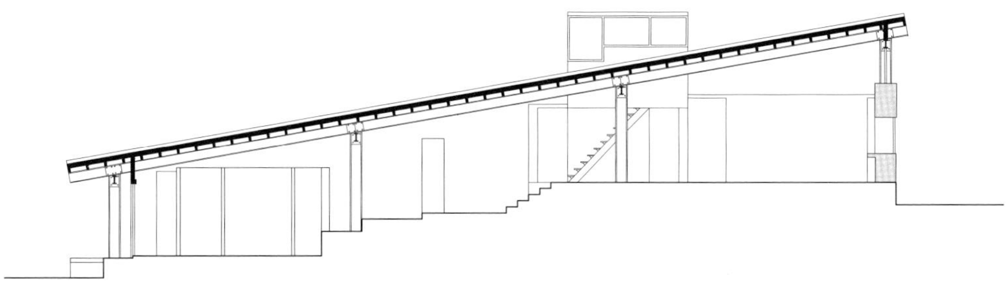
Section A-A'

Section B-B'

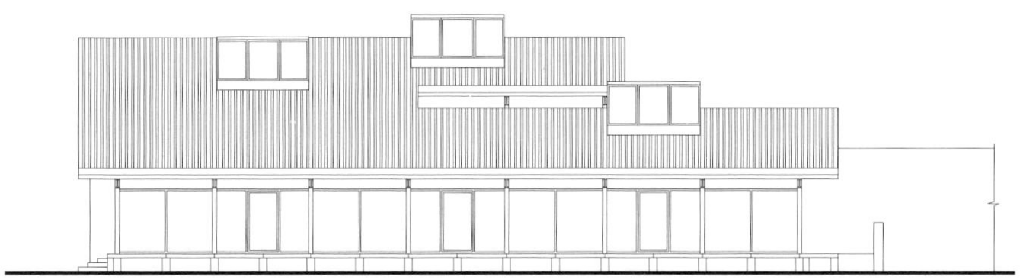
Elevation

0 2 5 10m

v Night view from the south

Ladder to attic guestroom

Attic guestroom

View from an attic guestroom

v View from the east

[EXPERIENCE of MOUNTAIN and WATER]

Split House

Beijing, China

2002

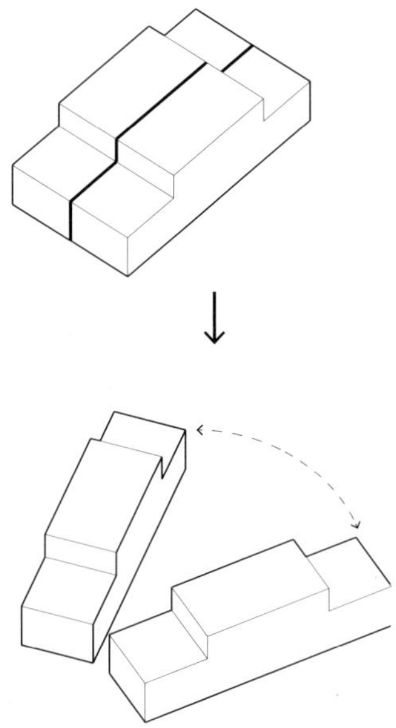

A courtyard house for an open landscape: Split House is located in a valley outside Beijing and is one of the eleven villas and one club house that make up the Commune by the Great Wall. The natural setting of the project inspired us to wonder what would and could happen if we were to transplant a traditional courtyard house from a high-density urban environment to the open country? We discovered that the transplanted courtyard could be situated between and surrounded by both nature and architecture. The name "Split," therefore, not only refers to the two wings of the house, but also reflects how the courtyard is enclosed half by the house and half by the hillside. The design further embraces the landscape by preserving all the trees on the site.

A contemporary *tu mu* structure: Another design objective was to build the house with materials that would have a low environmental impact, and which could be disintegrated when needed. Taking from the traditional Chinese use of *tu* (earth) and *mu* (wood) as primary building materials, Split House uses laminated wood for the structural frame and rammed earth for the walls, in order to gain good insulation. During the off-peak season, Split House may open one wing in order to conserve operation and maintenance costs.

A flexible prototype: This design is conceived as a flexible prototype that can change with site conditions. The angle between the two wings is not fixed and may be adjusted from zero to 360 degrees in order to suit different configurations and topography of land. This means that besides being a "split house," this dwelling can also potentially be a "line house," "parallel house," or a "right-angle house."

COMMENTS

Zhu Jingxiang
Associate Professor, School of Architecture, The Chinese University of Hong Kong

Observing the site, it's not hard to realize that the "force" of the "split" comes from trees and creeks. Trees can split the ground; water can split valleys, so why not architecture? Cut by the ground, the house defines the yard. This method is very different from creating a yard by enclosing a void with buildings around it, as in traditional residential architecture. Though the yard of Split House is inward and pleasant, it is also livelier and more natural.

The form of the rammed-earth wall comes from the tradition of building houses. A light, wooden frame may look traditional, but in fact comes from modern-day North America, on account of the standardization of material supply as well as the calculability and predictability of the performance of a wooden structure. This "earth house" shows a strong opposition to visualizing and symbolizing traditional dwellings which was popular at the time, and has unintentionally highlighted three skills that architects should work on: handcraft, engineering, and organization.

With a hinge-like system enabling its change of forms, the house can adapt to uncertain sites. What changes is the terrain and angle of the yard; what stays the same is the spatial system and the organization of functions inside. This spatial system has the ability of combining with other structures and materials. This design stems from the Eastern life experience of the designer but is reconstructed with modern design methods, coming to form a single house between the mountains and rivers.

> The two wings of the house embrace the existing trees on the site

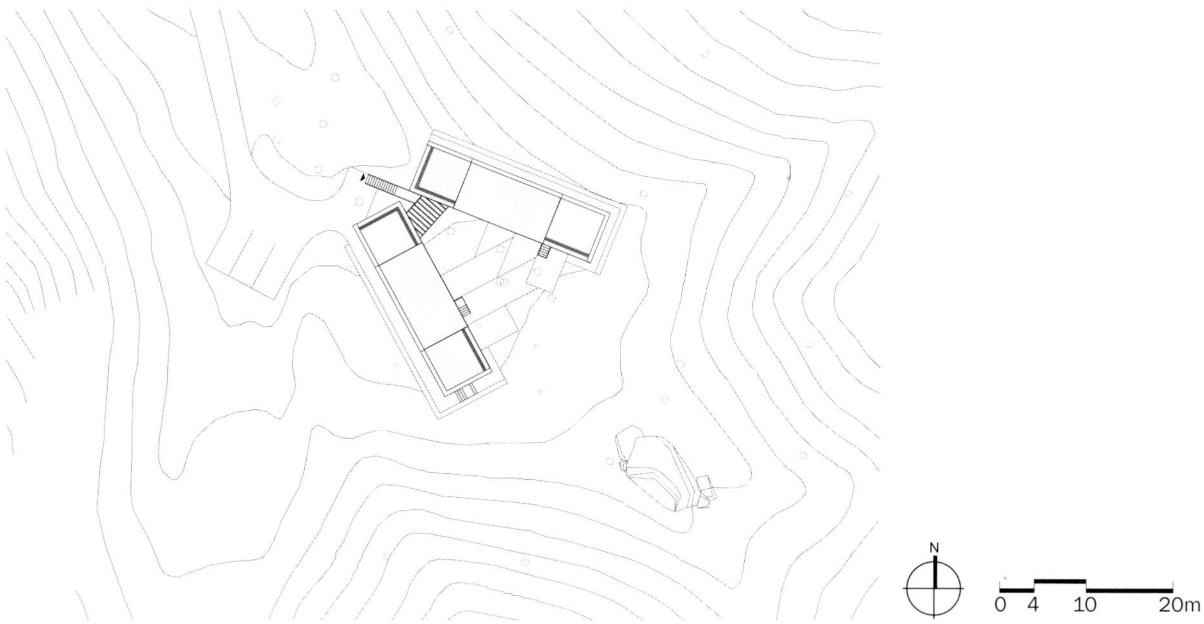

Site plan

v Variation diagram of the prototype

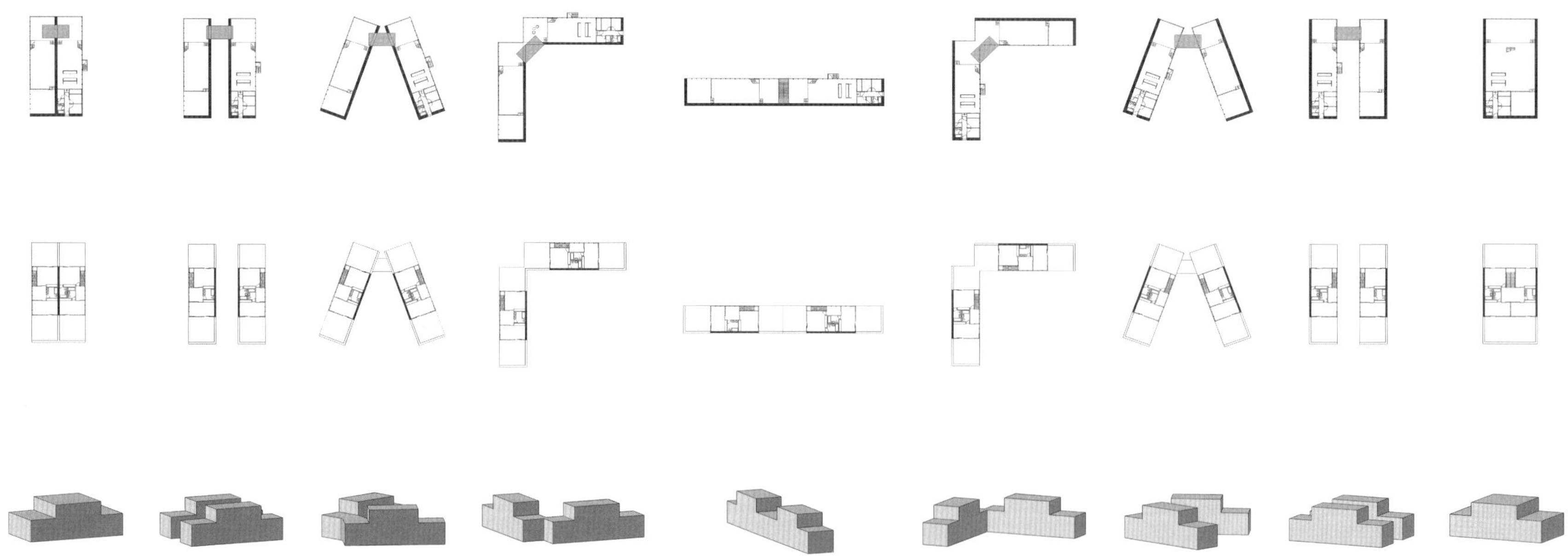

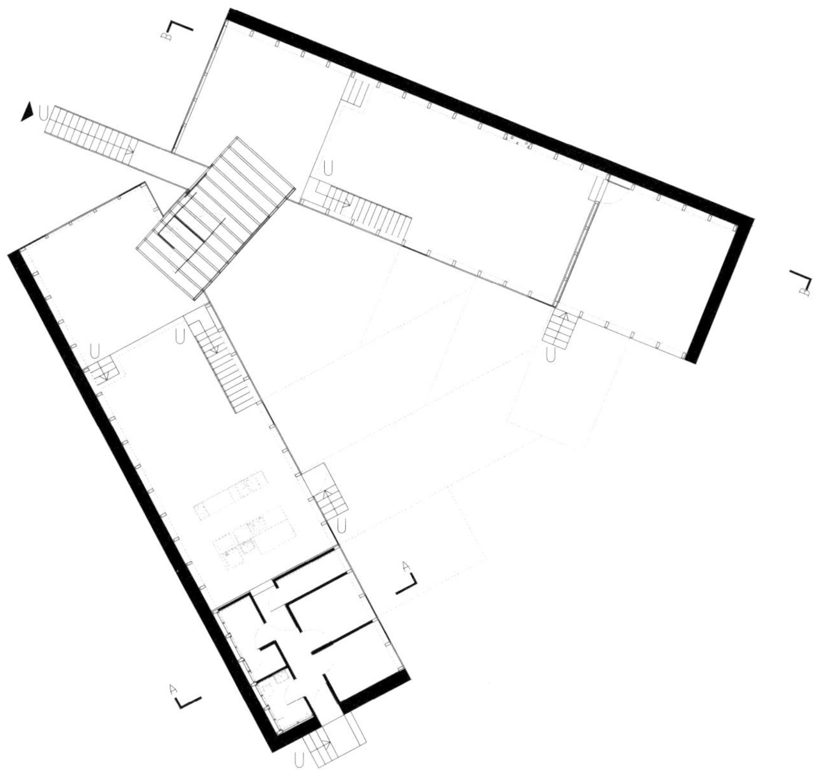

First-floor plan

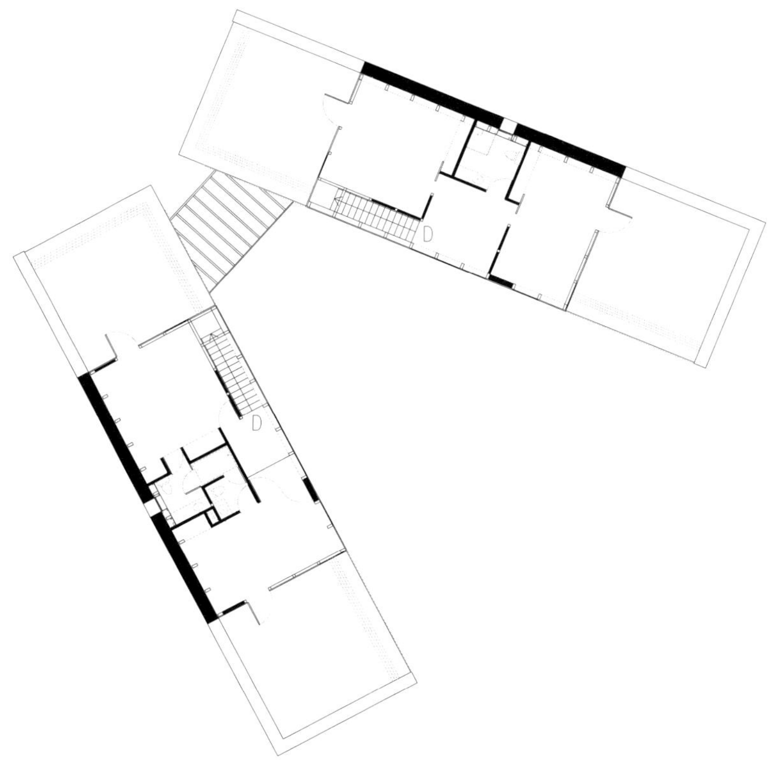

Second-floor plan

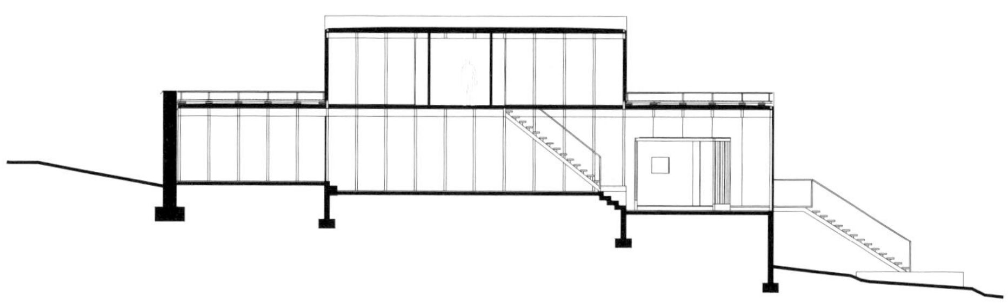

Longitudinal section

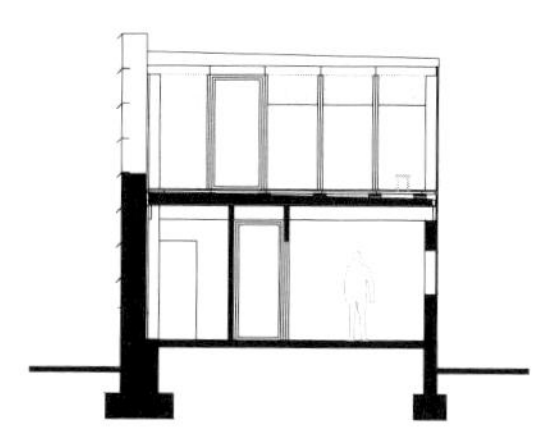

Cross section

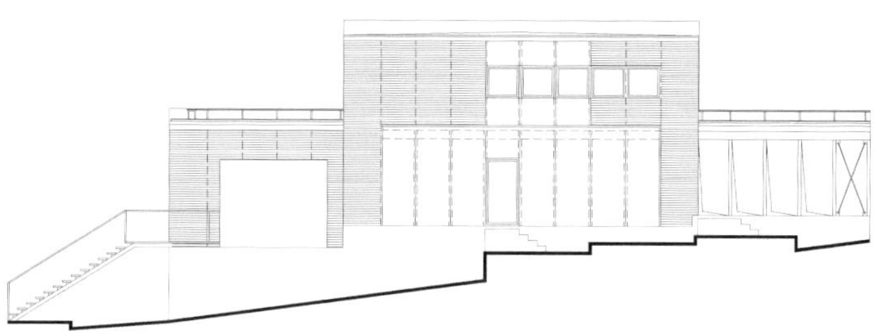

Elevation toward the courtyard

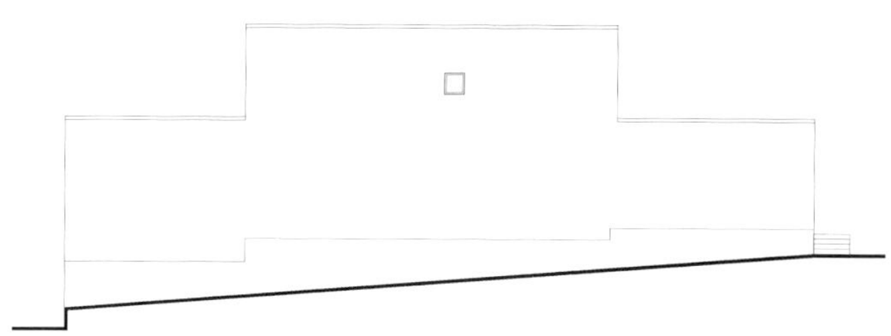

Elevation toward the outside

0 2 5 10m

> 1 Entrance
> 2 View of courtyard from the second-floor terrace

1
2

Construction process

v Rammed-earth wall

Sitting area next to dining room

v Front door

v Vestibule

[EXPERIENCE of MOVEMENT]

Xishu Bookstore

Beijing, China

1996

Site history: The site of the bookstore is a street-level space of an office building built in the 1950s. This space used to function as a passageway where bicycles would often be seen either parked or in motion. In later years, the passageway was closed down and used by the library next door to store books.

As we contemplated the project, we wondered: Would it be possible to present the history of the programmatic changes of the space in our design? And would it be possible to overlap the previous usage of the space—circulation—with its new one—a bookstore?

Conceptual art, installation art: Guided by the above observations as an idea and informed by conceptual and installation art—the thoughts and works of French artist Marcel Duchamp, in particular—we combined bookshelf and bike as a "ready-made" element to produce a "collage." The result was the Book-Bike, a rotating bookshelf with bicycle wheels; eight Book-Bikes in four pairs made up the core of the bookstore design.

More space, changeable space: We also took advantage of the height of the existing space to add a mezzanine. The circular steel pillars supporting the mezzanine were also bearing shafts for the rotating Book-Bikes. Each Book-Bike had two back-to-back bookshelves and shared the same thickness as the existing walls. This allowed the bookstore staff to rotate the shelves at will to alter the space in the shop.

A steel structure inserted: The mezzanine was a freestanding steel frame system within the original masonry load-bearing wall structure. The Book-Bikes and other bookshelves against the walls were made of profile steel.

A project with a short lifespan: The bookstore was the first built project of Atelier FCJZ. It opened in 1996 and was demolished in 2000, existing for four years. The space where it was located was eventually restored to a passageway, and bicycles made their return to replace the Book-Bikes.

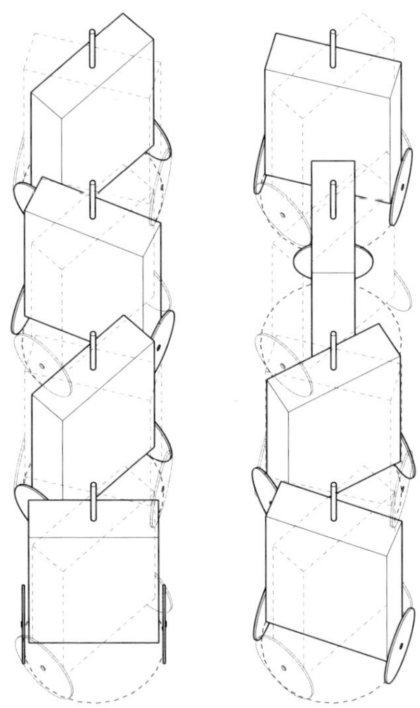

v The site used to be a corridor, with bicycles parked inside

> Xishu Bookstore entrance with Book-Bikes as doors

Nothing at First

Reminiscing Xishu Bookstore as a Gene for Thought

Zhou Rong
Scholar of architecture and urbanization
Associate Professor, School of Architecture, Tsinghua University

In the ecological realm of any field, the historical chance of influencing or even changing the evolutionary process of the whole ecosystem from the level of "genes for thought" is quite rare. However, the Xishu Bookstore, designed by Yung Ho Chang in 1996 historically took up the eco-revolutionary mission of providing a "gene for thought" for "restarting" Chinese contemporary architecture.

In the mid-1990s, when Chinese society was being swept up and agitated by the waves of "a second round of reform and opening-up," and people in Chinese architectural circles were looking for a change but couldn't find new ideas and methods to serve as the turning point, Xishu Bookstore—an "illegal building" with a footprint less than 100 square meters—was designed and built, and immediately produced a nuclear-explosion-scale impact on Chinese contemporary architecture.

To understand the unique historical contribution of Xishu Bookstore, we must place it back at its location and time twenty years ago, taking it back to that particular era of Chinese architecture. The time that Xishu Bookstore was born was the heyday of Chinese postmodernism. The so-called "Chinese postmodernism" is actually modern eclecticism and vulgar mannerism under the Pomo banner. The Chinese architectural circle was then addicted to the shallow semiotic game of "postmodernism" and lacked, for a long time, the inner driving force to push architecture thinking and discussion at the ontological level. At that moment, the appearance of Xishu Bookstore, undoubtedly, had the inestimable value of enlightenment.

Chang's first truly completed work, Xishu Bookstore could be considered a spatial textbook that presented all of his world views and architectural ideas. Briefly speaking, Chang's view of the world was postmodernist, entangled in diverse, rich, contradictory, and complicated interdisciplinary desires and mixed interest. But his architectural ideas followed utopian modernist creeds, almost as strictly as if of a fundamentalist manner—pure fictional ontology; the monist value system; abstract visual forms; self-consistent logical deduction; and dense integral construct, among other things. The inherent structural conflict between his world view and methodology made the "cause" of Chang's works and lent themselves naturally to dissemination and consumption and often appealed to the taste of the public, while the "effect" of the works carried the boring elitism, as well as the arrogance of anti-dissemination and anti-consumption without exception. The vast contrast and space between interpretation and operation that Chang's design commands, to the Chinese architectural community in the 1990s—which was short of both ideas and forms—proved to be fatal and attractive. Xishu Bookstore is the plainest, most vivid example.

Looking back today, the biggest achievement of Xishu Bookstore was raising the cognitive sensibility and intellectual complexity for Chinese contemporary architects: from Xishu Bookstore, some learned to see architecture as a fractal component of the city; some experienced the spatial possibilities of the rotating Book-Bikes; some discovered an "ontological architecture," which was reduced to minimal abstract volumes; some saw the architectural "skin" that was pushed in front of our eyes by the glass floor and simple joints; and some woke up to the value of propagation, a taste of ascetics, the control of orders, the submission of syntactics, and so on.

Just four years after being built, Xishu Bookstore was demolished and the space it occupied returned to the original passageway, and everything that was glimpsed in the bookstore was gone. Twenty years later, several generations of architects who were inspired, encouraged, and changed by Xishu Bookstore gathered in that passageway and the site of the bookstore to hang a memorial plaque. At that moment, perhaps, some would have faintly sensed that the "gene for thought" indeed has a fundamental power beyond time.

This essay was first published in *World Architecture* 328; translated by Chen Yuxiao

Collage of *hutong* scenes and Xishu Bookstore by Yung Ho Chang

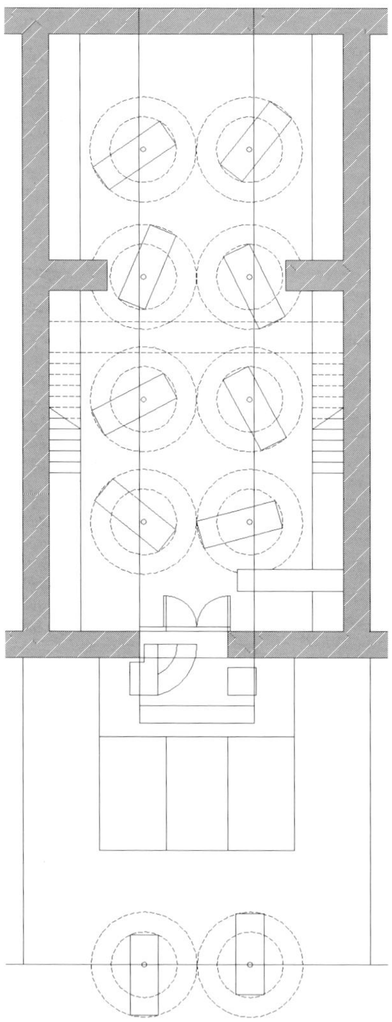

First-floor plan

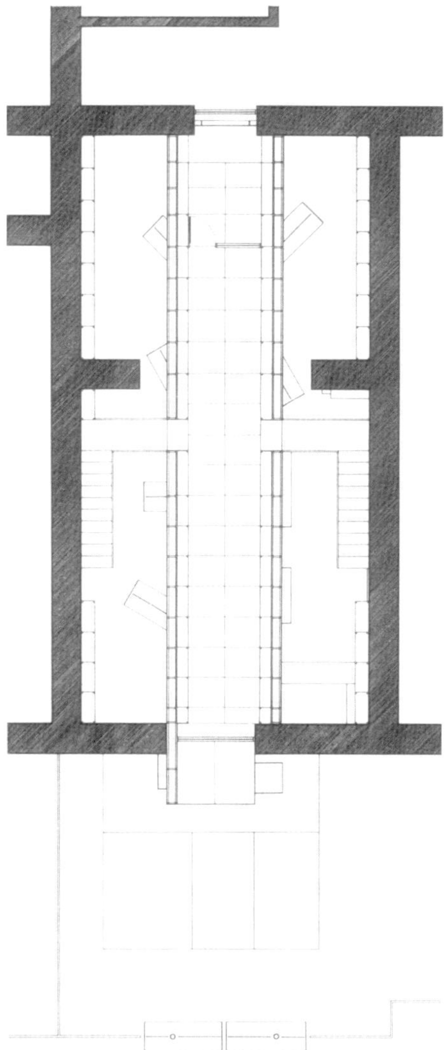

Mezzanine-floor plan

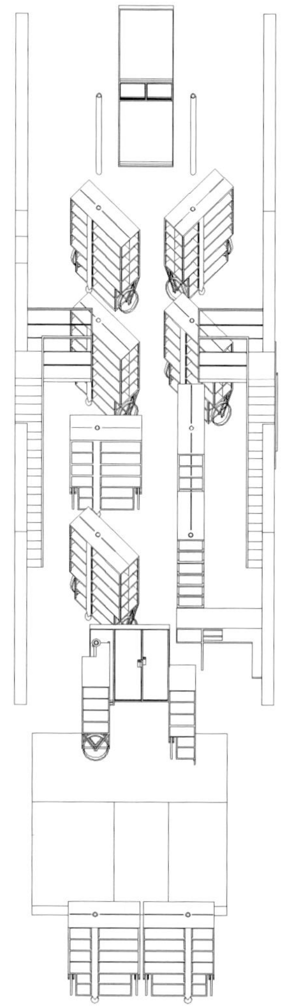

Axonometric

> 1, 2 Interior scenes 1 | 2

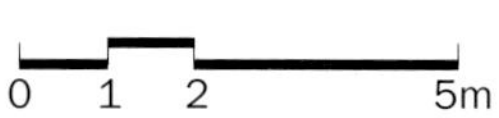

梁思成建筑画

1 | 2

< 1 Interior, with a chair designed by Atelier FCJZ
< 2 Interior, with Book-Bikes in different positions

The Book-Bike

v Mezzanine level

[EXPERIENCE of MOVEMENT]

Urban Cycling Wear

2014

Defining urbanity via clothes for cycling: The love for sports has heavily influenced and pervaded urban culture in recent decades, as far as attire and gear go. We, too, enjoy and believe in an active lifestyle, bicycle-riding in particular, since it is both healthy and green.

In our cycling outfit design, we combine traditional horseback riding gear and contemporary cycling attire, so that elegance and sportiness can coexist and biking in the city will have a distinctive appearance. Special attention is paid to details such as the way a mobile phone is pocketed, as well as accessories, including backpacks, to further facilitate the urban life of cyclists today.

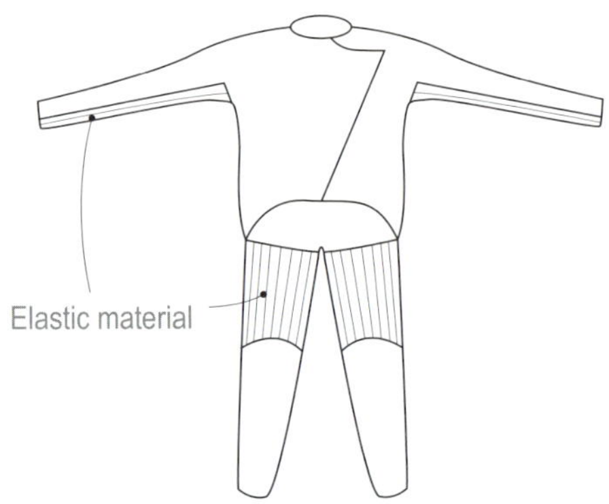

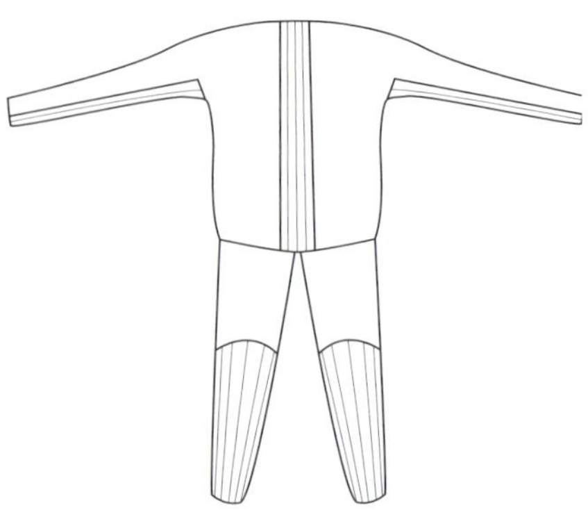

v Urban Cycling Wear installation at the Get It Louder exhibition in Beijing in 2014

v A “show” of Urban Cycling Wear worn by architects of Atelier FCJZ and the exhibition’s organizing team at the opening of Get It Louder 2014

Pleated skirt + shorts

T-shirt + cape

Dress + hoodie

Urban Cycling Wear jacket for men

Urban Cycling Wear jacket for women—an asymmetrical hem is convenient for getting on and off the bike

The elastic parts of the Urban Cycling Wear pants

[EXPERIENCE of MOVEMENT]

Bike Ring

Xiamen, Fujian Province, China
Design development

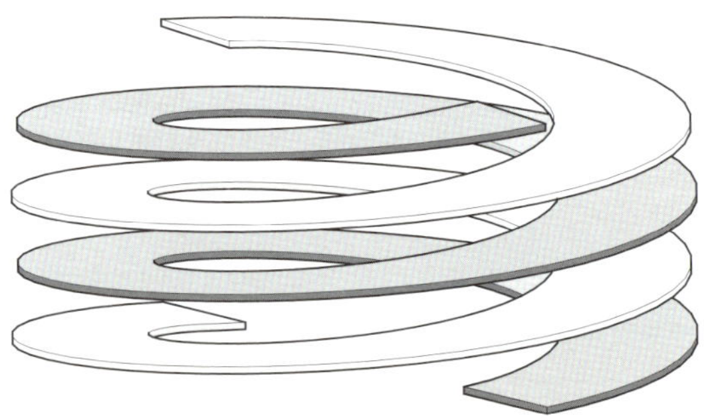

Bike building in the bike city: Xiamen, also known as Amoy, is a coastal city in Fujian Province. The site for this project is located on the waterfront of Maluan Bay, serving as a fitting initial implementation for Xiamen's current plans to develop an elevated bicycle network around the entire city.

Before learning of the city's ambitious plan, we envisioned a commercial complex that would allow cyclists to ride through it, and even access the rooftop, without having to dismount from their bicycles. At the time of the project, it had been decades since myself or Atelier FCJZ had thought about the possibility of building something for biking. When our client on this project entertained the idea of extreme sports as part of the program for this commercial complex, we suggested cycling. Following that, we were informed that the municipal government of Xiamen has not only a master plan, but had already built a stretch of the bike highway, which was being well-enjoyed by the citizens. This formed our realization that our proposition of a ride-through shopping center would then become a part of the larger urban infrastructure.

Spatial structure for riding: The building takes the form of two interlocking spirals: One is a spiraling ramp that houses an indoor megastore, with cycling as the theme; the other is lined with small specialty shops, bars, cafés, and eateries—which would appear somewhat like a street being extended upward. The two spirals are linked by passage-bridges at three locations, so that one has the choice to either make a shortcut, or ride continuously all the way up one spiral and down the other. The entrance of the building is directly connected with the city biking route. Bike parking can be found along both ramps, indoor, and outdoor. On the rooftop, the surfaces of the mechanical space serve as two back-to-back billboard-like signs, on which there are two words in English: "Bike Amoy."

v Completed portion of bicycle highway

> The bike ring is connected with the bicycle highway

BIKE

Research-based designs about the possibility of architecture for biking conducted by Atelier FCJZ, prior to Bike Ring project

Conceptual designs of an Eight-unit Bike Apartment
...

Model

Circulation concept

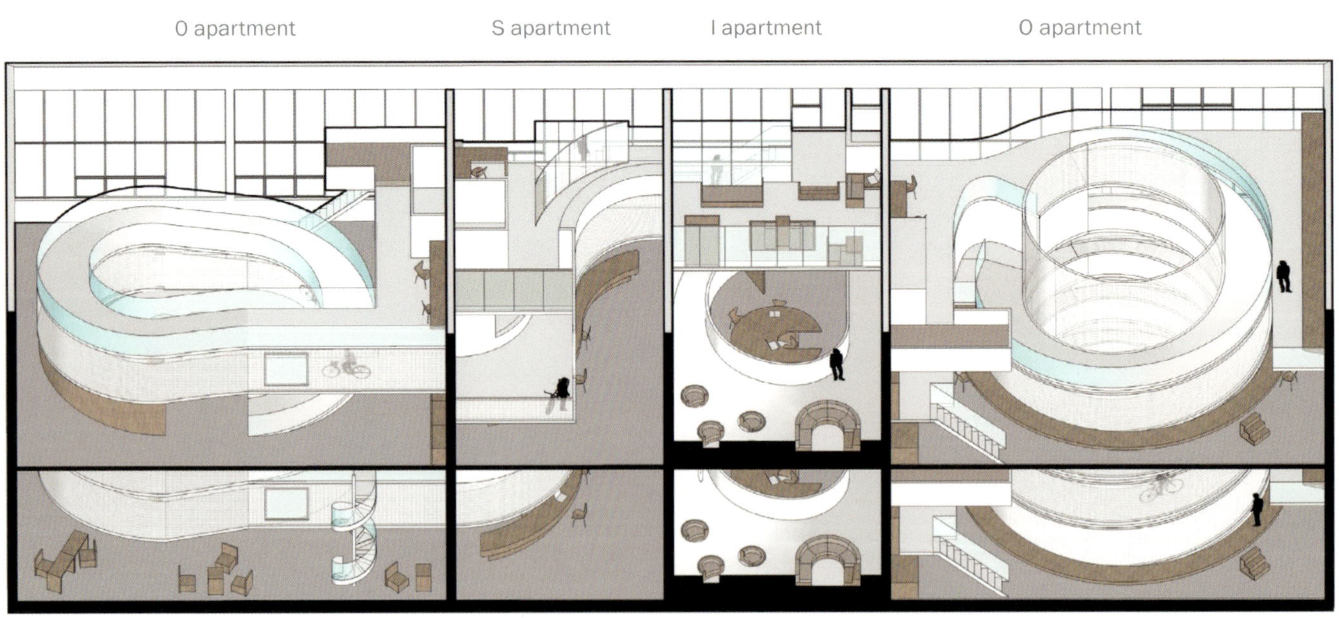

Sectional axonometric

... And a Bike House

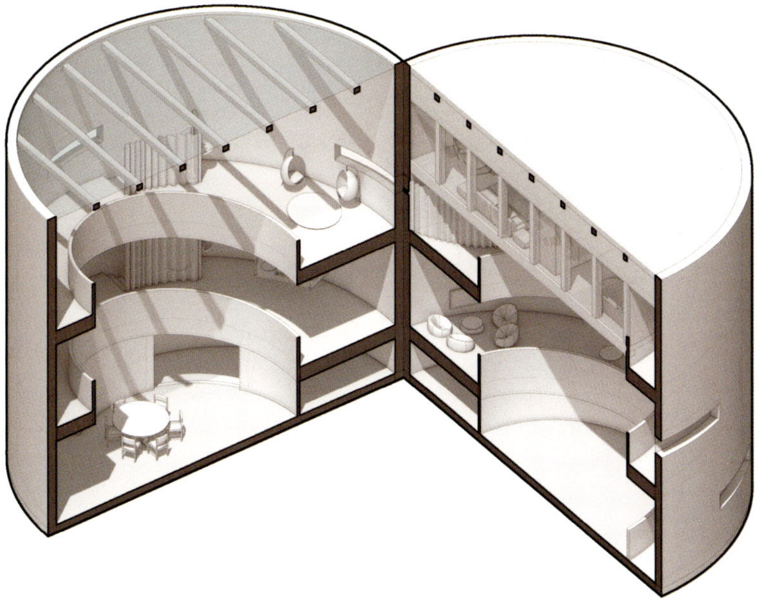

Sectional axonometric

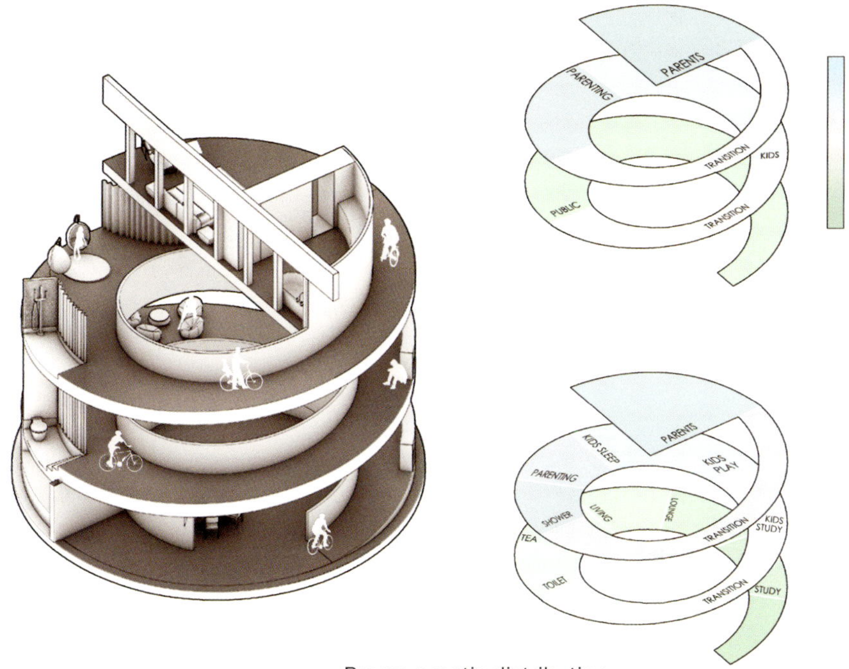

Programmatic distribution

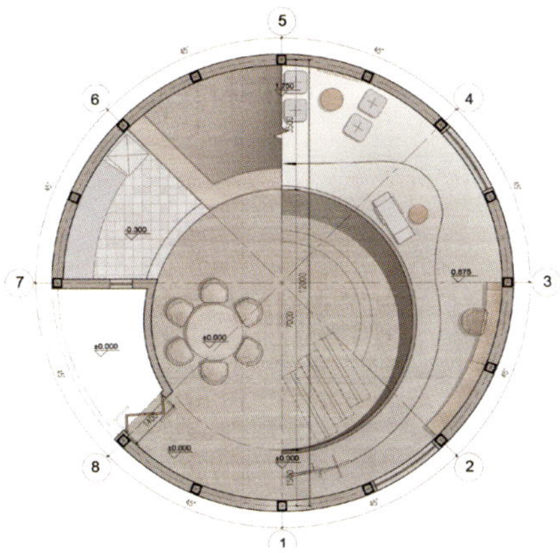

First-floor plan

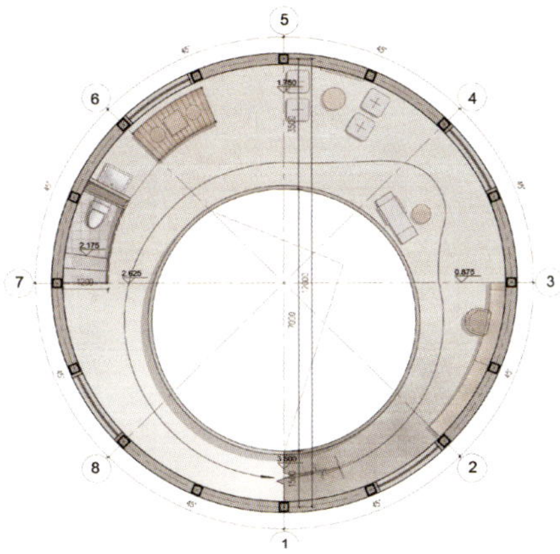

Second-floor plan

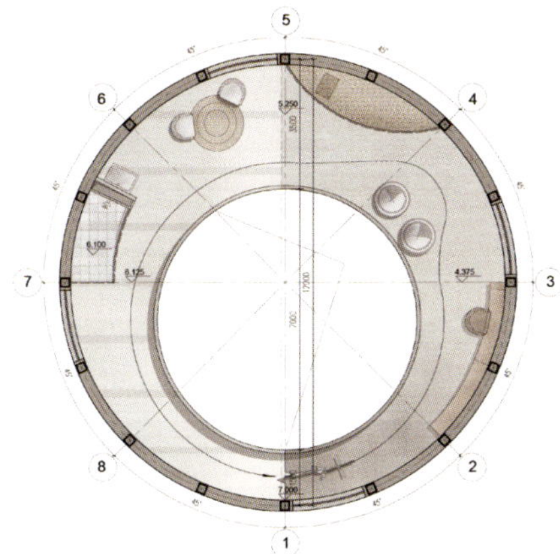

Third-floor plan

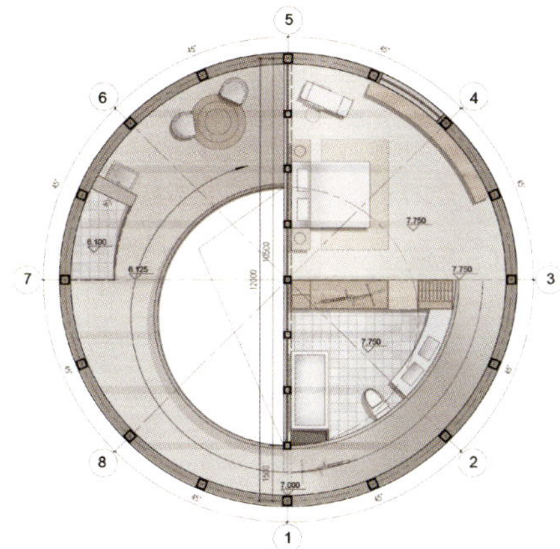

Fourth-floor plan

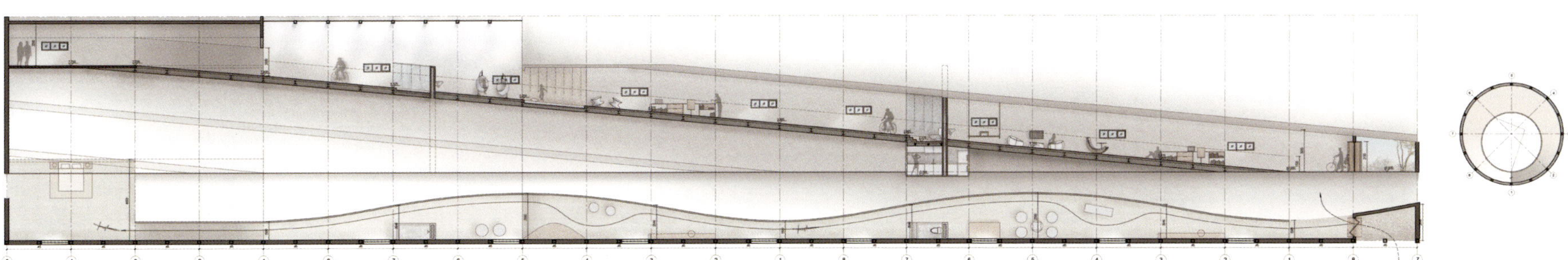

Flattened section

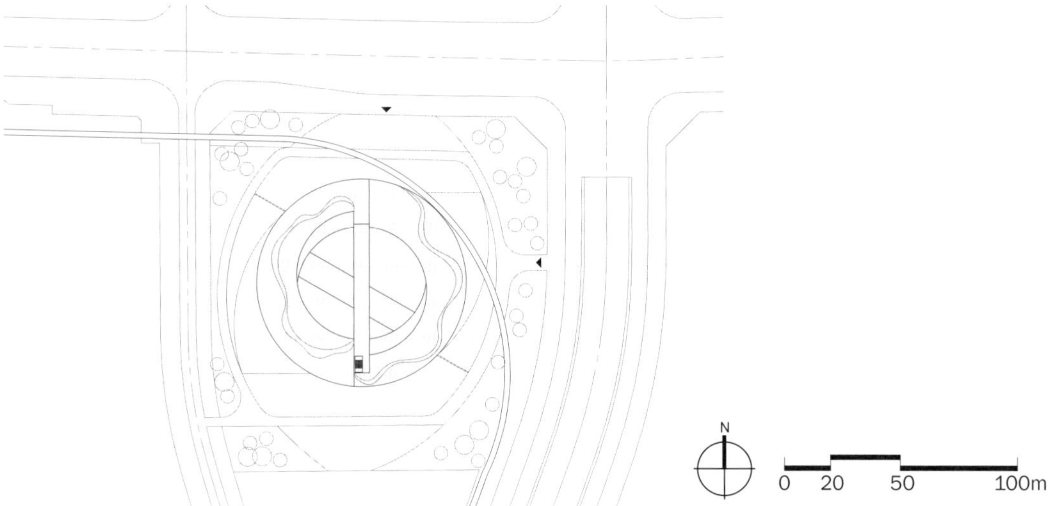

Site plan

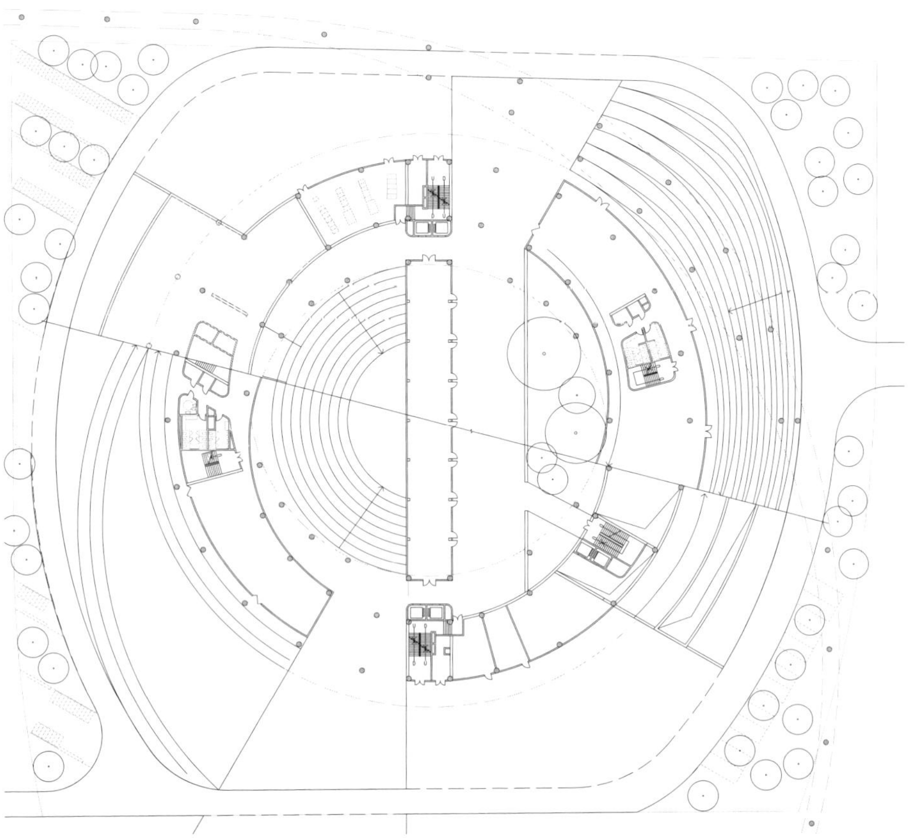

First-floor plan

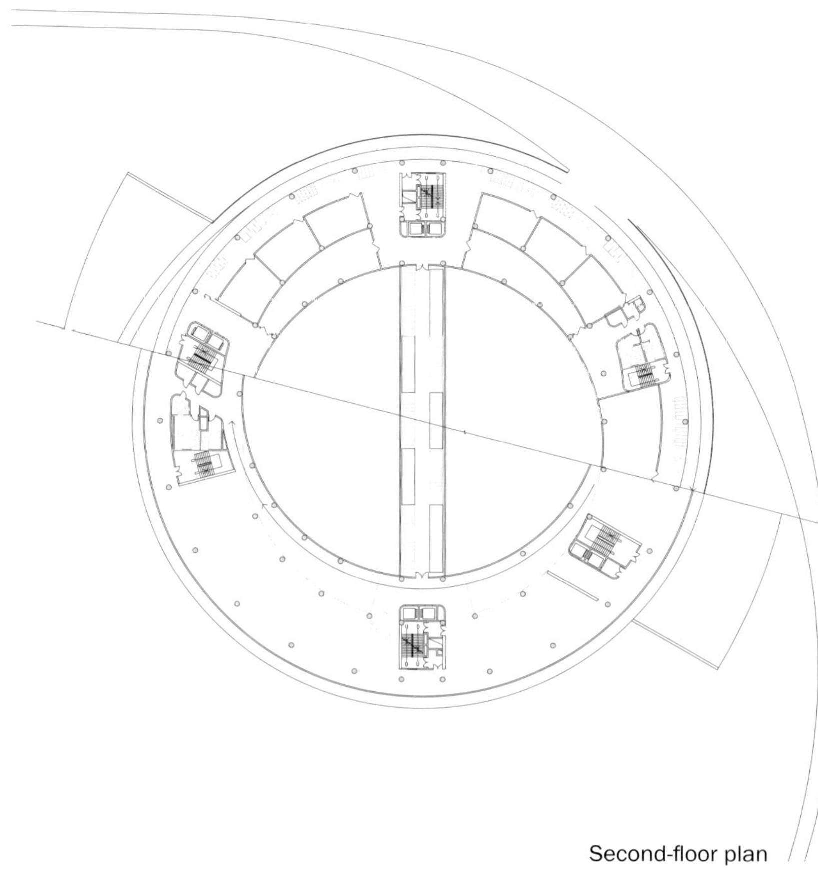

Second-floor plan

0 10 25 50m

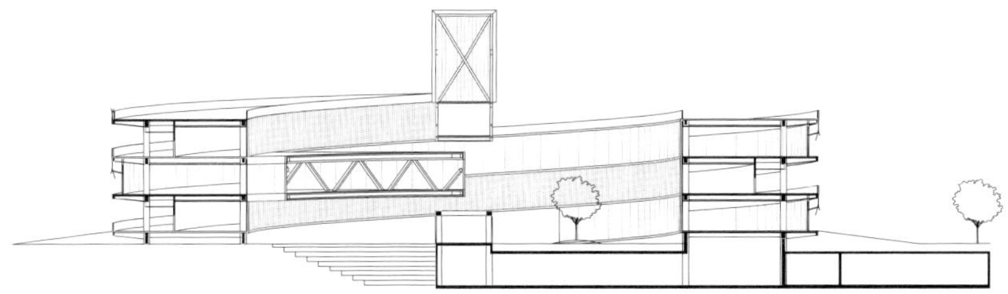

Section

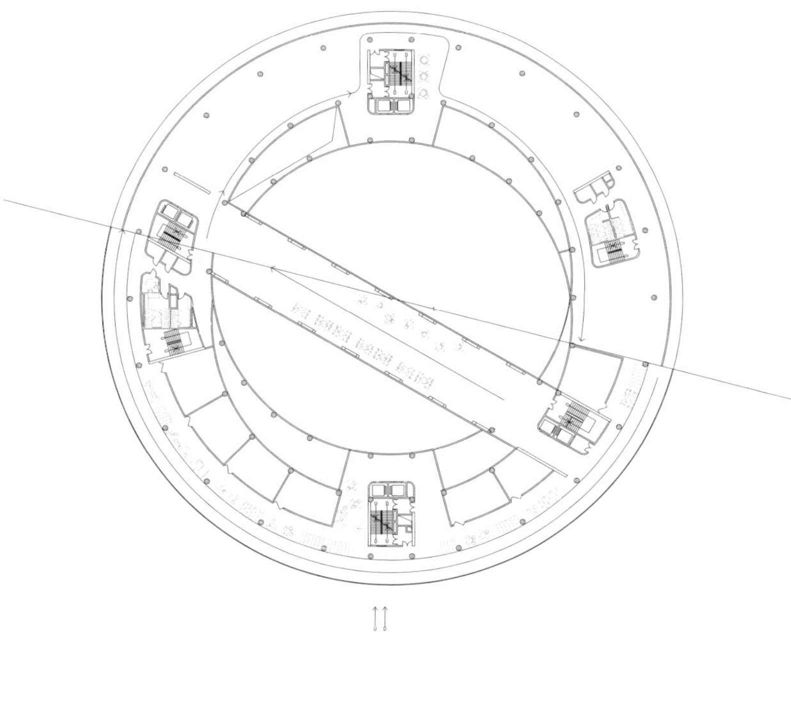

Third-floor plan

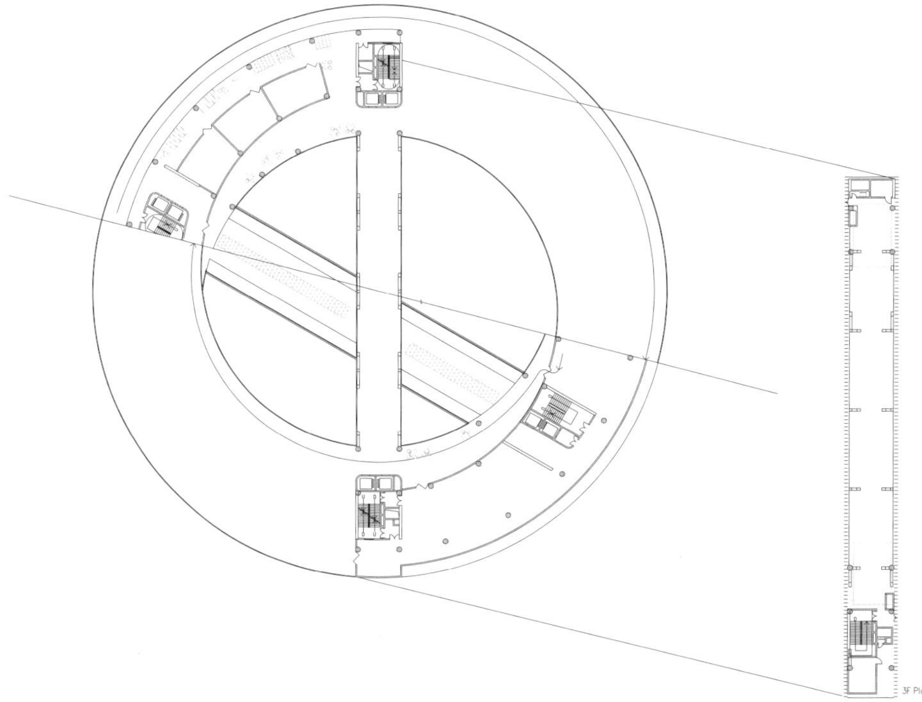

Fourth-floor plan

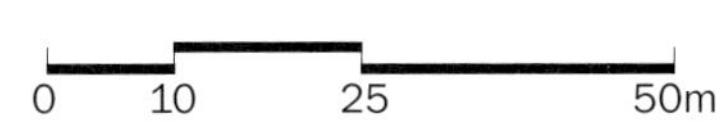

1 < 1 Flagship store interior

2 < 2 Street in the form of a rampway lined with stores

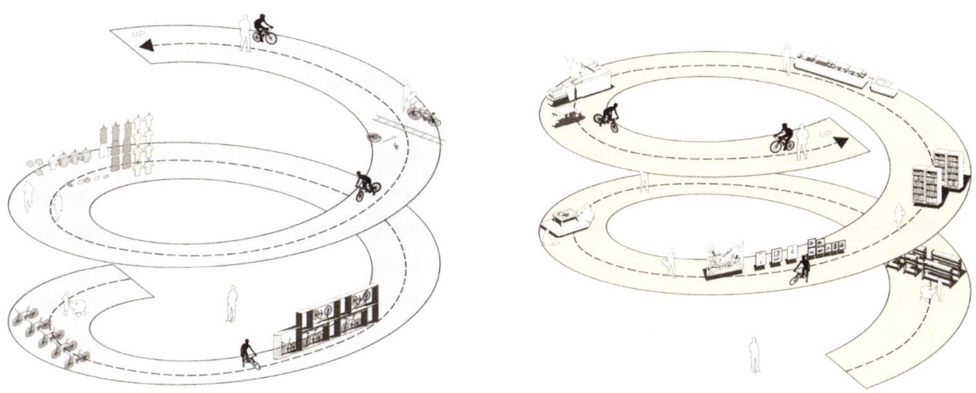

Rampways diagram

Section-perspective

v Bike ring approached from bike highway

[EXPERIENCE of STORIES]

Ocean Art Center

Beijing, China

2001

Save by cutting: Ocean Art Center is renovated from one of the textile factory buildings on the site of a real estate project, which is next to the east fourth ring road in Beijing. The decision to reuse the existing two-story facility indicates the client's acceptance of the particular quality of such construction. Therefore, our design attempts to enhance and further express the spatial order and the structural logic of the industrial architecture.

Due to planning reasons, the only way to save the building from demolition was to have three bays of the structure sawed off. However, the traces of the cuts made with water-drills turn into details of the revealed section, so that the evolution of the building is present in the latest transformation. Meanwhile, new channel glass curtain walls fill up the original large-span reinforced-concrete frame. The open space of the interior is kept intact wherever possible. On the north side, the spatial organization of the factory extends out to form a courtyard. The new functions of the project include the real estate sales office downstairs and the art center on the second floor, where various activities of contemporary art, such as exhibitions, films, or performances take place.

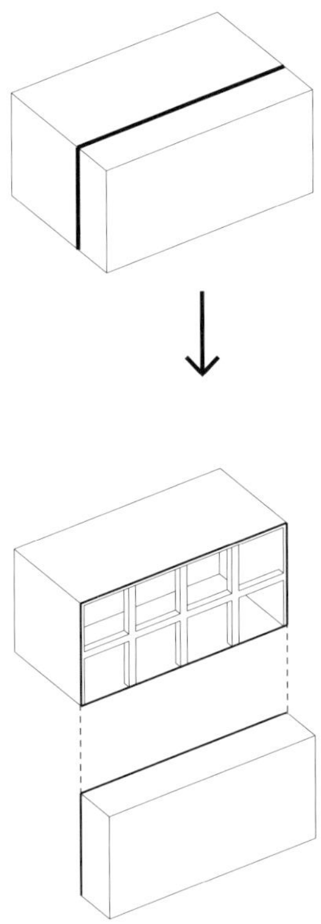

v Before renovation
v Channel glass elevation detail

Traces of water-drilling

A performance

v Art center interior

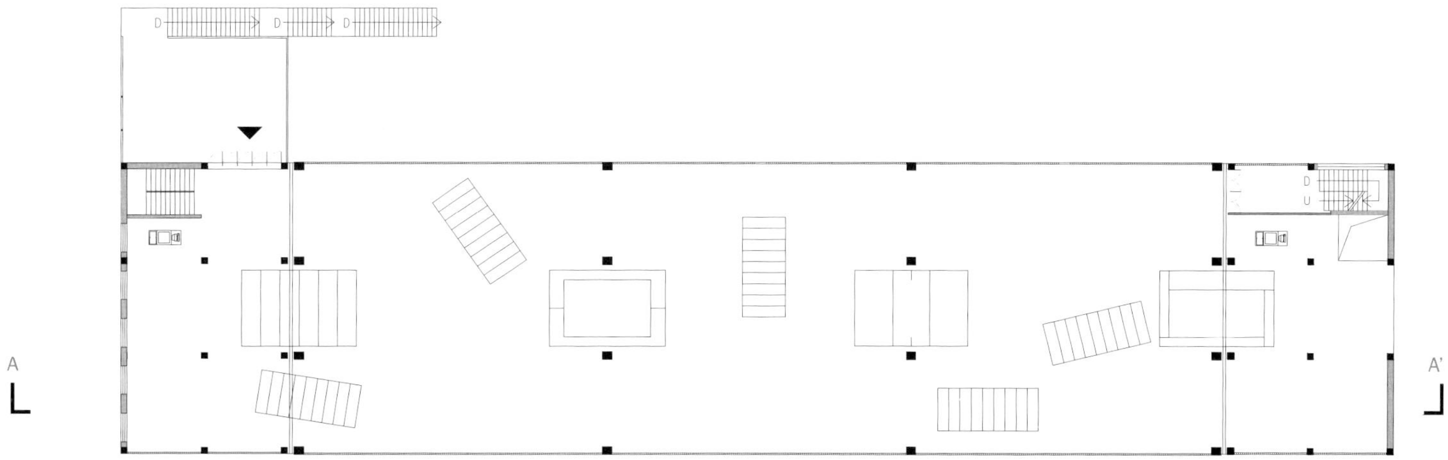

Second-floor plan

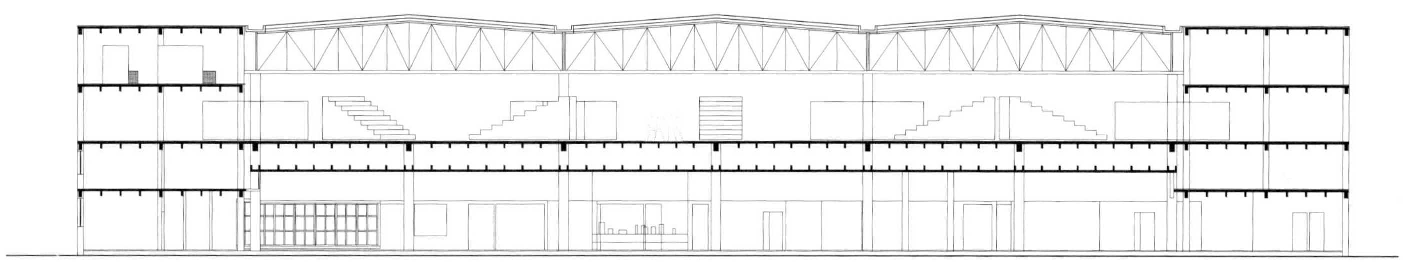

Section A-A'

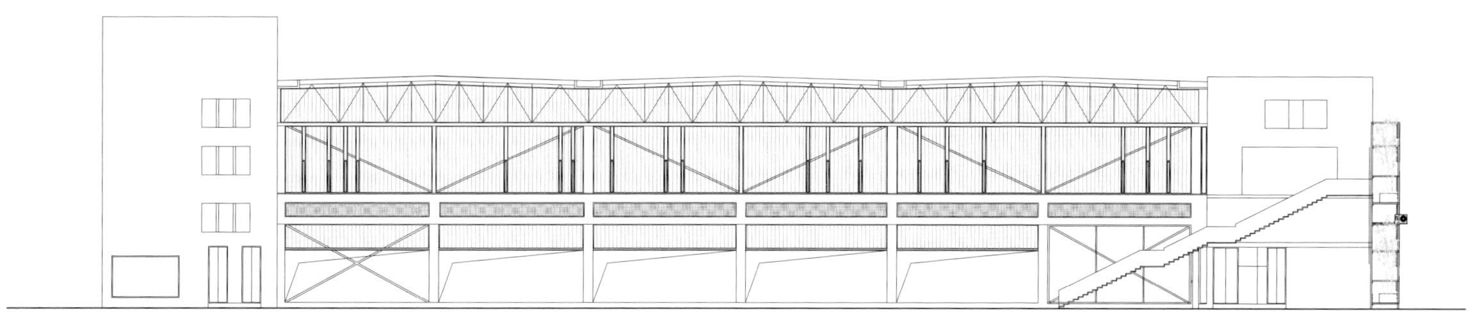

Elevation

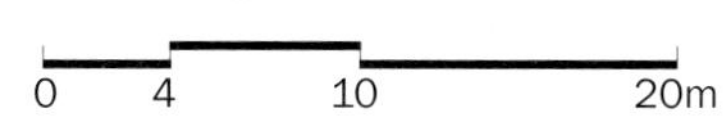

[EXPERIENCE of STORIES]

Shanghai Corporate Pavilion

World Expo 2010, Shanghai, China

2010

Addressing technology: Beginning 2010, the human race went through a long period of rapid technological advancement; the amount of infrastructure in a building has dramatically increased in modern-day, to the point that technologies are today's basic building blocks. For Shanghai Corporate Pavilion at World Expo 2010, we sought to manifest this observation in our design. The interior spaces of the Pavilion, shaped as a series of free, flowing forms, were not only enclosed by walls of the static kind, but also by a dense, cubic volume of infrastructural network, including a mist-making system and LED lights, which changed the appearance of the building from one moment to the next, as programed to do so through the computer.

Addressing energy: Through technology, we also took on the pressing issues of energy and sustainability. Components of the architectural infrastructure were designated for solar energy harvesting and rainwater collection and the external façade was made of recycled polycarbonate (PC) plastic.

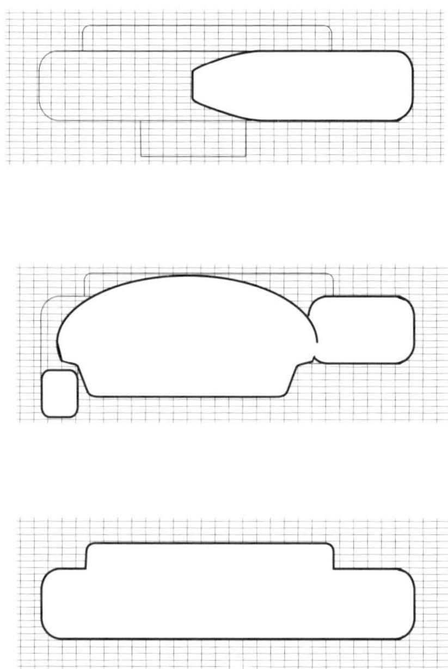

Three environmentally sensible measures

1. Solar energy system: Our design featured a 1,600-square-meter area of solar heat-collecting tubes on the roof. These solar tubes can collect solar energy to produce hot water of up to 95°C ultralow temperature; power generation technology is in turn used to convert heat into electricity.

2. Recycled plastic material: Shanghai produces nearly 30 million CDs in its overall waste every year, and only 25 percent of them are recycled. If these CDs are reclaimed and cleaned, they could be used to produce polycarbonate granules and manufacture new polycarbonate plastic products. The external façades of the Pavilion used polycarbonate transparent plastic tubes to create its dreamlike matrix. After the expo, the plastic tubes can also be recycled.

3. Water/mist system: Rainwater was collected and reused. After sedimentation and filtration, the collected rainwater was used for the Pavilion's daily water needs, in particular the mist spray. The mist enabled a lower temperature under the Pavilion, purified the air, and created a comfortable microclimate around the area.

> Thick skin with LEDs in PC tubes

上海企业联合馆
SHANGHAI
CORPORATE

Analysis of process graphic design

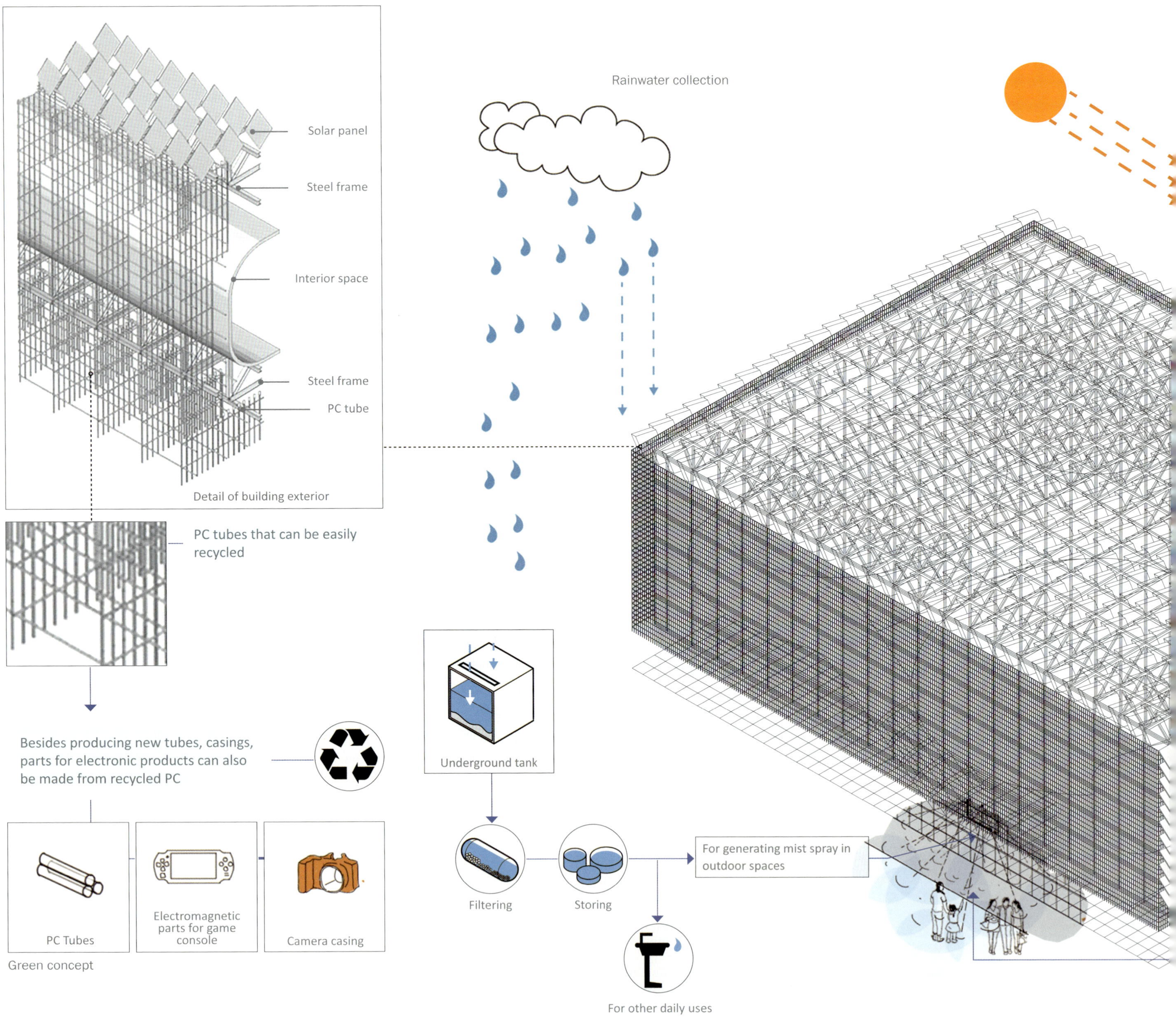

Solar energy collection

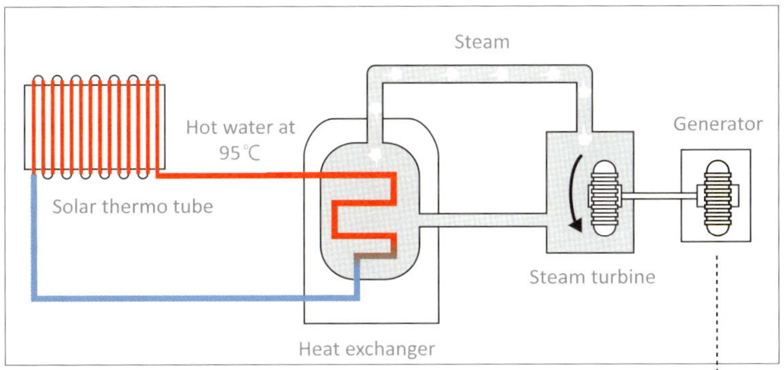

Design thinking process

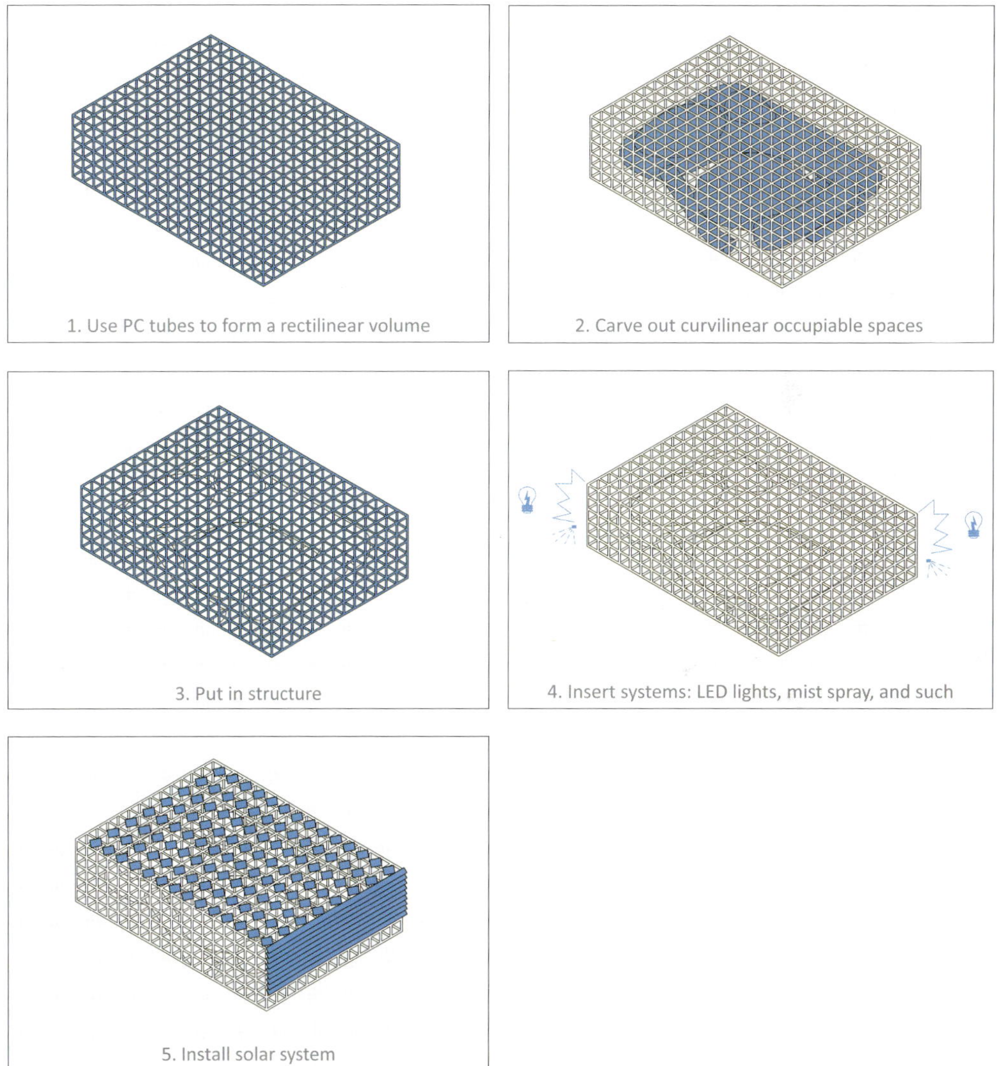

1. Use PC tubes to form a rectilinear volume

2. Carve out curvilinear occupiable spaces

3. Put in structure

4. Insert systems: LED lights, mist spray, and such

5. Install solar system

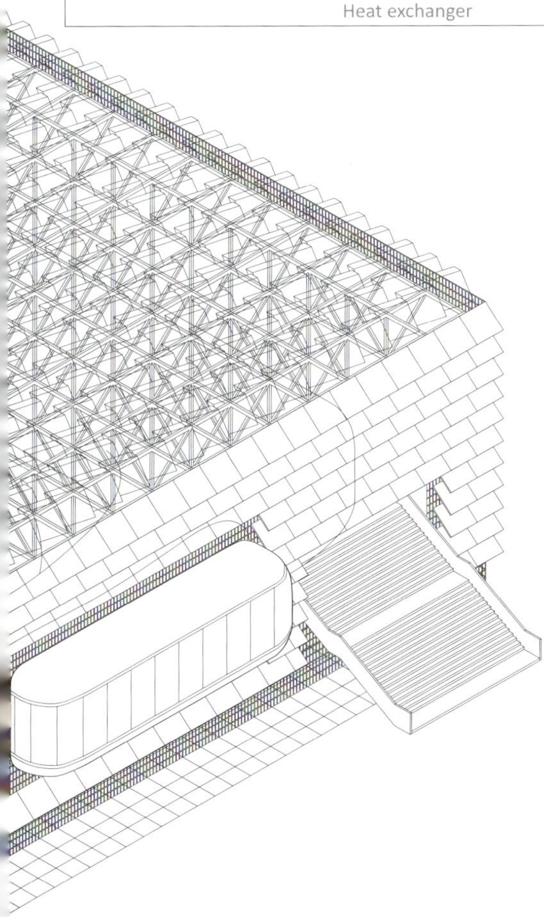

Building exterior changes with digitally programed moving images

Technology helps us to reduce energy consumption while enhancing the architectural experience

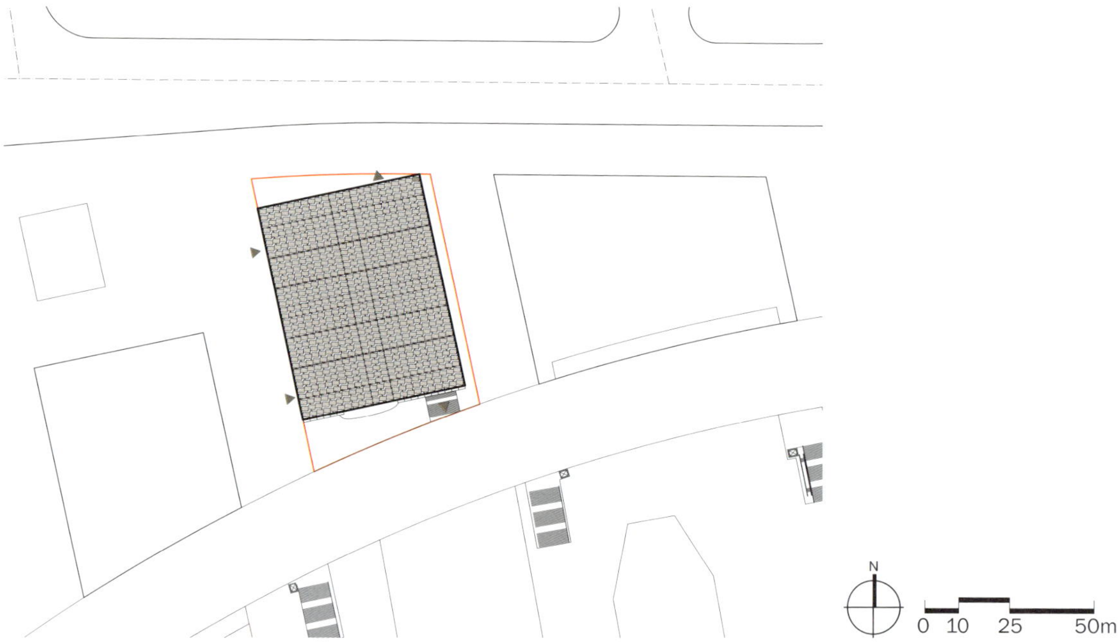

Site plan

v Entrance to exhibition and theater

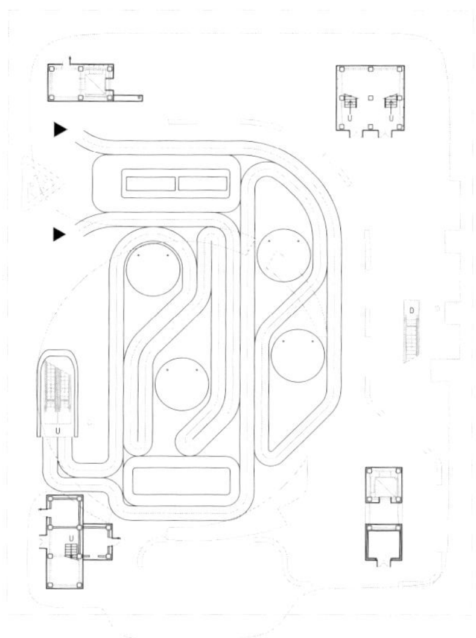

First-floor plan

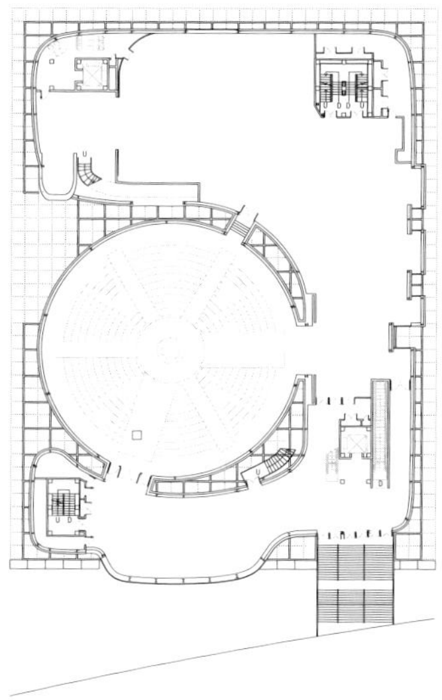

Second-floor plan

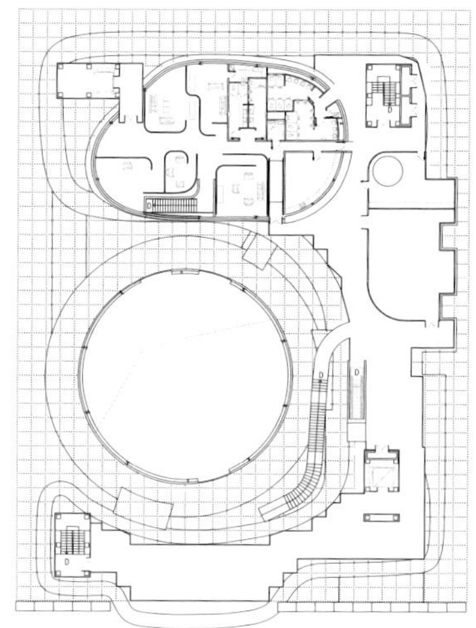

Third-floor plan

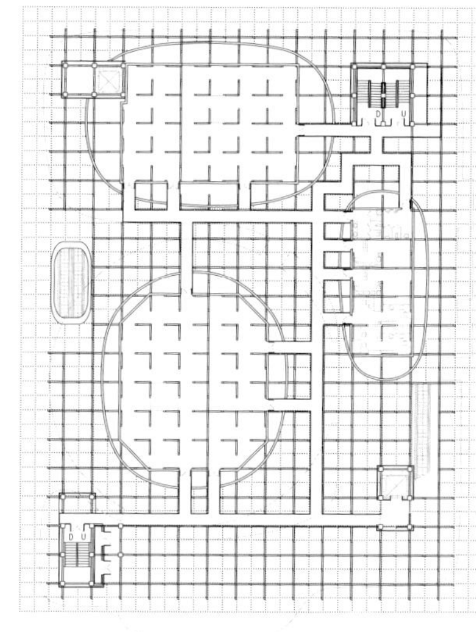

Fourth-floor plan

0 4 10 20m

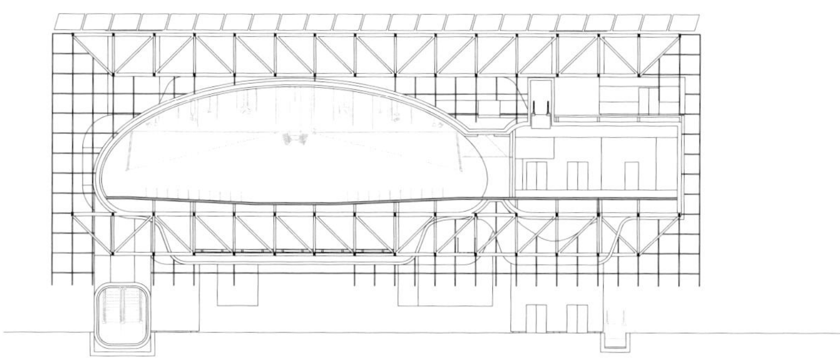

Section

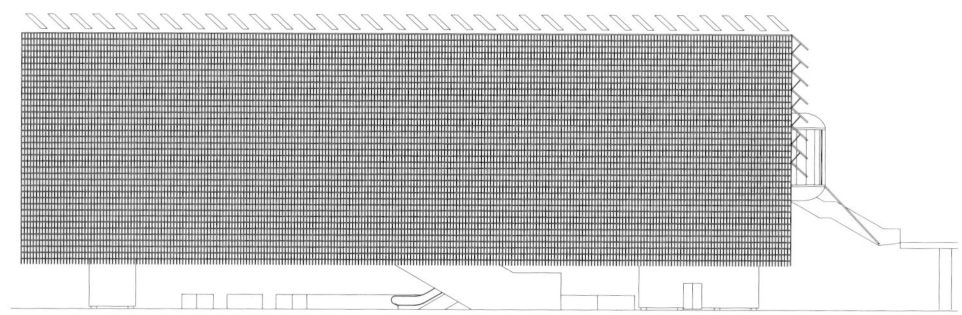

West elevation

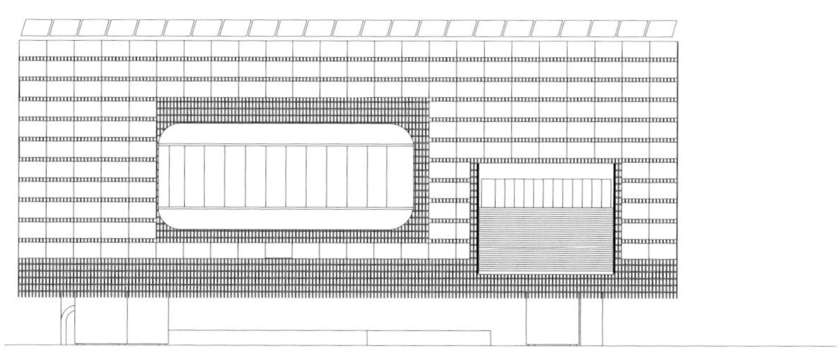

South elevation

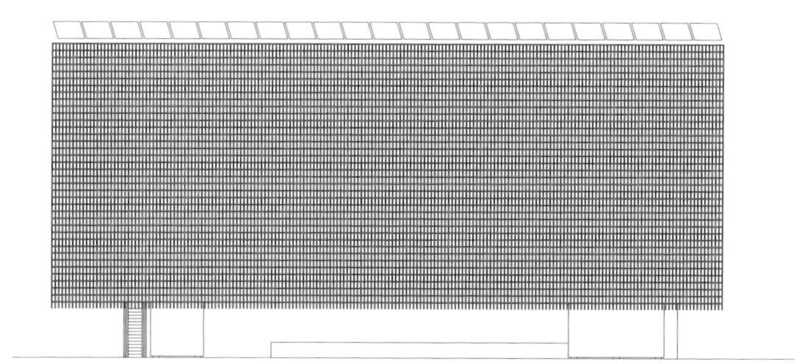

North elevation

0 4 10 20m

v West elevation during the day
v West elevation at dusk

v West elevation at night

Innovation

< Panoramic theater

LED lights in PC tubes

Utility ducts color coded

v VIP lounge

v Gift shop

[EXPERIENCE of STORIES]

Micro Stages

2012

Drama on body: In this design, jewelry is looked upon as micro architecture, or specifically tiny stages to be worn as accessories. Inspired by the simple yet ritualistic stage setting of Peking Opera, as well as architectural sections, these small silver boxes are open on one side; each depicts a scene of daily life with minuscule furniture pieces inside. Functionally, they are intended to be a ring, earrings, pendant, brooch, or pin.

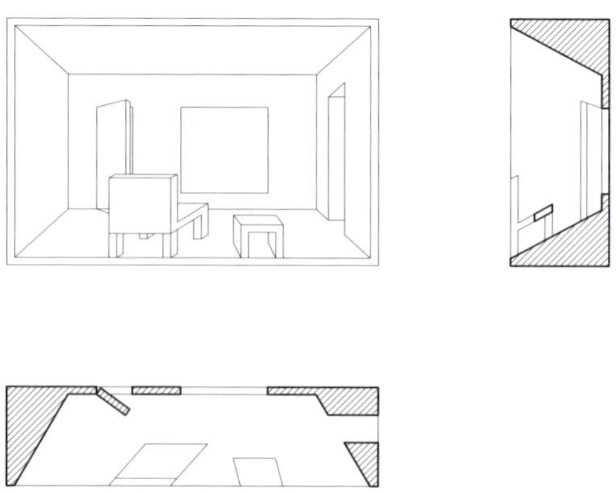

Plan, elevation, and section at full scale

v "Hotel" necklace

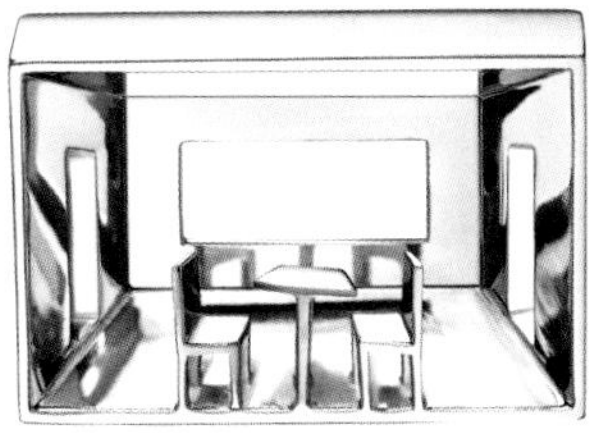

Dining-pin from Rear Window series

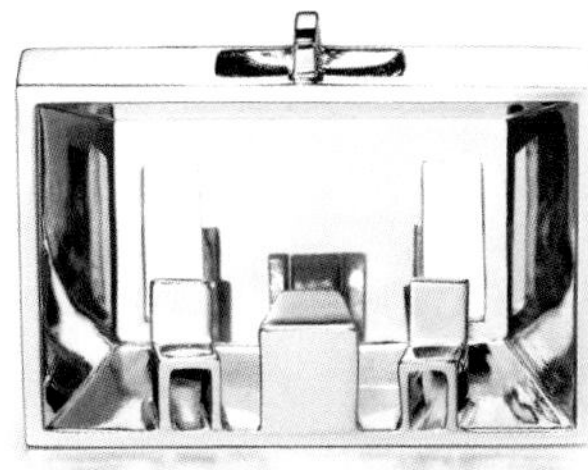

Pendant from Peking Opera series

Pin from Peking Opera series

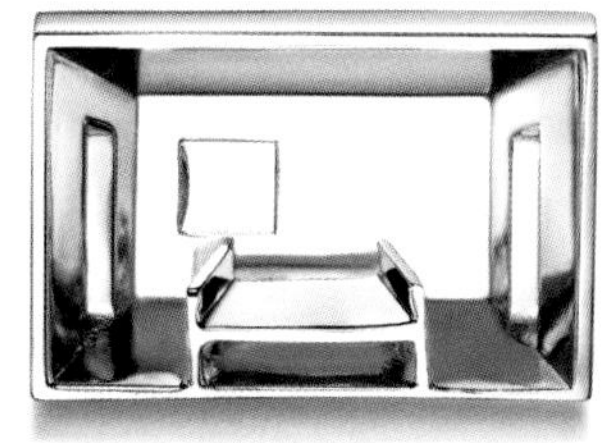

Bedroom-pin from Rear Window series

Ring from Old Mansion series

Ring from Peking Opera series

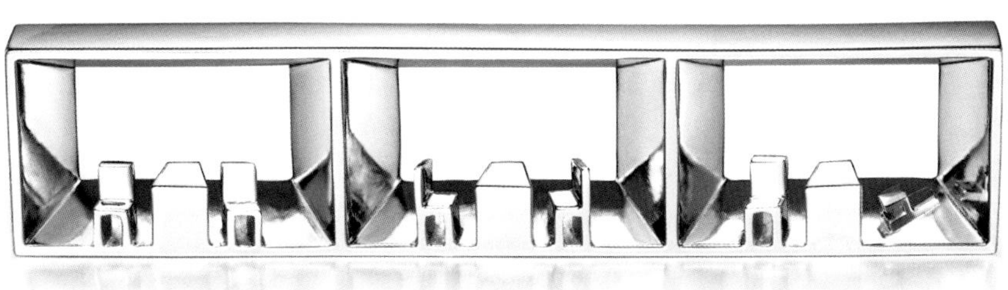

Brooch from Pina series

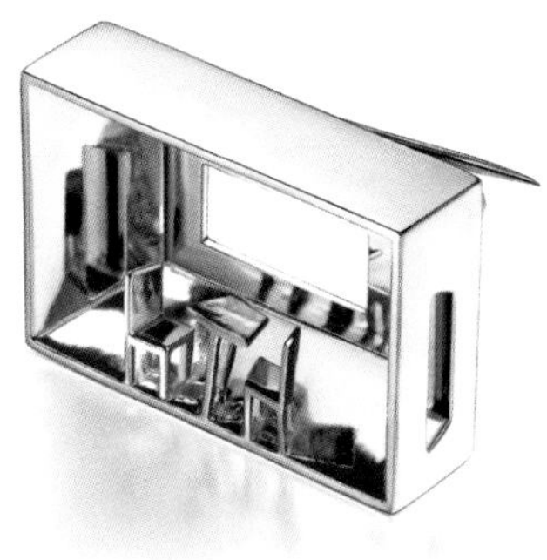

Dining-pin from Rear Window series

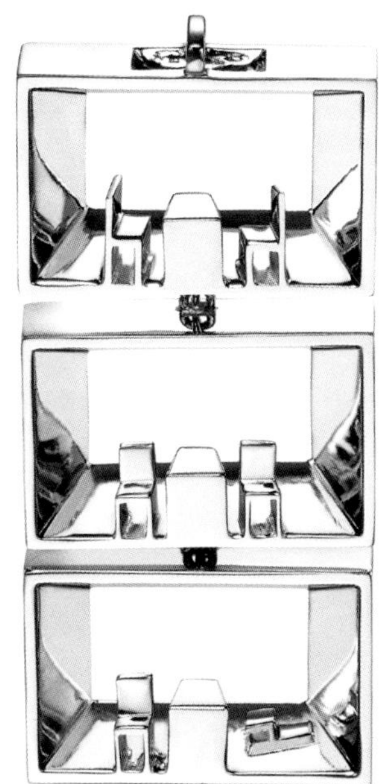

Pendant from Pina series

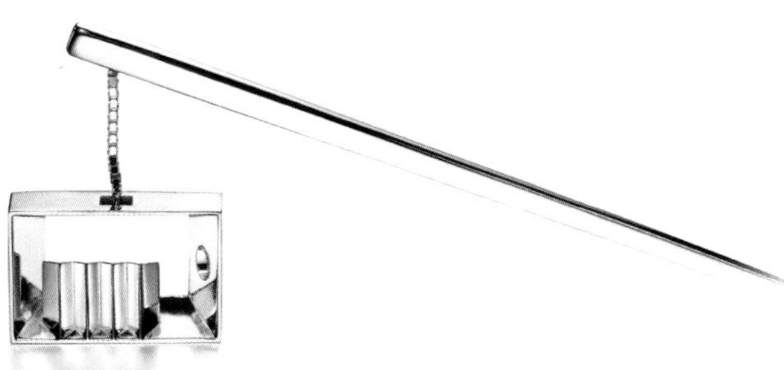

Fold-screen-hairpin from Old Mansion series

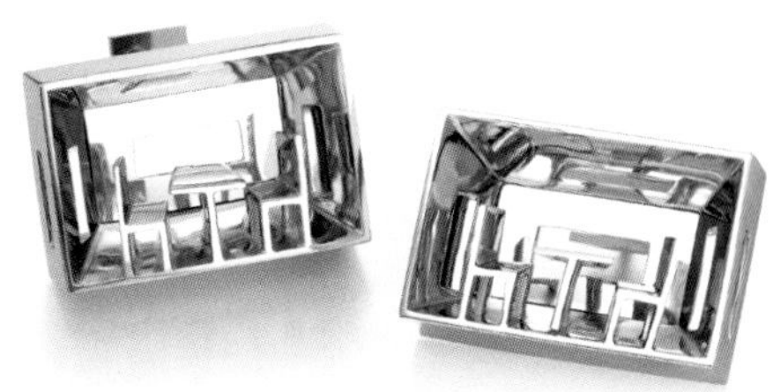

Dining-earrings from Rear Window series

[EXPERIENCE of STORIES]

Graphic FCJZ

2014

An observation: Our world is getting increasingly visual. Besides the bombardment of images—static or moving—via media of all sorts, we have also witnessed the reappearance and resurgence of graphic novels as a serious literary and artistic form. Architects are trained to communicate visually and are always good at absorbing and comprehending graphic information. It would be nothing unnatural that a monograph of an architect's work today could be done with only few words, a bit like a graphic novel.

A page of graphic storytelling for each project: In *Graphic FCJZ*, for each of the forty-eight projects by Atelier FCJZ presented in its pages, there is a graphic spread as the start of each project that depicts the site conditions, ideas and concepts, design processes, construction and technologies involved, and references and inspirations, and so on. There is even a thread of fictional human characters woven into the visual narrative to remind readers that endeavors of design never take only a linear, rational trajectory.

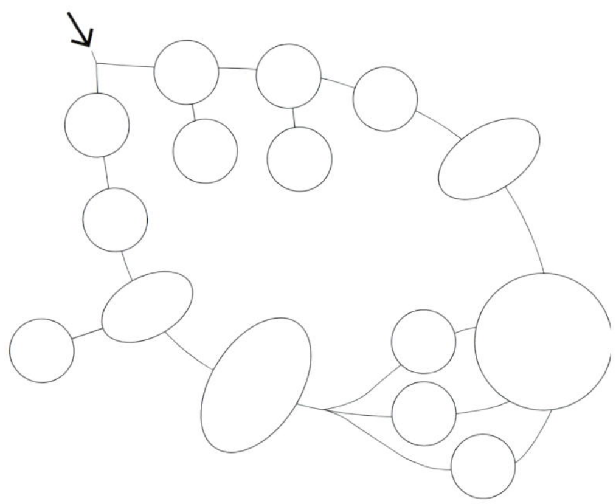

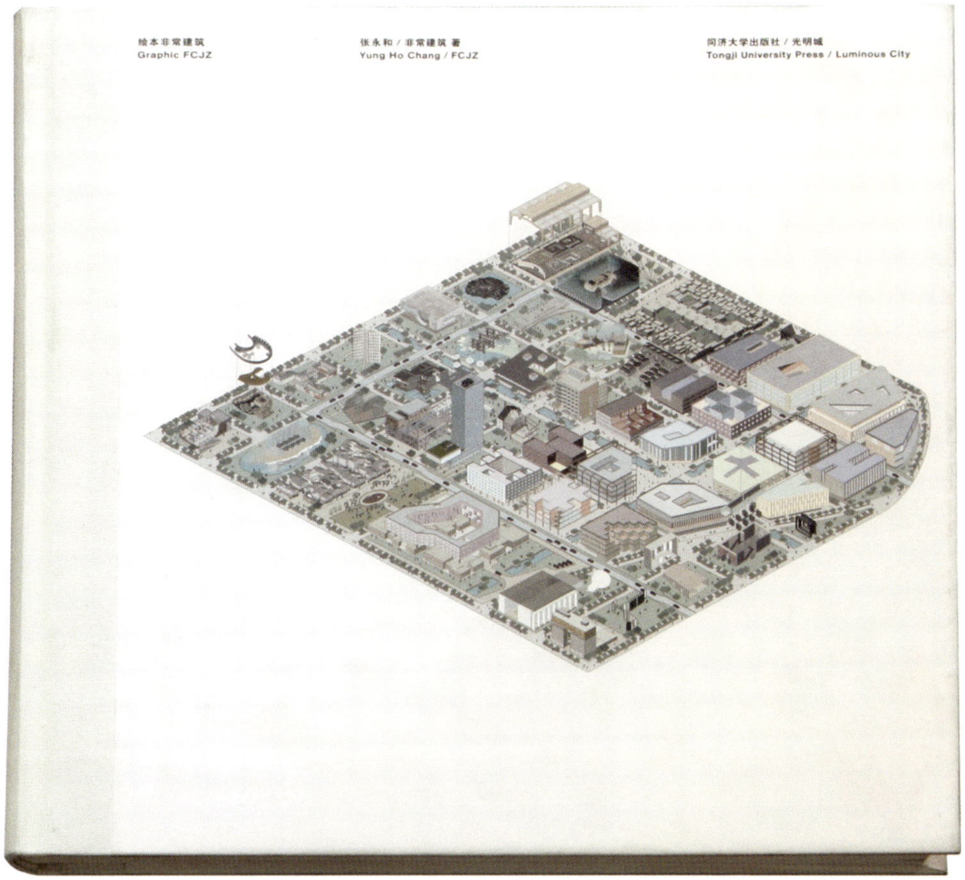
绘本非常建筑
Graphic FCJZ
张永和 / 非常建筑 著
Yung Ho Chang / FCJZ
同济大学出版社 / 光明城
Tongji University Press / Luminous City

Book cover

Images for Pingod Sales Center/Art Museum in *Graphic FCJZ*

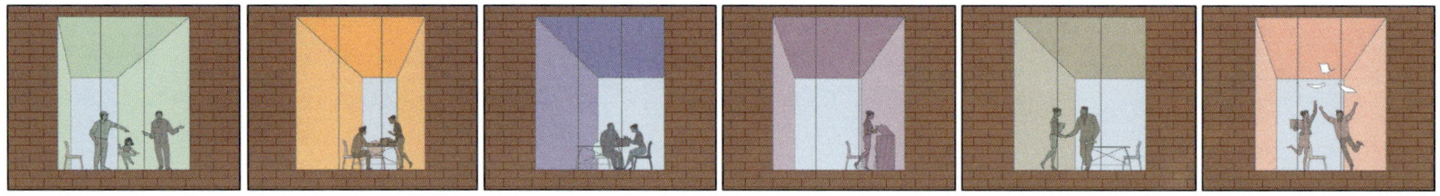

Conference rooms

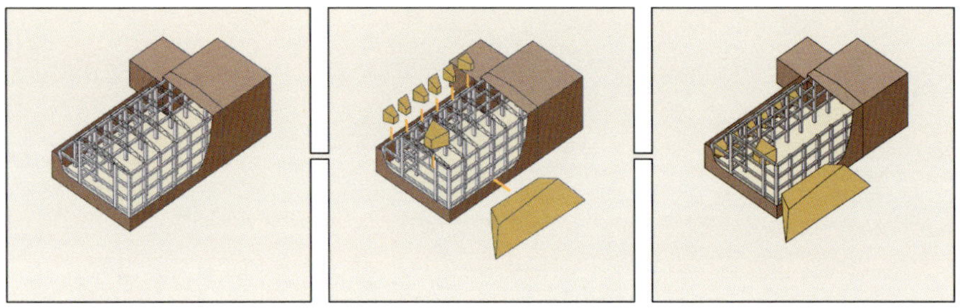

Renovation process

∨ Complete graphic narrative extracted from *Graphic FCJZ*

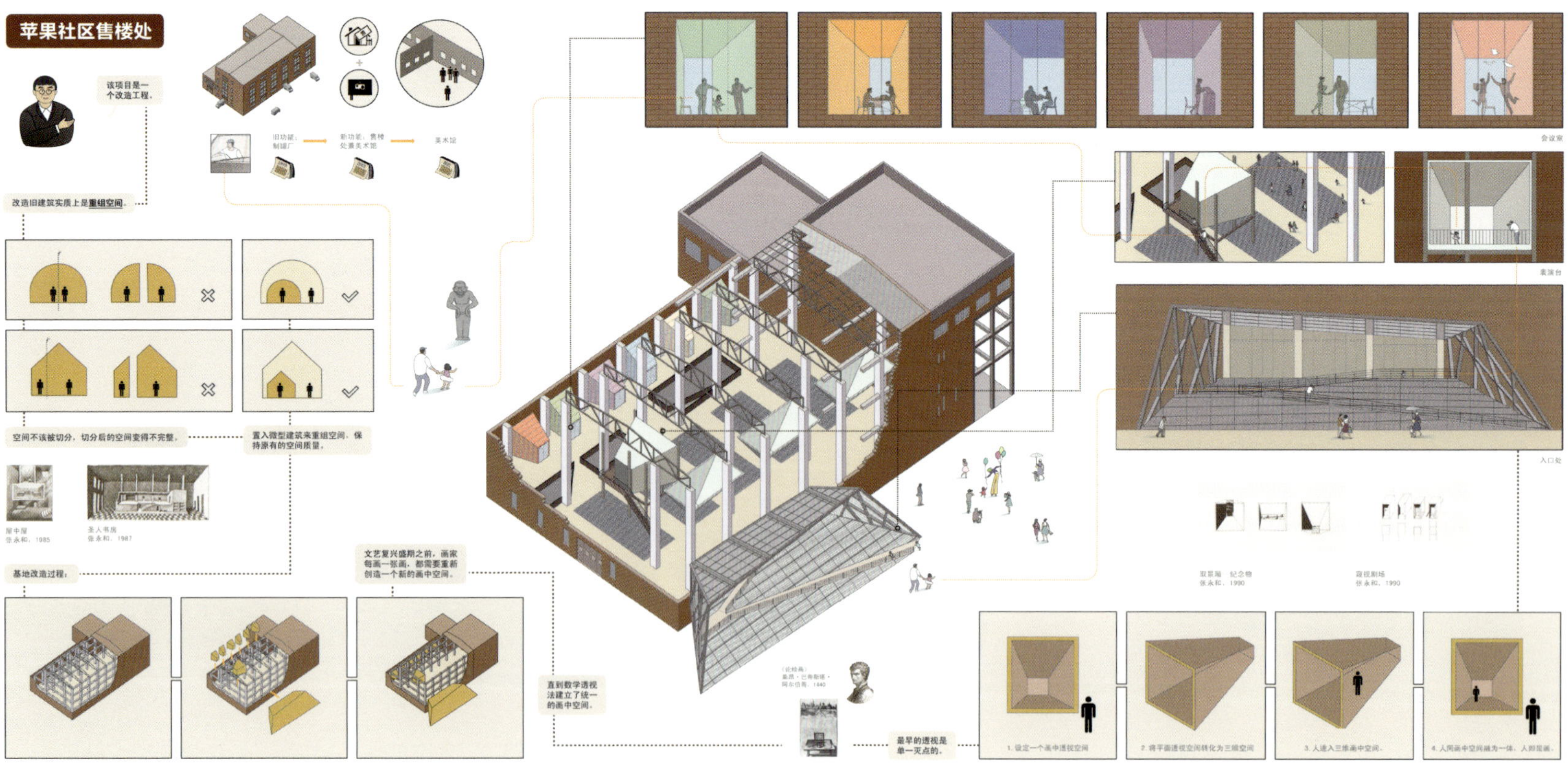

Images for Villa in Persimmon Grove in *Graphic FCJZ*

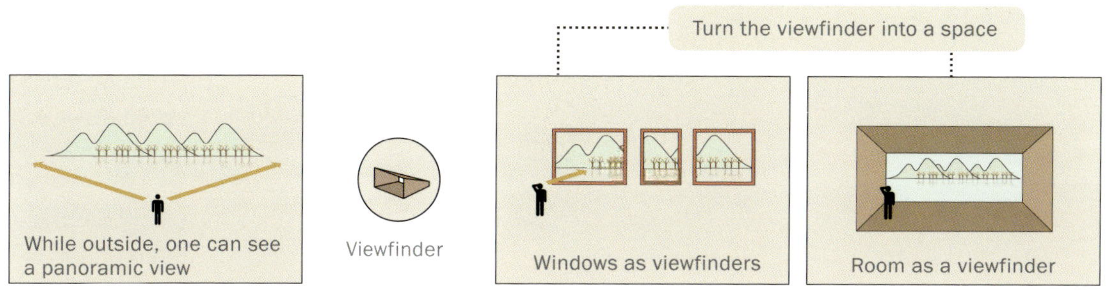

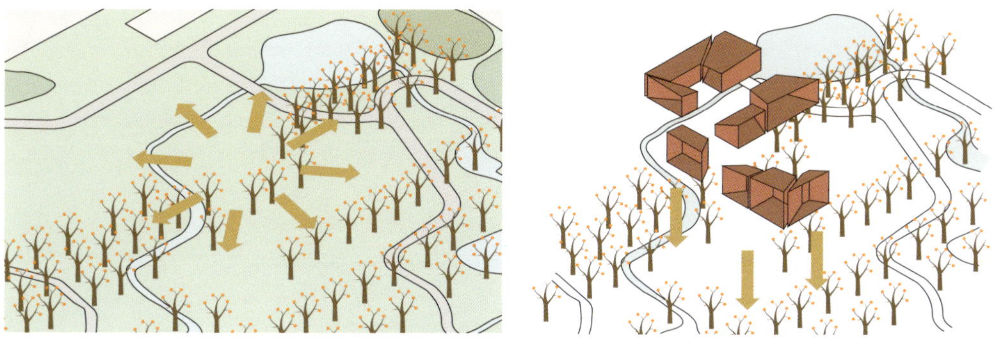

Nine tapered spaces are orientated toward nine different views

∨ Complete graphic narrative extracted from *Graphic FCJZ*

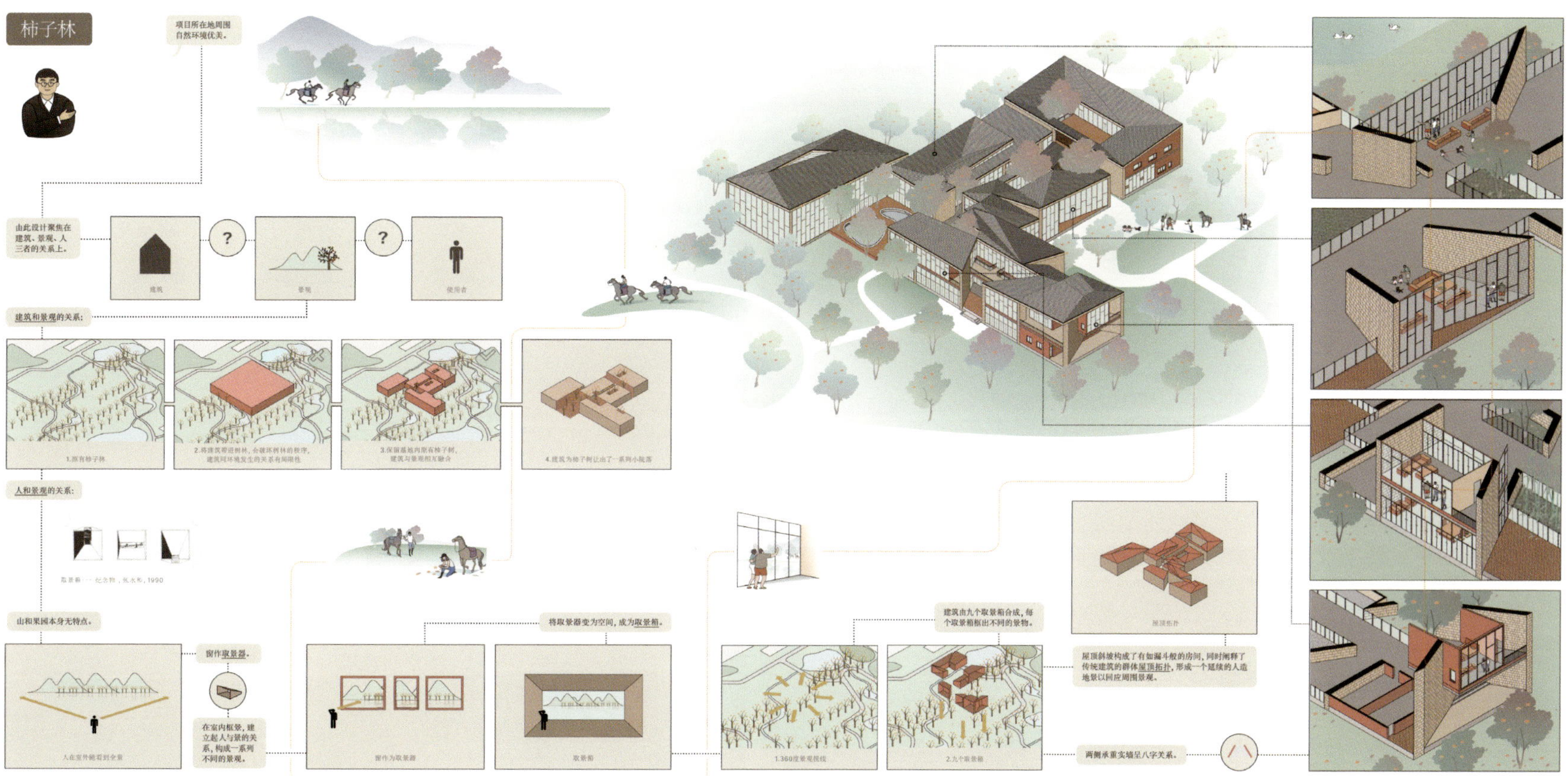

[EXPERIENCE of STORIES]

Little Detective

2015

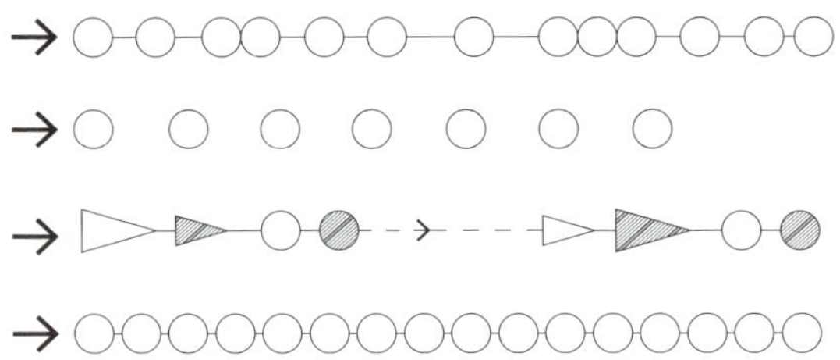

A memory lost: Yung Ho Chang's career as an architect and his passion for art have always been tightly interwoven. With *Little Detective*, he initiates an art project based on a story his architect father used to tell him when he was a child. Over weekends, Chang reinvents the character Little Detective in a graphic novel.

A story recreated: *Little Detective* is a fragmented story series that is told from different perspectives through four booklets presented in a box set: The *Pic Book* is about two mysteries that Little Detective solves, which are narrated in ink-line drawings and short captions; the *Word Book* narrates through text the encounters of Little Detective with Old Detective, in both Chinese and English; Flip Book portrays Little Detective in motion, and may be used as a sketch book; and *Color Book* contains a series of watercolor portraits of all the characters who appear in both the *Pic Book* and *Word Book*.

The book design tells a story too: Graphic designer Ma Shirui has conceptually reiterated the books, binding history in the design of this book set.

v *Pic Book*

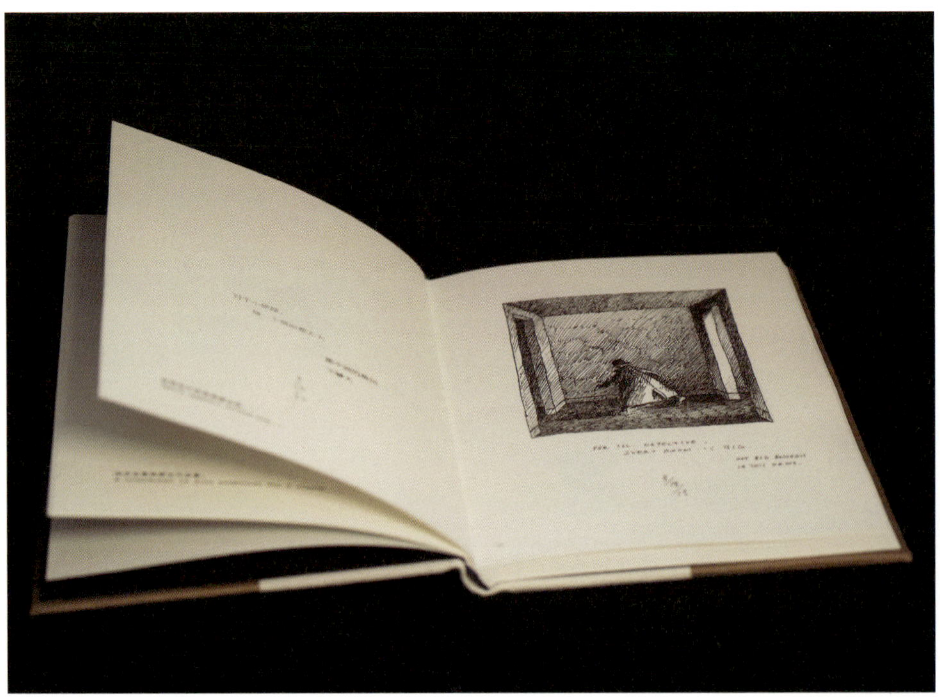

v *Color Book*

Book case

Book covers and binding

∨ *Flip Book*

∨ *Word Book*

Pages from *Color Book*

Little Detective

Aunt

Photographer

Old Detective

Little Detective

Little Detective

Pages from *Pic book*

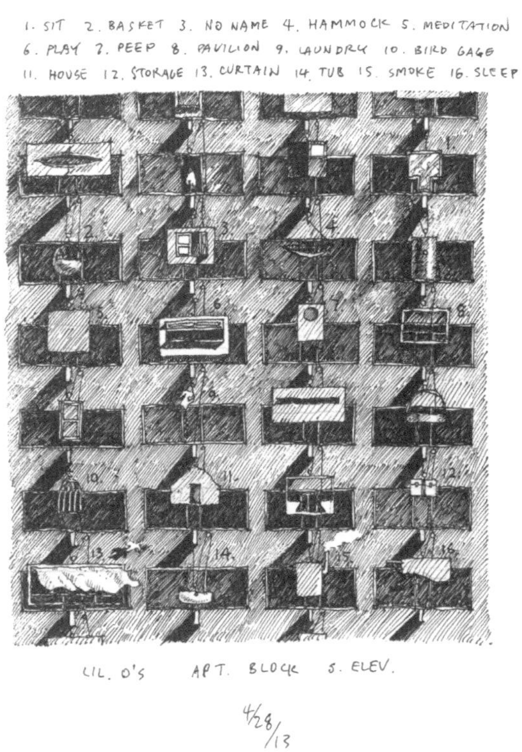

[EXPERIENCE of STORIES]

Little Detective Zumtobel

2017

History of a special annual report: The Austrian based lighting fixture company Zumbotel has a long tradition of inviting graphic designers, artists, and architects to create their annual reports. There is only one requirement: the artwork has to align with the concept of light and the book(s) also has to include the content of their annual report.

Little Detective looks for the annual report through light: We separate the artwork and the annual report into two books. Conceived as a sequel to the *Little Detective* graphic novel, the first volume is titled *The Little Detective: Search for the Book* and the second, *The Book: Zumtobel Group Annual Report 2016/17.* The two volumes are linked by a narrative. As the titles suggest, at the beginning of the art book, Little Detective is sent by his aunt to look for a book. He goes through a myriad of spaces, both indoor and outdoor, each with a unique lighting atmosphere. Finally, Little Detective switches on the light in a basement and finds the book, which is the second volume of the set—the annual report. The artwork is hand-drawn by Yung Ho Chang and interspersed with photographs of the built works of Atelier FCJZ. A case sleeve is designed in the spirit of an old Chinese book holder to contain the two books together.

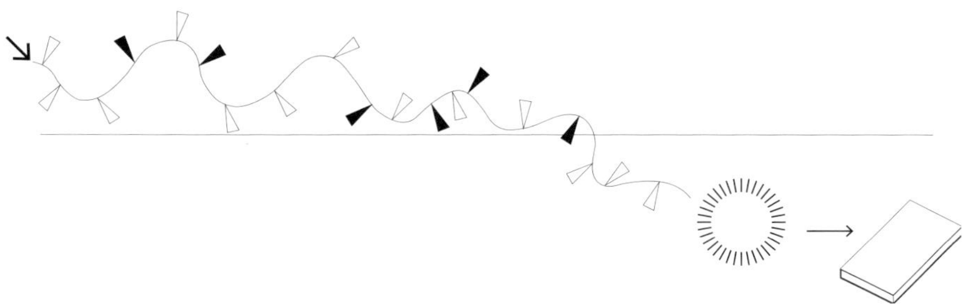

v Book case sleeve closed

v Book case sleeve opened to present the two volumes in the set: *The Little Detective: Search for the Book* (left) and The Book: *Zumtobel Group Annual Report 2016/17* (right)

v *The Little Detective: Search for the Book* flipped open

v Both books flipped open

Pages from *The Little Detective: Search for the Book*

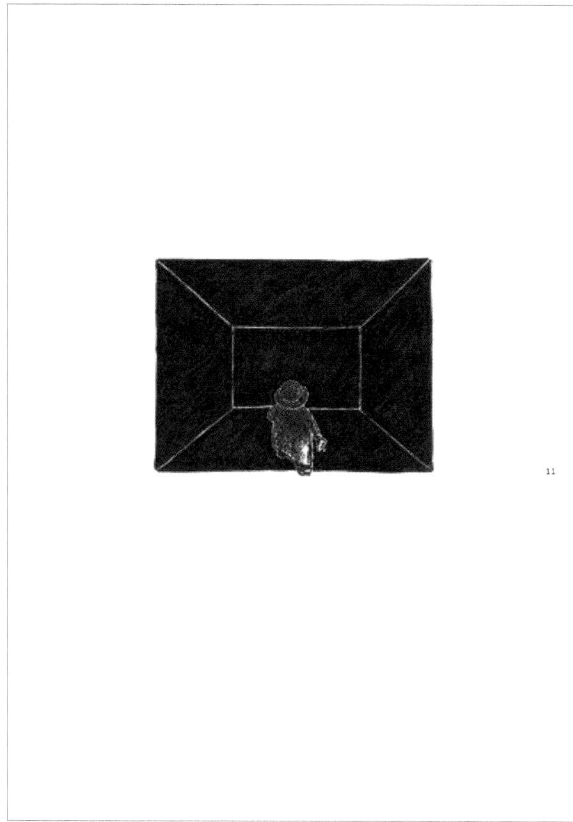

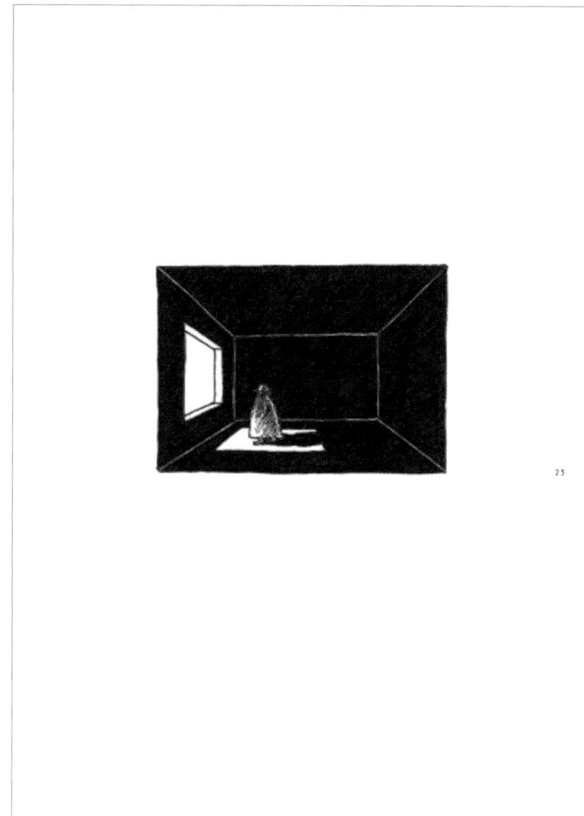

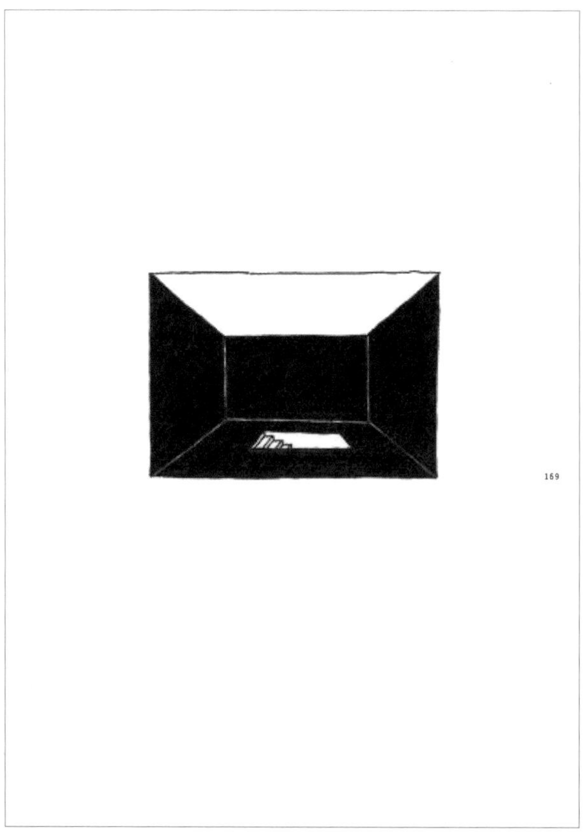

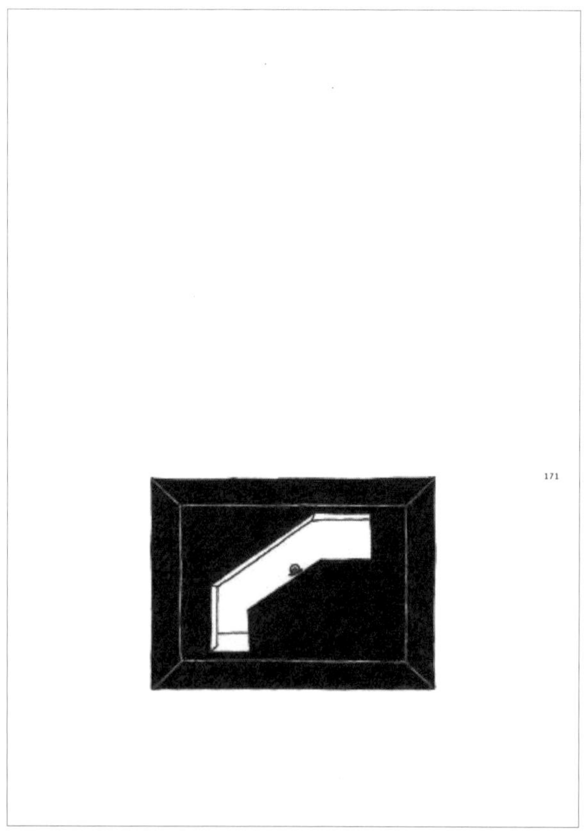

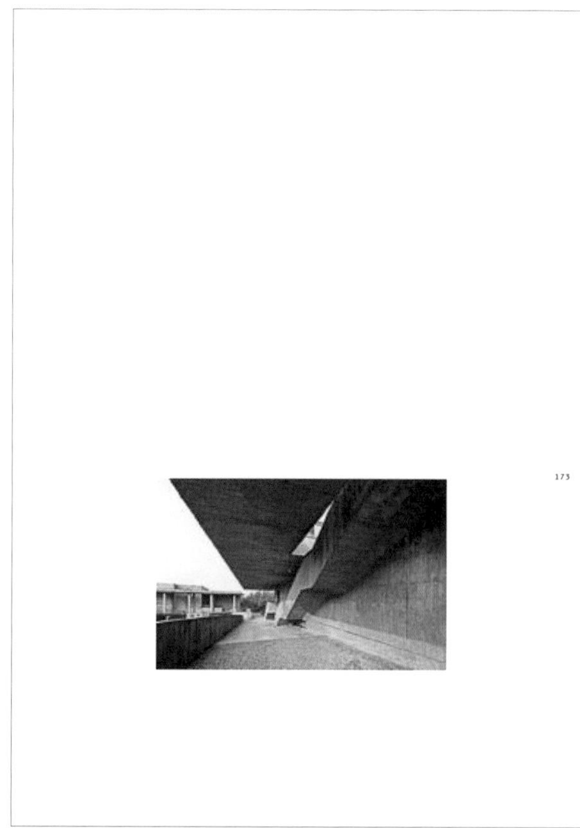

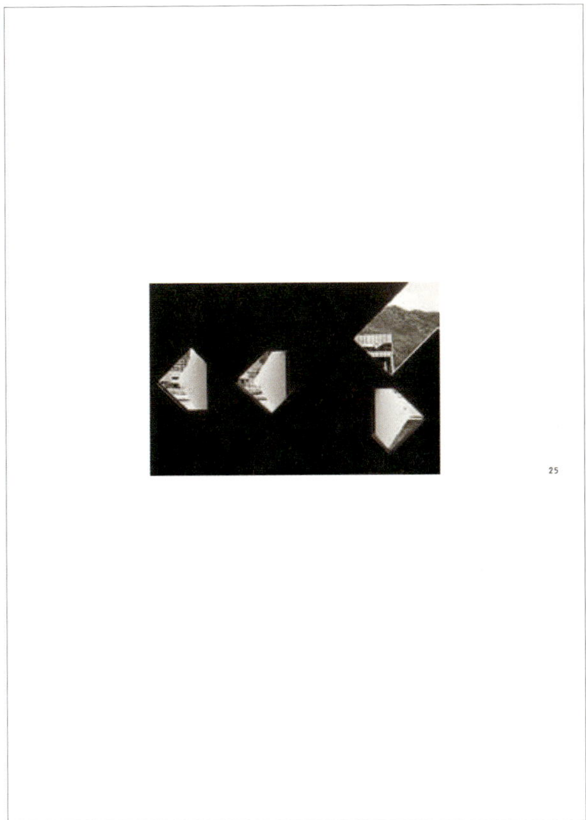

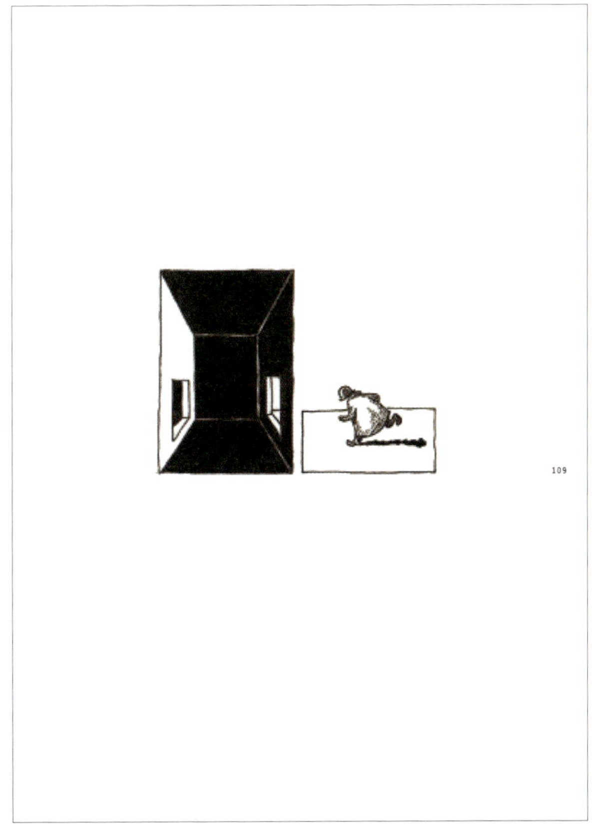

v Exhibition installation at Power Station of Art, Shanghai

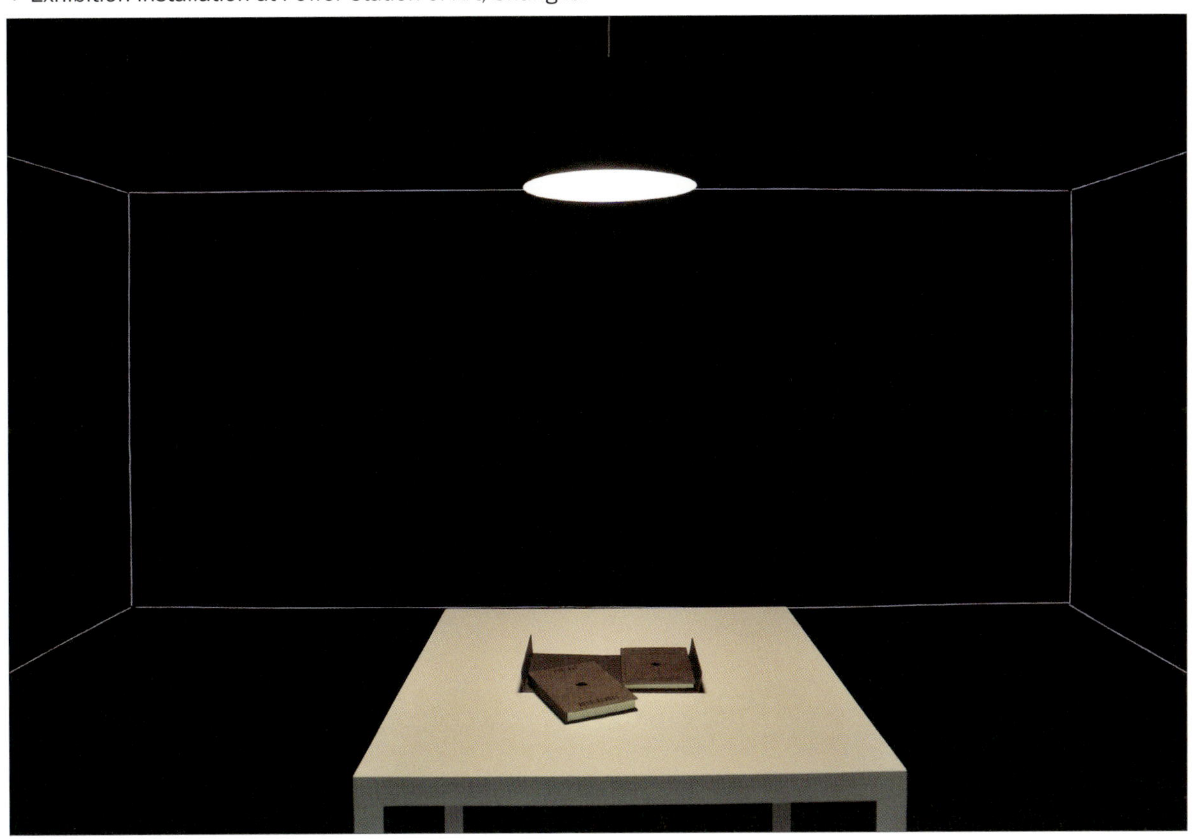

[EXPERIENCE of STORIES]

Forbidden City Cultural Relics Museum

Chongqing, China

2020

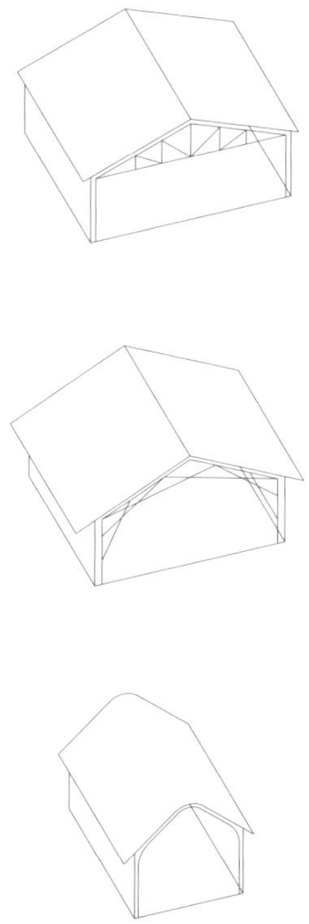

v The site by the Yangtze River

A history to be remembered: The project is located on a steep hillside on the southern bank of the Yangtze River, which courses through the city of Chongqing. In 1891, the Swedish trading company Andersen & Company began building offices and warehouses on the site. During the Japanese invasion, the treasures of the Forbidden City in Beijing had to be relocated to far south China. During their transit, they were kept under the protection of Anderson & Company and were retained in their storage holds for some time. Today, most buildings on the site are still standing, but are, unfortunately, in various degrees of deterioration.

Forbidden City returns: To commemorate that important event in history, the Forbidden City Museum in Beijing plans to open a branch facility on the old Andersen & Company site, consisting of a lecture hall, exhibition spaces, craft workshops, classes for children, and a design store and tearoom, among other facilities.

Restoration and more: Our work is unfolded along two parallel fronts:
1. Restore the existing buildings with traditional construction technologies, such as woodwork, rammed earth, and brick; and
2. Design new buildings that can be integrated into the historic complex.

We set the building section as the common denominator; that is, all buildings, old and new, should have a similar spatial configuration—specifically a rectilinear plan with a pitched roof. For the historic buildings, this translates to the sectional form being defined by wood frames and a clay-tiled roof. In some areas, where some parts of the existing timber structures were beyond repair, we reframed a single space, partly with the original wood trusses that could be saved, and partly with a contemporary timber bracket system. For the new buildings, the common section is shaped with bent steel frame and roofed with slates. Ultimately, what we strove for was for visitors to experience the changes of architecture and the continuation of time, from 1891 to present day.

COMMENTS

Rahul Mehrotra
Professor, Graduate School of Design, Harvard University
Founder Principal, RMA Architects (Rahul Mehrotra Architects)

What's particularly striking is how you have used the section to weave the historic and contemporary together through a skillfully articulated circulation system as well as the relationships of the roof forms. The subtleties in terms of the differences in the roof form as well as material, while maintaining the overall integrity of the contemporary additions and simultaneously reinforcing the historic skyline, makes it a stunningly beautiful intervention.

> View of the entire museum complex

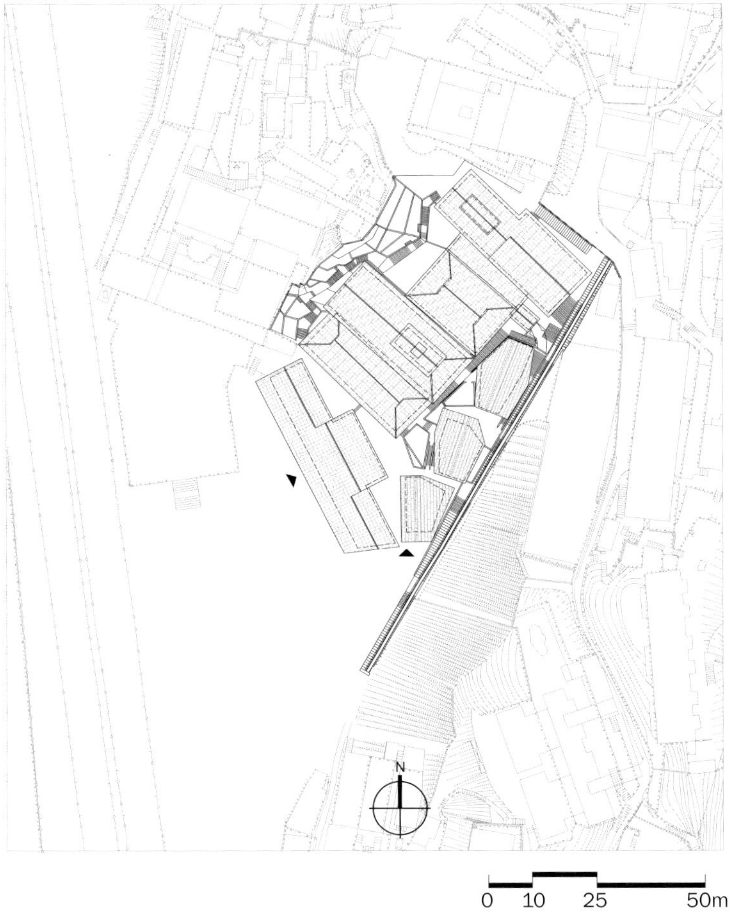

Site plan

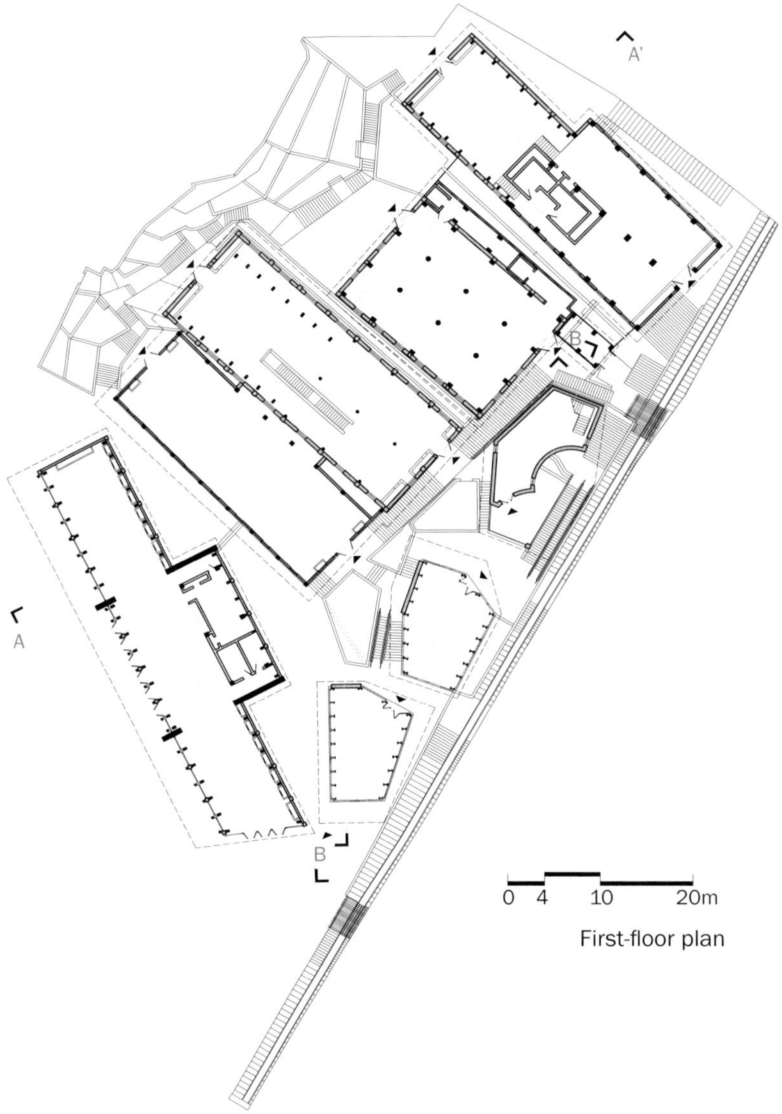

First-floor plan

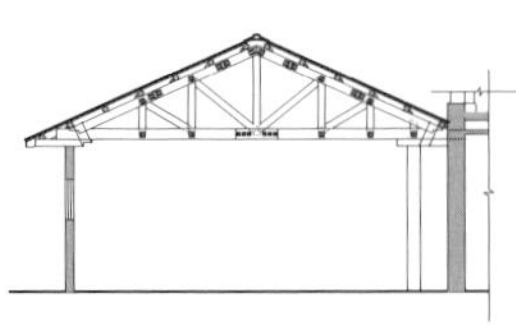

Preserved structure 1

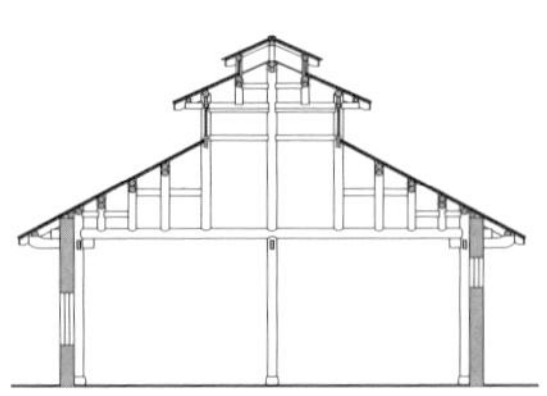

Preserved structure 2

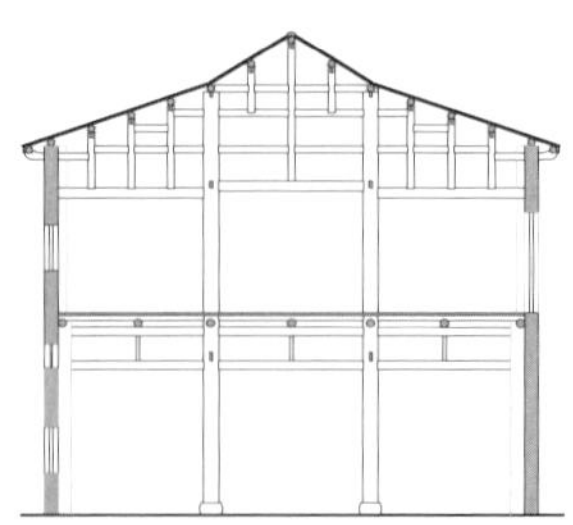

Preserved structure 3

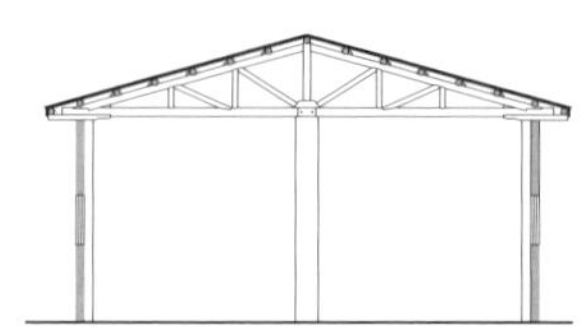

Preserved structure 4

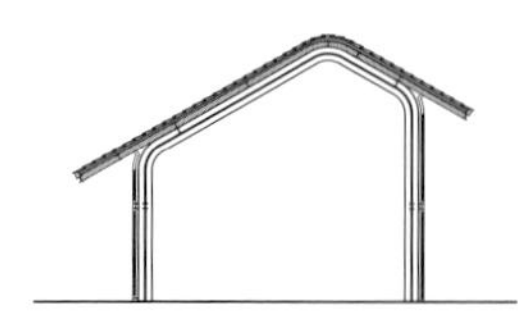

Steel structure

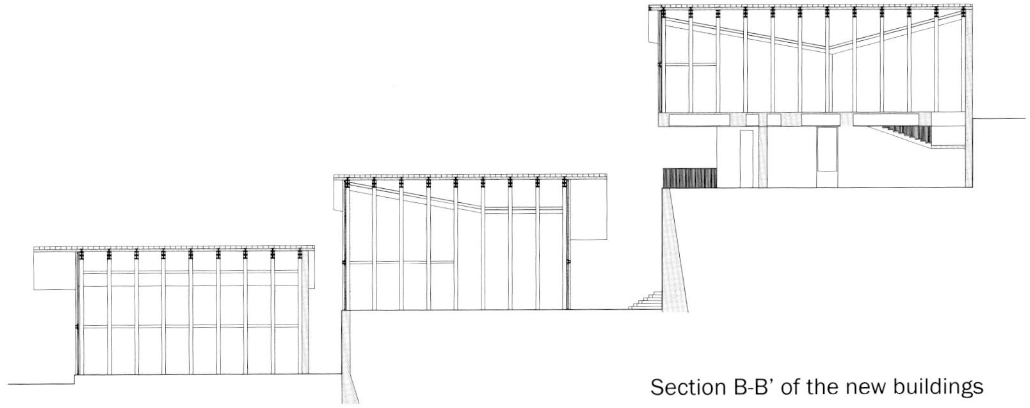

Section B-B' of the new buildings

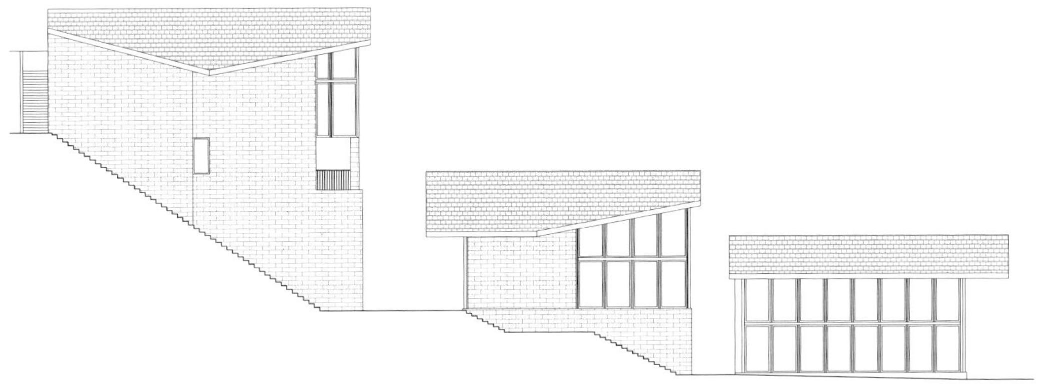

Elevations of the new buildings

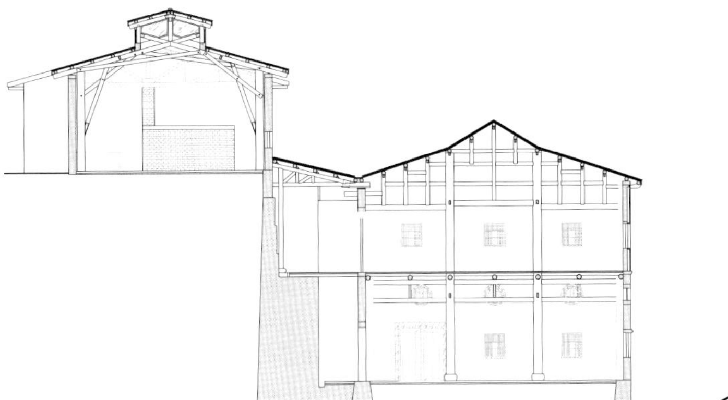

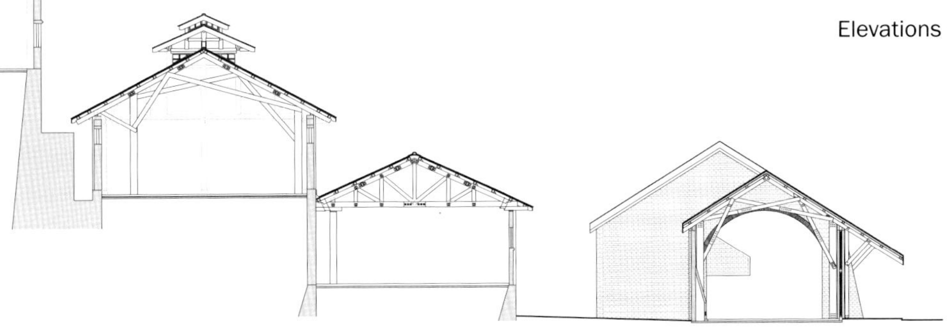

Section A-A' of the preserved and renovated buildings

0 4 10 20m

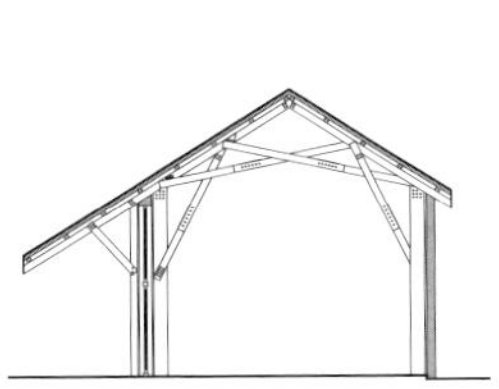

Wood truss structure 1

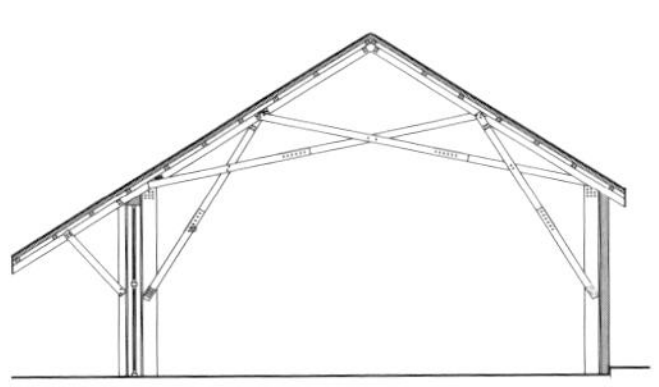

Wood truss structure 2

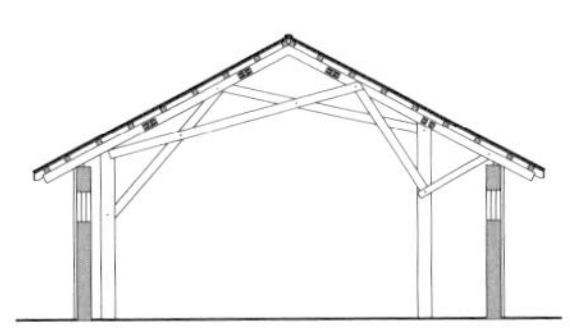

Wood truss structure 3

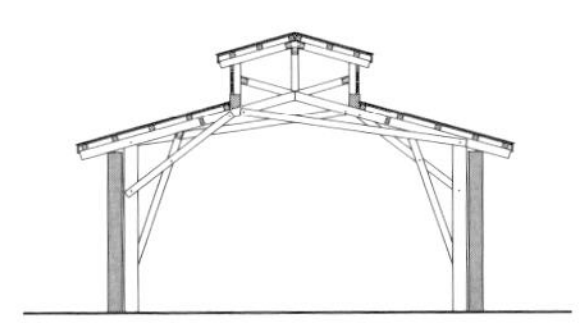

Wood truss structure 4

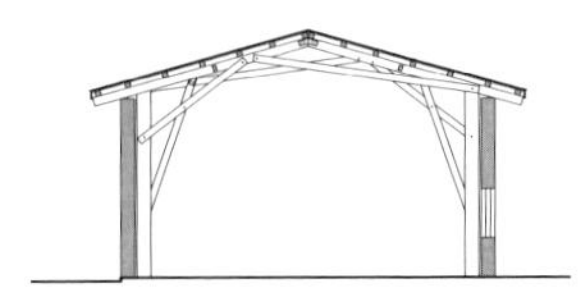

Wood truss structure 5

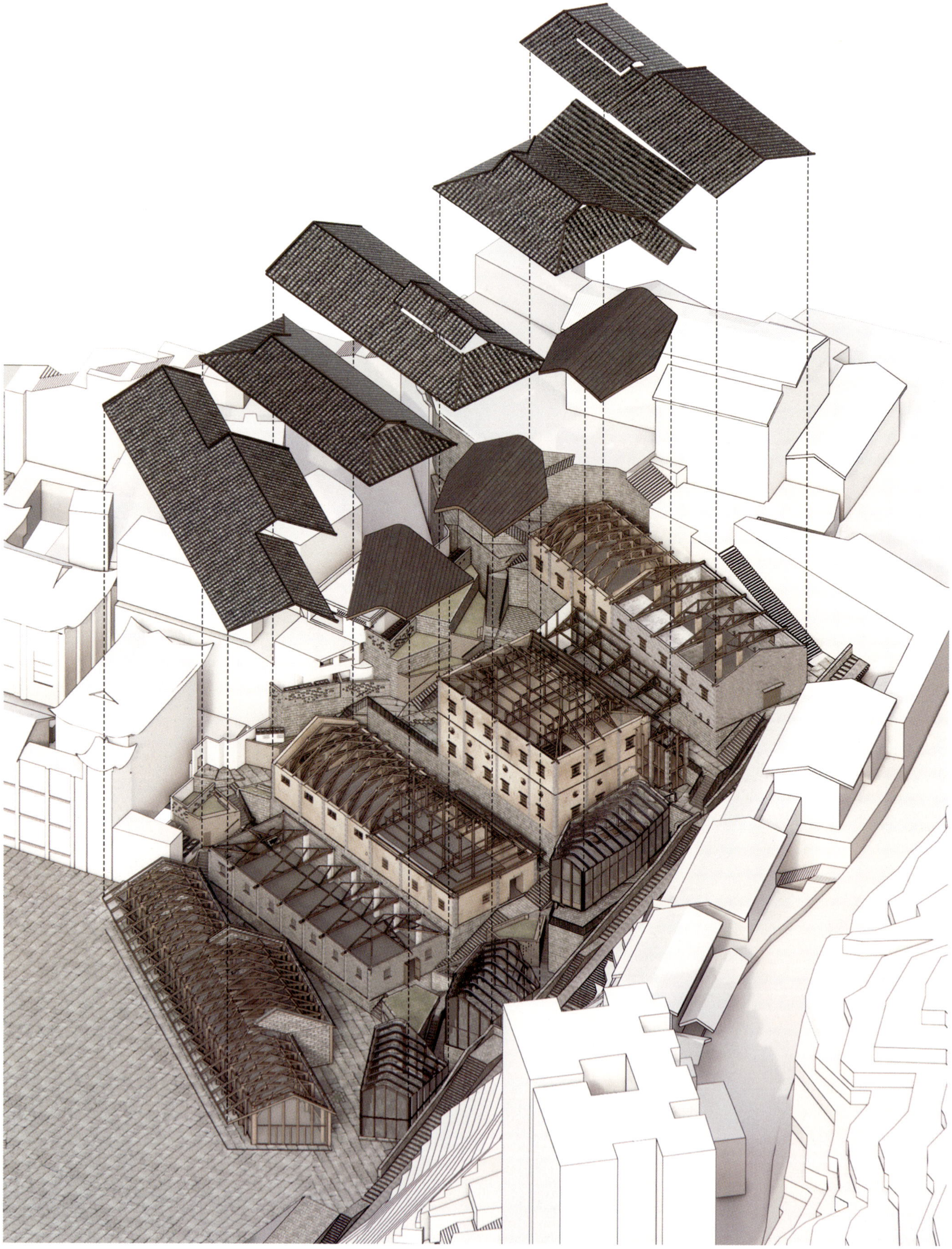

< Exploded axonometric

Slate tile roof

v Old and new roofs

> Buildings follow the hillside

View from the square in front

v Space under the eaves

< Preserved building—rebuilding the damaged structure with wood trusses

Original state of a preserved building

v Exhibitions in a preserved building

v Building No. 6: new building—steel curved frame

[EXPERIENCE of TIME and SPACE]

Seven Sages of the Bamboo Grove

Beijing, China

2015

The play: *Seven Sages of the Bamboo Grove* is a play that is a contemporary reinterpretation of a legend from the Chinese Wei-Jin period (220–420 AD) and tells the story of seven free-spirited literati.

A conceptual theater: Scaffoldings, which can be perceived either as the bamboo grove or as the columns in the palaces, are employed to build a highly abstract theater that opens on all four sides. On the top of the scaffolding frame are hoisted all stage props—mountains, clouds, a moon for the bamboo grove scene, and pitched roofs and folding screens for the palace scene—so that they can be lowered and raised for different scenes as the acts play out.

One piece of garment for all: All costumes are made from polypropylene fabric. Each robe is a piece of fabric rolled into a tube with multiple cuts in different places, which allows the actors to wear them in creative ways. Based on the clan that they belonged to in the story, the characters dress in either white, black, or red robes. Complex, main roles are given double layers of costumes; for example, a black outer layer on top of a red inner layer, or a white robe over a black one.

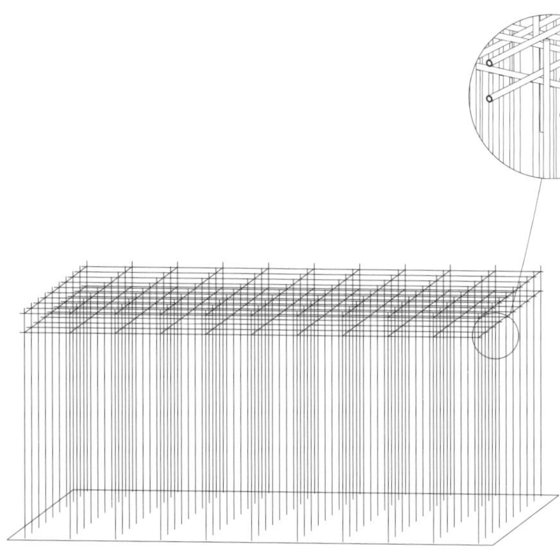

v Sketches for stage and prop design by Yung Ho Chang

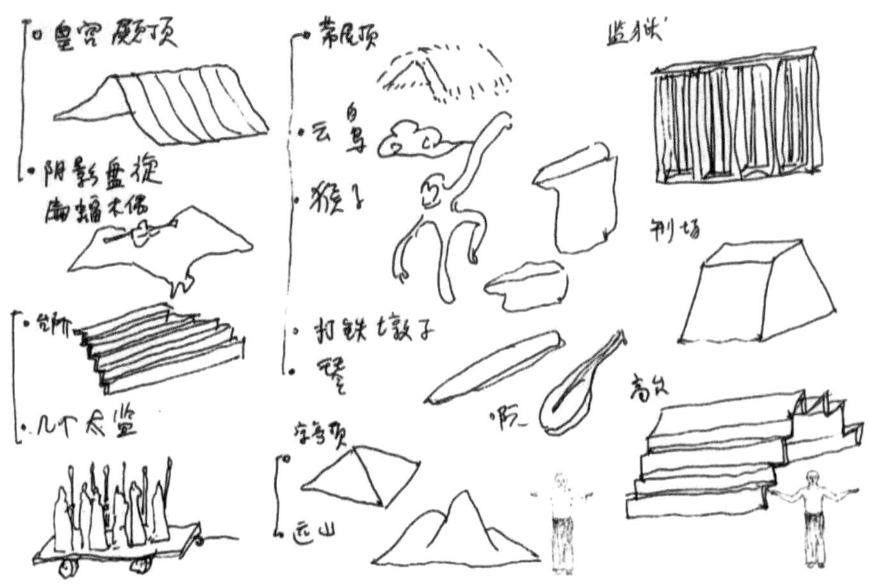

> During performance

1 < 1 Palace scene

2 < 2 Mountain scene

Conceptual sketches by Linmiao Zhang: tube with random cuts

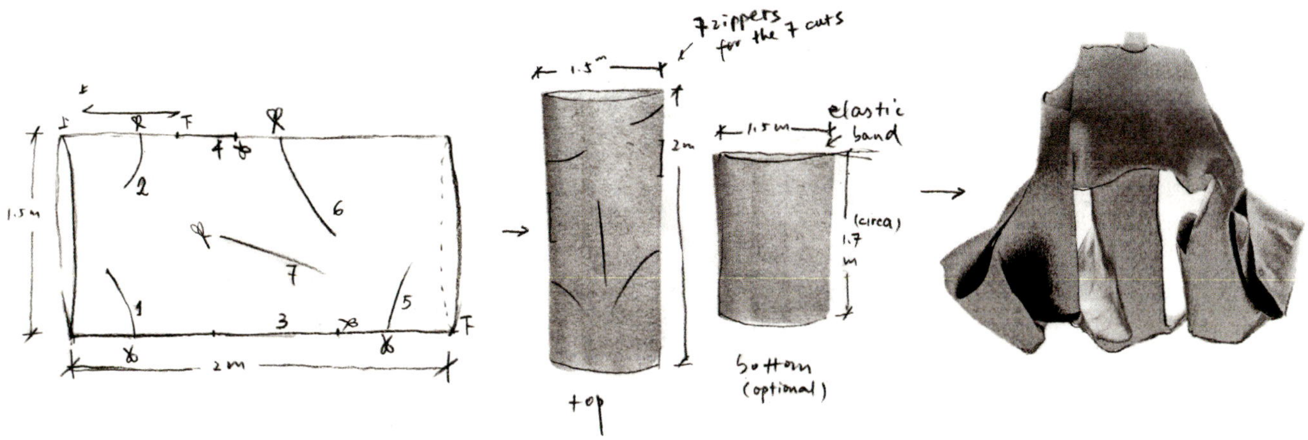

Costume design for the seven sages

v Close-ups of costumes worn by actors

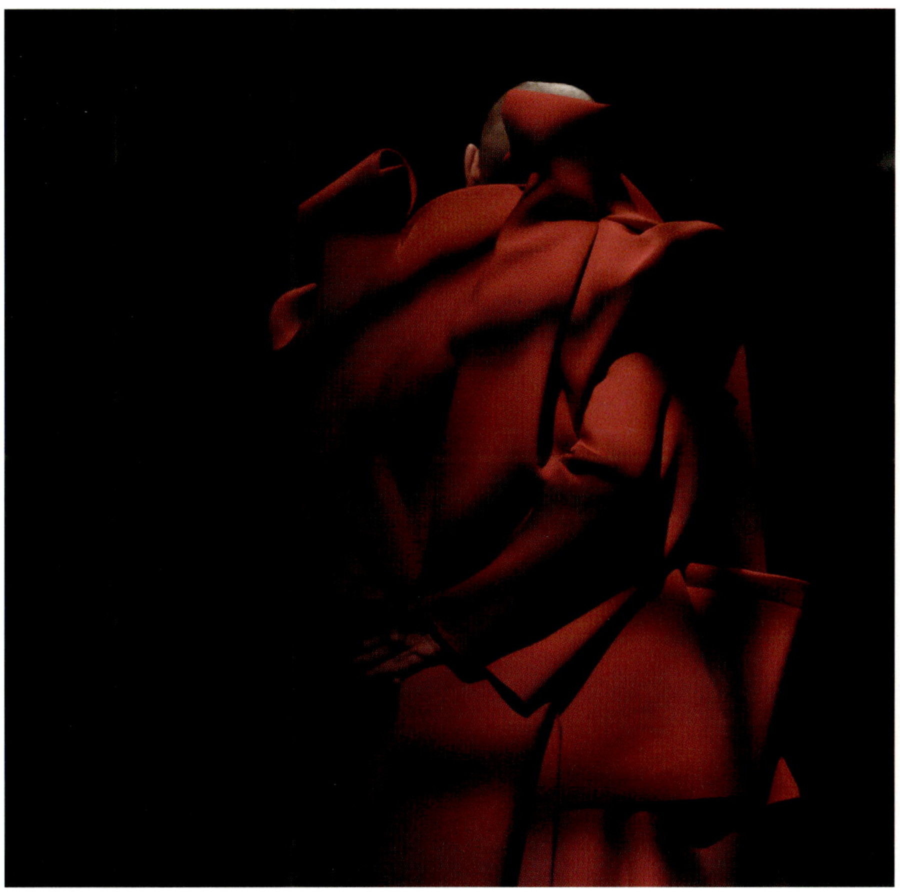

[EXPERIENCE of TIME and SPACE]

No Name Art Museum

Wuzhen, Zhejiang Province, China

2022

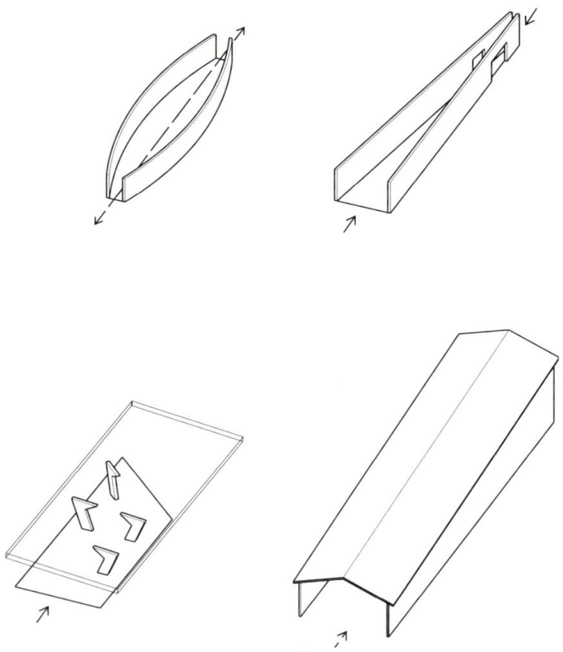

v Painting by Wu Dayu

v Wu Dayu's $10m^2$ studio

v $10m^2$ exhibition attic in No Name Art Museum

Our architectural design is influenced by Wu Dayu's paintings and poems.

Time: Wu's poem inspires us to explore the temporal dimension of architecture. Can time be designed?

Using French philosopher François Jullien's book, *On Time*, as a theoretical guideline, we compare the time of China and Europe.

The classic Western time—the observer is without time; time and space are separated; time is evenly paced, dividable, and one-directional, with a beginning and an end. Past and future are clearly defined but not present. This is the objective time.

The traditional Chinese time—the observer is within time; time and space cannot be separated; time varies, is continuous, and oncoming, without beginning and end. This time is always present and can be named as the subject time. The elasticity of Chinese time offers design possibilities.

The case of Bridge with Nine Bends—if a body of water can be crossed with three steps, with a nine-bend bridge, it may take twenty-seven steps, which means the time is nine times longer, and so consequently, the space feels much larger.

Here, we attempt to combine the Chinese and Western time. Both programed and pure spaces are stretched by perspective in one direction and compressed in the other. Thus, the temporal-spatial perception changes more dramatically with every move of the visitor. It demonstrates the immeasurability of time and space and enriches the experience to the point where one may get lost and embark on a journey of discovery. No Name Art Museum is a playground of space and time.

Space: The essence of an art museum is to provide a *you* or wandering experience. Therefore, besides perspectival manipulation, we introduce the concept of "pure architectural space"—a series of outdoor or semi-outdoor spaces serving as transitions among programs. They are configured to possess tensions, intensifying the temporal and spatial dynamics during the journey through the architecture. The overall spatial structure of this building complex is arranged in *yuan* (courtyards) and *jin* (layers), generating a dialogue with Chinese architectural traditions, while overlaying another layer of experience onto the perspectival play.

Form: Paying attention to time—space experiences allows us a break away from static compositions; which means the formal relationship between stereoscopic volumes and planar elevations are dissolved.

Structure: Partly beamless concrete slabs with irregularly shaped columns, and partly steel frames.

Regional culture and material: Besides space, we also pay tribute in our design to the vernacular architecture in Wuzhen, in terms of material and color. Hence, using clay roof tiles on the wall surfaces as well as exposing concrete cast-on-site with wood formworks constitute a rich and subtle color scheme of shades of gray.

> Bent Court

> Bird's-eye view

Wu Dayu's poem, *King Kong*, vividly portrays the dynamics and volatility of architectural experience.

Shadow wants to fool figure

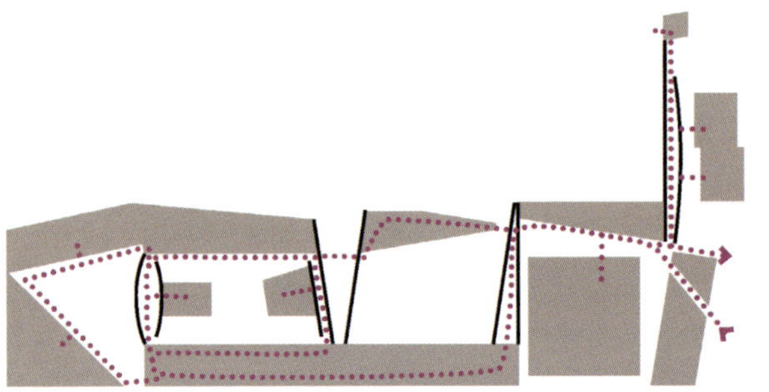

Time is laughing at space

With no sound and no trace

I come in and out of the darkness of time

Same wall, different perceptions

COMMENTS

Li Xiangning
Architectural critic and curator
Dean and professor, College of Architecture and Urban Planning, Tongji University

I have always thought of Atelier FCJZ's plan design as the most elegant among that of Chinese architects. From the rigorous and in-depth study on microcity of Morningside Center for Mathematics, to the conceptualization of the functionality and frugality of minimalist living in Vertical Glass House, in the control rationalistic and modularized rhythm has always been exactly where the beauty of FCJZ's works lie. However, with this project, FCJZ may have veered from its usual path, touching the edge and breaking the shackles of modernism.

Looking at Wu Dayu's paintings, we can easily find the same colors and lines of Henri Matisse's work from his Nice period. The bright and animated color blocks completely break away from a priori formal principles. In designing No Name Art Museum, located in a small township in southern China, it is impossible not to be influenced by the moist architectural aura typical of the Jiangnan area, as well as by the transparent artistic tendency of the paintings to be presented in the venue. How should architecture respond to these challenges?

One-story buildings, like this one, are particularly rare among FCJZ's work; in fact, this building does not show the rhythmic sense and logical norms produced by the repetition of floors in multiple-story buildings and because of this, it simply enjoys a very rare freedom of expression. The basic architectural component shows how FCJZ seems to be mesmerized by pure spatial elements; that is, small-scale prototypical forms, such as the box space, the see-through corridor, the camera obscura-like cone-shaped space, and the mono-pitched linear buildings. To draw a parallel—if Hejduk's "Masques" architectural installations have succeeded in connecting small spatial units through a rational system of grid, then Atelier FCJZ's floor plans have been able to go beyond Louis Kahn's Richards Medical Research Laboratories' division between service and serviced space, and even to bestow a privileged sacred role on the corridors connecting these microspatial units. While having the double identity of "functional" and "transitional," the corridors in No Name Art Museum have elevated to a pure spaces. The corridor is not only the spatial soul connecting and surroundings, but has also become a multifunctional open field—all kinds of activities, looking, moving, resting, entertaining, breathing, and meditating may happen within.

In the same way, the rationalistic expression of structures and materials—which, in the past, FCJZ has proven to be particularly skilled at—has been extremely constrained. Following the continuous changes of space and site in depth and perspective, architectural outdoor space has acquired—in a tangible way—a random spatial characteristic and improvised structure, in a fashion very similar to the matches dropping by and dispersing of the land artist Michael Heizer. Once abandoning, the rationality of the column grid and the limitation of modularity, the concrete columns of irregular shapes together with the very few and well-hidden steel framework structures offer the architectural plan surface the possibility to stretch out freely.

In this art museum, the natural color traits and atmosphere of southern China architecture and the ever-changing dynamic space created by Atelier FCJZ, as well as the brightly colored paintings by artist Wu Dayu mingle together, flying in the air.

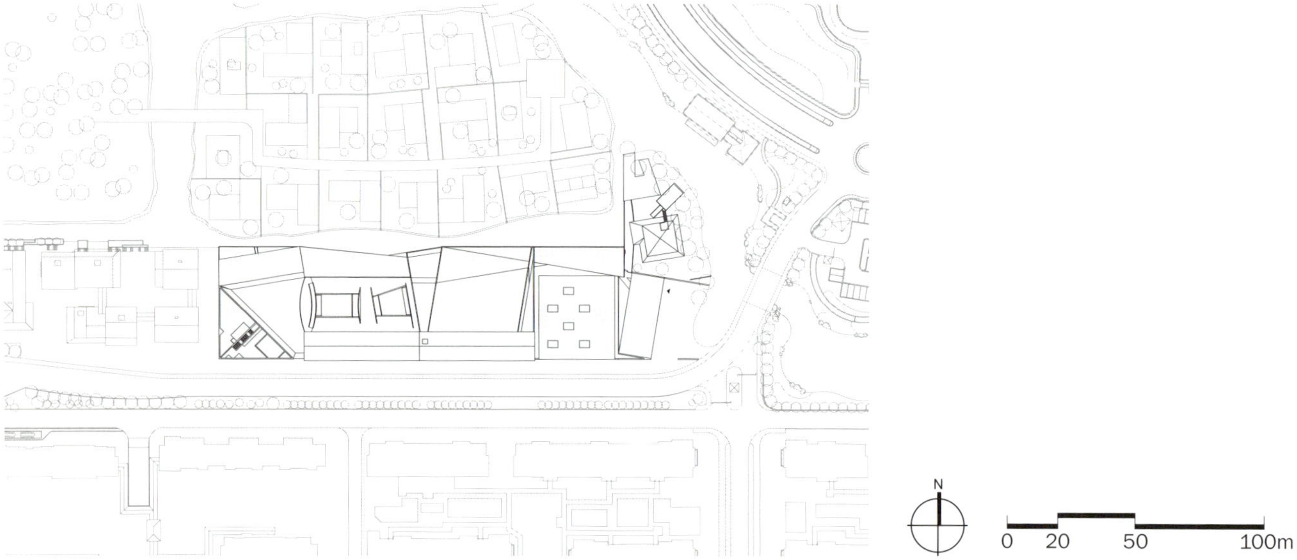

Site plan

v A composition of perspectival spaces

1 Reception and shops
2 Galleries
3 Office
4 Courtyard
5 Teahouse
6 Studios-residence
7 Commerce
8 Hotel rooms
9 Perspectival corridor
10 Multifunction hall

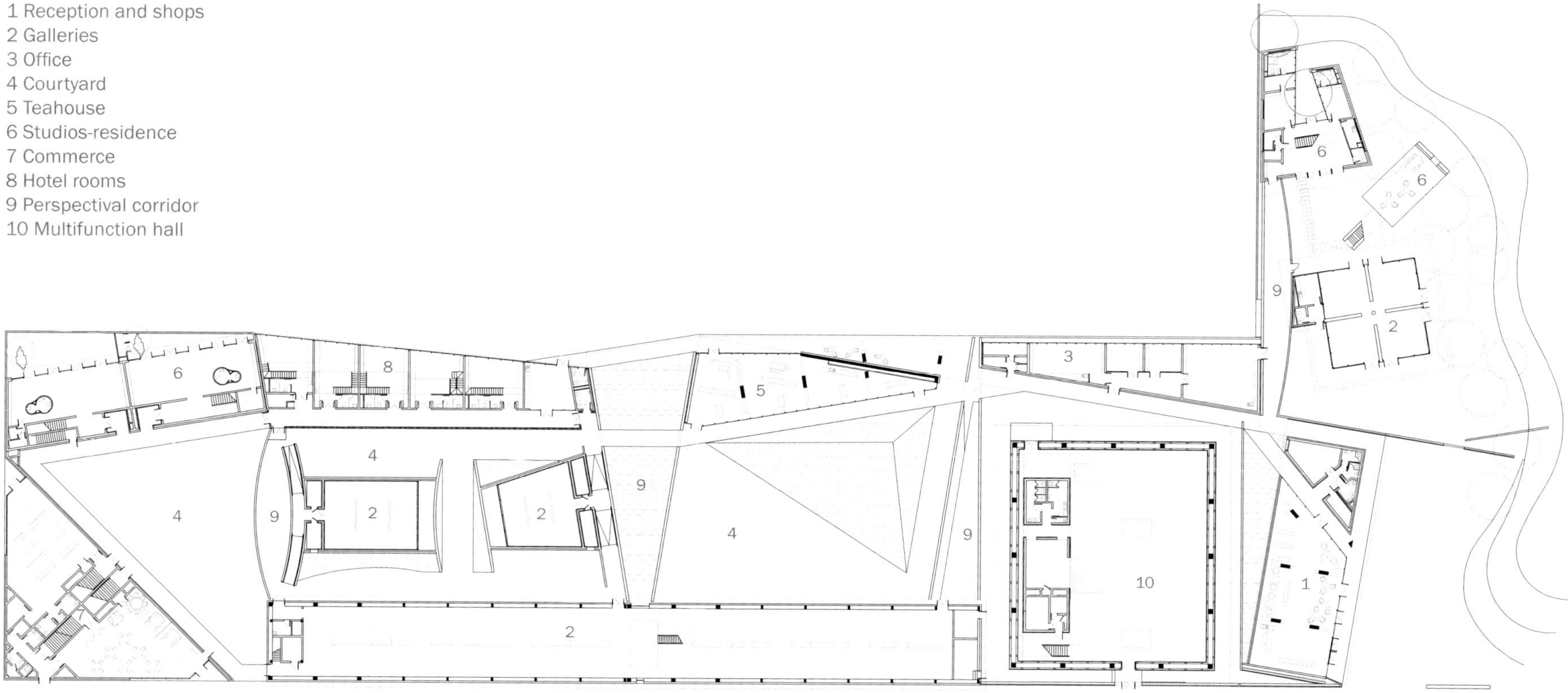

First-floor plan

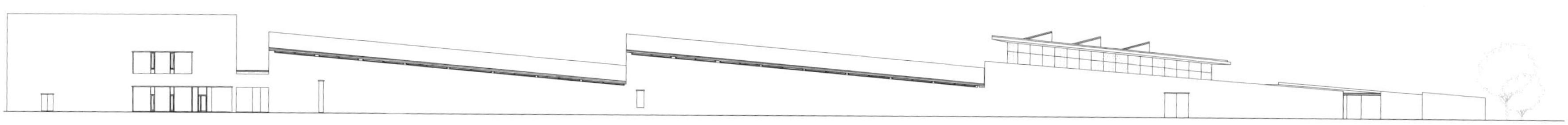

South elevation

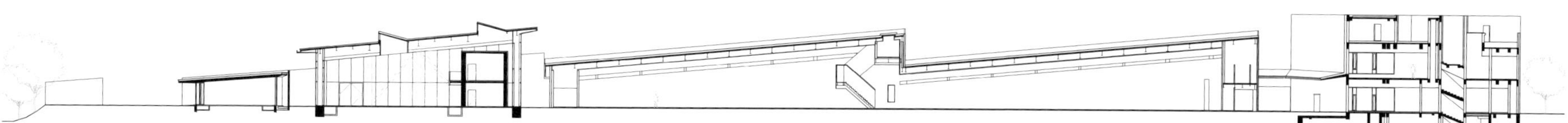

Section

0 10 25 50m

> Bird's-eye view of artist's studios-residence and multifunction hall

Crescent Passage

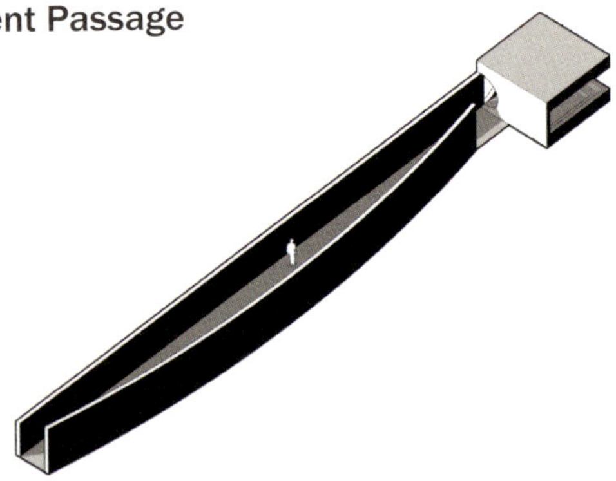

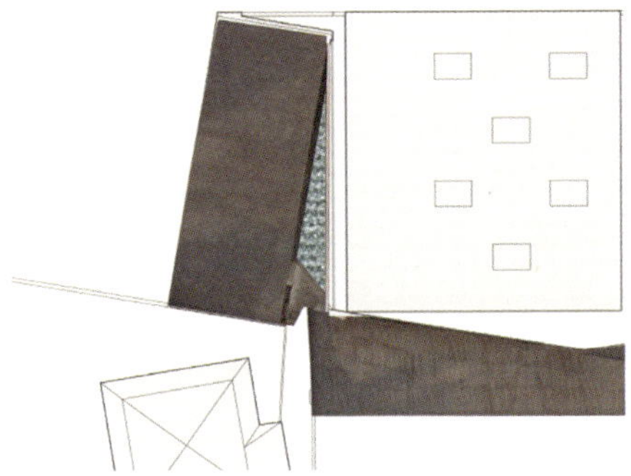

Water Triangle

Water Triangle
(waterscape to be constructed)

v Overlooking the Crescent Passage

< Between multifunction hall and offices

Sunlight filters in through the Wedge Passage

Wedge Passage

∨ Art gallery main entrance at one end of the Wedge Passage; a slit between the roof and wall brings in natural light

∨ An open cut-out at the riverside end of the Wedge Passage

Water Court

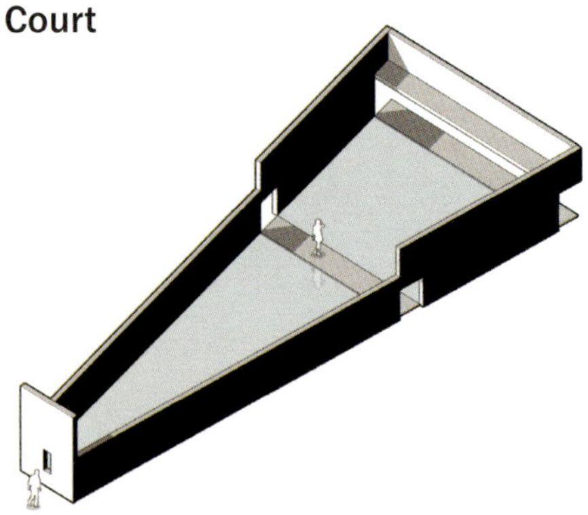

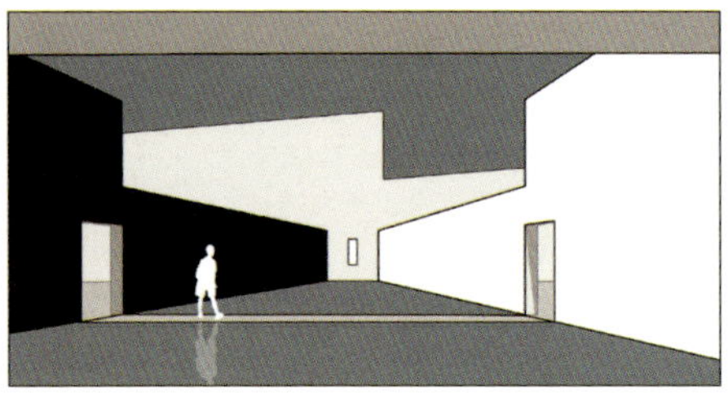

Footpath along the riverbank

v Water Court (waterscape to be constructed)

Spindle Court

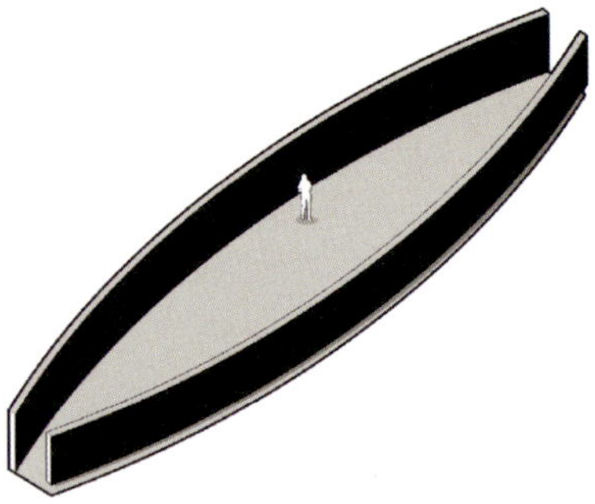

Overlooking the Spindle Court

v A dark space converges with a light one

1	3
2	4

< 1 Interior of shop at the reception
< 2 Structural system of concrete slab with irregularly shaped columns
< 3 Interior of multifunction hall
< 4 Interior of galleries

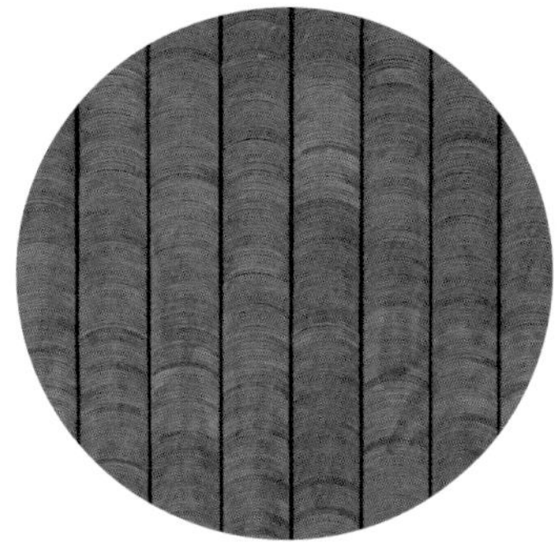

Tile wall cladding

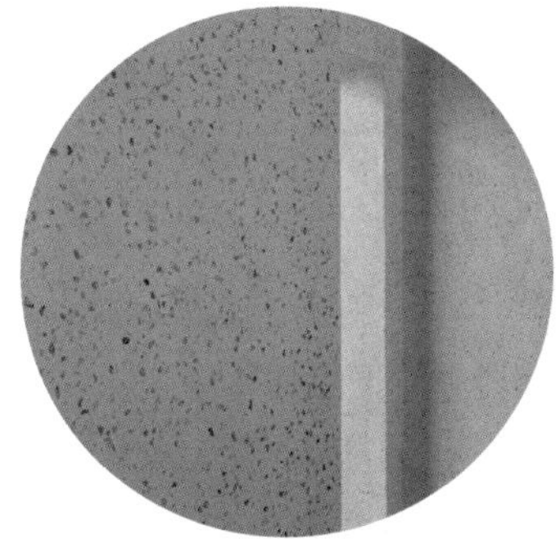

Plaster with broken shells

Tile-louvre wall

v Different materials form a variety of textures

POOL followed Yung Ho Chang and Lijia Lu around as they were in town on April 20, 2019, for a lecture at UCLA (University of California, Los Angeles). We went to the Art Center (College of Design), Norton Simon Museum, Gamble House, Schindler House, and Samitaur Tower in Culver City. Chang shared with us his insights on the topic of nostalgia, and the notion of constructing his own "castle" of interest, aesthetics, and knowledge.

A Day with Yung Ho Chang

Part 1: Art Center College of Design

POOL: I want to talk to you about nostalgia, the theme of our upcoming issue. In my opinion, in Chinese culture, the closest notion to that is probably something of homesickness. We can also talk about homesickness or nostalgia, if you like.

Yung Ho: What we are talking about is actually quite interesting. In Chinese, *xiangchou* (homesickness) immediately defines this issue in one way. But if you were to say nostalgia in English, the topic is defined in a totally different way. In fact, if someone wants to address the subject directly when asked, he has to convert the way he normally thinks into the linguistic system of this subject. However, I would like to try not to convert. Of course, you will be the judge to see if it works; if you sense "homesickness" or "nostalgia" [in] my response, then fine. If you don't think there is any element of "nostalgia," then that is fine too. But I wouldn't judge, because I've never thought about the topic; I don't even know where to start.

In my younger days, I formed an understanding of the world, which had been slowly but constantly evolving to where I am and [what] my views [are] now. The day before yesterday was my birthday; April 18; I am 63 years old. Now, I do have a tendency of looking back, but it doesn't mean that I used to be a futurist, and I may never be. This has to do a bit with watching movies, which is easy to explain. Let's say Stanley Kubrick's *2001: A Space Odyssey* is like constructing a plastic future. The material is not the concern but the newness is. This newness suggests a future without history. If this is the future, I have no interest in partaking in it. However, on the contrary, I am in line with *Blade Runner*'s future, which is older, dirtier, and more broken than the present. If that were so, would there be something in there that we don't have right now? For example, flight vehicles, androids, [etc]. This future, I can imagine and understand. In fact, the more we go forward, the older the world becomes. It is more interesting for me to look back. This has something to do with the fact that I like literature and art.

Let's still talk about movies first. It's not that there aren't good movies anymore, but there aren't any that make a breakthrough. I think radical movies were gone by the 1970s. Jean-Luc Godard had asked, "What is cinema?" To him, there was a definition. His definition was not that different from the ones before, but he stripped away all the complexity about cinema. [According] to him, "To make a movie is to put something in front of the camera." This thing can be an actor, a prop—[it] makes no difference. Acting, story—they all got thrown out in this definition. His logic is kind of funny: the lens, the camera—those were there first. Other directors, like François Roland Truffaut [and] Alain Resnais—their works we don't need to judge; at the end of a hard day's work, we don't want to watch something so painful anyway. Yet, Resnais's *Hiroshima mon Amour*—I did watch it seven times, not that I wanted to watch it over and over. I watched [it] seven times to see a whole movie

1 Still from the film *Last Year at Marienbad*

2 Still from the film *La Jetée*

once. Since I dozed off every time. I used to be quite diligent when I was young.

I first read the script of Marguerite Duras's in English. After reading it, I still felt insatiable, because Duras used simple sentences, like "This is a man. That is a woman;" I suspected that the original French version should not be that difficult, so I bought a French script and compared it with the English one. It was indeed not difficult. The literary approach of this film required the actor not to perform and express no feelings; just read like an off-screen narrator. The woman said, "I have seen it." The man said, "You have not seen anything." They were talking back and forth in this manner. The literalness emphasized by the film was not just a concept but also conveyed through the imagery, such as the documentary of the Hiroshima atomic bombing. It was an idea realized. It was revolutionary.

Now, let's talk about *Last Year at Marienbad* (image 1). The title of the movie is particularly important: "Last Year"—a specific time; Marienbad ("*bad*" means bath in German)—a specific place. You have to watch this film. It starts by giving you a clear notion of time and place. Bit by bit, that clarity is being undermined visually. By the end, you are no longer sure if it happened last year, or where? It's not a really difficult movie to watch, although very slow. It's not entertainment, so you may not enjoy it, but you won't forget it. Once again, it is a piece of revolutionary and groundbreaking work. To introduce uncertainty to people's perception of space and time is exactly what we are doing now with No Name Art Museum.

I will give you another example. (It seems now I am only talking about movies.) Chris Marker's *La Jetée* (image 2). This is an extreme example, but being extreme is not a problem, as long as he realized and clearly presented it; and that is great. Marker has a totally different understanding of the cinema than that of the New Wave directors. The entire [movie], *La Jetée*, is a set of photos, completely still. Someone once told me that at the end, there was a blink of an eye; one motion. I have seen the movie five or six times now, but I [have not seen] it. I don't really agree with the Chinese translation of this movie title, [which reads as] "Embankment." *La Jetée* is actually the observation deck on the roof of an airport terminal, where you watch the planes take off and land. There was an incident at the beginning and one person was narrating. Then, he was lying in a hospital bed, being treated and so on. In short, you listen to him up till the end to discover the incident, which was in fact [the] incident where "I" (he) was assassinated. So, the whole story was told after his death, and entirely by still photos, one frame after another; super static. This is probably an easy film to watch, unlike those of New Wave cinema, which can be very tedious.

I like such things very much. I use movies only as an example. We are, after all, at the Art Center, it would be a more appropriate setting to talk about furniture design, car design, and, of course, fashion design. Fashion is about how people wear clothes and the impact they have on people's behavior. If you wear casual clothes, like what we are wearing today, you can just sit down wherever with no concern of etiquette. Some professors at Princeton [University] conducted research on the decline of civilization, and their example was the United Kingdom. If you accept that the phenomenon which they described does exist, I would look no further than Italian TV. I do not understand Italian, and don't need to, since the vulgarity, and even obscenity, is all there—that is to say, from media itself, we can see the fall of Italian civilization. I feel that the Italian case is even worse than the British one [the professors] studied. Maybe this research can make sense of why I have a good impression of things before the 1970s. Otherwise, I am just a person who likes to watch movies; a person who enjoys design, architecture, furniture, and all kinds of things. And I like all sorts of things that happen to be old, and they are from different eras.

***POOL**: But it is not out of nostalgia that you talk about them.*

Yung Ho: It is not. I was born in Beijing in 1956 and never experienced some of the older eras that I am interested in now. Nostalgia implies that I was once like that but I am no longer like that, and so I long for that state. But not me, I have never experienced them before. For example, in 1983 or '84, I discovered The Beatles, whose music was brand new to me. I didn't realize that their music was from the '60s, since [only] I came to United States in 1981. Anyway, I liked their music very much, not because it's old, but because it's totally new, for me. So it is like that; I keep discovering these things of the past, so sometimes I do feel a confusion of time.

It's also like listening to Bach's music. I feel so tremendously happy when listening to it that I can't help but to think: [Could] this not [have been] written for someone like me? But it was composed three hundred years ago as religious music in the church? *[laughter]* I also think that the harpsichord is quite interesting; it is considered to be the predecessor of the piano, to [a] certain extent. Recently, I was listening to the contemporary adaptation of Renaissance lute music on the guitar. I'm now curious about the sound of the lute. What is more fascinating is the fact that in the postmodern era we are living in today, a person can choose to play a 500-year-old music, which means that you may choose your own time to live in. Because we did not choose the year we were born, that year has something and nothing to do with us. The world I am describing to you now is constructed with a little bit of music and a little bit of film. And it is completely my own. The time inside this world is convoluted, which is okay. [The] Belgian graphic novelist, François Schuiten, was labeled a futurist, which is inaccurate. The clothes worn by the people in his fictional city are from the Renaissance era; the architecture is art deco, a tradition of Brussels, many designed by architect Victor Horta; and the flying vessels belong to the future. That's the way it is.

***POOL**: A world one edits for oneself.*

Yung Ho: Totally fabricated, but ingenious.

Part 2: Norton Simon Museum

We were separated in the museum, looking at exhibitions on our own. Yung Ho found POOL and said [that] there were a couple of paintings he [wanted] to show us, which maybe would help us understand what he meant by constructing his own timeline of the world.

Yung Ho: Someone asked me yesterday about my experience in the East and West. I can't talk about it in any coherent way. Moving between the East and West has been my experience, whether I like it or not, and I can't change it. However, it has [had] a profound influence on me. As a matter of fact, there are paintings in this very museum that constitute part of my experience.

(Yung Ho took us to Allegory of Virtue and Nobility (image 3) by Giovanni Battista Tiepolo.)

This is a ceiling fresco by the eighteenth-century Italian painter Tiepolo. I had a teacher who was a South African Englishman. His name is Rodney Place. Rodney once asked me why Tiepolo was so good at painting figures, such as flying angels, from a lower angle. He didn't give an answer. Only much later, I figured out the answer to that question. The city where he painted in would have been in Italy, it [was] probably Venice. Of course, it was in Venice!

(walked over to check)

Why would I believe so? Only in Venice there are canals, and people sitting on the boats would look up and see the people on the sidewalk from a lower angle. Tiepolo knew more about how people look from below than other artists because he had seen it with his own eyes. My teacher gave me a lesson by asking this question, and I will remember it for the rest of my life. A few artists from the Early Renaissance period are also part of [this] castle of mine, which I have been slowly building over the years. Of course, architecture or things related to architecture, like perspective, are part of this castle. There are also things that don't have any relationship with architecture. It just keeps accumulating. I think the most empowering thing is to keep absorbing the culture of at least the past 500 years. If one can do this, then wouldn't his life [be] more interesting?

(we continued on to another painting)

That was Tiepolo. This is classicism; the Écoles des beaux-arts painter [Jean-Auguste-Dominique] Ingres. The brush strokes of paintings at his time were sanded off with fine sandpaper, so there aren't any strokes here. They [are] smooth. However, during his time, painting was already being threatened by photography. Ingres marked the beginning of the end of paintings of this manner. Meanwhile, [Ferdinand Victor Eugène] Delacroix began to show brush strokes, to express the production process, so that you can tell there was a hand that put the paint on. The artists started to "come out." These things are very interesting to me because I like to paint myself. My paintings are terrible, but it is enough to make me interested in these stories.

***POOL**: Time is misplaced.*

(we passed a small [Francisco] Goya painting)

Yung Ho: Here is Goya, a Spanish painter. His classical skill was also excellent. Hubert Robert, a French painter—his paintings are like architectural renderings. All this knowledge came from persistently looking and accumulating, and it now has an impact on my life; seeing these paintings here is like meeting old friends. That castle that I have been constructing, isn't it right here?

Part 3: Gamble House

Yung Ho: Rodney Place was not as good at talking or expressing himself as people are these days. But then, I also think that he might have been acting a bit, from time to time.

Lijia Lu: You were a student of his and have known him for so many years, you still think he was not pretending?

Yung Ho: The culture of AA [the Architectural Association] then (in the 1980s) was that one would never say a complete sentence. You would always just stop halfway.

3 *Allegory of Virtue and Nobility* by Giovanni Battista Tiepolo

Lijia: We know another person like this, deliberately not finishing a sentence, leaving you to guess; this is basically a self-inflicted problem.

Yung Ho: But if someone always puts on a persona, it becomes a pedagogy. He forces you to think. So, learning from people like that could be a painful thing. With every question you ask him, you would get [one] back from him: "What do you say to this? How do you feel about it?"

Lijia: I think students in those years were very different from students today. At that time, students did not have the access to information as students do now, so the students had no choice but to watch the teacher's mouth closely and wish that it would utter something fresh and useful. These days, students don't need that because the media is extensively developed; you can learn from practically everywhere and anywhere. That is the huge difference. So now, students do not believe in the teachers as much. Do students now believe in teachers? In the older days, listening to the teacher was like listening to a saint. Their words were gospel.

When the teacher at that time said something, you would not doubt it, right? They had so-called authority, which made you believe the teachers' words more easily. Now, it is an era of anti-authority. Anyone's words can be criticized. It is now completely opposite.

Yung Ho: It may have been some sort of idol worship at that time.

***POOL**: Did you get used to eating in the US while studying here? I am pretty curious about your experience.*

Yung Ho: When I first started school, I didn't like salad. In the dormitory, one could eat as much salad as one wanted; however, I felt like salad was for rabbits. I didn't eat much of it and was always hungry.

Lijia: When Yung Ho was a student, he was able to eat peanut butter sandwiches every day. He had a Hong Kong classmate who couldn't stand the sight of that anymore and ended up cooking him a hamburger. At that time, life for Chinese students overseas was hard. I am still amazed by the great difference. When Yung Ho first came here, he had in his pocket forty dollars (USD), which was the amount allowed to be taken out of China at the time. It wasn't even enough to take a taxi. What do you do after landing in the US? He was brave to come to the US with [just] forty dollars in 1981. When I came in 1989, I had more than 2,000 dollars in my pocket, but it felt like I was a millionaire.

Yung Ho: I married her for her money. *[laughter]*

Lijia: No way, Chang Yung Ho. I earned that money from moonlighting on a design project. Think about how big the difference is.

Part 4: Schindler House

***POOL**: I would like to go back to the metaphor of the castle. If your ambition was to know 500 years like you said, where do you think you are now?*

Yung Ho: Ah, that's a good question. I'm not sure. I am building it (the castle) very slowly, by picking things up here and there. For me, the starting point of the 500 years, since I am an architect, is relatively clear: it was early fifteenth century, because perspectives were invented then. Maybe it sounds too serious. But to me, that is important. With the invention of the one-point perspective, the concept of space was established and man became aware of his position in the space. I think this is very meaningful. The Chinese translation of perspective reveals exactly its meaning: "透视" *toushi* (*tou* meaning through or penetrate and *shi* meaning see or vision); the two characters are super spatial. They suggest depth. Furthermore, it changed the way architecture was perceived; for instance, depth has gained aesthetic value since. Perspective was pursued as a sensation, nothing was allowed [along] the way and not a baptistry, like in the first *Ideal City* painting. Something like a triumphal arch would be perfect, right? Ancient Rome had triumphal arches, but only the triumphal arch built in Paris later was truly incorporated into the perspective of urban space. Taking perspective as the beginning is to accept Renaissance as the beginning. I'm also very much interested in the evolution of pictorial space during that period. Revolution in painting was one after another. We were just talking about Delacroix and Ingres. Their debate was not only about smooth or textured painting surfaces. The texture comes from the acts of the painter and is the trace of his movement. That was why their debate was so significant. When we discussed movies, I mentioned how [a] movie could be defined as putting something, say an object, in front of a camera. Similarly, what is a painting? Not a figure, nor a shape, nor landscape, nor a story. Painting is about depicting light, which was the opinion of the impressionists in [the] late nineteenth century. Too many interesting things. I don't necessarily see them from a history's point of view, and [simply] follow a thread that I find interesting, all the way to the American art of [the] 1960s, to Abstract Expressionism.

POOL: *When [if ever] did you think that you have had a solid architectural view, or is it always evolving?*

Lijia: He has grown very slowly, and he is still confused. *[laughter]*

Yung Ho: It's been really confusing, and really slow. I am really thankful to be back to the ontological side of architecture. Sometimes, I wasn't so sure I would be. Lijia, do you think I'm back?

Lijia: Not sure. *[laughter]*

Yung Ho: I remember a long time ago, Rodney was having a conversation with a classmate of his from AA. They were talking about an architect, and how he would follow the new trends one after another. I thought, "That is also me!" I am always attracted by different ideas. So I asked my teacher and said, "Oh, I also have this problem." I think that was in 1983, about a year and [a] half after we had met. But he said, hey, you are fine, you will always come back in the end. He was like a fortune teller.

POOL: *What were you looking at when you felt that you were the most estranged in the process?*

Yung Ho: I was looking at everything! Social issues, environmental issues, technical issues. It was the most confusing time for me when I was at MIT (Massachusetts Institute of Technology). I was okay with teaching, as well as working as the department head, but in fact, my mind was totally mixed up.

POOL: *Although at first you said that you don't have nostalgia, and I agree with you there, but in some of your projects, is it inevitable to use symbols to produce nostalgia?*

Yung Ho: I don't think so. Because I believe that architecture has to be present. Architecture is a reality and not there to represent another one. To be present means whatever is there, is there, and if it's not, it's not. If in the presence of architecture, someone has certain associations with things not present, that is that person's business. As an architect, I don't think it is possible to tailor particular associations because everyone is so different.

[This article was first published in spring 2019 in *POOL* (issue No. 4). *POOL* is the student journal of the Department of Architecture & Urban Design (AUD) at the University of California, Los Angeles (UCLA).]

Yung Ho Chang / Atelier FCJZ

Yung Ho Chang studied in both China and the United States and received a Master of Architecture from the University of California, Berkeley, in the US, in 1984. He became a registered architect in the US in 1989, and has been practicing as Atelier Feichang Jianzhu (Atelier FCJZ) with Lijia Lu in China since 1992. Atelier FCJZ's work spans architecture, urbanism, landscape, interior design, furniture design, product design, clothing, jewelry, stage design, exhibitions, and art installations.

Chang and Atelier FCJZ have received numerous accolades and honors, such as first place in the Shinkenchiku Residential Design Competition, 1987, a Progressive Architecture Citation Award, 1996, the 2000 UNESCO Prize for Promotion of the Arts, the Academy Award in Architecture from the American Academy of Arts and Letters, 2006, an Achievement in Practice Prize in the China Architectural Media Award, 2016, and also won the design competition for Fondation de Chine, also known as Maison de la Chine at Cité internationale universitaire de Paris (CIUP) with Coldefy. The practice has participated in many international art and architecture exhibitions too, including the Venice Biennale in which they have participated six times since 2000. Products, architectural models, and installations by Atelier FCJZ are in the permanent collection at Victoria and Albert Museum (London, United Kingdom), Echigo-Tsumari Land Art Triennale (Japan), National Art Museum of China (Beijing, China), He Xiangning Art Museum (Shenzhen, China), and M+ (Hong Kong, China). Chang has also published several books and monographs with the team at Atelier FCJZ.

Chang has taught at various architecture schools in the United States and China. He served as the head of the Architecture Department of Massachusetts Institute of Technology (United States) from 2005 to 2010. He was also a Pritzker Architecture Prize jury member from 2011 to 2017. In 2019, Chang was elevated by the American Institute of Architects to its College of Fellows.

Project Information

Morningside Center of Mathematics
Client: Chinese Academy of Sciences
Location: 55 Zhongguancun Dong Lu, Haidian District, Beijing, China
Principal architect: Yung Ho Chang
Project team: Liu Hongwei, Wang Hui, Lijia Lu, Han Ruowei
Structural consultant: Beijing Institute of Architectural Design & Research, Chinese Academy of Sciences
Building area: 2,500 m^2
Structure: Concrete shear walls (painted)

Museum Bridge
Client: Sichuan Anren Jianchuan Cultural Industry Development Co. Ltd
Location: Anren Township, Dayi County, Chengdu City, Sichuan Province, China
Principal architect: Yung Ho Chang
Project team: Liu Lubin, Wu Xia, Guo Qingmin, Liang Xiaoning, Feng Bo
Collaboration: Shenzhen Xing Zhong Architectural Design Co. Ltd
Floor area: 2,114 m^2
Structure: Reinforced-concrete framework and bamboo formwork concrete

21Cake, Huangpu Shop
Client: 21Cake
Location: SOHO Fuxing Plaza, Huangpu District, Shanghai, China
Principal architect: Yung Ho Chang
Project team: Simon Lee, Han Shukai, Chang Cheng, Yin Shun
Design area: 33 m^2
Material: Corian, tile

21Cake, Baoshan Shop
Client: 21Cake
Location: Jingwei Hui, Baoshan District, Shanghai, China
Principal architects: Yung Ho Chang, Lijia Lu
Project team: Simon Lee, Zhang Min, Li Shuai
Cooperative R&D and production of *da fanzhuo* and *xiao tuiche*: Qumei Home Furnishings Group Co., Ltd
Collaboration: Beijing ZJHJ. Design & Engineering Co. Ltd
Design area: 167 m^2
Material: Terrazzo, stucco, and wood

Jishou Art Museum
Client: Jishou Qianzhou Historic Town Administration
Location: Qianzhou Historic Town, Jishou, Hunan Province, China
Principal architects: Yung Ho Chang, Lijia Lu
Project team: Liang Xiaoning, Yang Pu, Liu Kunpeng, Su Siqi, Rao Gang
Structural consultant: Chang Qiang
Collaboration: Hunan Provincial Communications Planning, Survey & Design Institute Co., Ltd
Floor area: 3,535.4 m^2
Structure: Steel truss and reinforced-concrete arch

Zigzag Tower
Client: CCCC Investment Co., Ltd (Zhengzhou)
Location: New district of east Zhengzhou, Zhengzhou, Henan Province, China
Principal architect: Yung Ho Chang
Project team: Yang Pu, Wu Xia, Liang Xiaoning, Feng Shuni, Rao Gang, Wang Yue, Zhang Bowen
Collaboration: China Institute of Building Standard Design & Research Co., Ltd
Curtain wall consultant: Beijing ZiZhong Curtain Wall Consultant & Design Co., Ltd
Lighting consultant: Toryo International Lighting Design Centre
Floor area: 39,172.10 m^2
Structure: Core-in-core beamless structure system

Jiading Mini-Block
Client: Shanghai Jiading Industrial Zone
Location: Jiading Industrial Park, Jiading District, Shanghai, China
Principal architect: Yung Ho Chang
Project team: (Not limited to) Dan Chen, Liu Jing, Liu Xianghui, Cai Feng, Dong Shuyin, Lin Fangjie, Liu Yang, Guo Qingmin, Wu Xia, Huang Shuyi, Shen Yuheng, Zhao Chunlei
Collaboration: Arcplus Institute of Shanghai Architectural Design & Research Co., Ltd
Floor area: 70,085.7 m^2
Structure: Reinforced-concrete arch and steel truss

Qingpu Bridge
Client: Shanghai Qingpu New City Development (Group) Co., Ltd
Location: Qingpu District, Shanghai
Principal architect: Yung Ho Chang
Project team: Cai Feng, Wu Huibiao
Building height: 745 m
Structure: Reinforced-concrete structure

Thick Thin Fold
Client: Formica
Principal designer: Yung Ho Chang
Project team: Jimmy Shen
Material: Artificial stone

Hulu
Client: JIA Inc.Limited
Principal designer: Yung Ho Chang
Project team: James Shen, Guo Qingmin
Material: Bone china, glass, stainless steel

Lotus Leaf
Client: Alessi
Principal designer: Yung Ho Chang
Project team: Lijia Lu, Du Baoli
Material: Stainless steel

Steel Unit Chair
Principal designer: Yung Ho Chang
Project team: Lu Bai
Material: Steel

2D-3D Qipao
Principal designers: Lijia Lu, Yung Ho Chang
Project team: Zhang Linmiao

Cheng Table
Principal designer: Yung Ho Chang
Project team: Xin Dawei, Guo Qingmin
Collaboration: WUUYO (无有)
Material: Wood

Bend It Like Yoga
Client: Qumei Home Furnishings Group Co., Ltd
Principal designers: Yung Ho Chang, Lijia Lu
Project team: Guo Qingmin, Han Shukai, Xing Dawei
Material: Bent plywood

***Mille-feuille* Reconstructed**
Client: 21Cake
Designer: Yung Ho Chang

King's Joy Restaurant
Client: Beijing King's Joy Food Culture Co., Ltd
Location: Yonghe Lama Temple Street, Dongcheng District, Beijing, China
Principal architect: Yung Ho Chang
Project team: Wang Yue, Guo Zhaowei, Xing Dawei, Dan Chen, Wu Xia
Floor area: 1,298.5 m^2 (aboveground)
Structure and material: Wood, bricks, and tiles

Campus Green Redux
Location: Haidian District, Beijing, China
Principal architect: Yung Ho Chang
Project team: He Zelin, Feng Shuni, Wu Xia
Structural consultant: Chang Qiang
Collaboration: Beijing ZJHJ Design & Engineering Co., Ltd
Site area: 28,995 m^2
Structure: Timber, reciprocal structure

Novartis Shanghai Campus
Client: Novartis Institutes for BioMedical Research (China)
Location: Pudong District, Shanghai, China
Principal architect: Yung Ho Chang
Project team: Simon Lee, Dan Chen, Keith Goh, Feng Shuni, Li Xiangting, Guo Zhaowei, Chang Cheng
Construction drawing collaboration: Tongji Architectural Design (Group) Co.,Ltd.
Landscape collaboration: Beijing Tsinghua Tongheng Urban Planning & Design Institute
Floor area: 1,298.5 m^2
Building height: 36.45 m
Structure and material: Reinforced-concrete structure and aluminum spandrel with terra cotta rain screen and sun shading

Brick Kiosk
Client: Bi-City Biennale of Urbanism/Architecture 2017
Location: Nanmen Park, Nantou Old Town, Shenzhen, China
Principal architect: Yung Ho Chang
Project team: He Zelin, Wu Xia, Liu Yang
Floor area: 75 m^2
Structure and material: Reinforced-concrete structure, brick

Shede Visitor's Center
Client: Sichuan Tuopai Shede Wine Co., Ltd
Location: Tuopai Zhen, Sichuan Province, China
Principal architect: Yung Ho Chang
Project team: Liang Xiaoning, Huang Shuyi, Zhang Bowen, Liu Chao
Interior design team: Simon Lee, Zeng Xiangyan, Zhang Min, Li Shuai
Collaboration: China Southwest Architectural Design and Research Institute Corp., Ltd
Floor area: 22,592 m^2
Structure: Reinforced-concrete framework

EP YAYING Fashion and Arts Center
Client: EP YAYING Fashion Group Co., Ltd
Location: 2029 Changsheng Zhong Lu, Jiaxing, Zhejiang Province, China
Principal architects: Yung Ho Chang, Lijia Lu
Project team: Yin Shun, Yu Yue, Liu Yang, Shi Qi, Pan Chenchao, Wu Xia, Li Xiangting, Liu Ping, Xie Yanxu, He Zelin, Long Bin, Interior design team: Zhang Min, Han Shukai, Zeng Xiangyan, Li Shuai, Landscape design team: Shi Qi, Yin Shun, Lin Shijie, Xie Yanxu
Construction drawing collaboration: Tongji Architectural Design (Group) Co., Ltd (No. 4 Architectural Design)
Landscape collaboration: Hangzhou Ruige Architectural Design Co., Ltd
Lighting consultant: TJAD-Architectural Lighting Studio, Shenzhen ShiYao Lighting Design Co., Ltd
Floor area: 25,000 m^2
Structure and material: Reinforced-concrete frame

Loop House
Client: Private residence
Location: Beijing, China
Principal architects: Yung Ho Chang, Lijia Lu
Project team: Liang Xiaoning, Cheng Yishi, Yang Pu, Rao Gang
Construction drawing collaboration: Beijing ZJHJ. Design & Engineering CO. Ltd
Floor area: 460 m^2
Structure: Reinforced-concrete frame

Maison de la Chine
Client: Cité internationale universitaire de Paris (CIUP), Beijing Capital Group
Location: 14th Arrondissement, CIUP, Paris, France
Principal architects: Yung Ho Chang, Lijia Lu
Project team: Cheng Yishi, Simon Lee, Meng Yao
Collaboration: Coldefy
Floor area: 8,287 m^2
Site area: 2,800 m^2
Building height: 24.3 m
Structure and material: Reinforced-concrete frame and brick wall

International Exchange Center of Wenzhou Medical University
Client: Wenzhou Medical University
Location: Chashan Campus of Wenzhou Medical University, Wenzhou, Zhejiang Province, China
Principal architect: Yung Ho Chang
Project team: Wang Yue, Yu Yue, Long Bin, Liang Xiaoning, Simon Lee, Yin Shun, Li Xiangting, Chen Youyou, Hou Jiali, Wu Xia, Liu Yang
Collaboration: Architectural Design and Research Institute of Ningbo Technology Co., Ltd
Floor area: 38,770 m^2
Structure: Dense ribbed-beam reinforced-concrete frame

CAA Liangzhu Campus
Client: China Academy of Art
Location: Liangzhu, Hangzhou, Zhejiang Province, China
Principal architects: Yung Ho Chang, Lijia Lu
Project team: Yin Shun (Phase 1), Wang Wenzhi (Phase 2), Wang Yue, Long Bin, Huang Shuyi, Liang Xiaoning, Liu Yang, Liu Chao, Zhang Bowen, Wang Shuo, Cheng Yishi, He Zelin, Shi Qi, Lin Shijie, Xie Yanxu, Jiao Huimin, Zhang Min, Han Shukai, Li Shuai
On-Site supervision: Li Shiqi
Construction drawing collaboration: Tongji Architectural Design (Group) Co., Ltd (No. 3 Architectural Design)
Lighting consultant: TJAD-Architectural Lighting Studio
Floor area: 18,000 m^2
Structure: Reinforced-concrete frame, vault

Open Kindergarten
Client: Education Committee of Beijing Haidian District
Location: Haidian District, Beijing, China
Principal architect: Yung Ho Chang
Project team: Liang Xiaoning, Liu Chao, Zhang He
Collaboration: Beijing Victory Star Architectural & Civil Engineering Design Co., Ltd
Site area: 4,300 m^2
Floor area: 4,980 m^2
Structure: Reinforced-concrete frame

Vertical Glass House
Client: West Bund
Location: Longteng road, Xuhui District, Shanghai, China
Principal architects: Yung Ho Chang, Lijia Lu
Project team: Bai Lu, Li Xiangting, Cai Feng, Liu Xiaodi
Construction drawing collaboration: Tongji Architectural Design (Group) Co. Ltd
Floor area: 144 m^2
Structure and material: Reinforced-concrete structure, steel column and beam, laminated panel glass, and tempered plate glass

Concrete Vessel
Client: Haier
Location: Chaoyang District, Beijing, China
Principal architects: Yung Ho Chang, Lijia Lu
Project team: He Zelin
Structure consultation: Xu Minsheng
Landscape collaboration: Original Ecology Landscape Co., Ltd
Material research and development: Beijing Baogui Stone Art Technology Co., Ltd
Floor area: 184 m^2
Structure and material: Steel frame and GRC panel

Four Studio-Houses
Client: Ningbo Huamao Education and Culture Investment Co., Ltd
Location: Ningbo, Zhejiang Province, China
Principal architects: Yung Ho Chang, Lijia Lu
Project team: Liang Xiaoning, Huang Shuyi, Wu Zhuqing, Han Shukai, Zhang Min, He Zelin
Collaboration: China Shanghai Architectural Design & Research Institute Co., Ltd
Design management: Zhejiang Huazhi Architectural Design Co., Ltd
Floor area: 1,255 m^2
Structure: Reinforced-concrete shear walls

Villa Mountain Dialogue
Client: Private residence
Location: Huairou District, Beijing, China
Principal architect: Yung Ho Chang
Project team: Xu Yixing, Wang Hui, Lijia Lu
Structural consultant: Zhong Chang Sheng Architects and Engineers
Floor area: 380 m^2
Structure: Steel frame, timber joists, granite retaining wall

Split House
Client: Red Stone Industry Co., Ltd
Location: Shui Guan (Water Gate) of the Great Wall (Commune by the Great Wall), Yanqing District, Beijing, China
Principal architect: Yung Ho Chang
Project team: Liu Xianghui, Lucas Gallardo, Xu Yixing, Wang Hui, Lijia Lu
Structural consultant: Xu Minsheng
Site area: 6,729 m^2
Floor area: 449 m^2
Structure: Laminated plywood frame, rammed-earth wall

Xishu Bookstore
Client: Xi Shu
Location: Chegongzhuang Street, Xicheng District, Beijing, China
Principal architect: Yung Ho Chang
Project team: Yin Yimu, Lijia Lu
Floor area: 133 m^2
Material: Steel frame, frosted glass

Urban Cycling Wear
Designers: Lijia Lu, Yung Ho Chang
Project team: Zhang Linmiao

Bike Ring
Location: Xiamen, Fujian Province, China
Principal architect: Yung Ho Chang
Project team: Huang Shuyi, Cheng Yishi, Zhang Bowen, Wang Shuo
Floor area: 21,056 m^2
Structure: Reinforced-concreted frame, steel frame (partial)

Ocean Art Center
Client: Sino-Ocean Real Estate Development Co. Ltd
Location: Balizhuang, Haidian District, Beijing, China
Principal architect: Yung Ho Chang
Project team: Wu Xuetao, Wang Hui, Du Jinli
Structural consultant: Yu Zhixiong
Floor area: 2,900 m^2
Material: Channel glass

Shanghai Corporate Pavilion
Client: Shanghai Guosheng Group Co., Ltd
Location: Huangpu District, Shanghai, China
Principal architect: Yung Ho Chang
Project team: Zang Feng, Liu Lubin, James Shen, Wong Siuming, Wang Kuan, Qiu Yukui, Liang Xiaoning, Wang Lin, Wu Xia, Deng Honghui, Chen Guannan
Structural consultant: Center for Engineering Design and Research under the Headquarters of General Equipment
Floor area: 4,949 m^2
Structure and material: Steel frame, recycled PC tubes, and LED lights

Micro Stages
Client: TTF
Principal designers: Yung Ho Chang, Lijia Lu
Project team: Du Baoli, Lin Yixuan, Zhang Sitian
Material: Silver

Graphic FCJZ
Publishing house: Luminous City/Tongji University Press
Author: Yung Ho Chang / FCJZ
Project team: Zhang Sitian, Vince Sze Wing Ho, Yang Fan, Dai Panpan

Little Detective
Publishing house: Luminous City/Tongji University Press
Author: Yung Ho Chang
Project team: Zhang Linmiao
Graphic design: Ma Shirui

***Little Detective* Zumtobel**
Client: Zumtobel Group
Designer: Yung Ho Chang
Project team: Ji Yaqiong

Forbidden City Cultural Relics Museum
Client: Sunac China
Location: Nanbin Road, Nanan District, Chongqing, China
Principal architects: Yung Ho Chang, Lijia Lu
Project team: He Zelin, Yu Yue, Long Bin, Pan Chenchao
Collaboration: Brother Cooperation Group
Site area: 4,692 m^2
Floor area: 2,700 m^2
Building height: 13.7 m
Structure: Plywood truss and steel curved beam column

Seven Sages of the Bamboo Grove
Client: Xincan Drama Centre-CHINA-UK Literary Theater Exchange
Location: Beijing, China
Principal architects: Yung Ho Chang, Lijia Lu
Project team: Zhang Linmiao, Ji Yaqiong, Xing Dawei
Floor area: 660 m^2
Material: Steel scaffolding

No Name Art Museum
Client: Zhejiang Yada International Health Ecologic Park
Location: Wuzhen, Zhejiang Province, China
Principal architects: Yung Ho Chang, Lijia Lu
Project team: Simon Lee, Wang Yue, Cheng Yishi, Li Xiangting, Wu Xia, Liu Yang, Chen Youyou, Hou Jiali
Site supervision and technical collaboration: Hu Youbin
Structure & MEP: Tongji Architectural Design (Group) Co., Ltd (Dujing Architectural Design Institute)
Site area: 124,244.34 m^2
Floor area: 6,159.59 m^2
Structure: Reinforced-concrete shear wall and steel structure

Image Credits

All the illustrations, renderings, diagrams, plans, and photography are provided by Atelier FCJZ.

The Meaning of Things

Thomas Child: 20 （top）

South by Southeast

The Art Institute of Chicago/Art Resource, NY; gift from George E. Danforth: 24 （top）

Taipei Palace Museum of China: 27

Ludwig Mies van der Rohe / VG Bild-Kunst, Bonn - SACK, Seoul, 2023: 29

Morningside Center for Mathematics

Cao Yang: 30 (bottom), 32 (bottom left, bottom right)

Museum Bridge

Cao Yang: 35, 36 (bottom), 38, 39 (bottom left, bottom right), 40 (top left, bottom), 42–43

Arch-Exist Photography: 40 (top right), 41 (bottom)

21Cake, Huangpu Shop

Tian Fangfang: 44, 45, 46 (bottom left, bottom right), 47

21Cake, Baoshan Shop

Tian Fangfang: 48–51

Jishou Art Museum

Tian Fangfang: 53, 54 (top left, bottom), 56 (bottom), 57 (top right, bottom), 58–64, 65 (bottom left, bottom right), 66–67

Zigzag Tower

Tian Fangfang: 69, 70 (top right, bottom), 72 (bottom), 73 (bottom left, bottom right), 74–75

Jiading Mini-Block

Tian Fangfang: 77, 80–89

Hulu

Domus: 98 (bottom right), 99 (bottom)

The PLAN: 99 (top four)

JIA Inc.: 100–101

Bend It Like Yoga

Qumei Home Furnishings Group Co., Ltd: 113–115

***Mille-feuille* Reconstructed**

21Cake: 116 (bottom right), 117 (bottom)

King's Joy Restaurant

Shu He: 119, 120, 122, 123, 124 (bottom), 125, 126 (bottom), 127

Campus Green Redux

Tian Fangfang: 133 (top left)

Novartis Shanghai Campus

Lyu Hengzhong: 137, 138, 142–146, 148–151

Brick Kiosk

Tian Fangfang: 152 (bottom left, bottom right), 153, 154 (bottom), 157 (bottom left, bottom right), 158–159

Shede Visitor's Center

Arch-Exist Photography: 160 (bottom), 161, 162 (bottom), 164 (bottom), 167, 170–171

EP YAYING Fashion and Arts Center

Tian Fangfang: 172 (bottom), 173, 174, 176–182, 183 (bottom left), 184–185

Loop House

UK Studio: 187, 188 (bottom), 190–192

CAA Liangzhu Campus

Tian Fangfang: 212 (bottom), 213, 222, 224, 227, 230, 231 (bottom left and right), 232 (bottom), 233, 234 (bottom left, bottom right)

Wu Qingshan: 223, 225 (top), 229 (bottom), 232 (top), 235

Li Shiqi: 228 (bottom left and right), 229 (top), 231 (top left and right),

China Academy of Art Press; extracted from Retrospect on the National Academy of Art, pg 31: Yongchang, Huang. Retrospect on the National Academy of Art [M]. Hangzhou, China Academy of Art Press, 2020: 234 (top left)

Open Kindergarten

Tian Fangfang: 237, 238 (bottom), 240–245

Vertical Glass House

Lyu Hengzhong: 250, 252–255

Tian Fangfang: 247, 256

Concrete Vessel

Tian Fangfang: 260 (bottom), 264, 267 (bottom right), 268–269

Japan Design Center: 266

Haier: 267 (bottom left)

Four Studio-Houses

Tian Fangfang: 271, 272 (bottom), 273, 274 (bottom), 276 (top right, bottom right), 280, 283–287, 289 (bottom), 291

Li Keliang: 275, 276 (left), 277 (bottom), 278–279, 281, 290

Villa Mountain Dialogue

Fu Xing: 293, 294 (bottom right), 296, 297, 298 (bottom right), 299

Split House

Shu He: 301, 304 (bottom), 305 (top), 308 (top), 308 (bottom right)

Fu Xing: 305 (bottom), 306–307, 308 (bottom left)

Asakawa Satoshi: 309

Xishu Bookstore

Cao Yang: 311, 315–317

Ocean Art Center

Cao Yang: 331 (top), 331 (bottom right), 332

Shanghai Corporate Pavilion

Shu He: 335, 340, 343 (top right)

Nic Lehoux: 338, 341, 342, 343 (bottom left, bottom right)

Micro Stages

TTF: 344 (top right, bottom right), 345

***Little Detective* Zumtobel**

Zumtobel Group: 354 (bottom left, bottom right), 355 (bottom left, bottom right), 357 (bottom right)

Forbidden City Cultural Relics Museum

DID-STUDIO: 358 (bottom), 359, 364 (top), 365, 366 (bottom), 367 (right), 368, 369 (bottom right), 370–371

Bai Yu: 364 (bottom)

Fang Ziyu: 367 (left)

No Name Art Museum

Tian Fangfang: 378 (bottom right), 379, 381, 384 (bottom), 386 (bottom), 388, 389 (bottom left, bottom right), 390 (bottom), 391, 392 (top right, bottom), 393–395

A Day with Yung Ho Chang

The Norton Simon Foundation: 399

Published in Australia in 2023 by
The Images Publishing Group Pty Ltd
ABN 89 059 734 431

Offices

Melbourne
Waterman Business Centre
Suite 64, Level 2 UL40
1341 Dandenong Road
Chadstone, VIC 3148
Australia
Tel: +61 3 8564 8122

New York
6 West 18th Street 4B
New York, NY 10011
United States
Tel: +1 212 645 1111

Shanghai
6F, Building C, 838 Guangji Road
Hongkou District, Shanghai 200434
China
Tel: +86 021 31260822

books@imagespublishing.com
www.imagespublishing.com

The Images Publishing Group Reference Number: 1615

NATIONAL LIBRARY OF AUSTRALIA

A catalogue record for this book is available from the National Library of Australia

Title: Design as Experience Research
Author: Yung Ho Chang / Atelier FCJZ
ISBN: 9781864708820

FSC www.fsc.org MIX Paper from responsible sources FSC® C019910

Printed by Everbest Printing Investment Limited, in Hong Kong, China